CW00430540

A NEW INTRODUCTION TO OLD NORSE

PART III: GLOSSARY AND INDEX OF NAMES

A NEW INTRODUCTION TO OLD NORSE

PART III

GLOSSARY AND INDEX OF NAMES

COMPILED BY

ANTHONY FAULKES

FOURTH EDITION

SUPPLEMENT I: GLOSSARY AND INDEX OF NAMES TO EAST NORSE TEXTS

SUPPLEMENT II: GLOSSARY AND INDEX OF NAMES TO RUNIC TEXTS

COMPILED BY

MICHAEL BARNES

VIKING SOCIETY FOR NORTHERN RESEARCH
UNIVERSITY COLLEGE LONDON
2007

© VIKING SOCIETY FOR NORTHERN RESEARCH

ISBN: 978-0-903521-70-3

First published 2001
Second edition with corrections and additions 2002
Third edition with corrections and additions 2005
Fourth edition with corrections and additions and two supplements 2007
Reprinted 2008
Reprinted 2011 with further corrections
Reprinted 2016
Reprinted 2019
Reprinted 2020
Reprinted 2021

Printed by Short Run Press Limited, Exeter

GLOSSARY AND INDEX OF NAMES

References to the Grammar are to paragraphs (e.g. *Gr* 3.5.2.1; ex. = exercise) and those to texts are to the number of the text followed by the line number (e.g. II:62). A second occurrence of the same word in a line is indicated by (2).

Syntactical explanations and common pronouns and conjunctions are referred to the appropriate paragraphs in the Grammar for full information. Cross-references are given for verbal and nominal forms where the vowel in the first syllable differs from the head-word form, except for some forms involving the alternation of *a* and *ǫ*.

Principal parts of verbs are identified by *pres.*, *past*, *past pl.*, *subj.*, *pp.* For *pres.* and *past*, the 3rd person sg. is given, for *past pl.* the 3rd person pl., for *pp.* the nom. m. sg., except for those verbs that are more often found in the n. form (supine), where the nom./acc. n. sg. is given. See *Gr* 3.9.7.1.

In the alphabetical order the acute accent is disregarded; *d* and *ð* are treated as one letter, *þ* comes after *y* and is followed by *æ*, *œ*, *ǫ* and *ø*, and *ę* is not distinguished from *e*. Words from Text XXII with lengthened or diphthongised vowels before *-ng* are not listed separately from words without these changes.

Abbreviations

acc.	accusative	*pl.*	plural
act.	active	*pos.*	positive
adj.	adjective	*poss.*	possessive
adv.	adverb(ial)	*pp.*	past participle
art.	article	*prep.*	preposition
aux.	auxiliary	*pres. (part.)*	present (participle)
comp.	comparative	*pret.-pres.*	preterite present
conj.	conjunction	*pron.*	pronoun
dat.	dative	*refl.*	reflexive
def.	definite	*rel.*	relative
f.	feminine	*sf.*	strong feminine
gen.	genitive	*sg.*	singular
imp.	imperative	*sm.*	strong masculine
impers.	impersonal	*sn.*	strong neuter
indic.	indicative	*subj.*	subjunctive
inf.	infinitive	*sup.*	superlative
interrog.	interrogative	*sv.*	strong verb
m.	masculine	*vb.*	verb
n.	neuter	*wf.*	weak feminine
neg.	negative	*wk.*	weak
nom.	nominative	*wm.*	weak masculine
num.	numeral	*wn.*	weak neuter
pass.	passive	*wv.*	weak verb

For abbreviated bibliographical references see *NION* II, p. x.

á¹ *prep.* (*Gr* 3.7.4); *with acc.* on I:18, 77, II:27, VI:251, XXII:5/3,
    XXVII:7; onto II:30, III:86, VI:272, X:47, XIX:80, XXI:120,
    XXV:77, XXVI A: 28, 38, XXVI B:11, 27; over VIII:120; in, to
    XXV:97; to II:46, VI:6, VIII:18, X:110, XXI:14, XXII:33/1,
    XXIII:84, XXVI A:9, 16 (to *or* at); at I:119, XXII:49/1, XXV:72,
    92, XXVI A:30, B:194; in III:9, XXII:24/1, XXIII:70; into I:2, II:74,
    VI:10, VII B:76, XXI:181, XXII:44/3 (postposition); for X:29, XXI:52;
    with dat. in I:121, 129, II:23, VI:19, VIII:5, 7, IX:37, XVI:122,
    XIX:4, XXI:38, 94, XXII:52/3, XXIII:33, 60, XXVI B:98, XXVII:2,
    26 (i.e. over); on I:27, 76, II:66, V:171, VI:36, 312, IX:19, X:6, XI:48,
    XIX:44, XXI:15, XXII:45/4, XXIII:6, XXV:1, 12, 99, XXVI A:15,
    B:116, 229; upon XXI:129; from in/on VIII:78, 116; at III:84, V:3,
    VII B:25, IX:53, XV:33 (in a place-name, cf. *Gr* 3.1.8 ex.), XXII:35/1,
    XXVII:38; **í smáþarma á Þorvaldi** at Þorvaldr's guts XXI:175–80,
    textual note; in relation to, against VII B:30; about I:72; for XXII:26/1,
    XXVII:39; *as adv.* (*Gr* 3.7.7) I:55 (*see* **leita**), 130 (*see* **halda**), III:54
    (*see* **horfa**), VI:111 (*see* **sjá**), VIII:19 (*see* **leggja**), X:49 (*see* **láta**),
    X:64 (*see* **leggja**), XXII:34/3 (*see* **leggja**); on it XXI:27, i.e. on her
    breast XXI:142 (1), 159, XXVI A:52, were on it XXI:46; in them
    XXVI B:88; in it VII B:61, about this VI A:32; **á upp** on it at the top
    XXI:45; **er hon stóð á** which it stood on XIII:6, 38; **var á veðr gott**
    it was fine weather (on that day) XV:48; **á braut** *see* **braut**; **á miðli**,
    á milli *see* **milli**; **á mót(i)** *see* **mót²**; **á at sjá** *see* **sjá**;

á² *see* **eiga**

á³ *f.* river, stream (*Gr* 3.1.7.5 (2), 3.1.8.(16), 3.1.9 ex. 8) XXI:87, 169;
    yfir ár across the rivers XXVI A:4; *with suffixed def. art.* XXI:89,
    við ána niðri down by the river VII B:59, **eptir ánni**, **með ánni**
    along the river VII B:75, 80, XXI:130

-a *neg. suffix with verbs* not V:54, IX:100, X:77, 95, 97, 108, 124, 168,
    XXV:5

ábóti *m.* abbot XIV:180, 181

ábyrgðar(h)lutr *m.* matter involving responsibility XXVI B:104

Aðalból *n.* 'chief dwelling, manor' *Gr* 3.1.8 ex.

áðr *adv.* before, earlier, previously I:25, 54, 69, III:45, IV:76, VIII:45,
    94, 99, 140, 160, 165, XI:39, 40, XV:32, XVI:37, XIX:39; already
    XXVI A:75; just now XXVI A:47; just before III:58; first X:149,
    XIV:68, XXI:175–80, *textual note*; at first XV:123; **næstr áðr**
    preceding XXVII:33; **kvámu áðr** had already come VIII:108; *as*

conj. (*Gr* 3.8.2.4) before II:38, III:104, 114, IV:83, V:6, VIII:42, 60, XIV:70, 100 (. . . **þá**), XVI:7, 123, 157, XIX:108, XXI:44, XXVI B:35, XXVII:7, 34, 49, until XXV:65; **áðr en** *as conj.* before, until VI:73, 310, XI:72, XIV:5, XVI:189, XXIV:13

aðra, aðrar, aðrir *see* **annarr**

áeggjun *f.* instigation, urging VI:5 (*dat. with* **af**, *parallel to* **atkalli**)

af *prep. with dat.* (*Gr* 3.7.3); from, of I:31, II:25, VI:19, 212, X:9, 31, 148, XI:38, 43, XV:12, 71, XVI:15, XIX:3, 7, XXI:15, 33, 83, XXIV:68, XXVI A:8, 44, 61, 90, 153, 220, XXVII:37; by VIII:150, 178, XXII:7/4; from among II:63, VI:213, VII A:33, 78 (2); from on VI:221, 259; off I:124, V:145, 147, VI:256, X:79, XV:84, XIX:34, XXI:56, XXII:48/2, XXIV:46, XXVI A:31, B:90; away from V:162; beyond XXII:13/4; out of III:81; **tíu vikur váru/eru af sumri** ten weeks of summer were/have passed VIII:92, XXVII:29; by, because of III:13, 53, 114, VIII:182; by means of, with XIV:2, XXII:58/2; as a result of VI:5, 254, 315, 366, VII A:66, VIII:151, XXI:179, XXII:54/4, 55/4, 58/4; for XXII:3/4; caused by XXIII:107; as a consequence of VI:324, VII B:86; consisting of II:55; made of XIII:31; about, concerning VI:107, XXII:24/3; with II:29, V:131, VI:152, XXII:31/2, 40/2; **af þessu** for this reason II:116; **af því** from this VIII: 23; **af því at, af því . . . at** (*Gr* 3.8.2.2) because VI:289, 314 (*see* **því**), VII A:35–36, VIII:22, XXI:160; *as adv.* (*Gr* 3.7.7) II:6 *see* **þar**; off II:59, X:49, 50, 114, 158, XXV:98, XXVI A:60; away VIII:40; of them II:64, 74, of it (them) VIII:154, 157; from it II:99, XXI:76; (some) of it XXI:75; with it XVI:29; by it, as a result of it VIII:127; from among them VII A:78 (1); about it XXVI B:23; **þá er . . . af** those from whom XXVII:34; **bera af** *see* **bera**

afarkostr *m.* harsh treatment *Gr* 3.3.5 ex. 9

áfenginn *adj. pp.* strong (of drink) II:12

afhuga *adj. indeclinable with dat.* **verða afhuga** having one's mind turned from, have out of one's mind XIV:52

afi *m.* grandfather XIV:129

afl *n.* strength II:29, VII B:9; the majority XXVII:13; **með ǫllu afli** with all his strength XIV:78

afla (*past* **aflaði**, *pp.* **aflat**) *wv. with gen. and dat.* bring (about), cause something for some one XXII:53/4

aflangr *adj.* very long XXIII:11, 46

afroð *n.* cost, price, penalty XXVI B:53

ágjarn *adj.* covetous, ambitious, impetuous; *acc. sg. n. as noun* an ambitious (etc.) person XXIII:91

ágæti *n.* glory, renown; **til síns ágætis nǫkkut** something in which they take pride, something which brings them fame (by which they are remembered?) XXVI A:85

ágætliga *adv.* splendidly, excellently XVI:178

ágætr *adj.* excellent, famous VII A:49; *sup. n.* **ágætast** most excellent (i.e. because it relates to divinity or theology) XXIV:31

áhyggja *f.* concern, responsibility XXIV:63, 64; anxiety XXIV:73

aka (*pres.* **ek,** *past* **ók,** *pp.* **ekinn**) *sv.* drive (*Gr* 3.6.9.3 ex. 1) IX:47, 52, 84

ákafliga *adv.* extremely VII A:97, XVI:89, XXIII:31, 106; furiously *Gr* 3.5.3 (3)

ákafr *adj.* furious, violent, vehement, impetuous XXIII:2; *n. as adv.* **ákaft** violently I:100; *sup. n. as adv.* **sem ákafast** as hard as he could II:154

ákall *n.* invocation XXIV:33, 42

Áki *m.* King Sveinn's steward XVI:45, 47, 56, 66, 67

akkeri *n.* anchor XXI:47

ákveðinn *adj. pp.* agreed, appointed *Gr* 3.3.9 ex. 27, II:38, IV:70, 102 (*understand* **var**); *n.* **ákveðit** IV:110

ál *f.* strap, saddle-strap; **við álar sér** to his saddle-straps V:157

ala (*pres.* **elr,** *past* **ól,** *past pl.* **ólu,** *pp.* **alinn**) *sv.* nourish (thoughts *or* feelings) IV:59; breed, rear, bring up XXV:105

albúinn *adj. (pp., cf.* **búa**) completely ready XVI:136

albyggðr *adj. (pp.)* fully settled, fully colonised, occupied VIII:56

aldinn *adj.* ancient; *acc. sg. f. wk.* **ǫldnu** IX:127

aldr (*gen.* **aldrs**) *m.* age; generation XIV:166; **at aldri** in age XIV:34, 89; **á fulltíða aldri** in adulthood XIV:167; **við aldr** advanced in years III:65, XXI:11

aldrbót *f.* 'life-betterment', advancement, fame, glory VI:204 (*object of* **fekk**)

aldri *adv.* never II:34, III:36, IV:14, 74, V:3, XII:27, XIX:42, XXVI A 56, 64, 81, XXVI B:49, 172, 214; not at all, not in the least XXVI A:83

Aldrian *m.* young son of King Attila XI:44, 45

aldrigi *adv.* never VI:119, 184, XIV:67, 74, XVI:74

aldrlag *n.* death XXV:29

álengðar *adv.* for the future, indefinitely XVI:116

alin *f.* (*pl.* **álnar**) ell (a measure of length; in early Icelandic = 49 cm., later 54–57 cm.; ells of homespun were used as a standard of currency) XXVII:37 (*gen. pl.*, cf. *Gr* 3.4.2 (5))

álit *n.* face, looks XXIII:61

álfr *m.* elf IX:23, X:57, 67, 147, XXV:2

alldjarfliga *adv.* very boldly I:138

alldýrr *adj.* very fine, very worthy VI:264

allfróðligr *adj.* very wise, very sensible XXIV:22

allfrægr *adj.* much spoken of, very famous II:60

allfúss *adj.* very eager (**til** for it, to do it) I:125

allkátr *adj.* very merry, very cheerful XI:62

alllítill *adj.* very small; **ekki alllítill fyrir sér** of no small importance or ability I:55

allr *adj.* all *Gr* 3.3.9 ex. 12, 18, I:83, II:80, 127, VI:43, 151, 274, 366, IX:53, 54, 96, 118, XII:14, XIII:14, XIV:165, XV:31, XIX:8, XXI:108 (2), XXII:2/4, XXIII:19, XXIV:4, 40, XXVI A:119, B:46; the whole IX:49; *acc. sg. m.* **allan** II:153, VI:286, X:27 (*sc.* **vetr**), all over I:24, every XXIII:35, the whole XXVI B:4, 91, his whole XXIII:103; *dat. sg. m.* **ǫllum** XXII:61/4; *f.* **ǫll** the whole VII B:22, entirely XIII:5, XIV:10; *acc. sg. f.* **alla** IV:30 (*with* **hǫll**), IX:126 (with **ætt**), XI:47, XVI:11, XXVI A:62, all over XIV:10; **alla stofuna** the whole room XXVI B:28; *dat. sg. f.* **allri** all XIII:36, every VI:318, XXIV:74; *n.* **allt** all I:113, III:86, VI:148, 294, XVI:90, XXII:34/3, the whole VI:275, VII A:128, 169, XVI:76, XXVI A:63, B:29, the whole of VIII:42, his whole XXVI A:3; everything II:152, V:106 (*subject of* **koma**?), VIII:93, XIII:16, XV:57, XXVI B:14, 65 (anything); everywhere III:107; **allt þat er**, **allt þat es**, **þat allt er** everything that VI:22, VII A:130, VIII:84, XII:64, XIV:107, XXIV:25; **þetta allt** all this XXVII:30; **allt saman** altogether XIV:145, the whole business XVI:57; **allt eitt** all the same XIV:117; *gen. sg. n.* **alls** of everything XV:9, XXI:161, **alls þess** (*gen. with* **þurfa**) all that (care) XI:71 (*or* **alls** *adv.* entirely?); *dat. sg. n.* **ǫllu** II:29, it all, everything; **því ǫllu er** everything that XV:147; **ǫllu saman** everything together III:60; **með ǫllu** altogether, entirely I:93, XIV:76, XVI:142; *pl.* **allir** they all, everyone I:86, VI:100, 111, 298, VIII:137, XII:74, XIII:7, XXIV:69; **allir menn** everyone XXVI A:76, XXVII:7; **allir er** all those who V:144; **þeir allir**, **allir þeir** they all

V:69, 143, VI:131, XXVI B:16; **þeir allir er, allir þeir er** all those who XXIV:33, XXVI A:6; **vér allir, allir vér** we all V:64, VI:91; *acc. pl. m.* **alla** all X:38, XXVI B:10, XXVII:26, every X:149, **þá alla** them all XIX:69, 84, **alla þá er** all those who XII:58; *f. pl.* **allar** IV:82, XXVII:38, they all XI:50; *n. pl.* **ǫll** II:11, III:88, VI:86, 223, 305, VII A:35, XI:50, XIX:97, XXVI B:221, XXVII:27, complete II:61, the whole I:50, them all XXII:4/2, XXVI B:195, **ǫll váru þau** they were all XV:40, **ǫll ein** all the same XXI:192; *gen. pl.* **allra** IV:70, VI:193, VII A:123, VIII:44, X:133, XXII:65/4, of all XIX:104, **til allra þeirra** to all those who XXIV:81, *with sup.* of all *Gr* 3.5.3 (12), *with num.* all told, in all X:48; *dat. pl.* **ǫllum** I:17, 84, VIII:179 (everyone), XXII:9/2, XXVI A:105, B:121, XXVII:39, they/them all XXI:76, XXII:13/4, XXVI B:30, **allum** XXIV:60, *dat. of comparison* than/to all XXIV:16, **allum þeim er** for all those who XXIV:68; *n. as adv.* **allt** all the way, right VII A:3, 153; **allt í heilann** right to the brain XXVI A:18; **allt saman** altogether, the whole of XXIII:54; **allt um** all over, over the whole of VII B:24; **allt þar sem** everywhere where XXI:91; *gen. sg. n. as adv.* **alls** in all V:82, VI:49, VIII:193, XV:133, at all VI:211, **alls fyrst** first of all IX:5, **alls engi** no . . . at all XXI:108; **alls/allz** *as conj.* since VI:329, XXV:92

allsannr (*n.* **allsatt**) *adj.* very true XI:184

allsárliga *adv.* very bitterly XI:8

allsherjarfé *n.* public property VIII:53 (not recorded elsewhere)

allsherjargoði *m.* supreme priest/chieftain XIX:113 (his chief duty was to open or hallow the proceedings of the Alþingi every year)

allskǫruligr *adj.* very splendid, magnificent XV:79

allstórr *adj.* very large VI:127

allsvaldandi *adj. (pres. part.)* 'all-ruling', almighty XXIV:18

allumveginn = **ǫllumveginn** *adv.* on all sides VI:276 (*cf.* **megin**)

allvaldr *m.* all-powerful one, ruler (King Óláfr; *subject of* **vá**) VI:159

allþarfliga *adv.* most earnestly II:34

allþurr *adj.* very dry X:54 (*f. with* **fura**)

almáttigr *adj.* almighty; **almáttkum Guði** to almighty God XIV:65

almenning *f.* (land) where common rights exist (*Laws* II 29 note 19, 414) VIII:54

álna(r) *see* **alin**

Álptafjǫrðr enn syðri *m.* fjord in south-east Iceland XIX:28

álptahamr *m.* swan-shape, swan form X:7

alroskinn *adj. (pp.)* quite grown up VII B:6

alsnotr *adj.* very clever, absolutely clever IX:102

alsvartr *adj.* completely black, pure black IX:90

Alvini *m.* (*spelled* **Alfvini** *in K and some other manuscripts*; *variants*: **Alvini, Alfini**) fictional Englishman VII A:76, 80, 97, 99, 102, 104, 106

alvitr *adj.* all-wise, absolutely wise; *as a byname* X:9; **Alvitr** *f. as a personal name* X:11, 18, 30, 59

alvæpni *n.* full armour; **með alvæpni** fully armed VIII:110, XXVI B:11

Alþingi *n.* general assembly (legislative and judicative assembly for the whole of Iceland held annually in late summer at **Þingvǫllr**) VIII:42, 44, 53, 54, 95, 97, 99, 182, XV:4, 137, XIX:108, XXVII:29, 49; **á Alþingi hér** here at the Alþingi XXVII:39

alþýða *f.* general public; **at alþýðu tali** according to the common reckoning VIII:149

ambátt/ ambótt *f.* handmaid IX:79, 102; female slave XIX:100

amen *interjection* (ecclesiastical Latin, ultimately from Hebrew) 'so be it' XIII:49

áminna (*past* **áminnti,** *pp.* **áminnt**) *wv.* remind, admonish; *pres. part.* **áminnandi** insistent XIV:137

amma *f.* grandmother; in address XXVI B:171

ámunr *adj. with dat.* reminiscent of, similar to X:83

án *prep. with dat.* (*Gr* 3.7.6) without, lacking; **án ráði** *with gen.* without consultation with VI:16; **þóttisk varla án** felt he hardly lacked V:114

ána *see* **á³**

ánauð *f.* hardship, torment (of Hell?) XXII:49/4

andaðr *adj. (pp.)* dead VII A:75

andask (*past* **andaðisk,** *past pl.* **ǫnduðusk**) *wv. refl.* die III:131, VII A:92, XIV:168, 171

anddyri *n.* entrance, porch III:12 (*with suffixed def. art.*), III:21 (*with suffixed def. art.*), III:48 (*with suffixed def. art.*)

andi *m.* spirit; **heilagr andi** the Holy Spirit XIII:48, XIV:101

andligr *adj.* spiritual XIV:147

andlit *n.* face VII A:85, XII:11, 50, XXIII:54; *with suffixed def. art.* his face XXVI B:92

andskoti *m.* enemy, adversary IV:40 (*pl. subject of* **sitja ok hvetja**), VIII:106

andsvar *n.* reply, answer; *pl.* VII A:40, 44, 51, XXIV:2, 49, responsibility XXIV:73

andvaka *adj.* sleepless *Gr* 3.3.8.5 (6)

andverða *see* **ǫndverða**

angra (*past* **angraði**, *pp.* **angrat**) *wv. with dat.* distress XXVI B:176
ann *see* **unna**
annar(r) (*f.* **ǫnnur**, *n.* **annat**) *pron. adj.* (*Gr* 3.4.1) other, another, a
second II:20, 81, 148, VI:67, 274, VII A:62, 103, VIII:16, 40, 62,
XIX:2, 89, XXII:18/1, XXIV:8, 36, XXVI A:40, B:102, 226; the
second X:4, XV:98; next XV:81, XIX:9, XXVI B:125; another (man)
III:57, 85; other XXVI B:148; any other II:6, VII B:14; different
XXVI B:138; **engi annarr** no one else XXVI A:66; **sá annarr er**
some other person who XXIV:70; **sá annarr (kostr)** . . . **hinn annarr**
the first (choice) . . . the second/other XXVI B:103; *f.* **ǫnnur** another
XV:133, **annr** VI:31; *n.* **annat** other XII:68, next XV:82, (*i.e.* **lið**)
other troops, more men VI:222; **annat sumar** for the following
summer XXVII:39; **eigi annat** nothing else I:102; **margt annat**
much else VIII:178; **annat . . . en** something other than V:137,
anything other than XII:11, 60, XVI:35; **annat lið hans** the rest of
his troops VII B:60, **annat lið þeira** the rest of their party XXI:86,
annat liðit the other troop XXI:147; *gen.* **annars** another XXVI
B:124, something else XXVI B:78; **eigi annars ván** no other
expectation VIII:90; **eigi annars en** no differently than if VI:257;
einskis annars en nothing else than XXI:129; **ens annars hundraðs**
of the second hundred (*Gr* 3.4.2 (9)) VIII:148, XXI:18; **annars dags**
tomorrow X:106; **annars staðar** elsewhere XIV:179, XXI:47, XXVI
B:208; *acc. m. sg.* **annan** I:146 (another), II:31 (the other), VIII:111
(the next), X:110 (the other), XI:47 (the other), XXVI B:77 (another),
XXVII:50 (another); **annan veg** in any other way XXVI B:65; *dat.*
sg. m. **ǫðrum** II:70, XXVII:11, a second II:153, the other XXV:46;
gen. sg. f. **annarrar** VII A:47; *dat. sg. f.* **annarri** (help) the other
XXV:48; *dat. sg. n.* **ǫðru** V:1, 147, XXVI A:117; **ǫngu ǫðru en**
nothing else than XVI:36; *m. pl.* **aðrir** others VII A:81, XIV:181,
XVI:34, 187, XXIII:32, XXVII:16, 46, other VII A:36, 161, VIII:81,
IX:58, XIV:105, the other VI:270, XXIII:83, the others XXVII:19;
acc. pl. m. **aðra** VII A:68, VII B:10, other XXIV:78, the other XXVI
A:60, another XXVI A:88, the others VIII:114, other people
XXIII:81; **þá luti aðra** the other things XXIV:49; *f. pl.* **aðrar** others
XXVI B:126, other, different IV:13; *n. pl.* **ǫnnr** VI:303; **annr þau**
the other VI:74, **annur þau** those other XXIV:83; **sem ǫnnur** like
the others VIII:143; **skip hans ǫll ǫnnr** all his other ships VI:223;
gen. pl. **annarra** VII A:155, of others (other people) XXIII:73, 85;

einnhverr annarra anyone else XXIV:63; **hverr maðr annarra** any other man VIII:150; **enginn annarra** no one else I:126; *dat. pl.* **ǫðrum** other XXVI B:31, others, other people VII A:51, XXV:30, XXVI B:33; one (of two): **ǫðru(m) megin** on one side III:6, XII:52, on the other side XXI:205; **annarr/annat/ǫnnur ... annarr/annat/ ǫnnur** one ... the other III:31–32, XIX:62–63, XXI:203, **ǫðrum ... ǫðrum** IV:8–9, XII:52–58; **annarr/annat þessara/þeira ... annarr/ annat** one of them ... the other XII:19–20, XXI:49–50 (cf. *Gr* 3.2.1 (1), 3.9.6.1); **á aðra hlið** *(with dat.)* ... **en á aðra** on one side of someone ... and on the other XI:74; **annarr at ǫðrum, hvern at ǫðrum** one after another VIII:113, XI:10; **hverjum at ǫðrum** each (group, rank) after the other XI:58; **hverr við annan** with each other VI:150; **hverr annan** each other II:44; **hverr ǫðrum** *(poss. dat.)* II:130; **hvárr ǫðrum** each to the other III:17

annask *(past* **annaðisk,** *past pl.* **ǫnnuðusk)** *wv.* **-sk** *form* take care of; **ǫnnuðusk um** were occupied with XIV:134

ánni *see* **á³**

annmarki *m.* fault, wickedness XIV:105, 106

annr = ǫnnur, *see* **annarr**

annt *n. adj. with dat.* desirous; **er annt til** (someone) wants (something) XXI:64

aptann *m.* evening XV:67, XVI:98; **þenna aptan** this evening XXVI B:21, **þenna aptan inn sama** that same evening XXVI B:19

aptr *adv.* back I:32, 42, 116, III:123, 124, V:78, 95, VI:14, 272, VII A:42, 106, IX:29, X:12, 59, XVI:12, 39, 87, XIX:30, 74, 88, XXI:43, 165, 180, 193, XXVI B:195; backwards II:159, VI:215, XXVI B:92, 215, leaning backwards? XXIII:102; aft VI:268, 285, to the rear of the ship VI:279; **fallinn aptr** closed XV:104

ár¹ *f.* oar VI:125

ár² *n.* year XIX:48, 50

ár³ *adv.* early XXV:3

Arabíagull *n.* Arabian gold XII:31

áraburðr *m.* protection XV:126

árbakki *m.* bank of the river VII B:83 *(with suffixed def. art.)*

arðr *(gen.* **arðrs)** *m.* plough; *with suffixed def. art.* XIX:64

arfasáta *f.* heap of chickweed; **arfasátu þá er** the heap of chickweed which XXVI B:117

arfr *m.* inheritance II:79

argr *adj.* effeminate, perverted IX:66; dastardly, wicked XXII:30/4 ('some wicked Búfinnar')

Ari Ingimundarson *n.* 1226–1258; one of the incendiaries at Flugu-mýrr III:71, 107

ármaðr *m.* steward XVI:44, 55 (*with suffixed def. art.*)

armgrjót *n.* 'arm-rock', stones of the arm, gold rings or jewels, wealth VI:307 (*gen. with* **ógrœðir**)

armleggr *m.* arm V:21, XXIII:82

armr[1] *adj.* miserable, wretched IX:114

armr[2] *m.* arm *Gr* 3.1.7.1 ex. 3, 3.1.7.2

arn- *see* **ǫrn**

Arnardóttir *f.* daughter of Ǫrn Bjǫrnólfsson XIX:11, 39

arnarhamr *m.* eagle shape, eagle form II:41, 53 (*with suffixed def. art.*), 154, 155

Arnarhváll *m.* a hillock in Reykjarvík XIX:92

Árni Ármóðsson *m.* XXII:18/1, 40/1; **Árna synir** = Finnr and Þorbergr XXII:40/1

Árni beiskr *m.* III:52, 64, 67

Arnljótr gellini *m.* a robber XXII:27/2, 39/1

arnsúgr *m.* 'eagle-sucking' or 'eagle-noise', the wind (or its sound) caused by an eagle's wings II:53

áróss *m.* river-mouth, mouth of a river XXI:88, 169

árr *m.* messenger, servant, user; **árr oddflagðs** *is a kenning for an unnamed* warrior VI:333 (subject of **var samr**)

ásamt *adv.* together XV:32

Ásbrandr Þorleiksson *m.* XXVI A:71

Ásgarðr *m.* the home of the Æsir II:3, 45, 62, IX:70; the fortification round the home of the Æsir II:36, 39, 55, 157

Ásgrindr *f. pl.* the gates of the (home of the) Æsir II:60

Ásgrímr *m.* died in the fire at Flugumýrr III:75

ásjáandi *m. (pres. part.)* onlooker (cf. **sjá**); **enginn ásjáandi maðr** no person looking at it XII:11

ásjána *f.* look, face; **ásjánu þína** the sight of your face IV:79 (*object of* **meina mér**)

asni *m.* ass, donkey; *dat. pl.* **ǫsnum** XXIII:60

Áss *m.* a god, one of the Æsir, q.v.; = Þórr IX: 8 (i.e. the speaker), 65

ássendi *m.* end of roof-beam (projecting at the gable; cf. **brúnáss**) XXVI A:59

ást *f.* love (**við** of *or* for someone) XII:36, 39, XIV:93, 97; *pl.* affections IX:117, love XIV:90, *note*

ástarþokki *m.* feeling(s) of love XII:83

Ástríðr *f.* daughter of Búrizleifr VI:23, 44, 46, 47

Ástríðr af Djúpárbakka *f.* wife of Grímr Njálsson XXVI B:143, 146

ástsamligr *adj.* loving, affectionate XII:83

ástsæld *f.* popularity VIII:151

ástsæll *adj.* beloved, popular (**við** with) XIV:113; *comp.* **ástsælli af** more popular with VIII:150

ástvinr *m.* close friend VI:321, XIV:155

Ásum *see* Æsir

Ásynja *f.* a goddess, female **Áss**; *pl.* **Ásynjur** II:10, IX:54

at[1] *prep. with dat.* (*Gr* 3.7.3) at II:91, X:45, XVI:109, 111, XIX:10, XXI:45, XXV:110, XXVI A:13, B:2, XXVII:27 (2), 30; in VI:24, 246, 308, VIII:147, XIX:65, XXII:61/4; of VIII:30; to I:23, 28, II:7, III:29, 39, VI:244, 285, VII B:70, IX:131, XI:30, XVI:130, XIX:23, XXI:87, XXII:28/1, 37/4, XXV:35, 54, 101, XXVI A:101, B:155; into I:128, IX:82, X:136; towards, up to I:17, 39, 116, 138, VI:135, XIX:60, 83 (2), XXI:35 (2), XXVI A:32; in, over XIX:48; after VIII:113; against IV:45 (*i.e.* of), VI:289, XXVI A:6; beside IX:89; with respect to, by II:64, XVI:2, XXV:55; in XXIII:96, XXIV:65; with, in XXV:28; with regard to VI:226, 357 (*with* **orði**), XII:10, as regards XII:21, (of) XXV:17, 18; according to VI:330, VIII:8, 61, 149; (swear) by X:150; in, to be gained from I:66; about, concerning I:58; from V:85, VI:18; for IX:90; for, in search of IV:32, X:34, 35; with, (while engaged) at XXV:71; engaged in, busy with XIX:83 (1); as IV:91, IX:30, 43, 87; in accordance with VIII:42, 44, 173; **at því sem** in accordance with how VIII:38; **at því er/es** about how VIII:144, according to what VIII:14, 73; *in 'dat. absolute' construction* (*Gr* 3.9.7.3) VIII:195, **at óbyggðu landi** while the land was uninhabited XIX:104; *of time* at, in II:37, 38, 138, IX:93 (to?), towards I:73, at the beginning of XV:14; *with gen.* at the house of VIII:172, X:79 (*Gr* 3.1.5 (13)); *with acc.* **at þat** after that X:26; *as adv.* about it I:3, in it II:77, XV:21, XXIV:5, of them XIV:41, **er ... at** in which XIV:126; busy, employed XIV:133, XVI:131; **hér at** to this I:54; **at þar er** to where VI:271

at[2] *conj.* that (*Gr* 3.1.2.1, 2) I:6, 27, 29, 46, 51, 54, 74, 83, 94, 113, 115, 116, 119, 125, 134, 136, 143, 144, 145, II:16 (*after* **þar**), 19, 22 (*after* **mál**, saying that), 63, 145, VI:75, 147, 151, 203, 335, 346 (*with* þess 342), VIII:2, 15, 23, X:42, 109, 152, XV:20, 23, XVI:31, XIX:10 (2), XXI:50, XXII:47/2, XXIII:1, XXIV:1 (2), 11, XXV:67, 103, XXVI A:2, 35, B:33, XXVII:2, 25; *as rel.* (*Gr* 3.8.2.1, p. 212) which XXVI A:117, such that XII:27, XIV:96 (2)?, XVI:125 (1), in which, by which I:124; so that III:111, V:109 (2), VIII:90, XIII:46, XIV:72, XXIV:26? 42 (2)? 45? 51? 83, XXVI B:20; in such a way that, so that XIV:33, 96 (2), XXII:60/2; when, if I:79; **attu = at þú** that you XXVI B:218; **til at** in order that XXVI B:65; **þeir at** such that VI:82; **þat at** that which, what XXV:80; *after* **svá** I:17, 26, 36, 43, 97, 109, II:5, 73; **þó . . . at** though, even if IX:15

at³ *particle with inf.* to I:33, 34, 52, 53, 63, 84, 86, 89, 93, II:11, 35, 69, IV:5, 20, 56, VI:20, 160, 331, VII A:32, VIII:3, 6, IX:3, 44, X:12, 13, 19, XIX:12, 24, XXI:2, XXII:1/2, XXIII:36, XXIV:1 (1), 8, XXV:9, XXVI A:9, XXVII:17, 18; in order to IX:120, XXII:33/2, XXV:42; intending to II:62 (see **taka**), 94; engaged in: **at hirða** looking after XIV:135, **at lúka** finishing XXVI A:3

at⁴ *adv. with comparative* because of this; **at lengrum** the longer V:18; **þess at meir** all the more VII A:43; **at heldr** the rather, all the more XXVI A:105; **eigi at síðr** none the less VI:212

-at *neg. suffix with verbs* V:149, VI:138, 177, 246, 348, X:152, 170, XXV:33, 35, 62

át¹ *n.* eating VIII:141

át² *see* **eta**

atburðr *m.* event, what had happened II:106, VIII:144; *acc. pl.* **atburði** IV:77

atferð *f.* attack VII B:87

atflutning *f.* supplies, provisions; **til atflutninga** fetching supplies XIV:136

atganga *f.* attack V:137, VII B:73 (*with suffixed def. art.*), VII B:74

atgeirr *m.* halberd, thrusting spear XXVI A:30, 35, 69

atgørvi *f.* ability VII B:9

athugaleysi *n.* heedlessness, carelessness XXIII:44

athugasamr *adj.* attentive, careful, thoughtful, reflective XXIII:12

athugi *m.* attentiveness XIV:22; **með athuga** with devotion XIV:62, 161

athœfi *n.* conduct, way of behaving XII:74

átján *num.* eighteen *Gr* 3.4.1

átjándi *num. adj.* eighteenth *Gr* 3.4.1

atkall *n.* demand VI:5

atkvæði *n.* expression XXIV:3; mode *or* form of address XXIV:41, 52, 62

Atli Buðlason *m.* Attila the Hun, former husband of Guðrún XXV:28 (cf. **Attila**)

Atli enn mjóvi *m.* XIX:6, 15, 24. Cf. *Landnámabók, ÍF* I 370–76, and *Flóamannasaga, ÍF* XIII 231–45

atmælasamr *adj.* given to finding fault, abusive XXI:12

atreið *f.* ride XXVI A:1

atseta *f.* residence I:2

atsókn *f.* attack VI:315; *with suffixed def. art.* his attack V:141

átt¹ *see* **eiga**

átt² *f.* family line; **seggja átt** the race of men; *gen. with* **sætt** (*i.e.* among) VI:56

átta¹ *num.* eight (*Gr* 3.4.1) VII B:33, IX:28, 95, 104, XIX:50, XXVI A:75

átta² *see* **eiga**

áttartala *f.* genealogy (perhaps collective) VIII:4

átti¹ *ordinal num.* eighth X:27

átti², **áttir** *see* **eiga**

Attila *m.* (*indeclinable*) king of the Huns (died AD 453) XI:14, 38, 44, 51, 52, 53, 55, 57; cf. **Atli Buðlason**

áttrœðr *adj.* 80 years old VIII:29

attu = **at²** **þú**

áttu, áttum, áttusk *see* **eiga**

átu *see* **eta**

auðigr *adj.* wealthy *Gr* 3.3.8.5 (1), 3.3.9 (10), (20), XV:3

auðit *pp. with gen.* fated XXVI B:78

auðkenndr *adj. pp.* easily recognised VI:290

auðn *f.* wilderness, uncivilised wasteland XXV:105

auðna (*pres.* **auðnar**, *past* **auðnaði**, *pp.* **auðnat**) *wv. impers. with gen.* something is granted by fate; **ef þess vildi auðna** if it were granted by fate III:92 (*unless* **auðna** *is here a f. noun and the subject, meaning* fate); **eptir því sem auðnar** as fate determines I:85

auðr¹ *adj.* empty VI:269, X:32 (*with* **sali**); *acc. with* **sá Tranu ok báða Naðra fljóta** VI:306

auðr² *m.* wealth VI:351 (*gen. with* **kenni**)

Auðr *f.* wife of Þórðr Ingunnarson XV:49, 64, 69, 70, 71, 83, 84, 86, 91, 98, 103, 106, 109, 115, 119, 120

auðræði *n. pl.* property, wealth, XIV:9

auðsóttr *a.* (*pp., cf.* **sœkja**) easily won, soon granted (with dat., to someone; **við** by) XV:78

auðsær *adj.* easy to see V:46

Auðunn *m.* a young Icelander, apparently a member of farmer
Þorsteinn's household XVI:1, 2, 4, 6, 8, 10, 13, 18, 36, 41, 47, 60,
75, 78, 97, 99, 105, 107 (**honum Auðuni** *Gr* 3.9.6.1), 115, 117, 121,
130, 132, 136, 146, 162, 165, 169, 172, 176, 181, 188, 189, 191
auðveldliga *adv.* easily XIII:24, 45
auðveldr *adj.* easy; compliant, tractable XXIII:70; *comp. n. as adv.*
því auðveldara mun okkr it will be the easier for us V:67
auðœfi *n. pl.* wealth, income VIII:161, 162
auga *n.* eye *Gr* 3.1.8.(30); *pl.* II:74, IX:108, X:83, XIV:26, *note*, XXI:68,
XXIII:21, 24, 29; *pl. with suffixed def. art.* **augun** XXIII:33; **í augum**
in his looks XII:57; **mínum augum** with my own eyes XIV:172
augsýn *f.* sight; **mér í augsýn** into my sight XVI:75
auka (*pres.* **eykr,** *past* **jók,** *past pl.* **jóku,** *pp.* **aukinn**) *sv.* increase,
add to V:161; **auka við, auka þar viðr** add to it VIII:3, 40; **jók nú
miklu á** it was now become much worse XVI:99; *past with suffixed
1st person pron.* **jókk** *with dat. object* VIII:4; *pp.* **gengr barni aukin**
is great with child X:166
aumr *adj.* poor, needy XXII:31/4
aungr = **øngr**, *see* **engi**
aura, aurar, aurum *see* **eyrir**
austan *adv.* from the east, westwards VI:60, 64, XXVI B:15; i.e. to
Iceland VIII:91; **fyr austan** east of VIII:18
Austfirðingafjórðungr *m.* the Eastern Fjords Quarter (of Iceland)
VIII:165
Austfirðir *m. pl.* the Eastern Fjords (of Iceland) VIII:50
Austmaðr *m.* easterner, Norwegian *Gr* 3.1.9 ex.12, XXVI A:29
austr *n.* the east; **ór austri** from the east XXI:169; *as adv.* eastwards
VI:21, 352, VII A:162, X:34, XVI:42, XXVI A:4, 10, *Gr* 3.5.3 (8);
i.e. to Norway VIII:84; in the east VIII:41 (of Iceland), 69 (of
Greenland); i.e. in Norway VIII:87
Austrvegr *m.* 'the eastern route', the countries east of the Baltic XVI:129
austrœnn *adj.* from the east, i.e. Norwegian VIII:35
auvirðismaðr *m.* worthless wretch, contemptible person XXI:133
Ávaldamon *m.* a native king in North America XXI:203
ávalt *adv.* constantly X:98, 143, always XIV:31, XXVII:2
ávant *adj. n. with gen.* someone (is) lacking IX:92
áverki *m.* wound III:86, XV:107, 111, 113; *gen. pl.* **til áverka við
hann** for the wounding *or* butchering of him III:106
ávǫxtr *m.* increase, interest XIV:123; *dat. pl.* **ávęxtum** fruit XXIV:37

bað, baðat *see* **biðja, -at**

báðir (*n.* **bæði,** *gen.* **beggja**) *pron. adj.* both (*Gr* 3.4.1) II:139, III:26, XII:54, XV:108, XVI:57, XXVI A:69, 74; we both I:64 (*with* **vit Họttr**), I:65 (*with* **vit**), XXVI B:204; **ok báðir þeir** as were they both VII B:69; *n.* (*Gr* 3.9.6.1) **okkr bæði** us both XXVI B:164; **þau bæði** XXVI B:165; *acc. m.* **báða** II:28, VI:309, **okr báða** both of us XXV:38, **þá báða** both of them III:94, VII A:137; *gen.* **beggja vinir** friends of both of them VII B:57; **ykkur beggja** of you both X:167; *dat.* **báðum** XXII:48/2, **þeim báðum** them both III:63 (*see note*)

báðu *see* **biðja**

bagall *m.* crozier VIII:23

bak *n.* back XXV:50; **at baki** *with dat.* behind someone III:18; **á bak** on horseback III:120, XV:98, 110; **á bak þeim** behind them V:86; **fell á bak aptr** fell over backwards XXVI B:92; **af baki** off one's horse XV:101; *with suffixed def. art.* **á bakinu** on its back I:76

baka (*past* **bakaði,** *pp.* **bakat**) *wv.* bake XXVI B:111

bakborði *m.* port side of ship; **á bakborði þeim** on their port side XXI:168

bakki *m.* bank XXI:170

Bakki *m.* farm in northern Iceland III:2

bál *n.* fire XXVI B:107, 120 (*pl.*)

baldr *adj.* bold (or *m.* lord) XXV:91

Baldr *m.* a god, one of the Æsir, son of **Óðinn;** *dat.* **Baldri** II:66

ballr *adj.* dangerous, destructive, fatal; *n. pl.* **bọll** XXV:95

bana (*pres.* **banar,** *past* **banaði,** *pp.* **banat**) *wv. with dat.* kill I:15, 21

banamenn *m. pl.* slayers VII B:82

banasár *n.* mortal wound III:56, XXVI A:116

banasótt *f.* mortal sickness, last (final) illness XIX:111

bani *m.* death I:44, 88, 131, II:47, V:102, 103, 129, VI:132, XXVI A:77; **við bana** close to death XXVI A:89; ; cause of death, slayer IV:42, V:156, XXV:23; **verða at bana** *with dat.* cause the death of someone X:153, XIX:77 (*understand* of him); **þat sé þeira bani** it would be (lead to) their death XXVI B:66; **þat er várr bani** that will lead to our deaths XXVI B:86

bann *n.* ban, prohibition XXII:5/3

banna (*pres.* **bannar,** *past* **bannaði,** *pp.* **bannat**) *wv. with dat. of person(s)* forbid I:83, VIII:26, XIV:76, 79, XXI:114; **banna at gera** forbid its being done, forbid the practice XIV:85

banvænn *adj.* likely to die, appearing mortally wounded, deadly sick VII A:54

bar *see* **bera**

bardagi *m.* battle (*Gr* 3.1.7.1, 3.1.8 (9)) VI:85, VII A:53, VII B:88; fight VII A:100

barða, barði[1] *see* **berja**

barði[2] *m.* a ship with a projection at the front for ramming; **Barði** as name of a ship (= **Járnbarðinn**) VI:234 (*object of* **lagði**), VI:251 (*object of* **fœrðuð**); *with suffixed def. art.* **Barðinn** VI:273

barðisk, barðr, barðusk, barizk *see* **berja**

barma (*past* **barmaði**, *pp.* **barmat**) *wv.* complain, lament XXI:66, *textual note*

barn *n.* child VIII:140, X:166; *pl.* **bǫrn** XXVI B:3; **bǫrn tvau** two were children XXI:199; *dat. pl.* **bǫrnum** children XXVI B:134

barndómr *m.* childhood XIV:167

barsmíðir *f. pl.* fighting VIII:127

báru *see* **bera**

bast *n.* bast (rope), rope made of the inner bark of a tree X:47, *with suffixed def. art.* X:79

bátr *m.* (rowing) boat XIX:70, 81, XXI:22, 33

batt *see* **binda**

bauð *see* **bjóða**

Baugi *m.* a giant II:130, 131, 134, 135, 138, 139, 141, 142, 144, 145, 146, 147, 149

bauglestir *m.* 'ring-damager', one who breaks or uses up, *i.e.* gives away (gold) rings, *a kenning for* generous man (= Kormakr) IV:94 (*nom. phrase used in address*)

baugr *m.* ring; arm-ring X:47, 56, 82, 97, 122; *collective sg.* X:111; *descriptive gen. with* **serkjar**, shirt made of rings, mail-coat VI:261; *or* **baugr Heðins serkjar**, the circle of Heðins shirt (*gen. with* **verkendr**) = shield?

baukr *m.* (= **buðkr**) small box (for herbs) XII:17; the form **baukr** is generally only found in 17th-century texts; the form **bauðk** in line 18 appears to be a compromise between the two.

bazt *adv. sup.* best VI:224

beðit *see* **biðja**

beðr *m.* bed XV:109, XXV:23

beggja *see* **báðir**

beið *see* **bíða**

beiða (*pres.* **beiðir**, *past* **beiddi**, *pp.* **beiddr**) *wv.* **1.** *with acc. and gen.*

ask (someone for something) XV:20. **2. -sk** *form* **beiðask** (*with acc. and gen.*) ask (someone for something) for oneself, request, demand II:138, III:19; **beiddiz at** stirred himself up for, spurred himself to XXV:71 (*see note*)

beiðir *m.* demander, ruler; *in kenning for* shield-user, man, warrior (= Bjǫrn), **beiðir meiðs morðvandar** V:154

bein *n.* **1.** leg III:113. **2.** bone I:35, 52, XXVI B:177

beina (*past* **beindi,** *pp.* **beindr**) *wv.* assist; **beina at** (**með þér**) lend (you) a hand V:68, XXVI B:203

beinahrúga *f.* pile of bones I:6, 32; *with suffixed def. art.* I:7, 13

beini *m.* hospitality XIV:138

beiskr *adj.* bitter; *as nickname* III:52, 64, 67

beit *see* **bíta**

beita (*past* **beitti,** *pp.* **beitt**) *wv.* cause to bite; **beita á veðr** *with dat.* sail (**þeim** their ships; *unless* **þeim** *goes with* **hólmanum**) close to the wind VI:124, XXI:31

bekkr *m.* bench, seating platform I:29; *acc. pl.* **bekki** IX:86. *Cf.* **pallr**

belgr *m.* animal skin, pelt XXI:115; bellows X:157 (*acc. pl.*); skin bag (i.e. the limbless body of Jǫrmunrekkr) XXV:94, 95 (*see note*)

bella (*pres.* **bellir,** *past* **belldi,** *pp.* **bellt**) *wv.* deal in, utter IX:39

belti *n.* belt II:125

ben *f.* wound *Gr* 3.1.7.3–5 ex. 4

benda (*past* **bendi,** *pp.* **bendr**) *wv.* (*Gr* 3.6.9.3 ex. 4) indicate, give a foreboding (**mér** to me) V:17

bera¹ (*pres.* **berr,** *past* **bar,** *past pl.* **báru,** *past subj.* **bæri** (*Gr* 3.6.5.2), *pp.* **borinn**) *sv.* (*Gr* 3.6.6) **1.** carry I:22, 89, 99, II:5, 55, III:49, VI:114, XI:45, XII:6, 67, XIX:110, XXI:56, 206, XXVI B:174; **berr þá** carries them, moves them XXIII:104; bear XXIV:63; put XXVI B:27; take XXVI B:117; wear X:79, 96, XII:28; hold VII A:160; **berr sik** holds itself XXIII:76; bear (witness) VI:324; overcome, overpower X:130; **bera ráðum** overrule XXVI B:69; **bera ofrliði** overpower (*or* outnumber?) XXI:145; **bera sigr** win victory VI:185; *imp. pl.* **berum** let us carry (it) XXI:101; **berið** bring IX:120; *subj.* **beri** were/is carrying XXIII:102; *1st person past* **bárum** we (*i.e.* I?) bore (*vb. after* **þá er**) VI:208; *pp.* **hefr borit** has been drawn XXVII:10; **hǫfðu borit** had borne them (*Gr* 3.9.5.1) VI:304; (**vera**) **borinn** be carried VII A:54, (be) taken X:94, 95, (be) born (*with dat.,* to someone) X:73, XXV:8 (i.e. she was his daughter); *pres. part.* **berandi** (able) to be carried (*with dat.*, by someone) I:132; **bera af** surpass XXII:13/4; **bera niðr af** stick out underneath further (*or* force them away down?) XXIII:21; **bera at** bring up III:2, put on III:127; **bera at eld** make use of fire, set fire to it (the house) XXVI B:103; *pp.* **borit fram** served out (*with var* line 93) IX:94; **bera fyrir** serve to XXVI B:21; **bera þar í** put into them III:3; **bera í** pour on XXVI B:114; **bera eld í** set it on fire, set fire to it XXVI B:119; **bera milli** take from one to the other, mediate, negotiate VII B:57; **bera saman ok** compare with II:41; **borinn til** born for XXII:1/4; **bera um** take them round XXVI A:59; **bera upp** announce, set forth, make known VIII:111; **bera sik vel** comport oneself well XXVI B:33, bear up well III:130. **2.** *impers. with acc.* **bar hann** he appeared IV:15; **berr þá** they are carried (by wind and currents) XXI:167; **bar at . . . skjǫldinn** the shield was driven against XXVI B:91; **þat bæri frá** it was outstanding, extraordinary VIII:112; **bera fyrir** appear (to someone in a dream) V:16; **bera til** come about, happen XIII:12, XXI:119, XXIV:1; **þik skal út bera** you shall be carried out XXVI B:169; **bar við** was carried, i.e. passed, against *or* in front of XXVI A:30; *with dat.* **berr þér** it behoves you, you ought XXIV:85; **-sk** *form* **at berask** happen, turn out XVI:182

bera[2] *f.* she-bear X:53 (*dat. of respect, Gr* 3.9.6.2)

berar *see* **berr**[1]

berðisk *see* **berja**

berfjall *n.* bear-skin X:56

berfœttr *adj.* barefooted III:22, 62

berg *n.* cliff XIX:85

Bergljót *f.* daughter of Jarl Hákon VII B:5, 77 (*see note*), 80

bergrisi *m.* mountain giant VII A:160

bergsalr *m.* rock-hall, cave VII A:142

Bergþóra Skarpheðinsdóttir *f.* Njáll's wife XXVI B:19, 156, 161, 163, 165

Bergþórr Hrafnssonr *m.* lawspeaker 1117–22, died 1123 VIII:170, 171, 173, 181

Bergþórshváll *m.* Njáll's home in the south of Iceland XXVI B:2, 40, 106

berhǫgg *n. pl.* open blows, *in the phrase* **ganga í berhǫgg við** come out openly against (**um** with) XV:141

berja (*pres.* **berr**, *past* **barði**, *pp.* **barðr/bariðr**) *sv.* **1.** (*Gr* 3.6.9.2 (3), (6), 3.6.10) beat, strike I:52 (pelt), VII A:23, 105, XII:58, 61;

overcome, defeat XXV:82; **berja í móti** attack XXII:45/2; **barða**
(pp. acc. pl. m.) chastised XIV:103. **2. -sk** *form* **berjask** *(Gr* 3.6.10)
fight VI:90, 94, 97, VII A:6, VIII:110, XXI:135; *past* **barðisk** was
fighting VIII:146, **bǫrðusk** fought XXI:125; *past subj.* **berðisk** were
fighting VI:257; *pp.* **hǫfðu barizk** had been fighting XIX:16; **at
berjask við** to fight against VI:166; *past pl.* **barðusk við** VI:185
berliga *adv.* plainly, fully, absolutely XII:8
Bern *f.* Verona XI:43, 46, 56
bernskliga *adv.* childishly, like a child XXIV:24
berr[1] *adj.* bare, exposed XV:62; naked XXI:47
berr[2] *see* **bera**[1]
berserkr *m.* berserk *Gr* 3.1.9 ex. 8
Bersi Véleifsson, Hólmgǫngu-Bersi *m.* first husband of Steingerðr
XVIII:122rb31
bestibyrsíma X:65 *see note*
betr *adv. comp.* better *(Gr* 3.5.2) I:88, II:126, V:138, 160, VI:121,
X:131, XVI:111, XXI:135, XXIV:14, 28, XXVI A:42, B:71; **betr
... en** better than XXIV:21; **betr en** more than XXIV:19; **er betr** it
will be better VI:80
betri *adj. comp.* better *(Gr* 3.3.8.3) VIII:175, X:128, XI:68, XV:123,
XIX:29; finer XV:11; *n. (as adv.?)* XXVI B:172; **betra er oss** will
be better for us VI:83
beztr *adj. sup. (Gr* 3.3.8.3) best I:3, VI:214, VII A:80, 123, X:175;
finest XII:8, 31; **er bezt megu vera** the best that can be XI:60; **inn
bezti** a very fine XIV:175; **einn inn bezta klerk** one of the best
scholars XIV:27
bezt *adv. sup. (Gr* 3.5.2) best, most advantageously XVI:173, XXVI
B:72, most finely XIX:110, 112; **manna bezt** very well, as well as
any V:31; **njót manna bezt** use it best of anyone I:137 *(see* **njóta***)*
bíða *(past* **beið,** *past pl.* **biðu,** *pp.* **biðinn)** *sv.* wait V:89, VI:104, 109,
XIV:100; linger XXV:62; **bíðum** let us wait VI:65; *with gen.* wait
for V:110 *(inf. with* **skyldi***)*, X:39, XV:67, be waiting for VII B:41;
bíða þess er wait until VI:98, XXVI B:197; *with suffixed neg. and
pron. and acc. object* **bíðka þess bót** I shall not see (experience)
redress for this X:97
biðja *(past* **bað,** *past pl.* **báðu,** *pp.* **beðinn,** *n.* **beðit)** *sv. (Gr* 3.6.9.1
(5), (10))* **1.** *with acc. and gen.* ask, beg (someone for something;
and with dat., for someone) II:34, 40, 113 (**sér** for themselves), III:40,

67, VI:18, VIII:183, IX:115, XVI:43, 45, XXV:35, XXVI A:27; **biðja sér matar** beg for one's food XVI:91; *impers.* **skal þik þessa eigi lengi biðja** you shall not be asked for this for long (i.e. repeatedly) XXVI A:86; pray (for something) XIII:8; *imp.* **bið þú** ask, tell X:176; *pp.* demanded IX:128, pressed for it VIII:186; *with gen. of person* ask for someone's hand in marriage IV:101, XV:3, 7, 77, *pp.* VII A:77, 93. **2.** pray XXIV:41; **biðr ek** I pray XXII:65/3; **biðja fyrir sér** pray for oneself, *i.e.* say one's prayers III:9; **biðja bœnar sinnar** say one's prayer, make one's request XXIV:16. **3.** *with acc. and inf.* order/tell/ask (someone to do something) I:22, 41, 91, 114, 117, II:128 (**sér** to them), 147; III:91, IV:48, 99, VI:15, VII A:34, 111, VIII:116, XV:101, XVI:86, 183, XXI:37, 39, 43, XXVI B:8, 30; **bað øngvan mann** said no one was to XXVI B:37; **baðat hyggja** told (them) not to think VI:177; **bað/báðu þá/hann** told them/him VI:102, XXI:70, 71, XXVI B:195; **bað þá Þorkel nefju** told Þorkell nefja and his companions VI:120; **biðja (vera) vel kominn** bid welcome XI:9, XVI:107; command VII A:106; pray XXII:50/3

bifask (*past* **bifðisk**) *wv. refl.* shake IX:49

bikkja *f.* bitch; *with def. art. or demonstrative pron. as an insulting or contemptuous form of address* cur I:92

bil *n.* moment (of time); **í því/þessu bili** at that moment IV:64, V:129, VII B:79, XXVI A:68

bilt *adj. n. as adv.* startled, afraid; **varð þeim bilt** they hesitated, their hearts failed them IV:15

binda (*past* **batt**, *past pl.* **bundu**, *pp.* **bundinn**) *sv.* (*Gr* 3.6.9.1 (3, 6, 10), 3.6.9.2 (2)) bind, tie, fasten V:157 (**við** to; *see Gr* 3.9.5.1); tie up VII A:104, 105, X:65, XXV:76, 82, tether XXVI B:42; *with dat.* with, in something: *imp.* **bittu** IX:46; **bindu vér** let us tie IX:59 (*Gr* 3.6.9.1 (13)); **bindi menn** let men tie XXII:15/3 (**við** to); **batt sér** brought on himself XXII:52/2; **binda um** tie (a cord *or* a strip of cloth) round II:69 (*with the cord in the dat.*, **ǫðrum enda** II:70), XXI:116, wrap up, bandage XV:114; **-sk** *form for pass.* **bindask láta** let oneself be tied IX:67

birgðir *f. pl.* sustenance, provisions XXI:82

Birgir *m.* king of Denmark's reeve VII A:137, 142

birni *see* **bjǫrn**

Birni *see* **Bjǫrn Arngeirsson**

birta (*past* **birti**, *pp.* **birt**) *wv.* brighten, illuminate; reveal XXIII:38,

87; **birti** revealed it (**fyrir** to) XII:76; **-sk** *form* **birtisk** was revealed, was made manifest XIII:40

birti *f.* brightness XXIII:27, 33

biskup *m.* bishop III:32 (*as title*), XXVII:15 (**er biskup sá . . . með er** with whom the bishop . . . who)

bíta (*past* **beit,** *past pl.* **bitu,** *pp.* **bitinn**) *sv.* bite (*Gr* 3.6.6) IX:99, 100; cut II:126, 144, V:117, 145, 150, 155; **ok bíta vel** and that it cut well XXI:151; **bíta (á)** bite into, pierce, penetrate I:77, XXV:92; **ekki beit á** it did not make an impression on XXII:44/3

bitrligr *adj.* sharp, keen V:113

bittu *see* **binda**

bjálfi *m.* fur, (animal) skin with fur on it XXII:30/1 (*dat.* with an animal skin); *with suffixed def. art.* **hans bjálfan á** on/into that skin coat of his XXII:44/3

bjalla *f.* bell VIII:23, XII:46

bjarg (*pl.* **bjǫrg**) *n.* rock IX:83; *with suffixed def. art.* II:144, 145, 147; cliff XXI:80

bjarga (*past* **barg,** *past pl.* **burgu,** *pp.* **borginn**) *sv. with dat.* save XXII:65/3

bjarnar *see* **bjǫrn**

Bjarnar *see* **Bjǫrn Arngeirsson**

bjarndýr/bjarndýri *n.* an animal in the form of a bear, a (wild) bear XVI:11, 17, 63, 134, XXI:28

Bjarney *f.* 'Bear Island' XXI:28

Bjarneyjar *f. pl.* 'Bear Islands' XXI:20, 21

Bjarni Bergþórsson *m.* XIV:183

Bjarni Grímólfsson *m.* XXI:5, 66, 86, 162

Bjartey *f.* XXVI A:114

bjartliga *adv.* brightly, clearly XXIII:24

bjartr *adj.* bright, shining XXII:50/1, 62/3; *n. pl.* **bjǫrt** II:5

bjó *see* **búa**

bjóða (*pres.* **býðr,** *past* **bauð,** *past pl.* **buðu,** *pp.* **boðinn**) *sv.* **1.** offer XV:115, XIX:24, XXII:21/3; *with dat. and acc.* offer someone something I:60, II:62, 113, III:15, XXII:65/2, XXVI B:157; *pres. part.* **bjóðandi** offering it XII:50. **2.** *with dat.* invite II:102, 103, V:24, XVI:115, 169; challenge VII A:98; **bjóða út** summon, muster, levy VI:20, VII A:126. **3.** *with dat.* ask, command I:86, 119, VII A:146, B:22 (*inf. with* **vill**), XIV:62, 68, XV:97; charge XII:65,

26   *A New Introduction to Old Norse*

XIV:59, 60; *pp. (impers. pass., Gr* 3.9.3*)* **boðit** bidden (by nature or instinct) XXVI B:212

bjoggu, bjuggu *see* **búa**

bjórr *m.* beer; *instrumental dat.* with beer X:130

bjúgleikr *m.* curvature, crookedness XXIII:21

bjúgr *adj.* curved, bent, crooked XXIII:18, 90, 103; *pl. as substantive* **bjugir** cripples XXII:57/4

bjúgleitr *adj.* crooked-looking XXIII:55

bjǫllu, bjǫllur *see* **bjalla**

bjǫrg[1] *f.* means of subsistence, keep, maintenance XVI:7, 123

bjǫrg[2] *see* **bjarg**

bjǫrn (*gen.* **bjarnar,** *dat.* **birni** *Gr* 3.1.7.2 (2), 3.1.7.3–5 ex. 1) *m.* bear XIX:67 *(with suffixed def. art.)*, XXV:91; *as word-play on the name of* Bjǫrn Arngeirsson Hítdœlakappi V:63

Bjǫrn Arngeirsson Hítdœlakappi *m.* V:16, 27, 30, 33, 45, 47, 56, 65, 67, 77, 84, 85, 88, 91, 95, 97, 98, 103, 109, 111, 115, 119, 124, 126, 130, 134, 136, 142, 146, 159, 169; *gen. sg.* **Bjarnar** V:title, 98, 100, 129, 145, 157, 161; *dat. sg.* **Birni** V:1, 3, 93, 94, 114, 147, 169 (*poss. dat. with* **skǫr**)

Bjǫrn Gilsson *m.* bishop at Hólar 1146–62 XIV:178, 183

Bjǫrn Óláfsson *m.* died in the fire at Flugumýrr III:75

Bjǫrn stallari (digri) *m.* XXII:17/3, 45/1

Bjǫrnólfr Hrómundarson *m.* Icelandic settler XIX:2, 4

bjǫrtum *see* **bjartr**

bláhvítr *adj.* blue and white (striped) XXV:24

blaka (*past* **blakaði,** *pp.* **blakat**) *wv.* flap; *pres. part.* XII:33

blanda (*pres.* **blendr,** *past* **blett,** *past pl.* **blendu,** *pp.* **blandinn**) *sv.* with *dat.* mix II:98, XXI:157

blandask (*past* **blandaðisk,** *pp.* **blandazk**) *wv.* -sk *form* mix oneself, become mixed; **blandask við** be involved in, have dealings with, have to do with XXI:13

blár *adj.* (*Gr* 3.3.9 ex. 3) dark, blue-black; *acc. m. sg.* **blán** XXI:127

blása (*pres.* **blæss,** *past* **blés,** *past pl.* **blésu,** *pp.* **blásinn**) *sv.* blow II:145, 148; *with dat.* spit, belch forth VII A:152

Bláskógaheiðr *f.* heath near Þingvǫllr XV:47

Bláskógar *m. pl.* woods near Þingvǫllr VIII:48

blauðr *adj.* cowardly XXV:51

blauthærðr *adj.* (*pp.*) soft-haired XXIII:3

blautr *adj.* soft XXIII:88, 98

bleikr *adj.* pale XXIII:32; grey (of a wolf) XXII:41/2; **með bleikum** with pale or grey patches XXIII:106 (a word may be missing, or perhaps the word is here a noun, = **bleikja** *f.* white colouring)

blendu *see* **blanda**

blés(u) *see* **blása**

bleyði *f.* cowardice; **er engum manni blœyði at** it is not cowardice for any man to VI:167

blezan *f.* blessing XIV:148

blíði *f.* friendliness; **með blíði** graciously XVI:188

blíðr *adj.* happy; cheerful, friendly XII:50; kindly XIV:49 (*with dat.* towards), XXII:1/3 (**við** towards); *sup.* XXII:62/4; *n. as adv.* **þeim man vera blíðara** it will be pleasanter for them, they will find it is pleasanter VI:188

blik *n.* gleam, flash; *in kenning for* sword **randa blik** (that which flashes against shields; *gen. with* **rjóðandi**, *forming a kenning for* warrior) VII B:46

blíkja (*past pl.* **bliku**) *sv.* shine, flash, gleam X:44

blindr *adj.* blind; *dat. sg. with* **brœðr**, *i.e.* even if he were blind IV:93; *pl.* **blindir** blind people XXII:57/3

blóð *n.* blood I:101, II:96, 117, XXII:58/4, XXIII:37, XXV:84; *instrumental dat.* **blóði** with blood X:157; *with suffixed def. art.* II:98, III:86; **blóð eitt** nothing but blood XXVI B:29

blóðgagl *n.* 'goose of blood', *kenning for* raven (or other carrion bird); *pl.* V:170

blóðrás *f.* loss of blood XV:112

blóðslitr *m.* the colour of blood XXIII:33

blóðugr *adj.* bloody VI:196

blóm *n.* flower XXII:62/3

blómi *m.* flowering; **staðit með slíkum blóma . . . sem stóð** flourish as well as it did XIV:74–75; glory, blessedness, salvation XXII:25/2

blót *n.* (heathen) sacrificial feast XIX:41

blóta (*pres.* **blœtr** *Gr* 3.6.5.2, *past* **blét**, *past pl.* **blétu**, *pp.* **blótinn**) *wv.* worship, sacrifice (to heathen gods) (*Gr* 3.6.9.3) VIII:141, XIX:42, 78

blótbolli *m.* sacrificial bowl, cup used in heathen sacrifices VI:189

blótskapr *m.* heathen worship, pagan sacrifice XIV:77 *(pl.)*

blý *n.* lead XIV:10

blæss *see* **blása**

blœyði = **bleyði**

bóandaherr *m.* peasant army VII B:89 (*with suffixed def. art.*)

bóandi = **bóndi**; *gen. pl. with suffixed def. art.* VII B:74

boð *n.* feast, banquet (which might last several days) *Gr* 3.1.9 ex. 3, XIX:13 (*with suffixed def. art.*)

boða (*past* **boðaði,** *pp.* **boðat**) *wv.* proclaim, preach XXI:38

boði *m.* submerged rock, shoal II:104; breaker over a shoal XV:149

Boðn *f.* name of a vat II:98, 118, 153

boðorð *n.* commandment XIV:44 (dat. pl. object of **hlýða**)

bogastrengr *m.* bowstring XXVI A:69, 79

bogi *m.* bow XXV:76; *with suffixed def. art.* his/my bow XXVI A:64, 82

bógr *m.* shoulder; *acc. pl. with def. art.* II:28; *dat. sg.* **bœgi** I:97, X:151 (withers)

bók (*pl.* **bœkr**) *f.* book (*Gr* 3.1.7.2 and (6), 3.1.8 (19)) VIII:23, 172, XIV:32, 90, 91, 178; embroidered coverlet XXV:24

bokki *m.* buck; in an ingratiating form of address I:9, 11, 21, 39

bóklistir *f. pl.* literary skills, book-learning XIV:186

bókmál *n.* the Latin language; **at bókmáli** in Latin XVIII:97

bolr *m.* trunk (of the body): **ganga á milli bols ok hǫfuðs** *i.e.* sever the head from the body (the understood subject is probably the blow or the weapon, rather than Þórðr) V:147

bóndalið *n.* band of peasants, farmers VII B:79 (*with suffixed def. art.*)

bóndi (*nom. pl.* **bœndr**) *m.* farmer, peasant (*Gr* 3.1.7.2, twice) VII A:111, 115, 117, 120, B:24, 27, 29, 70, 87, XXII:12/2, XXVI A:8; *as title* XXVI A:14, in address XXVI B:157

bora[1] (*past* **boraði,** *pp.* **borat**) *wv.* bore (a hole in) II:144, 147; *pp. n.* II:145

bora[2] *f.* hole XII:16

borð *n.* board III:53, 54 (*with suffixed def. art.*), 64 (*with suffixed def. art.*); table XXVI B:27; *with suffixed def. art.* XVI:59, XXVI B:29, 35 (*pl.*: they would have been trestle tables); **til borðs** to table, to eat XI:44; **þar innan borðs** on board that ship VI:82; side (of a ship) X:150, *nom. pl.with suffixed def. art.* **borðen** VI:267; *dat. pl. with suffixed def. art.* VI:256; **borði hæstr** highest in the side, highest sided VI:224; **fyrir borð** overboard VI:294, 299, XIX:52

borðhús *n.* a cupboard or closet (in which the movable tables, trestles and related items were kept when not in use for meals) III:78

borði *m.* tapestry, embroidery IV:57 (*gen. pl.*)

borðmikill *adj.* high-sided (of a ship) VI:234

borg *f.* fortification, fortress, castle XXV:82, 87; *with suffixed def. art.* (*Gr* 3.1.9 ex. 7) I:116, II:56; city XI:3, 10, 61, 62, 76

borgarveggr *m.* wall of fortification II:57 (*with suffixed def. art.*); city wall XI:49

borgfirzkr *adj.* from Borgarfjǫrðr VIII:63

borin, borinn, borit *see* **bera**

bót (*pl.* **bœtr**) *f.* compensation *Gr* 3.1.7.2 (3); redress (*with gen.*, for something) X:97; cure XXII:57/3

bóta *see* **bœtr**

botn *m.* head, upper end (of a fjord) XIX:60 (*with suffixed def. art.*)

brá *see* **bregða**

bráð *f.* meat, food XXII:41/1

bráðr *adj.* quick XVIII:122rb12; *n.* **brátt** *as adv.* soon, quickly II:43, III:5, 130, V:60, VII A:55, XVI:16, XXI:64

bragð *n.* **1.** moment; **á skǫmmu bragði** in a brief period of time XIV:73. **2.** movement; **lítit bragð mun þá at** it must be a very slight thing, there can't be much sign of it XV:52. **3.** device; *especially in pl.* **brǫgð** stratagems (**til þess er** in order to bring about what) XIV:90, *note*; **þat bragðs taka** adopt this as our strategy XXVI B:105

bragða (*past* **bragðaði,** *pp.* **bragðat**) *wv. impers.* **bragðar** there is movement I:95

brágeisli *m.* 'eyelash-ray (of light)', *kenning for* eye; *dat. pl. object of* **rennda ek** IV:34

Bragi *m.* god of poetry (one of the Æsir) II:9, 13, 14, 77, 88, 123

bragnar *m. pl.* men XXII:1/3, 8/1, 57/2, XXV:84

bragníng(r) *m.* ruler, king XXII:12/1, 52/1, 65/4

bráhvítr *adj.* with white eyelashes X:176

brandr[1] *m.* firebrand, piece of burning wood XXVI B:193 (*with suffixed def. art.*)

brandr[2] *m.* sword(-blade) XXII:5/4, 16/4, 50/1; *collective sg. dat. as instrumental* with their swords XXII:20/4

branga *f.* battle XXV:71

brann *see* **brenna**[2]

brásk *see* **bregða; brast** *see* **bresta**

brátt *see* **bráðr**

brattr (*f.* **brǫtt**) *adj.* steep *Gr* 3.3.9 ex.14

braut[1] *f.* path, way XXV:51; road XXV:59; **á braut** on the road XXV:99; **á braut, í braut** *adv.* away II:42, IV:27, VI:10, VII A:155, VIII:22, 83, XVI:74, 126, 137, XXI:179, XXVI A:15, 107, B:85; **á braut af** away from, i.e. out from, up from XXII:60/3; *cf.* **brott**

braut[2] *see* **brjóta**

brautgangr *m.* separation; **brautgangs** *descriptive gen.* such that it would be grounds for divorce XV:27

brautgangssǫk *f.* grounds for divorce, accusation warranting divorce XV:62

bregða (*past* **brá**, *past pl.* **brugðu**, *pp.* **brugðit**) *sv. with dat.* move I:96 (*pp. with* **fær**); put VI:295; change II:51; bring to an end VI:364; break off, fail to fulfil IV:111; prevent (the fulfilment of something), cause to fail IV:86; **bregða á** move against, strike II:129; *subj.* **ok bregði á** tending (if it tends) towards XXIII:109; **bregða sverði/ saxi** draw a sword I:95, V:57, 115, VII B:68, XV:107; *imp. pl.* **bregðið sverðum** draw your swords VI:170; **bregða upp** lift up, raise XXI:112; **brá grǫnum við** drew back his lips (*i.e.* grimaced *or* grinned) at it XXVI B:95; *subj.* **hann brygði sér við** he was taken aback by, was affected by, flinched at *or* in the face of XXVI A:76; *impers. with dat.* **brá mǫnnum mjǫk við** people were very taken aback by XXVI B:35; *refl.* **bregðask** change oneself, turn II:148, 154; *pres.* **bregzk við** jerks away in response to II:30; *with dat.* **bregðask** fail someone XXI:79; *pp. n.* **brugðit** drawn IV:9

breiða (*past* **breiddi**, *pp.* **breiddr**) *wv.* spread VIII:120, XIII:3, XXVI B:180; *inf.* be spread out IX:63? *see* **breiðr**

Breiðafjǫrðr *m.* fjord in western Iceland VII A:156, 167

Breiðdalr *m.* valley in south-eastern Iceland *Gr* 3.1.8

Breiðfirðingafjórðungr *m.* the Breiðafjǫrðr Quarter (of Iceland) VIII:166

breiðfirzkr *adj.* from Breiðafjǫrðr VIII:65

breiðr (*n.* **breitt** *Gr* 3.3.8.2–5 ex. 4) *adj.* broad IX:63 (*see also* **breiða**), XXI:104; *with gen. of the amount of breadth* XXI:118; wide XV:92; *comp.* **breiðara** broader XXI:117; *comp. n. as adv.* **breiðara** with larger bites IX:100

brekvísi *f.* importunate demand, insistent begging for things (**við** from someone) XV:24

brenna[1] *f.* (house-)burning III:80 (*with suffixed def. art.*)

brenna[2] (*past* **brann**, *past pl.* **brunnu**, *pp.* **brunnit**) *sv. intransitive* burn, be consumed by fire (*Gr* 3.6.5.2) III:88, IX:83, 109, X:54, XIII:5, 17, 20; **brann upp ǫll** was completely burned down XIV:10; **ok brunnit** and it was burned XXVI B:201; **brenna inni** be burned in the house XXVI B:74, 157, 170

brenna[3] (*past* **brenndi**, *pp.* **brenndr**) *wv. transitive* burn *Gr* 3.6.10,

XIII:10, 14, 16, XXVI B:125; **brenna inni** burn (someone) in their house VIII:50, XXVI A:65, B:64, 104, 162; **brennu vér hann inni** let us burn him in his house XXVI A:55; **brennt gull** refined gold XII:19

brennumenn *m. pl.* burners XXVI B:1, *textual note*

bresta (*past* **brast,** *past pl.* **brustu,** *pp.* **brostinn**) *sv. intransitive* burst *Gr* 3.6.6; **brast** it (i.e. the king's sword, see note) shattered XXII:44/4

brestr *m.* break, crack X:126

Bretland *n.* Wales VII A:7

breyta (*past* **breytti,** *pp.* **breyttr**) *wv.* change; **breytt hafa** to have it changed XXVII:20; *intransitive with adv.* behave (in a certain way) IV:37, act XXVI B:204

breytiliga *adv.* strangely, unexpectedly IV:104

brezkr *adj.* British (*i.e.* Welsh? The word usually refers to Celtic peoples, but occasionally appears to refer to the English) VII A:23

brigða *adv.* extremely XXII:16/3

brim *n.* surf VII A:163

bringusár *n.* wound in the chest XV:122

Brísingar *m. pl.* a family *or* people IX:50 (*see note*), 60, 73

brjóst *n.* breast, chest IX:63, 76, 123, XIV:100, XXIII:77, XXV:84 (collective sg.); **á brjósti honum** on his breast XII:43; *with suffixed def. art.* its chest XII:17, her breast XXI:141, the chest XXIII:80

brjóstkringla *f.* round brooch for the breast X:121, 165

brjóstvit *n.* mother-wit XIV:36

brjóta (*pres.* **brýtr,** *past* **braut,** *past pl.* **brutu,** *pp.* **brotinn**) *sv.* break (*transitive*) *Gr* 3.6.5.2; go against, force (stifle), crush XIV:116; **brýtr þú** should you wreck XVI:139; *pres. subj.* **þótt þú brjótir** though you should wreck XVI:142; *past subj.* **bryti** were to break, violate VII B:29; *impers. with acc.* be wrecked VII A:135, XVI:177 (*past subj.*); **skipit braut í spán** the ship was broken to pieces XV:152; *pp.* **er brotit hafði** which she had broken X:123; **brjóta upp** break into IV:35

Brodd-Helgi (Þorgilsson) *m.* 10th-century Icelander who lived at Hof in Vápnafjǫrðr VII A:116

bróðir (*dat. sg.* **brœðr,** *pl.* **brœðr**) *m.* brother (*Gr* 3.1.7.2 (7)) II:109, 131, 139, III:75, IV:4, 16, 65, 67, VI:13, VIII:50, 183, X:3, 111, XI:6, 17, XIV:105, XV:119, 140, XXV:94 (in address), 99, XXVI A:71; *as title for a monk* XIV:26, *note*, 166; *gen. sg.* **bróður** V:98, VI:17; *dat. sg.* **brœðr** IV:93 (Fróði's (half-)brother = Kormakr; *with* **mik festa**), XI:30; *nom. pl.* **þeir brœðr** the brothers XXVI B:5,

þeir Hólmsteinn brœðr Hólmsteinn and his brothers XIX:16; *acc. pl.* **brœðr** XXV:36, XXVI B:139; *gen. pl.* **brœðra** XI:2, XXV:87; *dat. pl.* **brœðrum** I:149

bróðurson *m.* nephew II:112 (*probably an error for* **son**, *which is what appears in other manuscripts; cf.* II:114)

bróka, brókum *see* **brœkr**

Bróka-Auðr *f.* 'breeches-Auðr', *nickname* XV:53

brókabeltispungr *m.* purse on the belt of one's breeches III:30

brosa (*past* **brosti,** *pp.* **brosat**) *wv.* smile (**at** at this) XV:26

brotit *see* **brjóta**

brotna (*past* **brotnaði,** *pp.* **brotnat**) *wv. intransitive* break, be broken IV:11, V:117, IX:83, XXI:151, XXVI A:74

brott, á brott, á brottu, í brott, á brutt *adv.* away III:38, 94, 117, IV:17, 70, V:110, 141, 163, VI:354, VII A:106, 117, 152, 158, XI:42, XV:110, XVI:84, XIX:70, XXI:105, 142, XXVI B:204, 217; off XIX:100; **fara í brott** leave IV:52

brú (*pl.* **brýr**) *f.* bridge *Gr* 3.1.7.2 ex. 4, 3.1.8 ex.

brúðfé (*gen.* **brúðfjár**) *n.* 'bride-fee', bridal gift IX:115, 128

brúðkaup *n.* (= **brullaup**) wedding XV:14

brúðr *f.* bride IX:46, 99, 100, wife X:96, 153; *acc. sg.* **brúði** (*Gr* 3.1.8 (17)) IX:120

brugðit, brugðizk, brugðu *see* **bregða**

brullaup *n.* wedding IV:110 (*with suffixed def. art.*), VI:7, XV:78

brullaupsstefna *f.* date for a wedding IV:102

brún (*pl.* **brýnn**) *f.* eyebrow XXIII:18, *gen. pl.* XXIII:22, *with suffixed def. art.* XXIII:21

brúnáss *m.* roof beam (longitudinal beam along the middle of the sloping roof lying on the tops of one of the two lines of pillars) XXVI A:25

bruni *m.* burning, fire XIII:42

brunnit, brunnu *see* **brenna**[2]

brúnn *adj.* brown (*dat. with* **beru**) X:53; *n. as substantive* **nǫkkut brúnu** brownish colour XXIII:109

brúnvǫlr *adj.* frowning V:4

Brúsi Sigurðsson *m.* XXII:16/3

brutt *see* **brott**

brutu *see* **brjóta**

brygði *see* **bregða**

bryggja *f.* quay, jetty XVI:128

brýna (*past* **brýndi,** *pp.* **brýndr**) *wv.* sharpen, hone II:124 (*subj.*), 125

brynflagð *n.* giantess or trollwife of the mail-coat, *kenning for* battle-axe VI:235

Bryngvet *f.* Ísǫnd's maidservant *or* lady-in-waiting XII:48, 84

brynja *f.* coat of mail (chain-mail) II:61, III:28, 95 (*with suffixed def. art.*), X:43, XI:4, 16, 19, 27, XXII:56/2; **í brynju** in his coat of mail XXV:91

Brynjubítr *m.* 'mail-coat biter', name of a sword III:29, 98

Brynjudalsá *f.* river flowing into the head of Hvalfjǫrðr XIX:97

brynjurokkr *m.* mail-gown, coat of mail XXII:20/3 (*collective*)

brýnn *see* **brún**

brýr *see* **brú**

bryti[1] *m.* steward, bailiff, reeve VII A:137, XXVI B:174, *with suffixed def. art.* XXVI B:180; *as surname* III:76

bryti[2] *see* **brjóta**

brytja (*past* **brytjaði,** *pp.* **brytjat**) *wv.* chop XXII:41/1

brýtr *see* **brjóta**

brœðr, brœðra, brœðrum *see* **bróðir**

brœkr *f. pl.* breeches XV:49, 98

brǫgnum *see* **bragnar**

brǫngu *see* **branga**

brǫtt *see* **brattr**

bú *n.* farmstead, dwelling (*Gr* 3.1.8 ex.) II:42, XXVI A:109; establishment XV:12, XVI:9

búa (*pres.* **býr,** *past* **bjó,** *past pl.* **bjoggu/bjuggu,** *pp.* **búinn, búit/bút**) *sv.* (*Gr* 3.6.9.1 (9), 3.6.9.3 and ex. 6) **1.** live, dwell XV:2, 35, XIX:95, 101; *past* II:1, IV:1; **er fyrir bjuggu** who dwelt there already XXI:154; inhabit, live in IX:70; live together, keep house X:11; **býr** is included XIV:90. **2.** prepare XVI:131, XIX:79, XXI:3; fit out VII A:34, XIV:9, XIX:26; array, station, position VI:163; **búa til** prepare for XXVI B:109, get things ready for V:28, fit out for (going to) XIX:43; **búa sik til** get ready for I:119; **búa um** prepare for burial, lay out VII B:84; **búa um okkr/sik** arrange us/myself, dispose us/ myself XXVI B:175, 189; **búum um** let us arrange it I:109; *pp.* **búinn** constructed I:19, fitted out VII A:80, 81 (*pl.* **búnir**), ready IV:7, XXII:8/2; **svá búin** thus equipped (*i.e.* without figureheads) VI:83; **lítt til búinn** ill-equipped, quite unable XXVI B:160; *pl.*

búnir, búnar ready, prepared XI:15, 74, XIX:45; finished XII:3; clothed, attired XVI:95, fitted out XXI:44; *pp. n.* **vel búit** well equipped (*Gr* 3.9.2) VI:68; **var til búit** had been prepared XII:7, was ready XIX:57; **er búit við** there will be a danger, you may expect XVI:53; **bút svá sé** it looks as if it is, maybe it is, probably it is XXVI A:23; **svá búit** *as adv. phrase* in these circumstances, without more ado I:64. **3. -sk** *form* prepare oneself, get ready VI:115, XIX:14; get ready to leave XVI:126; **býzk** gets ready XXI:140; **um búask** protect oneself all round I:15; *past pl.* **bjoggusk/bjuggusk í/á brott** got ready to go, started to leave III:117, XXI:154; **bjoggusk þar fyrir** set themselves up there XIX:71; **bjoggusk þar um** settled themselves in there, camped there XXI:56

búandakirkjugarðr *m.* the farmer's churchyard, the householder's churchyard XXVII:40

búandi (*pl.* **búendr**) *m.* farmer, freeholder VIII:165, XVI:3

búð *f.* booth, a shelter for use during the summer assembly VIII:119, XV:58; shelter, temporary dwelling (on an expedition) XXI:106, 145

buðkr *m.* small box (for herbs); *see* **baukr**

buðlúngr *m.* king XXII:50/2, 64/1

buðu *see* **bjóða**

búfé *n.* livestock XV:77; farm animals XXI:134

Búfinnar *m. pl.* 'farm Finns', settled (not nomadic) Finns, i.e. Lapps XXII:30/4

búinn *see* **búa**

bukkskinn *n.* (billy-)goatskin XII:56

búna, búnar, búnir *see* **búa**

búnaðr *m.* adornment, attire XII:49

bundinn, bundu *see* **binda**

búr *n.* store-house; *with suffixed def. art.* III:81, 96, 97, 108

burðr *m.* birth VIII:13, 149

Búrizleifr *m.* king of Vindland (Boleslav I Chrobri, r. 992–1025) VI:3, 7, 18, 24, 46, 47

burr *m.* son VI:336 (*gen. with* **ævi**), IX:4; *acc. pl.* **buri** XXV:36; **buri þá** those boys XXV:76

burt, í burt *adv.* away I:33, 65, 87, 89 (*cf.* **brott**); **í burtu** (gone) away XII:77

búsmali *m.* cattle, especially milch-cows VII A:111

bústaðr *m.* dwelling-place *Gr* 3.1.8 ex.; a site for a home XIX:94

bút, bý *see* **búa**

býðr *see* **bjóða**

byggð *f*. dwelling, abode; settlement XV:42; **byggð hennar** her staying, her to stay IV:68; **sér til byggðar** as its dwelling XIV:101

byggva/byggja (*past* **byggði**, *pp*. **byggðr**) *wv*. settle (on *or* in) VII A:169, VIII:17, XIX:47, 53, 98, 101; live in VIII:72; live XII:74; *pp. n.* **byggt** settled VIII:35, inhabited VIII:71 (*supine*), 158, XXVI A:102; **-sk** *form* **byggjask** be settled VIII:7, 64

byggvendr *m. pl.* inhabitants VII A:24

býr[1] *see* **búa**

býr[2] (*gen.* **býjar**) *m.* = **bœr**; town VII B:32, 33; *with suffixed def. art.* VII B:49, 52

byrðr *f.* load II:55, *Gr* 3.1.7.3–5 ex.1

byrja (*past* **byrjaði**, *pp.* **byrjat**) *wv.* **1.** begin, set out on XXII:12/1 **2.** *impers. with dat.* be fitting, be proper (**til** for this, in these circumstances) XXIV:4

byrr *m.* (fair, favourable, following) wind; *adv. acc.* **lítinn byr** with a slight wind VI:26, 122

byskup *m.* bishop VIII:1, 159, 187, 191, XIV:24; *as title* VIII:9, 150, 158, 182, 196, XIV:1, 169

byskupligr *adj.* episcopal XIV:116, 148

byskupsdómr *m.* bishopric, diocese VIII:163, XIV:170

byskupsstóll *m.* bishop's see, bishopric VIII:163

bystr *adj.* (*pp.*) bristled; fierce, violent, hostile XXII:45/1; **Hárekr ... bystr** the fierce Hárekr XXII:8/1

býzk *see* **búa**

bæði[1] *conj.* both I:133, III:13, 22, V:112 (*understand* **váru**), VII A:50, 155, VIII:2, 11, 69, XII:67, XIII:41, XIV:13, XVI:44, XXI:68, XXII:21/3, XXIV:50, XXVI B:57, 125; **var bæði at** it was the case both that XIV:17

bæði[2] *see* **báðir**

bægja (*past* **bægði**, *pp.* **bægt**) *wv.* **1.** cause to give way. **2.** **-sk** *form* **gerðisk bægja við** = **bægðisk við** did strive against, contend with VII A:12

bæri *see* **bera**[1]

bœgi *see* **bógr**

bœjarbruni *m.* farm-burning, burning of a farm XXVI B:106

bœkr *see* **bók**

bœn *f.* prayer XIV:62, 121, XXIV:16, 17, 27; **fyrir bœn þeira** at their entreaty XXVI B:145

bœnahald *n.* (saying of) prayers, praying XIV:162

bœndr *see* **bóndi**

bœr (*gen.* **bœjar**) *m.* farmstead VII A:129, XV:134, XXVI A:8, *with suffixed def. art.* XXVI A:9, B:44; (in Norway) town VII B:34, *with suffixed def. art.* VII B:78; settlement, city XXV:61; *cf.* **býr²**

bœta (*past* **bœtti**, *pp.* **bœtt**) *wv.* repair; *pres.* **ek bœti** I shall mend X:126

bœtr *f. pl.* atonement, compensation I:60, IV:70 (*gen. pl.*)

bǫð *f.* battle VI:260, 311

bǫðfrœkn *adj.* bold in battle XXV:99

Bǫðvarr bjarki (Bjarnarson) *m.* I:1, 2, 5, 7, 10, 12, 13, 20, 22, 25, 32, 35, 36, 38, 41, 42, 57, 59, 61, 63, 68, 71, 73, 79, 87, 88, 89, 91, 94, 95, 99, 100, 102, 104, 108, 123, 139, 143, 149

bǫðvaz (*past* **bǫðvaðiz**) *wv.* **-sk** *form* become eager for battle, become belligerent XXV:71

Bǫðvildr (*dat. and acc.* **Bǫðvildi**) *f.* daughter of Níðuðr X:3, 78, 82, 96, 121, 122, 137, 165, 166, 176, 178

bǫl *n.* misfortune, affliction XXV:3; evil, harm XXV:94

bǫll *see* **ballr**

bǫllóttr *adj.* ball-shaped, round like a ball XXIII:9

bǫlva (*past* **bǫlvaði**, *pp.* **bǫlvat**) *wv.* curse 3.6.9.2 (6)

bǫlvan *f.* curse, cursing III:37

Bǫlverkr *m.* 'mischief-causer', assumed name of Óðinn II:133, 136, 137, 140, 141, 145, 148, 150

bǫnd *n. pl.* bonds, *a term for the* heathen gods; **bergsalar bǫnd** *is a kenning for* giants, *but here seems to refer to* **landvættir** VII A:143

bǫrðusk *see* **berja**

bǫrn *see* **barn**

bǫrr *m.* conifer, tree, *in kenning for* warrior (King Óláfr), **dáðǫflgan bǫr dolga fangs** (*acc. in acc. and inf. construction after* **menn kváðu**; *Gr* 3.9.4) VI:176

Credo in Deum (Latin) 'I believe in God', the Creed XIV:65, 69, 70

dáð *f.* deed; ability to fight XXII:48/4 (*pl.*); manliness, courage, valour XXII:9/4 (*pl.*), 41/3, XXV:21

dáðǫflugr *adj.* mighty in deeds (*with* **bǫr**) VI:176

dagan *f.* dawn III:120 (**í dagan** just dawning)

dagleygr *m*. day's flame or fire, *i.e.* the sun V:22 (*gen. with* **hilmis**)

dagr (*dat. sg.* **degi**) *m*. day *Gr* 3.1.7.2, XIV:80, XXI:49, XXV:19; *acc. of time* **einn dag, einnhvern dag** one day II:50, IV:6, VII B:51, XV:47, XVI:128; **hvern dag** every day XI:71, XIV:61; **þann dag** that day V:126; **allan daginn** all day XIV:66, the whole day XXVI B:4; **þann dag allan** all that day VI:286, VIII:121; **þenna dag** on this day, today VI:90; **annan dag eptir** the next day VIII:111; **annars dags** tomorrow X:106; **nǫkkura daga** a few days VII B:49; *dat. sg.* **degi** (*Gr* 3.1.7.2) VIII:197; **á hverjum degi** every day XIV:70; **um daginn** during the whole day IV:47; **í dag** today V:10, 122, 134, XIV:12, XV:87; *in pl.* time VIII:7; **á várum dǫgum** in our time XIV:168

Dagr Hringsson *m*. XXII:54/1

dáligr *adj*. miserable XXII:6/3

Dálkr of Húsafell *m*. enemy of Bjǫrn Hítdœlakappi V:87, 113, 117, 159; *dat. with part of the body* V:116

dalr *m*. valley (*Gr* 3.1.7.1) II:18, IV:49, V:2; hollow XXVI B:42; *dat. sg. with suffixed def. art.* IV:52, VII A:151

Dalsfjǫrðr *m*. fjord in western Norway XIX:4

Danaherr *m*. army of Danes VI:119

Danakonungr *m*. king of the Danes VI:1, 21, 30, 34, 39, 107, 183, VII A:125, 126, 132, 134, 170, VIII:146

Danir *m. pl.* Danes, the Danes VI:94, 209, VII A:136; *dat. pl.* **Danum** VI:96, 222

Danmǫrk *f*. Denmark VI:45, VII A:136, VIII:128, 189, XVI:92; *gen.* **Danmarkar** VI:12, 25, **Danmerkr** VII A:169, XVI:13, 30, 42, 157

danskr *adj*. Danish VI:245; **á danska tungu** in the area where the Danish language (*i.e.* Old Norse) is spoken, in Scandinavia VI:317

dapr *adj*. sad XXII:56/3

dapreygǫr *adj*. dim-sighted V:31

darr (*pl.* **dǫrr**) *n*. spear XXII 41/4, 54/2, 56/4

datt *see* **detta**

dátt *adj. n. in phrase* **gera sér dátt við** become friends with, make friends with IV:4, XV:18

dauðadagr *m*. the day of one's death; **til dauðadags** until their dying day VI:304, until his dying day VI:324

dauði *m*. death III:31, VI:364, XXII:6/3, 39/4, 53/2, XXIV:39, XXVI B:75

dauðr *adj*. dead III:77, V:96, VI:327 (*acc. with* **hungrdœyfi**, *parallel*

to **eða þó kvikvan**), VIII:61, XIX:74, XXI:139, XXII:48/3, XXVI
A:19, 104, B:92,133; **saztu yfir dauðum** you sat over him dead
XXV:26; **sízt mína sonu dauða** since my sons died X:144; **(vann)**
tvá dauða caused two (men) to be dead, i.e. killed them XXVI A:100;
n. **dautt** I:98, 100, 139
daufr *adj.* deaf; *pl.* **daufir** deaf people XXI:57/3
degi *see* **dagr**
deila (*past* **deildi,** *pp.* **deilt**) *wv.* dispute, quarrel XIV:160
detta (*past* **datt,** *past pl.* **duttu,** *pp.* **dottinn**) *sv.* (*Gr* 3.6.5.2) drop, fall I:98,
XXVI B:194
deyða (*past* **deyddi,** *pp.* **deyddr**) *wv.* kill; **deyða sik** mortify oneself
XIV:122
deyja (*past* **dó,** *past pl.* **dó,** *pp.* **dáinn**) *sv.* die (*Gr* 3.6.9.1 (8), 3.6.9.3)
II:79, IV:66, VII A:20, XVI:52 (**fyrir þér** on you), XXI:179,
XXII:54/4, XXV:39, 108, XXVI B:173
digr *adj.* stout VIII:31
dirfð *f.* boldness (**til** for, to) VII B:26
dís *f.* lady; goddess, valkyrie *or* norn (perhaps a guardian spirit?) V:20
(*subject of* **bendir,** *though pl.*; *cf.* I:27, *note*; *Gr* 3.9.8.2), XXV:100
djákni *m.* deacon III:118
djarfr *adj.* bold I:30, XXIII:27, 75; *acc. sg. m.* **djarfan** a bold person
XXIII:91
Djúpárbakki *m.* farm in southern Iceland, east of **Síða** XXVI B:143
Djúpdœlir *m. pl.* people of Djúpidalr in northern Iceland VIII:37
djúpr *adj.* deep; **á djúpum sæ** on the open sea VI:316
djǫfull *m.* devil *Gr* 3.1.7.3–5 ex. 1; cf. 3.1.7.4 (1)
dó *see* **deyja**
dolgstœrandi *m.* (*pres. part.*) 'hostility increaser', warrior (*here* King
Haraldr; *dat. with* **hugnar**) VII B:17
dólg/dolg *n.* hostility; battle (*gen. pl.*) VI:175; *gen. sg. with* **runna** VI:242
dólgr/dolgr *m.* enemy; **Frísa dolgr** = Earl Eiríkr VI:201
dómandi *m.* judge (*Gr* 3.1.7.2 (7)); *pl.* **dómendr** II:8
dómr *m.* judgment; sentence XXII:36/4; decision; **með leyndum Guðs**
dómi, at leyndum dómi Guðs by the inscrutable decree of God
XIII:13, XIV:11; relic(s) (of a saint) XXII:62/1
dómsuppsǫguváttr *m.* witness of the announcement of judgment
XXVII:42
dóttir (*pl.* **dœtr**) *f.* daughter (*Gr* 3.1.7.2 (7), 3.1.8 (22)) II:61, 116,
VI:23, 38, 47, VII B:6, VIII:11, IX:88, X:2, 8, 58, 74, 78, XV:4

dóttursonr *m.* grandson (daughter's son) VIII:49

Drafdittr *m.* Irish slave XIX:37 (**Drafdrittr** in other manuscripts; perhaps from **draf** *n.* refuse, **drittr** *m.* dirt)

draga (*pres.* **dregr**, *past* **dró**, *past pl.* **drógu**, *pp.* **dreginn**) *sv.* (*Gr* 3.6.9.1 (4), 3.6.9.3) **1.** draw XVI:146, XXI:176, XXV:53, pull XIX:64, *i.e.* row VI:120; **draga fram** bring out II:143, bring forward, propose VII B:14; **draga (sverð)** draw *or* wield? XXII:40/2; *1st person pl. pres.* **dragum upp** let us hoist VI:166; **draga á tálar** entrap, betray VI:145; *impers.* make, cause (by pulling) II:53; **ef oss dregr undan** if we escape, get away XXVI B:67; **lítt dró enn undan við þik** there was no escaping you XXVI B:94; *pp. acc. pl. m.* **dregna** threaded, drawn X:47. **2.** wear X:23

drakk *see* **drekka**

drap, drápu *see* **drepa**

dráp *n.* slaying, killing VI:42, VIII:60, 149

draumr *m.* dream V:13, 23; *acc. pl. with suffixed def. art.* V:7

dregna *see* **draga**

dreifask (*past* **dreifðisk**) *wv.* **-sk** *form* scatter; spread out XIX:68

dreingr *see* **drengr**

drekahafuð *n.* dragon's head (as figurehead) VI:99; *pl.* **ok á drekahafuð** and on it dragon's heads VI:110

dreki *m.* dragon VII A:151; dragon-ship, large warship usually with a dragon's head on the prow and/or stern VI:78

drekka[1] (*past* **drakk**, *past pl.* **drukku**, *pp.* **drukkinn**) *sv.* drink I:101, 103, II:99, 151, 152, IX:97, 101, XI:59, XII:71; *imp.* **drekk** XVI:159; *inf. with* **skyldi** II:4; *pp.* (*impers. pass.*, **var** understood) II:13 ('there was much drinking'; *Gr* 3.9.3)

drekka[2] *f.* drink II:117

drengiliga *adv.* manfully III:130, VI:303, *Gr* 3.5.1–3 ex. 6 (b)

drengiligr *adj.* valiant VI:254, 315

drengr/dreingr *m.* (valiant) man, manly man I:133, XI:4; (*i.e.* the poet, Bjǫrn) V:18; (*i.e.* Þorfinnr Þvarason) V:59; **góðr drengr** a fine fellow XIX:77; **þeir drengir . . . at** such valiant men that VI:81; *in pl.* warriors, *nom. pl.* **dre(i)ngir** VI:239 (*subject of* **slitu**), XXII:56/3, *acc. pl.* **dre(i)ngi** VI:175, 280 (*acc. with* **hét á**), XXII:54/1; *gen. pl.* **drengja** V:55, VI:157, 266 (*gen. with* **vanr**)

drengskapr *m.* nobility XI:51

drepa (*past* **drap**, *past pl.* **drápu**, *pp.* **drepinn/drepit**) *sv.* (*Gr* 3.6.5.2) **1.** strike IX:125, 127; **drepa á** touch, stroke XXV:70; *with dat.* **drepa**

fótum í stumble against III:64. **2.** kill I:46, 47, 51, 142, II:59, 96, VII A:57, VIII:12, 86, XVI:73, XIX:21, 34, 65, 84, 86, XXI:158, XXVI A:11, 92; slaughter XXI:134; **hefði drepit** had killed it XIX:66; *imp. with suffixed pron.* **dreptu** I:125. **3. -sk** *form pp. in reciprocal sense* (*Gr* 3.6.5.3) **hǫfðu drepizk** had killed each other II:132

dreyma (*past* **dreymði,** *pp.* **dreymðr**) *wv.* dream V:8; *impers. with acc. of dreamer and of what is dreamed* **hvat dreymði þik?** what did you dream? V:12; *pp.* V:25

dreyri *m.* blood XXII:16/4, XXV:25; clotted blood XXI:157

drífa (*past* **dreif,** *past pl.* **drifu,** *pp.* **drifinn**) *sv.* drift I:28, be driven, surge, throng VII B:42, XIX:23 (*Gr* 3.9.8.2), XXI:73; hurry X:100; rush XXII:33/1

drjúgari *adj. comp.* more lasting, i.e. more successful; **verða drjúgari en** do better than, get the better of XXI:78

dró, drógu *see* **draga**

dropi *m.* drop II:140; *pl.* flecks? XXIII:30

drós *f.* lady X:20

drótt *f.* troop, following of a king or earl VI:362 (*gen. with* **stjóri**); men VI:155, 247 (*subject of* **vann**)

dróttinn *m.* lord VI:363 (*acc. in acc. and inf. construction; verb* to be *understood*), IX:19, 41, X:41, 66, 142; the Lord, = God, *dat.* **dróttni, Dróttni** XXII:2/2, 63/1; **Dróttinn** the Lord (Jesus) XIII:3, XIV:52, XIX:49; **Dróttinn várr** XIII:30; **Dróttinn minn** God XXIV:18

dróttinssvikari *m.* traitor, one who betrays his lord XXII:6/4

dróttinvandr *adj.* loyal to their lord (*refers to* **herr**) VII B:18

dróttning *f.* queen (*Gr* 3.2.7.4 (3)) VII A:73, XII:24; the queen X:80; *as title* XI:1, 2, XII:22

drukkinn *adj. (pp.)* drunk XVI:100

drukkna (*past* **drukknaði,** *pp.* **drukknat**) *wv.* drown (*intransitive*) XV:151

drýgja (*past* **drýgði,** *pp.* **drýgt**) *wv.* carry out, engage in; suffer? X:18, 30

drykkja *f.* drink, drinking, feasting, banquet II:6, 14, XVI:96

drykkjumaðr *m.* drinker XXIII:28

drykkr *m.* drink, draught I:37, II:134, 152, 162, 163, VI:9, XII:51, XIV:68

drœyri = **dreyri** *m.* blood VI:231

Dufþakr *m.* Irish slave XIX:36, 65 (Irish Dubthach)

Dufþaksskor *f.* overgrown sloping ledge in a cliff on Vestmannaeyjar XIX:85

duga (*past* **dugði,** *pp.* **dugat**) *wv.* be of use, be valiant I:117; be helpful XXVI A:57; **duga ekki** be useless V:127; *with dat.* **dugir illa** does not benefit, does no good for VII B:13

dugr *m.* valour, effectiveness I:124

dúkr *m.* cloth XIII:31, 37

dunði *see* **dynja**

dura, durum, durunum *see* **dyrr**

duttu *see* **detta**

dvelja (*past* **dvalði,** *past pl.* **dvǫlðu,** *pp.* **dvalinn**) *wv.* **1.** delay (*imp.*) VII A:114. **2. -sk** *form refl.* stay I:64 (*understand* **munu vit**), VII A:67, 107, B:49, XXI:104; wait XXVI B:43; *pp.* **dvalizk** XVI:88

dvergr *m.* dwarf II:95, 102, XII:42; *pl. with suffixed def. art.* II:99

Dyflinn *f.* Dublin VII A:74

dygð *f.* virtue XIII:22; valour; faithfulness, fidelity XXII:41/3

dyggr *adj.* trustworthy, faithful XXIII:30

dýja (*past* **dúði**) *wv. (transitive)* shake (up and down) IX:3

dynja (*past* **dunði**) *wv.* roar, boom, whirr IX:16

dynr *m.* noise; *in kenning for* battle, **dynr hjalma** VI:206

dynsæðingr *m.* 'noise-seagull'; *in the kenning* **Heita dýrbliks dyn-sæðingar** 'seagulls of the noise of the gleam of Heiti's beast'; seagulls of battle *means* carrion birds, eagles *or* ravens VI:327 (*gen. pl. with* **hungrdœyfi**; *a six-element kenning!*)

dýpri *adj. comp.* deeper (*cf.* **djúpr**) Gr 3.3.8.2

dýr *n.* (wild) animal, beast I:74, 80, 81, XVI:13; *pl.* game X:4, XXI:27, 94, 159; *dat. of comparison* **dýrum** than wild animals XXI:40; *with suffixed def. art.* I:84, 90, 91, 94, 97, 98, 100, 101, 109, 112, 116, 119, 121, 125, 131, 138, 139, 142, XVI:14, 161; **dýrit eitthvert** a beast of a kind XVI:21; **dýrin** wild animals; *in kenning for* ship, **ægis dýr** V:39, **Heita dýr-** VI:328

dýramergr *m.* animal marrow XXI:157

dýrblik *n.* 'beast-gleam'; **Heita dýr,** beast of the sea-king, *is a kenning for* ship; the gleam of the ship *is* a shield, since shining shields were fastened along the sides of viking ships VI:328 (*gen. with* **dyn-sæðinga;** the noise, **dynr,** of the shield *is* battle)

dýrð *f.* glory XIV:190; **þat er þá væri meiri Guðs dýrð en áðr** such that then (i.e. with it) would be to the greater glory of God than before (without it) XIV:14

dyrðill *m.* 'short tail'; *as a nickname perhaps means* 'dandy' VI:165

dýrðligr *a.* glorious XIV:44

dýrka (*past* **dýrkaði,** *pp.* **dýrkat**) *wv.* glorify; **ok dýrki þeir** and (that) they may glorify XIV:56

dýrligr *adj.* splendid XI:4; *sup.* most splendid XI:59

dyrr *f. or n. pl.* door(way) (*Gr* 3.1.7.2) IV:13; *with suffixed def. art.* II:109, III:15, 53, VII B:70, XXVI B:82, 84; *gen. pl.* **dyra** IV:9, XXII B:127, *with suffixed def. art.* **dyranna** (= of the doorway) XII:58; *dat. pl.* **durum** XV:103, **dyrum** XXVI B:121, 155, **-dyrum** IV:10, XIV:25, *with suffixed def. art.* **durunum** III:40, 51, **dyrunum** XXVI B:107

dýrr *adj.* precious II:114 (*Gr* 3.3.5), X:20, splendid VII A:21 (*gen. pl.*), B:17, XXII:19/2, *textual note*; high XXII:2/1; worthy, noble, glorious XXII:53/2, 60/4; expensive XV:17; dear (?) VI:362 (*with* **stjóri**); *n. pl. as substantive* precious objects, treasures X:100; *sup.* **dýrastr** most precious *or* expensive XII:15, 26

dýrshjarta *n. with suffixed def. art.* the animal's heart I:103

dœgr *n.* day (12 hours); *pl. i.e.* lucky and unlucky days? XIV:80; **in næstu dœgr áðr** during the preceding 24 hours XXVII:33; **tvau dœgr** for 24 hours, but in this text it is likely that **dœgr** has become just an alternative to **dagr**, so that **tvau dœgr** would mean two days (of 24 hours) XXI:21, 26, 30, **þrjú dœgr** three days XXI:44, 66, **á hinu fjórða dœgri** on the fourth day XXI:66

dœma (*past* **dœmði,** *pp.* **dœmðr**) *wv.* converse X:146; judge, adjudge, impose by judgment XXVII:39 (1); **skal dœma** (*impers.*) shall be fixed, enjoined by judgment XXVII:39 (2); **er fé lætr dœma** who has money awarded him by judgment XXVII:41;

dœmi *n.* example XIV:121, XXV:102; **eptir hans dœmum** following his example XIX:106; **vita dœmi til** know examples of it *or* precedents for it XIX:110

dœtr *see* **dóttir**

dǫglíng(r) *m.*king XXII:2/1

dǫgum *see* **dagr**

dǫrr *see* **darr**

døkkjarpr *adj.* dark chestnut, dark brown XXIII:7

døkkna (*past* **døkknaði,** *pp.* **døkknat**) *wv.* be darkened XIII:18

døkkr *adj.* dark *Gr* 3.3.8.5 (5)

Eadmundr *m.* St Edmund (841–69), martyr, king of the East Angles VIII:12, 60, 149

eða, eðr *conj.* or (*Gr* 3.8.1) I:124, II:1, 47, 83, 131, III:110, VI:40,

320, 328, 354, VII A:46, B:8, 33, VIII:3, XII:28, XIII:37, XIV:58, XV:10, 65, XVI:129, 167, XXI:118, XXIII:85, XXIV:46, 76, XXVI A:84, 110, XXVII:11, 33; and VIII:33, X:155; **eða . . . ella** or otherwise, or else XIX:11; *linking a question to a statement* (*Gr* 3.8.1) II:75, V:11, XXVI B:109; *linking two parts of a question* (*Gr* 3.8.1) I:10, VII A:90, XII:78, XVI:33, XXVI B:130

eðla *f.* adder VII A:152

eðli *n.* nature XIV:118, XXIII:1

ef *conj.* if (*Gr* 3.8.2.4) I:34, 137, II:48, 107, 108, III:33, IV:22, 51, V:45, VI:14, 82 (*or* whether?), 86, 147, VII B:82, VIII:124, 142, IX:52, 67, 117, XIV:170, XV:17, 52, XVI:25, XIX:67, 78, XXI:40, 134, XXIII:7, 18, 57, XXV:74, XXVI A:45, 53, B:23, 48, XXVII:4, 7, 13, 28, 32; **ef . . . ok . . . þá** XXVII:8 (*see* **ok** *and note 4*); if (as a result) IX:12; whether VII A:120, XV:113; to see if II:142, X:40, in case XXVI B:87

efna (*past* **efnaði,** *pp.* **efnat**) *wv.* perform, fulfil XVI:156

efni *n.* state VIII:124; material(s) XII:7; reason XXIV:61; **koma til efnis** come to pass, come about XIII:33; **mjǫk í annat efni** onto a very different course, into a very different direction XIV:48

efri *adj. comp.* upper XII:29, **hin efri** the upper one XXIII:57; topmost XII:31

efst *adv.* highest XXI:93

egg[1] *f.* edge X:151, XXII:48/2, XXV:54; *pl.* **eggjar** *i.e.* weapons, swords V:150, (neither) sharp weapons XXV:93

egg[2] *n.* egg XXI:55 (*with suffixed def. art.*)

eggja (*past* **eggjaði,** *pp.* **eggjat**) *wv.* (*Gr* 3.6.9.2 (6)) incite, urge I:95, IV:5, VI:273, VII B:71, 79, XXII:36/1, XXVI B:139

eggmóðr *adj.* wearied by edges (swords), i.e. slain by swords XXV:107 (*with* **val**)

eggver *n.* sea-birds' breeding ground, sea-birds' eggs XXI:84

Egill *m.* brother of Vǫlundr X:4, 10, 12, 21, 32, 34

ei *adv.* not XI:11, XXII:15/1, 40/3, XXIV:12, 41

Eið *n.* isthmus, neck of land in Vestmannaeyjar XIX:82

eiðr *m.* oath X:149

Eiðr (of Hurðarbak) *m.* father of Þórðr and Þorvaldr V:87, 93

eiga[1] (*pres.* **á,** *pres. pl.* **eigu,** *past* **átti,** *pp.* **átt**) *pret.-pres. vb.* have, own (*Gr* 3.6.7) II:49, 135, III:32, IV:2, 107, V:30, 58, 59, VI:30, 41, 67, 80, 90, VII A:112, 123, 135, VIII:48, IX:91, X:2, 48, 71, 155, XVI:9, 21, 151, XIX:26, 64, XXVII:14, 35; possess XI:24, XV:9

(*after* **skyldi**), 132; XVI:52, 65; **ok á** and owned it (*Gr* 3.9.5.1)
XVI:17; **en . . . áttu** and it belonged to XXI:119; **saman eiga** share
XXVI B:188; **hann á** he receives, there are due to him XXVII:38;
áttu do you have XVI:20; hold (a meeting) II:44, VII B:51, VIII:42,
XXVII:33; hold, engage in VII A:5, 45; marry VI:8, VII A:78, 88,
XIX:10; be married to VI:24, 31, 38, 48 (*pp. acc. f. sg.* **átta**), VII
B:5, 6, X:154, XV:34, **er hann hafði áðr átta** to whom he had
previously been married XIV:128; *3rd pl.* **hverir eigu** to whom
belong VI:190; *pres. subj.* **eigi lengra til** are further off from V:82,
at hon eigi that she may have XV:55, **þó at nauðsyn eigi til** though
they have urgent business requiring it XVI:34, **eigim** XV:23; *past*
átti had owned X:80, was married to XIX:107; **átti sér son** had a
son XXVI A:113; **slíkt sem hon átti** what she had to (do) XV:118;
átti skammt til was a short distance away from V:86; **eigu skammt
hingat** are not far off, will not be long in coming V:65; *reciprocal
past pl.* **áttusk þeir við** had with each other, exchanged, shared (*Gr*
3.6.5.3, 3.9.8.3; *cf.* I:15, *note*) II:13, wrestled with each other, fought
I:104; *past subj.* **ætta, ætti** had VIII:67, XVI:183, owned VII A:118,
XV:11, should have (possess) XV:16; *past subj. impers.* **ætti** ought
IV:97; *supine* **átt** been concerned in, been involved in II:15; **eiga
(at)** *with inf.* have to, need to V:42, 115, VI:36, have the duty to (of)
VIII:168, XIII:7, XXII:1/2; **á at** has to XXIV:64, XXVII:27, should
(be) XV:61, is to be XXVII:18; **eigu at** are to, shall (be) XXVII:17,
must, may XXVII:50; **átt/átti at** ought to VI:19, XV:89

eiga[2] *f.* possession VII A:107, VIII:19; **alla eigu sína** everything he
possessed XVI:11, *cf.* XVI:25

eigandi (*pl.* **eigendr**) *m. pres. part.* (3.1.7.2 ex. 4, 3.1.8 (10)) (its)
owner V:95

eigi[1] *neg. adv.* not I:15, 36, 37, 66, 85, 93, 102, 107, 147, II:23, 24, 37,
58, 68, 91, III:10, 68, 88, IV:16, V:14, 62, VI:5, 129, 184, 325, 357,
VII A:44 (**at hann væri eigi** of his being), VIII:22, 28, 57, 90, 110,
167, X:12, 69, XI:26, XII:39, XIII:17, XV:4, XVI:23, 33, XIX:37,
78, XXI:64, 74, XXIII:26, 36, XXIV:2, 47, XXVI A:7, 27, B:8, 50,
XXVII:13, 32, 41; not then XXVII:20; no XVI:28; **eigi meira** no
more VII A:37; **eigi minna** no fewer VI:222; **eigi at síðr** none the
less VI:212; **nema eigi** except not, but not VI:224

eigi[2] *see* **eiga**

eiginkona *f.* wife VI:16 (**sér** to himself)

eign *f.* property XIV:127, 134; possession XIX:25; *gen. pl.* VI:1, 2; **alla eign** all he possessed XVI:71

eigna (*past* **eignaði,** *pp.* **eignat**) *wv.* assign; *inf.* **eða eigna** or assigning XIV:80; **-sk** *form* **eignask** gain possession of, get VI:22, 148, 302

eik *f.* oak II:22 (*with suffixed def. art.*)

eilífr *adj.* eternal XIII:8, 45

Eilífr Qnundarson *m.* enemy of Gunnarr XXVI A:49

Eina(r) Gilsson *m.* fourteenth-century Icelandic poet XXII:*heading*

Einarr þambarskelfir (Eindriðason) *m.* 11th-century Norwegian chieftain VI:301 (*see note*), VII B:1, 2 (*see note*), 3, 4, 9, 10, 23, 24, 25, 29, 30, 32, 35, 38 (*acc. with* **sék ganga**), 47, 49, 50, 53, 55, 61, 64, 77, 78, 84, 86

Einarr Þorgrímsson *m.* one of the incendiaries at Flugumýrr, later killed on his own farm by **Óláfr gestr** III:55, 59, 119

einart *adv.* incessantly, without stopping *or* immediately, boldly? XXII:40/2

eindagi *m.* settlement day; **dœma eindaga á þeim** fix as settlement day for them (to be paid) XXVII:39

Eindriði *m.* son of Einarr þambarskelfir and Bergljót VII B:6, 7, 50, 62, 64, 68, 82, 84

einfalda (*past* **einfaldaði,** *pp.* **einfaldat**) *wv.* use in the singular, use a singular form in XXIV:6 (*subj.*), 56; **-sk** *form* **skal einfaldaz** should be used in the singular XXIV:51

einfaldr *adj.* single, simple XXIV:46, 53; singular XXIV:41, 58

einfœtingaland *n.* the land of the unipeds XXI:191

einfœtingr *m.* uniped (a mythical kind of man with only one very large foot) XXI:174, 175, 179, 185 (*object of* **eltu**)

einfœttr *adj. (pp.)* one-legged, on one leg XII:54

eingadóttir *f.* only daughter X:167

eingi = **engi**

einhverju, einhverjum *see* **einnhverr**

einmæli *n.* private discussion II:96

einn (*n.* **eitt**) *num. pron. adj.* one (*Gr* 3.4.1) I:47 (one of), II:50, 64, 81, 97, 134, VI:49, VIII:82, 164, X:2, 50 (*sc.* ring), 57 (*sc.* ring), 182, XIV:172, XV:20, XVI:128, XXI:166, 172, 182, XXIV:34, 36, XXVI B:224, XXVII:19; a single, any I:79, V:38, VII A:98; the same IV:41, VII A:118, VIII:125, 134, XV:9, XXI:192, XXVII:7; a certain I:74, II:1, 90, III:77, IV:13, 49, 55, VI:10, 11, 28, 58, 61,

165, VII A:70, 73, 75, 111, B:52, X:86, XIV:155, XVI:11, 130, XXI:53, 67, 159, 181, XXVI B:229; *as indefinite art.* a XI:2, XII:10, 16, 17, 27, 41, 79, XIII:1, 15, 19, XXVI A:25, B:179, 219; a single ('this one ox') II:18, XIX:64; one person III:92, IX:95?; **einn inn bezta klerk** one of the best scholars XIV:27; only XV:86; alone, only VI:119, IX:92 (*gen. sg. f.* **einnar**), X:89, XV:8 (1), XXIV:80; **sjá einn** that alone XVI:125; alone, on one's own I:142, II:51, VI:158, IX:24, 95 (*or acc.* one *with* **oxa**), X:36, XV:8 (2), 74, XXVI A:2, 9; to oneself II:136; *with gen. pl.* the only one (left) V:27; **einn heiðinna manna** alone of (among) heathen men XIX:109; **eitt** one of them (of the ships) VI:98, 110; **þat eitt** that alone XV:80; **þat eina** only that, that alone XXI:146 ('that must have been the only troop'); **hálft eitt** only half XVI:65; **ein(n) þeira** one of them X:21, XXI:149; **sú var ein (sǫk)** that was one (cause of resentment) VI:30; **af viði einum** entirely of wood XXVI A:24; **mér einum** me (when I am) on my own IV:44; **þér einum** to you alone X:124; **firi sér einum ... ok** for himself alone and for, just for himself and XXIV:63; **ne einn = neinn** no, not any XIV:93; **einn fyrir** (only) one to face, only one against them XXVI B:60; **einn/einir saman** on his own XXVI A:50, on their own XXIV:78; **eitt saman** alone, only XXIII:80; **einir tveir** just the two of you X:106; only VII A:129; alone, only, nothing but I:31, III:22, 29, 102, V:124, VII A:141; **eitt ráð** the only thing to do III:122, V:75 (**okkr** for us); **él eitt** only a passing storm XXVI B:123; **gull eitt** nothing but gold, pure gold VI:111; **vax eitt** nothing but wax (*i.e.* a pliable person, weakling) VII A: 141; *n.* **eitt** *as substantive* one thing, the same thing (*i.e.* the same fate) III:26, XXVI B:164; **allt eitt** all the same V:106, XIV:117; *dat. sg. n.* **einu** one XXV:49; **ok einu** and one *with* **sjau tigum** VI:50; **því at einu** only then XIV:141; *nom. pl.* **einir ér** only you XXV:15; **tveir einir** only two, just two XXV:81; **einar** only, nothing but XXI:168; *gen. pl.* **einna manna** of anyone, of all the men V:104; **allra nema einna** all except only? all except a few? X:133; **einna mestir** greatest of all I:78; *gen. sg. n. as adv.* **eigi at eins ... heldr ok** not only ... but also XIV:190, **nema því at eins at** except only if XXIV:70; *dat. sg. n. as adv.* **einu** only VII B:87; *gen. pl. as intensive adv.* **einna** (= by far) **miklugi gørr** very much more extensively XXVII:32

einnhverr (*n.* **eitthvert**) *pron.* (*Gr* 3.2.3) a certain, one IV:6; someone XXVI A:27; **einnhverr yðvar** any of you XXI:135; **einnhverr**

annarra anyone else, other people XXIV:63; **einnhverr hagastr** one of the most skilful XIV:16; **dýrit eitthvert** a beast of a kind XVI:21; *dat. sg. m.* **einhverjum** some I:5, a certain, one I:69; **einhverju sinni** one time, sometime *(the phrase belongs in the following* **at**-*clause)* XVI:115

einsetukona *f.* anchoress XIV:129

einsetumaðr *m.* hermit VII A:48 *(with suffixed def. art.)*, VII A:58, 64

einskipa *adj.* with one ship *Gr* 3.3.8.5 (6)

einskis *see* **ekki²**

einstœðr *adj.* standing alone, lonely XXV:16

Eir *f. name of* a goddess *or* a valkyrie; *dat. with* **at** (for, in search of) **þeiri Eir hárgeirs,** *kenning for* woman (= Steingerðr; *cf. SnE, Skáld-skaparmál* ch. 31) IV:32; *in kenning for* valkyrie **vápn-Eir** V:49

Eiríkr Hákonarson (Hákonarsunr) *m.* earl in Norway (died *c.*1024) VI:40, 65, 71, 79, 88, 94, 102, 117, 127, 146, 163, 192, 215, 217, 221, 227, 269, 275, 285, 302

Eiríkr (enn) rauði (Þorvaldsson) *m.* Eiríkr the Red VIII:64 (complement), 74, XXI:7, 8, 10, 14, 41, 174, 208

Eiríkr (Bjarnarson) *m.* king of the Swedes, father of **Óláfr enn sœnski** VIII:147

Eiríksfjǫrðr *m.* a fjord in south-west Greenland (Tunulliarfik) VIII:66

eirvǫndr *m.* copper wand or rod XII:29

eiskra *(past* **eiskraði,** *pp.* **eiskrat)** *wv.* howl *or* roar with rage XXV:41

Eitill *m.* son of Atli and Guðrún XXV:29

eitr *n.* poison VII A:152

eitt *see* **einn**

eitthvert *see* **einnhverr**

ek¹ *pron. first person* I (*Gr* 3.2.1) I:9, 11, 15, 16, 19, 53, 54, 56, 59, 63, 66, 79, 83, 85, 105, 107, 121, 127, 128, 131, 144, 147, VI:344, 357, 360, VIII:1, 101, IX:6, 14, 27, 40, 52, 67, 79, 91, 100, X:70, 126, XI:7, XVI:23, XXI:78, 134, XXII:15/1, XXIV:11, 81, XXV:16, 74, XXVI A:35, B:23; *referring to writer* XIV:171, 172 *or poet* XXII:4/2, 27/2, 44/2, 55/2, 65/2, 3; *duplicating suffixed* **-k** IX:12, X:93, 183, 184, XVI:69; *duplicating suffixed* **-k** *and with suffixed neg.* **-a** *or* **-at** VI:138, 246, IX:100, X:95, 97, 124; *see* **-k**

ek² *see* **aka**

ekkert *neg. pron. adj. n.* no I:18

ekki¹ *neg. adv.* not I:18, 22, 33, 55, 63, 66, 68, 77, 78, 79, 105, 107,

128, 132, 141, II:6, 20, 21, 159, III:67, IV:68, 75, 110, V:13, 77, 89,
VI:170, 188, 288 (2), VII A:41, 114, 164, XI:16, 68, XIII:17, XV:7,
12, 42, XVI:137, 167, XXI:70, 121, XXII:44/3, 55/3 (or **ekki²**?),
XXIV:46 (? or **ekki²**), 85, XXV:102, XXVI B:4, 31, 59, 62, 75,
228; **sumir ekki** others (that there was) not III:111

ekki² *neg. pron. n.* nothing (*Gr* 3.2.4) III:124, VI:288 (1),VII A:163,
B:73, 39, XI:39, XII:66, XIV:14, XV:78, XVI:47, XXI:60, 95,
XXIV:9, XXV:64, XXVI A:38, 42, B:79, 97; no, not a, not any I:81,
VI:112, VIII:121, XI:36, XV:21, XXII:55/3 (or **ekki¹**), XXIV:46 (?
see **ekki¹**), XXV:109; **þat ekki hús** no single building XIV:157; **ekki
meira skip** no greater ship VI:118; none (no men) VI:222; **ekki
dýrsins** none of the bear, no bear at all XVI:54; **ekki nema** nothing
but XIV:162; *gen.* **einskis** nothing XXI:58; **einskis annars** nothing
else XXI:129; **enskis** over no part (**af** of) II:135; **enskis metask** be
valued at nothing, be deemed worthless XXVII:17; *with partitive
gen.* (*Gr* 3.4.2.(5)) **ekki fleira** nothing else II:64, VII A:42. *Cf.* **engi**

ekkja *f.* widow XIV:111

él *n.* storm; **él eitt** only a passing storm (only one storm?) XXVI B:123;
él stála VI:337 *and* **darra él** XXII:41/4 *are kennings for* battle

eldask (*past* **eldisk**) *wv.* grow old; *1st person pres.* **eldumk** VI:203

eldhús *n.* kitchen III:88; the main living-room of a medieval house
XIX:96; a large public room with fires in it XV:103

elding *f.* lightning XIII:4, 13

eldistokkr *m.* blazing brand (piece of wood) XXVI B:226

eldr *m.* fire III:47 (*with suffixed def. art.*), IX:109, XI:15, 18, XIII:8,
15 (*with suffixed def. art.*), 25, XXV:89, XXVI B:64, 107; **bera eld
at** bring fire to it III:2; **bera (þar) eld í, leggja þar eld í, slá eldi í**
set fire to (it) II:57, III:3, 4, XXVI B:119

eldsbrunalitr *m.* colour of burning, scorch mark XIII:37

eldsbruni *m.* burning of fire XIII:44

eldshiti *m.* fiery heat XIII:9

eldsligr *adj.* fiery XXIII:107

ella *adv.* else, otherwise XIX:11, alternatively XXVI A:12

elli *f.* old age *Gr* 3.1.8 ex., XIV:171

ellifu *num.* eleven (*Gr* 3.4.1) VI:44

elligar *adv.* otherwise I:65

ellri *adj. comp.* elder (*Gr* 3.3.8.3) IV:2; older XIV:158, 162

elska (*past* **elskaði,** *pp.* **elskaðr**) *wv.* love XIV:105; *pp.* **elskaðr** loved
Gr 3.3.9 (11), (16)

elta (*past* **elti,** *pp.* **eltr**) *wv.* chase V:77, XXI:183

elztr *adj. sup.* oldest *Gr* 3.3.8.3

em *see* **vera**

embætti *n.* office XIV:116

en¹ *conj.* **1.** but, and (*Gr* 3.8.1); I:16, 18, 26, 27, 32, 53, 59, 66, 68, 77, 84, 102, 121, 141, 145, II:3, 17, III:1, IV:2, 43, V:38, 169, VI:3, VII A:142, VIII:2, 16, IX:63, 76, 107, 130, X:11, 24, XI:15, 68 (1), XIII:5, XIV:120, XV:5, 24, XVI:36, XIX:2, 9, 12, XXI:14, XXIII:2, 19, XXIV:4, XXV:23, 111, XXVI A:3, 35, 100, B:29, 64, XXVII:3, 8,19; while VI:86, XIV:189; whereas VIII:159. **2.** *with comp.* than (*Gr* 3.8.2.4) I:64, 70, 136, III:14, IV:15, V:41, 83, 133, 161, VI:8, 27, 65, 74, 97, 118, 189, 340, VII A:36, 160, B:14, VIII:5, 150, 162, 164, 175, 192, 196, XI:68 (2), XIII:37, XIV:115, XV:32, 123, XVI:155, XIX:29, XXI:117, 135, 164, XXII:28/2, XXIII:53, 57, 77, XXIV:9, 13, 29, 69, 84, XXVI A:63, B:33, 173, XXVII:29; than that he VII A:37; after **annarr/annat/annars** XII:11, 60, XIV:48, XVI:37, XXI:129, than that, but that VIII:91, than if VI:257, (different) from what XXVI B:138

en² *see* **enn², inn²**

enda¹ (*past* **endaði,** *pp.* **endat**) *wv. impers. with acc.* end I:149

enda² *conj.* (and) moreover VIII:131, XXVII:50; and also that XIV:18

endask (*past* **endisk**) *wv. refl. with dat.* serve, help, be of use to V:80

endi *m.* end II:31, 70 (*dat. with* **batt**), XII:29 (*with suffixed def. art.*), XIII:48, XXVI A:60 (*with suffixed def. art.*)

endlangr/ennlangr *adj.* the whole length of IX:107, X:46, 75, 140; **með endlǫngu landi** along the whole length of the coast VII A:162

endr *adv.* again IX:131

engi, enginn, eingi, øngr, aungr *neg. pron.* no one (*Gr* 3.2.4) II:93, 100, III:70, V:133, IX:7, XII:9, 63, 79, XIV:111, XXII:23/2, XXVI A:66, B:85, XXVII:31, none XXVI B:76; *acc. sg. m.* **øngvan** I:3; *dat. sg. m.* **engum** V:15; *gen. sg. n.* **engis** at nothing XXVI B:70; *dat. sg. n.* **engu/øngu** nothing VII B:63, XXI:69, XXVI A:107, for nothing XXI:152; **øngu ǫðru** to nothing else XVI:36; *cf.* **ekki²**; *dat. pl. of comparison* **øngum þessum** than none of these (*with* **lægri**) XIV:185; **sá kom náliga engi** there was almost no one came XIV:96; **engi sá er** none such that VII A:93; **enginn annarra** no one else I:125; **enginn . . . þeir er** no one who XII:59; *as adj.* **e(i)ngi/enginn** no XXII:2/3, 64/3, no, not any I:114 (*n. pl. with* **líkindi**), 124, VI:75, XII: 11, XIII:22, XV:11, 15; not a XV:3; **engi/enginn maðr** no one

I:111, VI:167, 316, IX:29, X:88, XII:73, XIV:106 (*pl.*), XV:150;
alls engi snjár no snow at all XXI:108; **engi varð (til)** there was no
(. . . available) VII B:74, 88; *acc. sg. m.* **engan/øngan/øngvan** no,
not any 1:54, VI:212, VII B:71, XII:5, XXI:136, XXVI B:162;
øngvan/engan mann no one XXIV:19, XXVI B:37, XXVII:17; *acc.
sg. f.* **øngva** I:121, XIX:11, **aungva** XXII:24/3; *gen. sg. n.* **engis** no
XIII:36; *dat. sg. m.* **øngum** *after neg.* any X:109; *m. pl.* **øngvir** none
of them XXI:80; *acc. pl. m.* **enga** VII A:169; *f. pl.* **engar** no, not any
XXI:46, *n. pl.* **engi** no XXI:204, XXVI B:6, (*after neg.*) any of
XXIV:3

engill *m.* angel XIII:12

engisax *n.* 'meadow-sword', 'meadow-chopper', *i.e.* scythe; *subject
of* **hneit við** IV:21

Englakonungr *m.* king of the English VIII:12

England *n.* England VII A:2, 9, 10, 70, 71, 75, 97, 107

Englar *m. pl.* the English VII A:11

enn[1] *adv.* in addition, further, again II:86, 147, V:47 (*i.e.* a second),
VI:93, 186, 190, 341, 350, 351, 359, XIV:130, XVI:164, XIX:22,
XXIV:76; still V:77 (2), VI:71, VIII:90, XI:71, XIV:179, XVI:143,
171, XIX:96, XXIV:4, 47, XXVI A:41, B:94, XXV:29; for ever
XXV:34; also V:71, XXVII:2; yet I:18, V:77 (1), VI:67, 72; any
further VIII:85; a little longer VI:65; **enn fleiri** still more V:70, 74;
Hvat er enn fleira? What else was there? XVI:168; **enn meira** still
more XV:55; **enn þá** still at that time VIII:119

enn[2] (*f.* **en**, *n. pl.* **en**) *def. art.* (*Gr* 3.3.5) the, *see* **inn**[2]

enni *n.* forehead XII:27, XXIII:51; **enni þat er** a forehead which
XXIII:13

ennlangr = **endlangr**

enskis *see* **ekki**[2]

enu *see* **inn**[2]

Epistolarum *gen. pl. of Latin* **epistola** *f.* letter; as title of Ovid's work
Heroides (Liber Epistolarum Heroidum) XIV:90

epli *n.* apple; *acc. pl.* II:36, 39

eptir *prep.* (*Gr* 3.7.4) *with acc.* after (*of time*) I:28, 98, 104, 110, III:11,
130, IV:35, V:161, VI:298, 323, VII B:57, 86, VIII:13, 60, 169,
XIV:170, XXV:109; **eptir þat** after this XV:57, 137, XIX:23, 31,
XXVI A:43; **eptir þat er** *as conj.* after VI:302; *with dat.* after I:26,
148, II:48, 149, III:49, VI:167, XXI:137, 180; to fetch V:89, VI:6,

XV:116, XVI:18; behind III:64, XVI:16; along VII B:75, 80, XXVI B:219; along, through III:35, V:78, VII A:153; in accordance with XII:48, XIV:120, XVI:135, XIX:106, XXIII:1; **nǫkkvot eptir sem** somewhat in accordance with what XVI:55; **eptir því sem** as I:85, 86, IV:110, as much as, to the extent that I:117; (in the likeness) of XII:47, 61; *as adv.* back II:70; to the rear XXV:14; after, behind VII A:111 (*see* **koma**), XXVI B:204, 211; about XXIV:8; afterwards (after him?) VI:43; after, following VIII:121, 173, 179, 187, 190; **annan dag eptir** the next day VIII:111; **et næsta sumar eptir, annat sumar eptir, um sumarit eptir** the following summer VIII:176, XV:82, XVI:9; **eptir um várit, um várit eptir** the following spring XV:124, XIX:14; **of vetrinn eptir** (for) the following winter XVI:8; **vera eptir** be left, remain VI:218, stay behind VIII:98, 107, XXI:166, XXVI A:113; **vera þar eptir** stay behind there XXI:162; **halda eptir** keep VII A:76; **ganga eptir** be fulfilled VII A:32; **lifa eptir** survive, be still alive VI:299

er[1] I:26, 36, 53, 81, 90, 94, 125, 133, II:1 (1), 2, 60, VI:105 (1), 340, VIII:5, 6, 30, IX:23, X:94, XV:73, 88, XVI:32, XXIII:13 (2), 35 (2, 3), XXV:7, XXVII:16 (1), 45: *see* **vera**

er[2] *conj.* (*Gr* 3.8.2.1) when, where, that, who, which, *etc.* I:6, 30, 55, 95, 130, II:1 (2), 3, 4, 8, 15, 18, 19, 20, 23 (**því er**), 40, 47, 49, 52, 54 (*twice*), 68, 110, III:3, 23, 27, 45, 77, 109 (while; *see note*), IV:6, 8, 111, V:3, 29, 32, 42, 86 (while), VI:1, 19, 24, 26, 33, 35, 42, 60 (while), 75 (1), 93, 105 (2), 120, 136 (as), 153 (when), 173 (which), 182, 190, 193, 219 (as), 255 (1; when), 270 (when), 293 (who), 315 (whereby), 316 (which), 317 (1; that), 317 (2; who), 334 (who), 342 (when), VII A:43, 63 (by which), B:87 (so that), VIII:4 (which), 6 (which), 9 (whom), 10 (who), IX:1 (when), 7 (which), 103 (who), 124 (when), X:5 (which), 48, 50 (which), 72 (when), 77 (who), 79 (which), 87 (which), 103 (when), 104 (which), 116 (which), 123 (which), 160 (which), 168 (which), 178 (what), 180 (what), XI:35 (which), XII:69 (that), XIV:26, *note* (who), 107 (which), 180 (who), 183 (who), 185 (who), XV:38 (who), 47, 71, 106, 111 (when), XVI:4 (who), 14 (when), 34 (where), 39 (when), 59 (whom), 100 (1) (since), XIX:8, 13 (when), 26 (which), 36 (who), 44 (when), 64 (while), 77 (that), 85 (where), 98 (so that), XXI:5, 16 (which, that), 31 (where), 42 (when), 44 (which), 49 (when), 79 (which), 80, 93 (when), 132, 133 (that), 138 (when), 146 (which), 152 (when, if), 197 (when),

XXII:*title*, 24/2 (which), 32/4 (who), XXIII:4, 35 (1) (which), XXIV:3 (which), 16 (1) (who), 49 (which), 75 (2) (those who? when they? *see note*), 76 (2) (when), XXV:8, 22 (when), 35 (which), 39 (who), 94 (when, in that), 97 (2) (when), 99 (whom), XXVI A:6, 8 (who), 32 (where), 47 (when), 52 (which), 104 (who), 106 (2) (when, that), 113 (who), B 99 (1) (whom), 104 (2) (when), 112 (that), 113 (1) (which), 149 (1) (when), 150 (who), 187 (2) (that *or* when?), 189 (where *or* how), 224 (who), XXVII:2 (2) (who), 21 (1) (at which), 35 (who); **nú . . . er** now that XXVI B:83; **þar er** where I:146; **þess er var** such as there was XVI:6; **þeim . . . er** to those who V:132; **þat er** which III:100, 102, XII:64, a . . . which XXIII:13; **þat . . . er** what XXVI A:66; **þeir er** they who IV:57, VI:255; **þær er** which IX:96; **sá . . . er** one . . . in respect of whom III:68; **er . . . þau** those which, such as VIII:175 (*see* **þau**); **er . . . í** in which XXVII:5, **er . . . í hag** in whose favour XXVII:10

ér *pron. pl. 2nd person* Gr 3.2.1, XVI:112, XXV:15 (note that this is not a dual form; perhaps Erpr is included), 92; *in address to the king* XXV:68, 69; *with imp. vb.* X:84

era, erat *see* **vera**

erendi *see* **erindi**

erfiði *n.* toil, trouble, labour IX:36, 40

erfiðr *adj.* difficult; awkward, demanding, hard to please XV:15; *n. as substantive or adv.* **var honum erfitt** he was exhausted III:13; **hefir oss erfitt veitt** it has proved difficult for us XXVI A:102

erfingi *m.* heir Gr 3.1.7.5 (4)

erindi, erendi, ørindi *n. pl.* **1.** errand, message, mission (*Gr* 3.1.7.3–5 ex. 4, 3.1.8 (28)) VIII:112; **þannug var þá mikit erendi margra manna** many people had important reasons for going there at those times XIV:42. **2.** result of an errand, news IX:36, 40

Erlingr Skjálgssunr (of Sóli, south-west Norway, modern Sole) *m.* son of Þórólfr skjálgr ('squinting') VI:80

ermr *f.* sleeve XXI:46

erni(r) *see* **ǫrn**

Erpr[1] *m.* son of Atli and Guðrún XXV:28

Erpr[2] *m.* son of Jónakr, half-brother of Hamðir and Sǫrli XXV:49, 98

ert, ertu, eru, erum, erumk, erut *see* **vera**

es[1] = **er**[1] VIII:5 (2), 14 (2)

es[2] = **er**[2] VIII:5 (1), 11 (1), 11 (2; when), 14 (1), 19 (where), 30, 33, 65, 93

et = **it,** *see* **inn**[2]

eta (*past* **át,** *past pl.* **átu,** *pp.* **etinn**) *sv.* eat (*Gr* 3.6.9.3) I:103, IX:95, 104, XII:71, XXI:75

ey *f.* island (*Gr* 3.1.7.5 (4), 3.1.8 (15)) II:1, XV:153, XXI:27, 53; *acc. sg. with suffixed def. art.* **eyna** XXI:54, 61; *dat. sg.* **eyju** X:137; *dat. sg. with suffixed def. art.* **eyjunni** VII A:31, **eynni** XII:4; *pl.* **eyjar** VII A:9, 129, XIX:71, 80; *dat. pl. with suffixed def. art.* **í eyjunum** i.e. on Vestmannaeyjar XIX:83

eyða (*past* **eyddi,** *pp.* **eyddr**) *wv.* (*Gr* 3.6.9.1 (7)) lay waste I:80, VII A:128; *with dat.* destroy VII A:15; **-sk** *form* **eyddisk** would be laid waste VIII:127

eyðimǫrk *f.* wilderness; *pl.* **eyðimerkr** desolate (forest) land II:17, XXI:168

Eyfirðingafjórðungr *m.* the Quarter of the people of Eyjafjǫrð (northern Iceland) VIII:167

eygðr *adj. (pp.)* having eyes of a certain kind; **eygðr mjǫk** with large eyes XXI:104

Eyjafjǫrðr *m.* fjord in the north of Iceland VII A:153, 166, VIII:38

Eyjar *f. pl.* = Landeyjar, the district where Njáll's farm Bergþórshváll was located, adjoining Fljótshlíð where Gunnarr's farm Hlíðarendi was XXVI A:3

Eyjólfr Valgerðarson *m.* 10th-century Icelander who lived at Mǫðruvellir in Eyjafjǫrð VII A:166

Eyjólfr Þorsteinsson (ofsi) *m.* (*c.*1224–1255) the leader of the incendiaries at Flugumýrr III:1, 82, 121

eyra *n.* ear XIV:21, XXIII:44

eyrir (*pl.* **aurar**) *m.* (*Gr* 3.1.7.2) ounce (of silver; one eighth of a **mǫrk**[2]) VIII:27; **í lausum aurum** in movable property VIII:161; *in pl.* money, treasures, gold X:68

eyrr *f.* sand- or gravel-bank XXI:88

eyverskr *adj.* of the islands (*probably* the Hebrides) VII A:20

fá[1] (*pres.* **fær,** *past* **fekk,** *past pl.* **fengu/feingu,** *pp.* **fenginn**) *sv.* (*Gr* 3.6.9.1 (8), 3.6.9.3) get, obtain I:61, II:49, III:70, 96, VI:11, 22, XIII:47 (*pres. part.* **fáandi**), XV:82; **fekk hann af** he got from it XXVI A:50; find XXI:177; *with suffixed neg.* **þú ne færat** you will not get XXV:35; receive VI:298, 299, VII A:40, 53, XII:86, XV:111, XIX:21, XXII:57/3, XXVI A:76; win (*1st person past* **fekk**) VI:202, XIX:35; suffer XXII:6/3, 56/3, 60/2, XXVI A:45, B:98; take (a

sickness), begin to suffer from VI:323, XIX:55; **fá bana** be killed
I:44, 131, V:102, 129; find, use, manage III:92; be able III:93; *past
subj.* **fengi** might get II:137; **at eigi fengi** that he did not get XIV:112;
with dat. of person provide someone with something VI:44, XVI:51,
hand over to, give to someone VIII:42, XXII:31/3; *imp.* **fá mér** give
me XXVI A:78; *with gen.* gain, win XXV:108; *with f. gen.* obtain (a
promise of) marriage with someone IV:99, marry VI:31 (*supine*
fengit; *understand* **hafði**), VII A:69, 107, X:10, XIX:39; **fekk at**
got provisions for XIX:41; **fá í hǫnd** *with dat. of person*, hand to
someone III:30; **fá í vald** *with gen.* put in someone's hands, hand
over to someone XII:65; **fá til** provide as, hand over for XXI:41,
subj. **fái til** but put forward for XXVII:16; **fá til** *with inf.* get, provide
(someone to do something) XIV:153; *with pp.* get (something done)
I:20, manage to (do something) I:96, XIV:72, 87, 96, XVI:34, 143,
XXVI B:97; **fá mik sótt** overcome me XXVI A:81; *impers.* **hvergi
fær** there is nowhere to be found XXII:3/3; **ei fær tǫlu á komit**
they cannot be numbered XI:11, **ekki fær nú at gert at** (*with inf.*)
nothing can now be done about XI:39; **-sk** *form subj.* **fekksk** was
granted, was brought about VIII:185; **fengisk** would be got, would
be gained VI:148; *pp.* **fengizk** been found XIV:110
fá² *see* **fár**
faðir *m.* father (*Gr* 3.1.7.2 (3, 7), 3.1.8.8) II:77 (*subject*), III:32, 79,
VI:3, 33, VIII:37, 46, 191, XIV:110, XIX:4, 114, XXIV:1, XXVI
B:72; *acc.* **fǫður** X:177, XIV:56, XXVI B:139; **ok fǫður** and (said
their) father (was called) XXI:202; *gen.* **fǫður** II:62, IV:64, 99,
X:138, XXVI B:74, 113, **faðr** VI:42, 95; *dat.* **fǫður** IV:109, VII
B:9, XXVI A:117, **feðr** X:127, XIII:48
faðmr *m.* outspread arms, embrace X:22; **í faðmi sér** in his arms
XI:45; *as a measure,* fathom (approximately 6 foot) XIX:62 (cf.
Gr 3.4.2 (7))
Fáfnir *m.* name of a dragon; = dragon-ship (**dreki**; *here* = Ormr inn
langi) VI:237
fagna (*past* **fagnaði**, *pp.* **fagnat**) *wv. with dat.* welcome; rejoice in
XXII:57/4, XXIII:73, 85; *impers. pass.* (*Gr* 3.9.3) II:3
fagnaðr *m.* joy XIV:148
fagr (*f.* **fǫgr**, *n.* **fagrt**) *adj.* beautiful (*Gr* 3.3.8.4 (1)) II:65, IX:9 (*with*
túna), 44 (*with* **Freyju**), X:22, XIV:162; **fagrt var at** it was beautiful
to XXI:58; fair, fine VI:26, XI:5, *dat. sg. n.* **fǫgru** XVI:130; *n. pl.*
fǫgr XXII:18/3; *dat. pl.* **fǫgrum** II:12

fagrferðugr *adj.* virtuous XXIII:24

fagrliga *adv.* beautifully, finely, splendidly XIV:43, 176; *sup.* **ok þetta hús væri sem fagrligast gǫrt ok búit** and that this building might be as beautifully built and fitted out as could be XIV:15

fagrvariðr *adj. (pp.)* fair-robed, beautifully dressed, with beautiful adornments X:177

fái *see* **fá**[1]

fáir *see* **fár**

fáklæddr *pp.* lightly clad, having few clothes on III:61

fal *see* **fala**

fala (*past* **falaði**, *past pl.* **fǫluðu**, *pp.* **falat**) *wv.* offer to buy, ask (*or* demand) to buy II:126

fála *f.* giantess, whose horse is a wolf (*SnE, Gylfaginning* 46/26) XXII:41/2

falda (*pres.* **feld**, *past* **felt**, *past pl.* **feldum**, *pp.* **faldinn**) *sv.* put a woman's head-covering on someone, cover someone's head XXVI B:144

fall *n.* fall (in battle), death IV:Chapter 5, *heading*, VI:323, 366, VII B:50, 77, 86, XVIII:121vb28

falla (*pres.* **fellr**, *past* **fell**, *past pl.* **fellu**, *pp.* **fallinn**, **fallit**) *sv.* (*Gr* 3.6.5.2, 3.6.6) **1.** fall I:139, II:110, V:101, IX:62 (hang down), XXII:49/4, XXVI A:19, 74; fall down III:57, 65, V:96, 130, 146, VII A:104, B:92, 198; collapse III:73, XXVI A:90; fall dead IV:66; (fall in battle) VI:212, 221, 223, 267, 317, VIII:145, XIX:18, XXI:144, XXV:110; **fellu Danir mest** the Danes had the most losses VI:209; *of water*, flow V:43, XXI:87, 169; **er út fell** when it (the tide) went out XXI:93; **fell þar á** there came to be about it XV:19; **falla aptr** close (intransitive) XV:104; **falla at** fall towards *or* close to XXVI B:220; **falla (í)frá** die XXIV:67, 71; **falla í fullting með** join in supporting XXVII:15; **falla til** fall at XVI:105; *supine* **fallit** VI:294, 319; *pp.* **fallinn at** deprived of, bereft of XXV:17. **2.** **-sk** *form with dat.* **fallask** fail someone, escape someone's memory IX:38; **fallask hendr** one's hands fail one, one is at a loss VII B:70; *refl.* **láta fallask** let oneself drop II:56, 71

falsguð *m.* false god XXIV:35

fálu *see* **fela**

fám *see* **fár**

fámálugr *adj.* of few words, reserved XXI:12

fámennr *adj.* having few men; with few companions XV:116; *comp.* **fámennari** having fewer troops, be outnumbered VI:293

fang[1] *n.* embrace; **í fang sér** in his arms XII:82; *pl.* **fǫng** provisions XI:60, XXI:83 (= **matfǫng**); means, opportunity (**á** for it) XIV:142

fang[2] *n.* tunic; *in kenning for* coat of mail **dólga fang** VI:175

fánga (*past* **fángaði**, *pp.* **fángat**) *wv.* = **fá**[1], receive XXII:39/4

fann, fannsk, fannt *see* **finna**

far[1] *n.* range, subject, ground; **of et sama far** on the same subject, covering the same ground, *or possibly* in the same way VIII:3

far[2] *see* **fara**

fár (*n.* **fátt**) *adj.* **1.** few *Gr* 3.3.9 ex. 13; *pl.* **fáir** VI:117, few people I:23, 144; *n. pl.* **fá** VI:71 (*with* **stór skip**); *dat. pl.* **fám** VIII:17, 143, XIV:72; **firi fá menn** for few people XXIV:64; **við fá menn** accompanied by a few men VII B:60; *n. as substantive* **fátt** few I:3, little II:66, few things XXV:7; **fátt er til** there is little choice VII B:20; **finnask fátt um** *see* **finna**. **2.** cold, hostile; **var/varð fátt um með** there was/came to be coolness (little warmth) between VII B:3, XIX:12

fara (*pres.* **ferr** *Gr* 3.6.5.2, *past* **fór**, *past pl.* **fóru**, *past subj.* **fœri**, *pp.* **farinn/farit**) *sv.* go (*Gr* 3.6.6, 3.6.9.3 ex. 2, 3.6.10) I:1, 32, 33, 87, 93, 98, 110, II:16, 17, 36, 109, 123, III:94, IV:50, V:2, VI:11, 14, 50, VIII:50, X:43, XI:5, XV:30, 34, XIX:6, 71, XXI:32, XXII:26/3, XXVI A:10, B:38; travel XVI:2, 42, 88; pass IV:103; sail VI:122, 136, VIII:65, XXI:7, 86, 122; come I:39, VI:72 (*supine* **farit**), 100, X:77, XVI:39; be coming VI:69; turn out VI:292, VII A:57; happen XXVI B:25; fare, suffer VII A:104; *with acc. of route*, travel along V:42; *pres.* **ferr** will go I:84; **farið** you are going V:167; **fǫrum** (we) shall go I:65, let us go V:78, let us go along (*with acc. of route*) V:75; **farum** let us go VI:63, 78; **ok fara** and (they are) coming (*inf. after* **sé**?) V:74; *imp.* **far, far þú, farþú** go I:125, V:89, XVI:153; *past* **þat fór** this went on, took place XXII:58/2; **fóru** they went XXVI A:107, men went XXV:66; **fóru vér** we have travelled XIX:98; *pres. subj.* **farir** XVI:38; *past subj.* **fœri** was going III:65, VIII:28, 32, was moving I:116, travelled VIII:15, went (on) VIII:106; **ok fœri hann** and he was to go XXVI A:9; **at þú fœrir** that you went V:10, that you should go XVI:126; **fœri** were behaving, were carrying on, acting XXVI B:36; *pp.* **farit** travelled (*supine*) V:43, gone on XXI:168; **hafi eigi farit** had not gone on XXI:163; **hvert hon hefði farit** where she had been XV:120, **þar farit** passed that way VIII:70; finished, done for, come to nothing IV:48, gone, been used up XVI:53; *with gen.* **fara leiðar sinnar** go (on) one's way XXI:51; *with dat.* **fara málum** bring a lawsuit XV:81; **fara af** leave VI:25, VII A:27, XVI:123, XIX:3, *subj.* **fœra af** left XVI:123; take off XI:15; **þá var af farit** then was past XV:149; **fara aptr** return VII A:42; **fara at** approach V:87, go to it, start to do it III:106 (*inf. after* **skyldi**), go against XIX:20, XXVI A:6; **hversu at skyldi fara** how they were to go about it XXVI A:7; **fara at** *with inf.* go to, start to V:91, XV:96, XIX:82; **fara eptir** go after *or* behind, follow, pursue V:70; **fara frá** leave III:91; **fara fram** come about VIII:177; **fór betr fram** went on better XXVI B:71; **fara með (meðr)** *with dat.* use, deal in VI:344, travel by VII A:109; go about something XIV:95; **hversu farit hafði með** what had passed between XVI:65; **fara með(r)** *with acc.* behave with, act with VI:211, XIV:164, go about with XXI:206; **fara leynt með** keep it secret XII:73; **fara ór landi brott** leave the country VII A:106; **fara til** approach X:88; **fǫrum til** let us go up (to it) I:108; **til hafa farit** have come there XV:116; **fara um** go across, go by VI:73, **fóru vel** went well XIX:8; *impers.* **fór** it went III:116, **fór svá fram** this went on XXVI A:40, **fór svá** this happened VII B:30, so it went on XXI:116, **fjarri fór þat** (it was) far from it XXVI B:226, **fœri** (*past subj.*) it went III:33, **ferr** it moved, the motion was XXI:98; **ferr vel/illa** *with dat.* someone behaves well/badly XXVI A:87, **vel mun þér fara** you will act well XXVI B:141; **-sk** *form* perish *Gr* 3.6.10; **farizk vel at** gone well in it VIII:93; *impers.* **fersk þeim vel** they get on well, they have a good voyage XVI:8

farar *see* **fǫr**

farmr *m.* cargo XVI:172, XXI:56

farskostr *m.* means of transport, conveyance II:118

fasta (*past* **fastaði**, *pp.* **fastat**) *wv.* fast, abstain from food XIV:121

fastna (*past* **fastnaði**, *pp.* **fastnat**) *wv.* betroth; *pp.f.* **fǫstnuð** IV:102, XV:7

fastr *adj.* (stuck) fast I:94; *f.* **fǫst** (**við** to) II:31; *n. as adv.* **fast** hard I:95, V:104, 134; tightly, fast VII A:104, XI:20; **svá fast** so hard I:97, XV:99, 109; thus hard, hard like this V:133

fátt *see* **fár**

fátœkr *adj.* poor XIV:109, 110; **fátœkar konur** beggar-women XXVI B:5

fávitugr *adj.* foolish, not clever or sensible XXIII:80

faxi *m.* 'maned one', horse VII A:141

fé (*gen.* **fjár**) *n.* property, valuables VI:18, 22, VII A:136, VIII:153, 156, XV:31, 76 (*with suffixed def. art.*), XIX:36; possessions XXII:49/3; wealth XII:68; livestock I:80, 84, 113; cattle, domestic animals XXI:57, 62, 95; money VIII:43, XIV:150, XV:7, 8, XVI:6, 53, 144, XIX:31, XXII:21/3; payment of money or equivalent XXVII:41; *with suffixed def. art.* **féit** the money XVI:90, **fjárins** of his money XVI:43; **fénu** the goods, cargo XVI:139; **fénu ǫllu** all the money XVI:183

feðgar *m. pl.* father and son XIX:25

feðr *see* **faðir**

feginn *adj. with dat.* pleased with someone (*i.e.* to see them, because they were there) III:25

fegrð *f.* beauty VII B:8, XII:21, 48

fegri *adj. comp.* fairer, more beautiful X:127, XII:13

feigr *adj.* doomed, near death, under the influence of death XXV:39, XXVI B:73, 83

feingu *see* **fá**

feitir *m.* fattener, feeder VII B:19 (**folkstara feitir** *is a kenning for a warrior, here* King Haraldr, *who kills his enemies and provides food for carrion birds*; *dat. with* **lýtr**)

feitr *adj.* fat XXIII:48, 86, 99; *n.* **feitt** XXI:177, XXIII:54

fekk *see* **fá**

fela (*past* **fal,** *past pl.* **fálu,** *pp.* **fólginn/folginn**) *sv.* (*Gr* 3.6.9.3) **1.** hide, conceal II:82 (*understand* it, gold, *as object* (*Gr* 3.9.5.1)); *pp.* II:85, IX:26, 27. **2.** entrust, commit XIX:111, XXVI B:182; **fela í hendi** *with dat.* commit to someone's charge XIV:124, 174

félagi *m.* comrade, friend I:108, 124; companion XII:5, 72

félagsfé *n.* shared possessions, joint goods XIX:44 (understand **hafði**)

félauss *adj.* without money XVI:142, 177

feldr *m.* cloak VIII:120

félítill *adj.* poor XVI:2

fell *see* **falla**

fella (*pres.* **fellir,** *past* **felldi,** *pp.* **felldr**) *wv.* fell, cause to fall, kill I:131, V:106 (*past subj.*), VI:147 (*past subj.*), VII B:69; **fella saman** fit together XII:6; **búit saman at fella** finished being fitted together XII:3

fellr, fellu, fellusk *see* **falla**

felmsfullr *adj.* fearful, panic-stricken XIX:84

fen *n.* fen, muddy ground; pool of water in a forge for tempering steel X:115, 159

fénaðr *m.* livestock XXI:108

fengi, fenginn, fengisk, fengit, fengizk, fengu *see* **fá**

fengr *m.* booty II:162

ferð *f.* journey, expedition II:2, 38, XV:129, XVI:86, XXI:4, 17, XXII:12/1; **fara ferðar sinnar** go on one's way XVI:87; **til ferða** on journeys, as messengers XIV:136; going, departure VII A:114; **gera ferð sína** make one's way, set out VI:20

ferhyrndr *adj. (pp.)* square XXIII:16, 67

ferja *f.* ferry, large rowing-boat, transport boat XV:130

ferr *see* **fara**

ferri = **fjarri**

fersk *see* **fara**

fertøgr *adj.* forty years old VIII:188

féskipti *n.* division of property XV:31, 75

festa (*past* **festi**, *pp.* **festr**) *wv.* **1.** stick, fix XI:36; fasten, make fast; gird on XXV:57; *inf.* **festa** (I would) fasten XXV:77; **festum** let us fasten XXVI A:60; **til at festa með** for securing XXVI A:58. **2.** betroth IV:94 (**sik** oneself), VII A:96 (**sér** to oneself). **3.** *impers. with acc.* **festa á** stick fast to, make an impression on (**ekki festi á** *i.e.* everything glanced off it) VI:288. **4.** -*sk form* **festisk** established himself, became more powerful VII B:12

festarmál *n. pl.* betrothal, engagement VI:37

fiðr *see* **finna**

fiðri *n.* feathers (*collective*) II:58

fimm *num.* five (*Gr* 3.4.1) VII A:129, B:33, VIII 27, XXI:155, 198, XXII:4/1, XXVII:33; **fimm saman** five in all, in a group of five XXVI B:13

fimmtán *num.* fifteen (*Gr* 3.4.1) V:32, VIII:72, XV:4, XXVI B:11

fimmtándi *num.* fifteenth (*Gr* 3.4.1); **meðr fimmtánda mann** *i.e.* with fourteen others, in a party of fifteen VI:270 (*Gr* 3.4.2 (8))

fim(m)ti *num. adj.* fifth *Gr* 3.4.1, XXIV:37

fingr (*gen.* **fingrar**, *pl.* **fingr**) *m.* finger XXI:117, XXIII:83, 87

fingrgull *n.* gold (finger-)ring III:30, 31 (*with suffixed def. art.*), XII:37

fingrgullssteinn *m.* ring-stone XII:31

finna (*pres.* **finnr/fiðr**, *past* **fann**, *past pl.* **fundu/funnu**, *pp.* **fundit/funnit/funnir**) *wv.* **1.** find, discover (*Gr* 3.6.9.2 (2), 3.6.9.3) II:39,

VIII:69, IX:103, X:6, 32; XII:13, XVI:185, XIX:27, 32, 73, 82, 91, XXI:22 (2), 51, XXII:46/2, XXV:59; visit, see IV:20, 33 (*inf.* with **fúsir at**), 68, 76, VII A:62; meet VII A:43, XVI:103, 139, 144, 149, XXI:143, XXV:43; meet with XXI:198; sight, come across XXI:22 (1); discover XII:74, XXI:193, find out, know XXII:22/4; realise II:146, XV:144; feel XIV:117; notice VI:203; **ef þú finnr eigi** if you don't notice it XV:52; **fann eigi fyrr en** did not notice until, the first thing [he] knew was that XXVI A:62, *similarly* XXVI B:119; **hafa þat funnit** thought it up XXIV:59; *pres.* **finn ek opt** I have often seen, noticed VII B:42; **þar fiðr þú** there you will find X:157; **finnr eigi** cannot see IV:26; *past subj.* **fyndi** met XV:85; **it fyndið** you have been to see X:109; **finna á** *with dat.* notice in someone, from someone's behaviour or demeanour III:34; **finna til** notice XV:51; adduce, call to mind, find to say XXIV:48; find for it, adduce XXIV:61, 76; **finna til saka** bring forward as the offence, give as reason XV:69. **2. -sk** *form for pass.* **finnsk** is found XXIII:60, **fannsk** was found III:48, was discovered VIII:64, **fundusk** were found VIII:52, *subj.* **fyndisk** were found III:105; *in reciprocal sense* **finnask** meet each other VII A:100, XIX:15, XXVI A:6; *impers.* **finnsk mikit um** *with dat. of person* one is greatly affected by III:34, XXVI B:30, **finnsk fátt um** *with dat. of person* one loses interest in something, one becomes unconcerned about something IV:105; **fannsk mǫnnum fátt um** people made no comment about, people took no notice of XIX:11

Finnakonungr *m.* king of the Lapps X:3
Finnason *m.* son of Finni XIV:28
Finnr Árnason *m.* XXII:17/1
firar *m. pl.* men; *gen. pl.* among men, human X:22
Firðafylki *n.* Firðir (a district in western Norway; Fjordane) XIX:23
firði *see* **fjǫrðr**
firðr *see* **firra**
firi, firir *see* **fyrir**
firra (*past* **firð,** *pp.* **firðr**) *wv. with dat.* remove from, free from XXII:59/2
first *adv. with dat.* furthest from V:87
fiskr *m.* fish XXI:92; *pl.* **helgir fiskar** halibut XXI:93
fit *f.* webbed foot X:134 (*see note*)
fjaðra *see* **fjǫðr**
fjaðrhamr *m.* feather-form, bird-shape IX:11, 16
Fjalarr *m.* a dwarf II:95, 107

Fjalir *f. pl.* district in western Norway (south-west Fiordane) XIX:4

fjall *n.* (*Gr* 3.1.7.1, 2) mountain (*collective*) VIII:20, XII:2 (*with suffixed def. art.*), XIII:1; *pl.* **fjǫll** II:17, VII A:130, 148, XXI:58, 192, XXV:41; *with suffixed def. art.* VII A:154, 160, XV:84; *dat. pl.* **fjarri fjǫllum** far from the mountains X:70

fjándmaðr *m.* enemy V:11

fjándskapr *m.* hostility, animosity XV:17, 142

fjár *see* **fé**

fjara *f.* (*Gr* 3.1.7.1) foreshore VIII:20

fjarðmýill *m.* 'fjord-lump' *is a kenning for* rock (in the sea) or skerry; *gen. with* **trǫð** VI:250

fjárfar *n.* money matters IV:104

fjarðskorinn *adj.* (cf. **skera**) indented with fjords XXI:52

fjárhald *n.* economic affairs II:131

fjárhlutr *m.* property, valuables XIX:79

fjárrán *n.* robbery, theft XV:127

fjarri, ferri *adv.* far off XXV:39; by no means, out of the question I:51; **eigi fjarri tekit** by no means rejected XV:5; **fjarri skyldu fara** should by no means be done XV:117; **fjarri fór þat** (it was) far from it XXVI B:226; *with dat.* far from X:70, 94; what is far from VI:340 (*with* **geta**)

fjárskipti *n.* division of property *Gr* 3.1.8 ex.

fjarst *adv. sup.* furthest away; **sem fjarst** the furthest away possible VI:214

fjórði *num. (ordinal) adj.* fourth (*Gr* 3.4.1) VI:127, VIII:194, XXI:66, XXIV:37, XXVII:44

fjórðungr *m.* Quarter (of Iceland) VIII:163, XXVII:9, 11; **ór þeim fjórðungi ... er hann hafði síðarst heimili í** from the Quarter in which he last had his home XXVII:4

fjórðungsmaðr *m.* man who lived in a certain Quarter of Iceland; **þeir fjórðungsmenn er ... í hag** the men of the Quarter in whose favour XXVII:9

fjórhyrndr = ferhyrndr *adj.* square XXIII:32

fjórir *num.* four (*Gr* 3.4.1) III:110 (**þrír eða fjórir**), V:83, VI:198, VII A:27, VIII:190, XII:60, XXI:18, 144, 164; *n.* **fjǫgur** VI:110, 123, XIV:145, XIX:50

fjórtán *num.* fourteen (*Gr* 3.4.1) VIII:72

fjúka (*pres.* **fýkr,** *past* **fauk,** *past pl.* **fuku,** *pp.* **fokinn**) *sv.* fly, be blown II:148

fjǫðr *f.* feather XII:32; *gen. pl.* **fjaðranna** in the feathers (*see* **litr**) XII:33

fjǫgur *see* **fjórir**

fjǫl *f.* board, flat piece of wood VII B:61

fjǫlð *f.* multitude, abundance IX:91, 130, X:104

fjǫlði *m.* a large number VII A:111, 155, 158, XI:61, XIII:12; multitude XXI:94, 110, 122, 159

fjǫlkunnigr *adj.* skilled in magic II:2, IV:1, XV:40

fjǫlkynngi *f.* witchcraft, sorcery XV:127, 136

fjǫll, fjǫllum *see* **fjall**

fjǫlmenni *n.* a large following, a large number of men VII B:31; **fjǫlmenni mikit** a very large number of people XIV:42; **hvat fjǫlmenni þat var** what the huge crowd had been XXI:145

fjǫlmennr *adj.* having a large following, well attended VII B:40 (*acc. with* **Einar þambarskelfi**); full of people XIV:144

fjǫr *n.* life IV:46 (*object of* **sœki**), XXII:49/3

fjǫrbaugsgarðr *m.* lesser outlawry VIII:142

fjǫrbaugsmaðr *m.* a man subject to the lesser outlawry VIII:99

fjǫrð¹ *adv.* in the former (year), last year VI:230

fjǫrðr (*acc.* **fjǫrð²**, *dat.* **firði**) *m.* fjord (*Gr* 3.1.7.1) VII A:150 (*with suffixed def. art.*), 153, B:76; XIX:60, XXI:53; fjord (and the valley leading into it; *with suffixed def. art.* **þar í firðinum** 'in that fjord', 'in that district') IV:69; **þar inn á fjǫrð** into that fjord VII A:157; **inn með firðinum** in along the fjord XXI:55; **vestr þar í fjǫrðum** (from) the Western Fjords (of Iceland) XVI:2; *as first part of compound* **fjǫrðjǫrð** 'land of fjords', *i.e.* Norway, *separated by tmesis* VI:248

fjǫrlausn *f.* deliverance (from death), ransom II:119

fjǫru *see* **fjara**

fjǫturr *m.* fetter X:63; part of the forge? X:115, 159

flá (*past* **fló,** *past pl.* **flógu,** *pp.* **fleginn**) *sv.* flay *Gr* 3.6.9.3

flabellum *n.* (Latin word) fan XIII:19

flagð *n.* giantess XXV:54 (see note)

flaug *see* **fljúga**

flaugun *f.* flight, flying; **á fǫr ok flaugun** a-coming and a-going, in bustle, commotion XXVI B:14

fleiri *adj. comp.* (*Gr* 3.3.8.3) more (in number) II:37, V:49, 74, VII B:31, XIV:140, XV:65, XXII:28/1, XXIV:10, 42; any more, any others XIX:37; in addition XVI:168; more numerous VIII:81; more people V:67; **váru inir fleiri** those ones were more numerous

XIV:146; **fleiri þeir** others of them III:71, XIX:85; **eða fleiri** or more (i.e. **lǫgmenn**) XXVII:33; **ekki fleira** no more, no other III:55, nothing else II:64, VII A:42; **fleiri en** more than, other than, other besides VI:65; **enn fleira** yet more XXIV:47, with yet more XVI:171; **því fleira** with more than that XVI:175; *n. as substantive* **fleira** more, other things I:135, XXVI B:23, 26

flekklauss *adj.* unspotted, immaculate XIII:42

flekkr *m.* spot, small patch (of ground) XXI:172

flestr *adj. sup.* most (*Gr* 3.3.8.3) VII B:13; *nom. pl.* **flestir** most of them VI:299, XXI:18 (subject of **váru**), most men, the majority XXVII:8; *n. pl.* **þau váru flest** they were most(ly), most of them were VIII:38

flík *f.* piece of cloth; *pl.* **flíkr** flags (probably) XXI:206

fljóta (*pres.* **flýtr,** *past* **flaut,** *past pl.* **flutu,** *pp.* **flotinn**) *sv.* float; drift, lie in the water without sail VI:109, 307 (*with* **sá Trana ok báða Naðra**); **fljóta í** swim (of bedclothes) in, be soaked in XXV:25

fljótliga *adv.* quickly XXIII:102

Fljótsdalsheiðr *f.* a high moor in eastern Iceland *Gr* 3.1.8 ex.

Fljótshlíð *f.* area in southern Iceland XXVI B:10

fljótvirkr *adj.* fast-working, fast-acting XXIII:101

fljúga (*pres.* **flýgr** *Gr* 3.6.5.2, *past* **flaug/fló** *Gr* 3.6.9.1 (2), *past pl.* **flugu,** *pp.* **floginn**) *sv.* fly I:76, II:30, 32, 42, 54, 154, 155, V:163, IX:16, X:11, 17; **fló upp á land** it flew up inland XXI:127

fló *see* **fljúga**

flóð *n.* high tide, flood tide XXI:93

flokkr *m.* **1.** herd II:18; flock V:166; band of men, gang VII A:52; troop, army XXII:20/1, 27/4; party XXVI B:12; *with suffixed def. art.* company, army, force VI:221, their men, their followers XXVI A:14. **2.** a poem comprising a series of stanzas without refrains VI:200

Flosi Þórðarson *m.* leader of the burners XXVI B:1, *textual note*, 40, 44, 47, 52, 83, 87, 88, 97, 98, 115, 120, 128, 129, 132, 149, 153, 155, 156, 161, 195

floti *m.* assembly of ships, fleet VI:29, 35, 83; *with suffixed def. art.* VI:60, 191

flótti *m.* flight, running away VI:170, 180; **koma á flótta** take to flight VI:155

flugr *m.* flight, flying II:53 (*with suffixed def. art.*), II:59 (*with suffixed def. art.*), II:155

flugstyggr *m.* who shuns flight, who is reluctant to flee VI:367

flugu *see* **fljúga**

flúr *n.* flower-shaped ornament XII:29

flutu *see* **fljóta**

flutti, fluttar, fluttr *see* **flytja**

flýgr *see* **fljúga**

flýja (*past* **flýði,** *pp.* **flýiðr**) *wv.* flee VI:305, VII A:130, XIX:19

flytja (*past* **flutti,** *pp.* **fluttr** *Gr* 3.3.8.5 (2), 3.6.9.1 (7)) *wv.* carry, transport II:112, 115, V:117 (*pp. with* **varð** *forming passsive*), XV:131; bring II:119; move (one's home) IV:70; **flytja upp** carry ashore XVI:155; **flytja fram** propose, argue for, present a case VII B:26, deliver XIV:45, perform, repeat XIV:61, 161, present XIV:115; **flytja við** present to, perform to, offer to XXIV:18

flæma (*past* **flæmði,** *pp.* **flæmt**) *wv.* cause to flee, drive away, cast out (*supine with* **hafðu**) VI:42

flærðsamr *adj.* false XXIV:41

flœðarsker *n.* skerry, rock covered at high tide II:113

fnasa (*past* **fnasaði**) *wv.* snort IX:48

fól *n.* fool XXIV:5 (*pl.*)

fólginn, fólgit *see* **fela**

fólk *n.* people II:89, VII A:130, XIV:75, 113, XXVI B:135, 148: **þat fólk** these people XXI:113; **fyrir fólkinu** before the people XIV:32

folkharðr *adj.* strong in battle (*with the implied subject of* **fœrðuð**, you, Eiríkr jarl) VI:251

Fólkher *m.* kinsman of (Gunnarr and) Hǫgni XI:21, 76

folkstari *m.* 'battle-starling', *kenning for* carrion bird, eagle or raven, *gen. with* **feiti** VII B:19

fór, fóru *see* **fara**

forða (*past* **forðaði,** *pp.* **forðat**) *wv. with dat.* save V:76

forðum *adv.* in the past, once upon a time XXIV:35

forgǫngumaðr *m.* leader VII B:71, 88

forkirkja *f.* porch of a church III:85 (*with suffixed def. art.*)

forkuðr *f.* strong desire *Gr* 3.1.7.4 (5)

forkunnar adv. exceptionally *Gr* 3.5.3 (9), II:65

forlǫg *n. pl.* future, destiny XIX:41

formáli *m.* prayer(s) III:10

formera (*past* **formeraði,** *pp.* **formeraðr**) *wv.* form, fashion, shape XIII:30 (Latin *formare*)

formæli *n.* prayer; exhortation XIV:31, 125, 141

forn *adj.* ancient VIII:141, 175, X:14, XXIII:1; old (from early times) XXV:112; **fornir menn** men of olden times XIV:79; *comp.* **fornari** older, earlier, longer ago XXV:7

forneskja *f.* heathen practices, witchcraft XIV:77

forráð *n. pl.* management; **hafa til forráða** have administration of VII A:128; **til forráða fyrir** for the administration of XIV:126

Forseti *m.* a god (one of the Æsir) II:9

forsjá *f.* prudence; **af forsjá** out of prudence XIV:33

forsjáll *adj.* prudent, foresighted XXIII:12, 39

forstjóri *m.* leader (**fyrir** over) VII B:24

fortǫlur *f. pl.* arguments, representations, persuasive speeches VII A:66, XXVI B:126

fóru *see* **fara**

forvitna (*past* **forvitnaði,** *pp.* **forvitnat**) *wv.* enquire into, want to know about XXIV:26; *impers. with acc.* **slíks sem mik forvitnar** whatever I want (am curious) to know XIV:23; **-sk** *form refl.* desire to know VII A:65; enquire, find out I:114

forvitni *f.* curiosity (**á** about something) VII A:32

forvitnisbót *f.* cure for curiosity I:123

fóstbróðir (*pl.* **-brœðr**) *m.* foster-brother *or* sworn brother (in pl. can also refer to two men brought up in the same household) VIII:41, XIX:6, 9, 38

fóstra (*past* **fóstraði,** *pp.* **fóstraðr**) *wv.* foster, bring up; **þar váru þeim fóstruð bǫrn** there their children were being fostered, brought up XXVI B:3

fóstrfaðir *m.* foster-father, tutor? guardian? VI:10

fóstri *m.* fosterer, foster-father VIII:9; foster-son, foster-brother; fosterling XXVI A:22 (in address to dog)

fóstrland *n.* native country XII:5

Fótar-Ǫrn, Ǫrn *m.* III:121 (*see note*), 125

fótkistill *m.* box-pedestal XII:41

fótleggr *m.* leg XXIII:96

fótr *m.* (*Gr* 3.1.7.2 and (2), (4), 3.1.8 (7)) foot, leg III:57 (*with suffixed def. art.*), V:116 (*with dat. of owner*), XXV:47, XXVI B:153 (leg); **sem fótr ǫðrum** as, like one foot (helps) the other XXV:46; *acc. sg.* **um fót sér** round his leg V:56, *with suffixed def. art.* **fótinn** the leg XXIII:97; *gen. sg.* **Fótar-** *used as a nickname* III:121; *dat. sg.* **fœti**

XXV:47, **fœti niðr koma** put down one's foot XXI:55; *pl.* **fœtr** II:32 (*i.e.* Loki's), II:64, III:23 (*with dat. of person* (*poss. dat.*)), X:115, 159, XXIII:99 (probably feet rather than legs), 100, XXV:88 (probably legs rather than feet; obj. of **sér**); **undir fœtr sér** under her feet XII:44; *with suffixed def. art. and dat. of person* XXVI A:31; *gen. pl.* **fóta** IV:18, XXI:46 (legs), **til fóta konungi** at the king's feet XVI:105; *dat. pl.* **fótum** II:64, III:64, X:63, XII:41, 60; **á fótum** on one's feet, up V:1; **fœtr linna Loddu lǫgðis** *is a kenning for* sword-blades (legs of swords) IV:81(*object of* **hafa at vinna**)

fótstallr *m.* pedestal XIII:38

frá[1] *prep. with dat.* (*Gr* 3.7.3) from I:89, 107, 147, III:58, VIII:28, 80, XIII:8, 25, XVI:186, 191, XIX:48; away from III:60, V:10, VIII:115, XXII:9/3 (*after noun*); *of direction,* of V:168; *denoting origin or residence,* of XXVI A:21; about I:149, II:14, 78, III:90, V:1, VI:353, VIII:128, XIV:184; concerning VII A:124, B:1, 11, 23, X:1, 16, XI:1, XXVI B:1, *textual note*; about XIV:19; absent, excluded III:20; **frá sér** from him, down; **í frá** away from VI:153; **þar út í frá** out there beyond VI:191; **frá því er** from where V:43, about that which XXIV:75 (see note 6); **koma frá** *see* **koma**; *as adv.* away XXVI A:41, 48, free VI:217; **þar frá** from this III:39; **í frá** away VI:210, 227; **upp frá** above XXI:106; **þar út í frá** out there beyond VI:186; **bæri frá** *see* **bera**; **falla frá** *see* **falla**; **næmi frá** *see* **nema**[2]; *cf.* **ífrá**

frá[2] *see* **fregna**

fram *adv.* forward VI:242, XVI:103, XXII:21/1, XXVI B:71; (to go) forward, (to) advance VI:258; ahead XXV:59; on(wards) XXI:167; forward on a ship, towards the prow VI:268, 275; (down) to the front XXIII:51; out IX:94 (*see* **bera**), (from one's clothing) II:143, (towards the entrance of a building) III:24, (into view, from behind the headland) VI:93; **fram at** (*with* **þraut**) on to XXII:33/4; *of time* on, by IV:111, back VIII:10, into the future IX:58; **fyrir fram** *with acc.* along, past II:104; **um fram** beyond, in greater measure than VII B:10, XXIII:35; **um fram hátt** beyond moderation XXIII:62; **fram fara, fara fram** *see* **fara**; **koma fram** *see* **koma**

framan *adv.* from the front, *i.e.* towards the rear, aft VI:271; **framan í** on the front of XII:27; **framan á** *as prep. with dat. or acc.* on the front of III:85, 113; **framan at** up to from the front XXVI B:88; **rétt framan í hann** straight in his face I:43

framar *adv. comp.* more, further XXII:32/2

framarliga *adv.* greatly, fully XIII:36

frami *m.* boldness, courage; **at eigi hafði frama til at** that he did not have the courage to XVI:101

framvíss *adj.* prescient, having knowledge of the future V:20

fránn *adj.* sharp X:94; gleaming (*with* **leggbita**) VI:243, glittering X:83

franzeis *m.* Frank, Frankish person XIV:155

frásaga *f.* story VI:320

frásǫgn *f.* story, narrative, account II:16; description V:85

fregn *f.* intelligence, news I:45; knowledge XXII:24/3

fregna (*past* **frá,** *past pl.* **frágu,** *pp.* **freginn**) *sv.* (*Gr* 3.6.9.3 and ex. 8) hear (of), learn (of) XXII:27/2, 44/2, 55/2, 4; *pp. in agreement with direct object* (**ógn**) V:19

freista (*past* **freistaði,** *pp.* **freistat**) *wv. with gen.* try II:141; find out II:137, VII A:147

freknóttr *adj.* freckled V:31

frelsa (*past* **frelsaði,** *pp.* **frelsat**) *wv.* free, deliver XIII:25, 45

frelsi *n.* freedom XIX:100

fremja (*past* **framði,** *pp.* **framit**) *wv.* promote, perform, do XXIII:36; **fremja gunni** wage war VI:156

fremr *adv. comp.* further off, further back (in time), earlier; **hálfu fremr** twice as far off, twice as early XXV:7

fremri *adj. comp.* superior (to) XXIV:16; foremost XXVI B:92

frétt *f.* intelligence, reply, oracle XIX:42

frétta (*past* **frétti,** *pp.* **frétt**) *wv.* **1.** hear, get intelligence (**til** about) VI:331, XXII:11/2; *pp.* **frétt** heard, learned XXVI B:37. **2. frétta (eptir)** ask (about) XXIV:8

Freydís *f.* daughter of Eiríkr rauði XXI:132, 136, 162

Freyja *f.* a goddess (of fertility, i.e. a sex-goddess) VIII:102, IX:9, 11, 13, 30, 43, 44, 46, 48, 87, 92, 104, 108, 112; one of the **Vanir**, though here described as an **Ásynja** II:10, 48

Freyr *m.* a god, one of the **Vanir**, though here described as one of the **Æsir** II:8

friðarmaðr *m.* man of peace V:69

friðill *m.* lover X:138

fríðleikr *m.* handsomeness VII B:8

friðartákn *n.* sign of peace, token of peace XXI:100

friðr *m.* peace VI:239 (*object of* **slitu**), 366, VIII:129, 131 136 (*with suffixed def. art.*), XVI:72, 187, XXII:51/3; quarter, truce II:34;

fara með friði travel peacefully VII A:71; **í góðum friði** very
peacefully XI:62

fríðr (*n.* **frítt**) *adj.* handsome VII A:95, XXII:19/2; beautiful XII:12;
magnificent XXII:1/1; *comp.* VII A:36; *sup.* VII A:34

friðstefna *f.* peace-conference II:89

Frigg *f.* a goddess, one of the Ásynjur, wife of Óðinn II:10

Frísir *m. pl.* Frisians VI:201

frjáls *adj.* free *Gr* 3.3.8.4 (1); *n.* **frjálst** freely, without restraint XII:68;
comp. **frjálsari** more free XIV:124

frjósa (*past* **frøri,** *past pl.* **frøru,** *pp.* **frørit**) *sv.* freeze *Gr* 3.6.9.3 and ex. 11

Fróðadóttir *f.* daughter of Fróði Vémundarson XIX:107

Fróði *m.* son of Qgmundr and half-brother of Kormakr; *gen. with*
brœðr IV:96

fróðleikr *m.* knowledge, learning, information II:101, XXVII:32
(**honum** in him, i.e. his knowledge)

fróðr *adj.* well informed, learned II:101

frón *n.* land, earth XXII:59/1 (*instrumental*, 'with earth')

frú *f.* lady; **vár frú** Our Lady, the Virgin Mary XIII:10, 26; *in address*
XI:28, 33

frýja (*past* **frýði**) *wv.* taunt; *with dat. and gen.* taunt someone for lack
of something, challenge someone's something V:152

frægð *f.* fame, renown; *pl.* famous deeds XXII:2/4

frægiligastr *adj. sup.* most likely to bring renown I:145

frægr *adj.* renowned (**af** for) VII A:35, XI:50; famous, bringing fame,
glorious (*with* **sið**) VI:160; *comp.* **frægri af** more renowned for
XXII:3/3; *sup.* **frægastr** most famous, most renowned VI:317,
XIX:104; *f.* **frægust** the most famous VI:314

frækn (**frœkn**) *adj.* valiant, brave XXII:17/1

frændi (*pl.* **frændr**) *m.* relative, kinsman III:36, 41, 91, IV:111, V:161,
VI:105, VII B:81, XI:55, XII:76, XIV:131, 182, XIX:17, XXV:17, 46

frœða (*past* **frœddi,** *pp.* **frœddr**) *wv.* instruct XIV:187

frœðamaðr/frœðimaðr *m.* man of learning, scholar II:99; writer
XXIII:1

frœði *n.* knowledge, learning II:94; *in pl.* history, learned work VIII:5;
spells XV:143

frœðinám/frœðinæmi *n.* acquisition of knowledge, learning, study,
education XIV:174, 185

frœknastr *adj. sup.* boldest XXVI B:94

frœknliga *adv.* bravely XXVI A:88

fugl *m.* bird VII A:154, 155, XII:32, XXIII:69; fowl, sea birds (*collective sg.*) XXI:54

fuku *see* **fjúka**

Fulla *f.* a goddess, one of the Ásynjur II:11

fullafli *adj.* having complete power (refers to Einarr þambarskelfir, the implied subject of **bíðr**) VII B:41

fullgǫrr *adj.* (*pp., cf.* **gera**) completed XII:9; **fullgǫrt at** complete with XII:33 (*with* **fugl**, *cf. note* 3)

fullhugi *m.* dauntless, courageous man V:131

fullkomliga *adv.* perfectly XIII:44

fullleiksa *adj. indeclinable* **hafa fullleiksa** have enough to do, have one's hands full V:144

fullr *adj.* full *Gr* 3.3.9 ex. 23, XI:61; **fullr af** full of VII A:149, XI:10, XII:17, XVI:141, XXI:92, complete VI:226, XXIV:48; *n.* **fullt** rounded, bulging XXIII:97; **til fulls** thoroughly (done), adequate XIV:141, fully, absolutely XXIV:34, 47

fulltíða *adj.* full-grown *Gr* 3.3.8.5 (6); **á fulltíða aldri** in adulthood XIV:167

ful(l)ting *n.* help XIV:73, XXV:46; support XXVII:15

fulltingsmenn *m. pl.* supporters VIII:105

fulltrúi *m.* patron; *with suffixed def. art.* my patron XXI:79

fultingja (*past* **fultingði,** *pp.* **fultingðr**) *wv.* help XXV:44

fundit *see* **finna**

fundr *m.* find II:162; meeting, encounter V:92, VI:197; rendezvous (*with gen.* with; *gen. object of* **hafði krafða**) VI:57; **á hans fund** to meet him, to see him VII A:45, XIV:96, 112; **á fund, til fundar** *with gen.* to meet, to see someone, to the home of someone VI:7, 15, XVI:14, 44, XIX:24, to engage (battle) with someone XXII:33/1, **sœkja á fund** go to visit someone XIV:139; **til konungs fundar** until your meeting with the king XVI:51; **til fundar við** to see, to speak to someone XXVI A:103; **ætlaði til fundar við** planned to go to meet XVI:94

fundu, funnit, funnu *see* **finna**

fura *f.* pine-wood X:54; fir (tree) XXV:17

furðu *adv.* wonderfully, amazingly VII A:119; **furðu mikit skip** an amazingly large ship VI:112

Furðustrandir *f. pl.* 'amazing strands *or* coastline' XXI:34, 42

fúss *adj.* eager; *nom. pl. complement of* **erum** *referring to the implied pl. subject* (Kormakr, 'authorial' we) IV:33

fylgd/fylgð *f.* support, help, service, attendance XXII:21/3; company, assistance: **til fylgðar við** to accompany *or* assist someone XXI:41

fylgðarmaðr *m.* follower III:52

fylgismær (*dat.* **-mey**) *f.* female attendant, maidservant XII:48

fylgja (*past* **fylgði**, *pp.* **fylgt**) *wv. with dat.* follow, accompany III:91, V:36, 88, VI:242 (*inf. in acc. and inf. construction after* **kváðu**), VII A:151, 158, VIII:74, XII:4, XV:46, XXII:17/2; keep up with XV:99, XXI:136; come with XXI:6; serve VI:201; take, convey VI:6, 13; go with VI:45, XI:44, XIV:36; be attached I:42; belong to XXIII:34, apply to VIII:117; **þar fylgir** there goes with it, in addition XI:25; *impers. pass.* **er þeim fylgt** they are conducted XI:14; **-sk** *form* **fylgjask** stick together XXVI B:76

fylkir *m.* leader of troops, war-leader, ruler XXII:11/1, 28/1, 64/3

fylla (*past* **fylldi**, *pp.* **fyllt**) *wv.* fill; fulfil, carry out XIV:50; *impers.* **fylldi af** was filled with it XII:14

fyllr *f.* fill (of food or drink) II:25, 117; *with gen.* **fyllr hilmis stóls** the filling of the throne (*gen. object of* **bíðr**; *i.e.* he is waiting to fill the throne himself) VII B:41

fyndi, fyndið, fyndisk *see* **finna**

fyr *prep. with acc. or dat.* (= **fyrir**) before, in front of IX:94, X:55, XVI:58, XXII:21/1, 38/2; for XVI:6, 44, in return for XXII:36/4; instead of IX:129, 130; as a result of XXII:58/3; in the face of, in despite of (= *dat. of disadvantage*) XXV:69; *in complex prepositions with acc.* (*Gr* 3.7.1) **fyr austan** east of VIII:18; **fyr innan** inside IX:18; **fyr . . . neðan** beneath IX:28; **fyr útan** outside IX:17, except for VIII:3, X:50; **fyr vestan** west of VIII:19; *as adv.* for it XVI:71; **fyr þikkja í** be displeased about it XVI:84; **þar fyr** with its help, by means of it XXII:37/3; *see also* **sjá, þykkja**

fyrðar *m. pl. poetical word for* men; *gen. pl.* V:19, XXV:28/2

fyrir/firir/firi *prep.* (*Gr* 3.7.4) **1.** *with dat.* in front of III:111, IV:5 (*see* **sitja**), VII B:89, XXI:88, XXVI B:121; before XIV:55, 188, XXI:26, XXVI B:104; **fyrir sér** in front of her XXI:138; before, in the face of I:33, V:38; at the head of XXII:8/1; for XXIV:63, 64 (2); **firi þér** for you XXIV:13, 25, **firi mér** for me XXIV:54; **fyrir þeim** before them, for them XI:15; over VI:181; off (the coast of) VI:28, X:87, on the coast of XVI:138; because of III:11, XXVI A:110;

presaging V:8; **fyrir honum** to him, in addressing him II:133, for him (*equivalent to dat. of disadvantage*) XXVI B:90, *similarly* **fyrir þeim** XXVI B:114, **fyrir hánum** on his side, from his troop VI:226, **fyrir þér** on your hands, on you XVI:52; **fyrir litlu** a short while before XV:38; **minni firi sér** of less consequence XXIV:75 (*cf.* **mikill**); **verða minni firi sér** be diminished, lose their power and importance XXIV:69; **alllítill fyrir sér** of very little importance or power I:55; **fyrir því at** *as conj.* (*Gr* 3.8.2.2) because II:100, 118, VI:27, 123, 224, 289, XI:70; **firi því . . . at** for this reason . . . that, in order that XXIV:32–33, 40–41, 51–52; **fyrir því at heldr þótt** any the more because of this that, even though VII B:55. **2.** *with acc.* for II:134, IV:100, 105, V:155, VI:34, 136, VII A:79, XIX:3, XXIV:21; on behalf of XXII:32/3, XXIV:64 (1); **fyrir oss** for ourselves XXVI B:102; before I:45, 50, 57; to the entrance of VII A:150, 153, in front of VII B:70, XXVI:84; over VI:294, 299, XIX:52; **fyrir land** along the coast XIX:55; past XXI:42; in return for I:60, XXI:78, XXVII:38, in exchange for XXI:115; **fyrir sik** in front of himself XXVI A:72; **fyrir þá** (from) in front of them V:87, for them, on behalf of them VII B:25; because of, as a result of XXIV:52; **fyrir hvat** why XV:52; **at firi þat** so that for that, so that in relation to it, so that as a result? XXIV:26; **firi þat at** because, as a result of the fact that XXIV:42; *of time,* before XV:97, XXVI B:41; *in complex prepositions with acc.* (*Gr* 3.5.1, 3.5.3 (7), 3.7.1) **fyrir norðan** to the north of VII A:148, XXVI A:13; **fyrir sunnan** south of V:151, XXVI A:96; **sunnan fyrir** from the south round XXI:111; **fyrir vestan** west of XV:36, XIX:91, west of it XXI:167; **fyrir innan** inside II:60, XV:132 (*see* **innan**); **fyrir neðan** below III:57, XIX:92 (see **heiðr**); **fyrir ofan** above XXI:172, XXVI B:118, **fyrir . . . ofan** down over XXI:80; **fyrir útan** beyond, outside IV:49, beyond, west of XIX:97, without VI:21; **sunnr fyrir** in the south off VI:207; **suðr firir** southwards along XXI:86, south past XXI:105; **vestr fyrir** west along (the coast) VII A:153, west past XV:146; **fyrir fram** along II:104; **fyrir sakar þess er** for this reason, that VI:316. **3.** *as adv.* there, in front III:110, 112, XXVI B:47, in front VII A:145 (*with* **varð** *line* 140), there present IX:102; there already XXI:154, to be found XI:17, in residence XVI:15; in the way, in its path V:128; **eigi lokan fyrir** the bolt was not across XV:105; in advance VII A:64; ahead VI:26, XXVI A:28; past VI:59, 61, past it, along its/the coast

XXI:22, 155; for it, as a punishment VIII:87; in return XVI:48; for it XXI:118; **einn fyrir** only one to face XXVI B:60; **sem . . . var fyrir** where . . . was positioned XXVI B:89; **út fyrir** out in the sea off it XXI:53; **fyrir útan** round the outside, round the edge (of the shore) VII A:163, round the seaward side of the island(s), on the open sea VI:87; **úti fyrir** out in front of the house XXVI B:49; **þeim er úti váru fyrir** those who were out there (on that side) XXVI B:221; **þar fyrir** in front of them XVI:A:25, in front (of the doorway) there, in front of it III:82, 83, ahead there XXVI A:16; **vera þar fyrir** be (already) present there VII B:32, XI:11; **þar . . . firi** about that XXIV:57; **gaf þar firir** gave for it XVI:11; **þar fyrir . . . at** for this reason . . . that XII:35

fyrirrúm *n.* 'forward place', the position on a warship in front of the raised stern section; *with suffixed def. art.* VI:268, 285

fyrr *adv. comp.* previously, earlier, before III:16, VI:8, VII B:52, VIII:186, XIV:103, XV:45, 141, 150, XVI:99, XXIV:24, the last time XVI:155; above (in a book) VII B:5, XV:35, XIV:154, XV:35; **fyrr sǫgð** aforesaid, aforementioned XIII:34: **var fyrr** had previously been XXII:9/1; **viku fyrr** a week earlier VIII:96; **fyrr en** *as conj.* before V:41 (lines 38–39 belong in the clause **fyrr en** introduces), VI:92, 115, VIII:73, 106, XIV:171, XXVII:29; until XV:100; **eigi fyrr en** not before, not until XXVI A:63, B:119, 133

fyrri[1] *adj. comp.* former, first (of two) *Gr* 3.3.5 ex. 6, XXVII:44, earlier XXIV:82

fyrri[2] *adv.* first, in front XXVI B:206, 210; before XXII:64/4

fyrst/fyst *adv.* first III:73, V:93, VIII:1, 7, 15, 18, 35, IX:5 (*adj. n.?*), XIV:64, XXIV:31; at first I:35; firstly VI:254, XIV:43; to begin with VI:267, XI:58, 145

fyrstr *adj. sup.* (*Gr* 3.4.1) first II:152, VIII:171, 181, IX:125, XXII:14/2, XXIV:77; the first XIV:180; the first one VIII:192; **byggði fyrstr landit** was the first to settle in the country XIX:105 (*Gr* 3.9.8.1); **inn fyrsti** the first XI:73, **hit fyrsta** XXI:196; *wk. n. acc. as adv.* **it fyrsta, hit fyrsta** first of all, to begin with II:28, 63

fýsa (*past* **fýsti,** *pp.* **fýst**) *wv. with acc. and gen.* give encouragement to someone for, encourage someone into something VIII:67; *impers. with acc.* **fýsti hann** he was eager VII A:43; **braut fýsir mik** I want to leave XVI:79; **þá fýsti einskis annars en** they desired nothing else but XXI:129; **þat er mest fýsir til** what he most longs for XXVI

B:20; *pres. part.* **fýsandi** desirous, importunate VI:39; **-sk** *form* **fýsask** *with gen.* be eager for, desire something XXI:13; **fýsask á** become eager for X:29; **fýsask í brott** be eager to leave, want to leave XVI:84

fýsi *f.* desire XIV:116

fyst *see* **fyrst**

fýst *f.* desires, eagerness XXIII:2

fæða *see* **fœða**

fælask (*past* **fældisk**) *wv.* **-sk** *form* be frightened (**við** by it, by this) XXI:120, 142,

fær, færat *see* **fá**

færa *see* **fœra**

færi, færri *adj. comp.* fewer *Gr* 3.3.8.2–5 ex. 4, V:83

fæstr *adj. sup.* very few I:136; **sem fæstum sinnum** as infrequently as possible XXIV:12

fœða/fæða (*past* **fœddi**, *pp.* **fœddr**) *wv.* feed, give food to, *Gr* 3.6.9.3 ex. 5; **fœddu sik sjálfir** provided for their own maintenance XIV:151; **-sk** *form* **fæddisk** there has been born XXII:64/3; **fœðask af** feed on, rejoice in, exult in? XIV:106

fœra¹/færa (*past* **fœrði/færði**, *pp.* **fœrðr/fœrt/fært**) *wv.* bring II:46, IX:30 (*subj.*), XI:23, 25, XIV:47; present XVI:50, 63, 167; take (*with dat.* to someone) V:159; *imp. pl.* **fœrið** IX:87; *past* **fœrðuð** you brought VI:250; **færði** presented, delivered XXII:63/1; **fœra fram** perform, discharge XIV:43, 125; **fœra upp** raise up XXI:126; **-sk** *form* **fœrðusk þar á upp** got up onto it XV:142

fœra² *see* **fara**

fœri, fœrir *see* **fara** *and* **fœra**

fœrr *adj.* passable, safe (*with dat.*, for) VII A:165; **til fœrr** capable of, able to do XXIV:25

fœti, fœtr *see* **fótr**

fœzla *f.* food XIV:147

fǫður *see* **faðir**

fǫðurbróðir *m.* (paternal) uncle III:32, VIII:10

fǫðurgjǫld *n. pl.* compensation for one's father's death II:114

fǫðurlauss *adj.* fatherless, orphan XIV:111

fǫðursystir *f.* (paternal) aunt XIX:107 (see note 6)

fǫgr, fǫgru, fǫgrum *see* **fagr**

fǫgnuðr *m.* joy *Gr* 3.1.7.1, 3.1.8 (6)

fǫlr (fǫlv-) *adj.* pale *Gr* 3.3.8.1, 3.3.8.2–5 ex. 4, 3.3.9 (6), (20)

fǫluðu *see* **fala**

fǫng, fǫngum *see* **fang¹**

fǫr (*gen. sg.* **farar**) *f.* journey; fate III:69; movement I:121; coming XI:2; going, departure X:138; migration VIII:25, 67; expedition XXVI B:50; **á fǫr** a-travelling XXVI B:14; *dat. pl.* **fǫrum¹** travels, movements V:13, XV:121, XIX:21; **í fǫr með** travelling with, in company with XV:45

fǫrull (fǫrl-) *adj.* rambling 3.3.8.2–5 ex. 4

fǫrum² *see* **fara**

fǫrunautr *m.* companion; **ok hans fǫrunauta(r)** and those who were with him XV:144, 154

fǫruneyti *n.* following VII A:67, XXI:5; company; **allt fǫruneyti hans** everyone with him XV:152

fǫstnuð *see* **fastna**

fǫstudagr *m.* Friday; *acc. of time* on the Friday XXVII:6; **fǫstudag inn fyrra í þingi** on the first Friday of the Assembly XXVII:44

fǫstuígangr *m.* the beginning of Lent; *gen. pl.* **fǫstuíganga(hald) the** (dates) of the observance of the beginnings of fasting, i.e. the date of the beginning of Lent XXVII:30

-g = -k

gá (*past* **gáði,** *pp.* **gát**) *wv. with gen.* give heed *or* thought to XXI:58, care about XXV:27

gaf *see* **gefa**

gafl *m.* gable, gable-wall X:45, XXV:110

gaflveggr *m.* gable wall XXVI B:29 (*with suffixed def. art.*)

gaft, gaftu, gáfu *see* **gefa**

gagn *n.* advantage, help, use; **koma at gagni** do (him) any good XXII:40/4

gagnvart *prep. with dat.* opposite *Gr* 3.7.3, XXI:205

gakk *see* **ganga**

Galarr *m.* a dwarf II:95, 109

galdr *m.* magic; *pl.* **galdrar** incantations, sorcery XIV:77, XV:143

gáleysi *n.* heedlessness, wantonness, irresponsibility XIV:164

gálgi *m.* gallows XXV:77

gall *see* **gjalla**

galt, galzk *see* **gjalda**

gamall (*f.* **gǫmul,** *pl.* **gamlir**) *adj.* (3.3.8.1, 3, 5 (1), 3.3.9 (8), (14), 3.3.9 ex. 7, 16) old II:44, III:22, 46, V:32, VIII:16 (*Gr* 3.4.2 (7)),

XXVI B:159; **enn gamli** *as nickname* XIX:17, 107; *with the number of years in the gen.* XV:4; **tólf vetra gamall** at the age of twelve XIV:174

gaman (*dat. sg.* **gamni** *Gr* 3.1.7.3–5 ex. 4) *n.* delight, pleasure; **jǫtni at gamni** for the giant's pleasure IX:90

ganga¹ (*pres.* **gengr,** *past* **gekk,** *past pl.* **gengu/gingu/geingu,** *pp.* **gengit/gingit**) *sv.* (*Gr* 3.6.9.1 (3, 4, 12), 3.6.9.3) walk, go I:3, 7, 25, 57, 68, 84, 89, 93, 121, II:45, 55, III:12, 41, V:34, 147, VII A:151, IX:89, X:33, 137, XI:8, 74, XVI:128, XIX:33, XXI:102, XXII:27/3, XXIII:102, XXIV:46, XXV:40, XXVI A:14, 32, B:44, XXVII:21; come I:96, X:177; lead XV:83; flow (of water) XXI:93; *with gen. of destination* go to, approach IX:9; *with acc.* walk through *Gr* 3.1.9 ex. 14 (*cf.* **fara**), X:46, 75; *pres.* **gengr** is going X:166; **gǫngum** let us go X:111; *imp.* **gakk** come XI:28, **gakk þú** go X:156, you go XXVI B:136, **gakktu** XXVI B:143, you come XXVI B:161; *past subj.* **gengi** II:110, IV:8, XV:102, XVI:94; **hafði þangat á gengit** (men, **liðit**; *Gr* 3.9.5) had boarded it VI:225; **ganga á** intrude on XXVII:35; **ganga á hǫnd** *with dat.* submit to someone, join someone's band XXII:10/1; **ganga at** come up/over, approach XXI:77, go against, attack I:138, XXVI B:101, enter upon, begin II:7, intervene VII B:57, **ganga framan at** approach from the front XXVI B:88; **ganga eptir** follow XXI:137, be fulfilled VII A:32, be proved true XXVI B:25; **ganga frá** leave, be finished with III:60; *impers.* **skal eigi frá ganga** there will be no going away, no finishing with it XXVI B:133; **ganga fram** come forward XVI:101, 105, advance, attack XXII:43/2; *subj.* **gangi sá nú fram** let that one now come forward XVI:103; **at gánga fram at** to come on to XXII:33/4; **ganga í** wear XXI:205; **ganga í mót** advance, oppose, go against the enemy, meet the enemy VI:256; **gánga oss í móti** are/will be fighting against us XXII:32/4; **ganga ór** go from, leave VI:271; **ganga saman** close, engage XXI:125; **ganga sleitum** *see* **sleita; ganga í sundr** break in two V:100; **ganga sundr** be broken VI:56; **ganga til at** result in, lead to XXIV:43; *impers. with dat.* **hvernug honum mundi ganga til** how successful he would be in obtaining VII A:46; **ganga undan** get away, escape V:107; **láta undan ganga** let off VII B:54; **ganga undir** undergo, accept XIV:99; **ganga upp** go ashore VII A:159, VII B:34, 40 (*inf. with* **sé ek Einar**), XVI:15, go aboard VI:269, 273; be used up XVI:89; **ganga upp á** board, go aboard VI:189,

220; **nú er þeim út at ganga ǫllum er** now it is for all those to go out to whom, now all those are to go out to whom XXVI B:135; **gengr vel** *with dat.* someone gets on well, things go well for someone XIV:107; **ganga yfir** befall III:26, VIII:85, XXVI B:164; *impers.* **gekk því** this went on XXVI B:194, *subj.* **gangi eigi** it be impossible XXVI B:209; *as aux. with inf.* go to, begin to X:53; **-sk** *form* **gangask í gegn** confront each other, enter into conflict VIII:133; *pp.* **var of genginn** had gone IV:21, **fram genginn** departed (from life) VI:361, **sem inn var gengit** where one went in, i.e. at the entrance XII:53

ganga[2] *f.* going; visit IV:60

gangr *m.* movement, activity; **snarpra sverða gangr** *is a kenning for* battle (*subject of* **gerðisk**) VI:241

Gangr *m.* a giant II:81

gangtamr *adj.* trained in its paces (of horses) XXV:13

gapa (*past* **gapði,** *pp.* **gapat**) *wv. with dat.* open wide XXI:67

Garðafylja *f.* 'Filly of Garðar'; Garðar is a common farm-name in Iceland, and the nickname may refer to Hallfríðr's place of birth or abode III:128

Garðaríki *n.* Russia VII A:37

garðr *m.* courtyard XI:74, XXV:40; *with suffixed def. art.* II:156, VII B:60, 61; *in Iceland*, farmyard *or* hayfield enclosure IV:49; *pl. with suffixed def. art.* buildings *or* enclosures XXVI A:13; farmyard, farm enclosure, farmyard wall; **hér at garði** beside this enclosure IX:89; **ór garði** off the premises III:121; (in Norway and other continental countries) premises, house (in a town) VII B:35, XI:49; *pl.* courts, dwelling, abode IX:17; *gen. of place* **miðra garða** in the middle of the courts IX:34

garpr *m.* brave man, soldier XXII:13/2,19/4, 22/1, 28/1, 32/3

Garpsdalr *m.* valley in Gilsfjǫrðr XV:2, 14

Garpsdalsgoði *m.* **goði** of Garpsdalr XV:2

gat *see* **geta**

gata (*pl.* **gǫtur** *Gr* 3.1.7.1 ex. 3) *f.* path; *acc.* **þá gǫtu** along that path V:42

gátu, gátum *see* **geta**

Gauka-Þórir *m.* robber XXII:23/3

Gaular *f. pl.* district in Norway south-east of Trondheim XIX:7

gaumr *m.* heed, attention I:24, 54, XXI:136

Gautland *n.* Götaland (southern Sweden) XIV:28

gaztu *see* **geta**

gefa (*pres.* **gefr,** *past* **gaf,** *past pl.* **gáfu,** *past subj.* **gæfi,** *pp.* **gefinn,** *pp. n.* **gefit**) *sv.* give II:25, 127 (**við** in exchange), III:17, IV:100, VI:3, VII A:112, VIII:43, 66, IX:14, X:78, 107, XVI:14, XIX:100, XXI:24, 38; give away XVI:150; pay I:23, 54; *imp.* **gef** I:130 (**til** for this purpose), XVI:152, XXII:32/3; **gaftu** you have given XV:23; *subj.* **gæfir** were giving XVI:76; **annat mun þér betr gefit** you are better disposed to other things, you are more talented at other things V:138; **gefa af sér** give out, proclaim XXIII:50; **gefa (þar) firir/ fyrir** give for it XVI:11, XXI:118; **firir at gefa** to give in return XVI:48; **gáfu fé með sér** gave money with themselves (i.e. for their maintenance), brought money with them (on entry to the foundation) XIV:150; *pp. f.* **gefin** given in marriage XXVI B:163; *impers.* **gefa** be found, be obtainable XXI:61; **gaf þeim** it was given them, they were enabled XXI:81

Gefjun *f.* a goddess, one of the **Ásynjur** II:10

gegn[1] *adj.* advantageous; worthy, reliable VII B:15

gegn[2] *adv.* (cf. *Gr* 3.7.3) against VIII:133 (*see* **ganga**); **í gegn** against it VIII:180 (*or prep. with* **því**); in opposition VIII:81; *as prep. with dat.* against XXII:34/1

gegna (**gegndi**) *wv. with dat.* mean, signify, be caused by II:22; meet, pay, discharge VIII:168; amount to (= **sæta**) XXII:55/2; be suitable for XXVI B:72

gegnum, í gegnum *prep. with acc.* through (*Gr* 3.7.1) VI:21, XXVI A:70, 72

gegnvart *prep.* opposite *Gr* 3.7.3

geigr *m.* hurt, injury XXVI A:45

geil *f.* lane, sunken path between fields or enclosures XXVI A:16

Geila *f.* daughter of Búrizleifr VI:47

geimi/geimr *m.* sea XXII:64/2

geirr *m.* spear VI:308, VII A:25, XXV:92; *dat. (instrumental)* **geiri** with a spear XXVI A:95

Geirr goði Ásgeirsson *m.* XXVI A:4, 110, 112

Geirrøðr *m.* Irish slave XIX:36

geirvarta *f.* nipple XII:16, XV:62, 108; **honum í geirvǫrtur** as far as his nipples III:103

geisli *m.* shaft of light XXII:60/3

geit *f.* (she-)goat II:69, XXIII:69 (*gen. pl.* with **rǫdd**)

Geitdalr *m.* valley in eastern Iceland *Gr* 3.1.8 ex.

geitskǫr *f.* (*or* **geitskor** *f. or* **geitskór** *m.*?) nickname (= 'goat-hair'?)
VIII:41
gekk *see* **ganga**
gella (*past* **gelldi**) *wv.* roar, bellow VII A:158
Gellini *m.* = **Arnljótr gellini**
gellir *m.* 'bellower', a nickname VII A:167
Gellisson *m.* son of Gellir Þorkelsson (1017–73) VIII:10, 34, 74
geingu *see* **ganga**¹
gengi¹ *f.* support, following, troop VI:157 (*gen. object of* **misstu**)
gengi², **genginn**, **gengit**, **gengr**, **gengu** *see* **ganga**¹
genja *f.* large frightening creature; a kind of axe; *as nickname* III:47
(perhaps with reference to the first meaning, or to an axe that the
man owned)
gera/gjǫra/gøra/gørva (*pres.* **gerir/gørir,** *past* **gerði/gørði/gjǫrði,** *pp.*
gerr/gjǫrr/gǫrr/gert/gjǫrt/gǫrt/gjǫrvir) *wv.* (*Gr* 3.6.7) **1.** do I:10,
53, 77, 86, 88, 110, 115, 118, 142, II:68, 69, 73, 111, 144, IV:12,
VI:122, VII A:101, VIII:185, X:86, XII:84, XIV:85, XV:89, 90, 97,
XVI:74, 127, 160, 47/1, XIX:105, XXVI B:74, 145, 213; **gera nú**
svá now do so XXI:72; *imp.* **gǫr** I:15, **ger þú eigi** do not do XXVI
A:47, **gerðu honum** make (for) him XV:27; **gerum vér** let us do
XXVI B:72; *subj.* **geri** should do VII A:101, **ok gera ek þat** where
I might (*or* so that I may) do it XV:65; perform, hold VI:7; make
I:11, 16, 29, 145, II:74 (**af** of them), VI:146, VIII:1, 31, 129, 174,
XII:16, XV:13 (*see* **ógetit**), 18 (*see* **dátt**), 30, XVI:116, XIX:65,
XXI:45, 92, XXVI B:107, provide, hold (*with dat.*, for someone)
XIX:9; **gerum** let us make XI:38; **gørði** was doing XII:78, was
making XII:77; **gjǫrði svá** did so XXI:72, **svá gjǫrðu þeir** they did
so XXI:102; **gjǫrðuð þér** you did XXVI B:70; **gerðu** they carried
out XXVI A:43; get ready XVI:113; devise X:99; set, calculate, pay
VIII:154, 157; enact VIII:172; perform XIII:20; build VI:113, X:5,
156, XIV:11, 152, XV:142, XIX:62, 102, XXI:106; bring about VII
A:17, XXII:26/1; put up, i.e. fight XXII:39/2; cause VI:39, XV:126;
gera ferð sína make one's way, set out II:2, VI:20; **gera kost** *with*
dat. give someone a choice XXVI A:11; **gera orð** send word
VIII:104, 122; **gera orð á** make remarks/comments about XXVI
B:32; **gera annat ráð** make another plan, try another course of action
XXVI B:101; **af gera** do with it XVI:29; **gjǫra af** banish, exile,
outlaw from XXI:157; **gera at** do something about XI:40, attend to

XV:24, make into VI:16; **fengu/gátu ekki at gert** achieved nothing XXVI A:38, B:97; **margir hlutir aðrir at gjǫrvir síðan** many other repairs *or* improvements (have been) done on it since XIV:13; **slíkt hafa at gǫrt** had acted in such a way in this matter XV:118; **gera eptir** make in the likeness of XII:61; **gera ráð fyrir** look after XXI:71; **gøra mót** *with dat.* act against, oppose someone XIX:21; **honum í móti gjǫra** do anything (*or* go) against him XIV:113; **gera til** earn I:61, direct at XV:145; **gera mikit um** make much of it V:72; **gera sér mikit um** be much concerned about, care much about VI:318; **gørið betr við mik** act better towards me, treat me better XXIV:21; **ekki við því gera** to do nothing to prevent it XXVI B:79; *pp.* **gerr** built XXVI A:24, done, committed XXVI B:140; **gǫrr** prepared, brewed (*with dat.,* for) XII:51; *f.* **ger, gjǫr** made, fashioned XIII:2, 14, built XIV:6; **gjǫr** *as adj.* fulfilled, complete II:72; *acc. f.* **gǫrða** made, constructed I:20; *n.* **gert/gǫrt/gjǫrt** made XII:59; XIII:19, XXI:45, XXII:30/4; **vel gǫrt** well made XII:12; **gjǫrt/gǫrt** done XIV:138, XVI:178; *m. pl.* **gervir** (are) made (*i.e.* lit) XI:15, **gǫrvir at** ready to, on the point of XXV:40; *f. pl.* **gǫrvar** made, *i.e.* told VI:321; *as aux. with inf. as meaningless periphrasis* X:40, *imp.* **gerið** XXII:22/2, *with suffixed neg.* **-t, gerðut** did not VI:261; *impers.* **gjǫrir hann** he becomes XVI:89. **2. -sk** *form* **gørask** become XVI:169; **gerðisk, gjǫrðisk/gerðusk/gørðusk** became I:73, II:43, XIV:22, 48, XXI:35, it became XXI:60; **sem gerðisk** however it might turn out (*or* if it happened?) IV:95; **gerðisk/gjǫrðisk** took place VI:238, there came XXI:59; there came to be (*with dat.,* in someone, *i.e.* someone came to have) VII A:32; **gørðisk** would take place VIII:127, turned out, worked VIII:130; **gørðisk af því** came about as a result of this VIII:113; **hafði gǫrzk, hafði í gǫrzk** had taken place XV:121, 140; **gjǫrðisk til** set about, took the trouble to XVI:70; **gǫrðumz** we forced ourselves (we were forced?) XXV:101 (see note and *Gr* 3.6.4, 3.6.5.3); *used as auxiliary with inf.* **gerðisk bægja við = bægðisk við** did contend with VII A:11; *with suffixed neg.* **gerðut** did not XXV:64

gerð/gjǫrð *f.* doing, deed; **í ǫllum sínum gerðum/gjǫrðum** in everything he does XXIII:19, 42; activity XXIII:40

Gerðr *f.* a goddess, one of the **Ásynjur** II:10

gerla *adv.* (= **gǫrla**) extensively, completely, fully, comprehensively XXVII:31

Gernoz *m.* brother of Gunnarr and Grímhildr XI:54

gerr[1] *adv. comp.* more clearly, more completely VIII:5

gerr[2] *see* **gera**

gersemi/gersimi/gjǫrsimi/gørsimi *f.* treasure, jewel, precious gift VIII:131, X:88, 105; valuable thing XV:15, XVI:11, 34, 140, 145, 167, XXI:151

gerv- *see* **gera**

gerzkr *adj.* from **Garðaríki**, Russian VII A:38

gestahús *n.* visitors' quarters III:78

gestr *m.* guest XIV:138; a rank of retainer at the Norwegian court (*Gr* 3.1.9 ex. 6) III:119 (see *MS* 284)

Gestr Oddleifsson *m.* XV:43, 45, 58 (*see note* 6)

geta (*past* **gat**, *past pl.* **gátu**, *pp.* **getinn**) *sv.* **1.** get; *with suffixed 2nd person pron.* **gaztu** did you get X:67 (*Gr* 3.6.9.1 (10)); **geta af** gain (knowledge) from, learn from XXVII:34; **geta at** *with dat.* obtain from VIII:97; **þat geta at** get to do it XXVII:12; *as aux. with pp.* manage (to do something; *Gr* 3.9.7.1) III:62, VI:10, XV:99, XXVI A:38; **get ek ei** I cannot XXII:15/1, **þá aldri sótta geta** never manage to defeat them XXVI B:49, **getum þá eigi með vápnum sótta** will never be able to defeat them with weapons XXVI B:100; *as aux. with at and inf.* **geta at** get to do something, happen to do something XXI:110. **2.** *with gen.* mention, speak of VI:173, XIV:130, XXIV:81; **getum eigi** let us not speak of them XI:38; **þess er við getit** it is further said/told XVI:10; tell VI:339, 348 (*inf. in nom. and inf. construction with* **þykkjat**; *Gr* 3.9.4); **er getit** *with gen.* someone is mentioned (**við** in connection with) VI:199. **3.** guess, gauge, predict XXVI B:177. **4. -sk** *form impers.* **getask vel at** *with dat.* (one) thinks well of someone, likes someone: **hafði honum vel getizk at manninum** he had thought well of the man VII B:53

geyja (*past* **gó**) *sv.* bark at; abuse, blaspheme VIII:101

geyma (*past* **geymði/geymdi**, *pp.* **geymdr**) *wv.* take care of XXII:58/1; *with gen.* **geyma þess at** make sure that XXVI B:85

geysaz (*past* **geysti**) *wv.* -sk *form* rush XXII:39/1, surge XXII:34/1

geysigrimmligr *adj.* very, exceedingly terrible XXII:30/3

geysistríðr *adj.* extremely severe; *n. as adv.* **geysistrítt** very harshly (*or as substantive,* very harsh treatment?) XXII:36/3

geystr *adj. (pp.)* rushing furiously XXII:38/1

geyst *adv. (or adj. (pp.) n.)* furious(ly), at great speed I:116

-gi *intensive suffix*; **miklugi gǫrr** more extensively by far, by very much XXVII:32. Cf. XXV, note 25.

gildi *n.* feast, banquet II:7

gildr *adj.* fine, worthy XXI:133, XXII:11/3; *with gen.* great, mighty, doughty in XXII:42/1

gilja (*past* **giljaði**, *pp.* **giljaðr**) *wv.* beguile, seduce XIV:90, *note*

Gillingr *m.* a giant II:102, 103, 105, 112

Gilsfjǫrðr *m.* fjord in north-west Iceland XV:3

gimfastr *adj.* X:37, *see note*

Gimsar *f. (?) pl.* estate near Trondheim, Norway (modern Gimsan) VI:67

gimsteinn *m.* precious stone, jewel XII:26

gin *n.* mouth (of animal), maw XXIII:63

gingu, gingit *see* **ganga**

gipt *f.* good fortune, grace XIV:36

gipta[1] (*past* **gipti**, *pp.* **gipt**) *wv.* give in marriage *Gr* 3.9.1, VII A:75, 91; **-sk** *form for passive* be married (to) *or refl.* marry oneself (to) VII A:93

gipta[2] *f.* luck (= **gæfa**) XVI:33

giptumaðr *m.* person of good luck (= **gæfumaðr**) XVI:125

girnd *f.* desire, lust XIII:43

Gíslher *m.* brother of Gunnarr and Grímhildr XI:30, 33, 54

Gísli Finnason *m.* XIV: 28, 154

gista (*past* **gisti**, *pp.* **gist**) *wv.* lodge, stay (overnight) XV:44

Gizurr glaði (the Cheerful) *m.* III:15, 19

Gizurr hvíti Teitsson *m.* VIII:80, 88, 111, XXVI A:4, 32, 33, 42, 52, 56, 66, 101, 110, 112, 118

Gizurr Ísleifsson *m.* bishop 1082–1118 VIII:150, 158, 181, 185, 188, 193, 195, 196

Gizurr Þorvaldsson *m.* 1208–68 III:6, 8, 9, 11, 12, 17, 20, 27, 29, 34, 35, 90, 91, 94, 96, 99, 101, 109, 111, 114, 122, 125, 126, 130

gjá *f.* ravine *Gr* 3.1.7.3–5 ex. 4, VIII:52

gjafar *see* **gjǫf**

gjald *n.* tax (*Gr* 3.1.7.1 ex.5) VIII:30

gjalda (*pres.* **geldr**, *past* **galt**, *past pl.* **guldu**, *pp.* **goldinn**) *wv.* pay (*Gr* 3.6.9.1 (3)) VII A:169, VIII:27, 32, XIV:123, XXVI B:53; hand over XIX:25; give XXVII:19; repay with XV:16; **-sk** *form past* **galzk** was paid VIII:30

gjalla (*pres.* **gellr**, *past* **gall**, *past pl.* **gullu**) *sv.* resound, clang VI:240,

XXII:18/4; bellow; **ok gall hátt við** and it bellowed loudly at the same time XXI:119

gjarn *adj.* eager (*with gen.*, for something) VII A:22

gjarna/gjarnan *adv.* (*Gr* 3.5.2) willingly, gladly I:31, V:78, VII A:121, XXIV:25; eagerly, is keen to XXIII:81

gjóðr *m.* osprey; **gjóðr geira hríðar**, osprey of battle VII A:26, *is a kenning for* a carrion bird, eagle or raven (*dat. of respect*, 'in or for the raven'; *cf. note to* I:12); when his hunger is diminished a battle has taken place

Gjúki *m.* father of Guðrún, Gunnarr and Hǫgni XXV:8, 77 (see note 4)

gjǫf *f.* gift II:163, IV:100 (*pl.* **gjafar**), XVI:188; *with suffixed def. art.* XVI:135, 188

gjǫld *see* **gjald**

gjǫr, gjǫra, gjǫrði, gjǫrðisk, gjǫrðuð, gjǫrr *see* **gera**

gjǫrð *see* **gerð**

gjǫrningr *m.* sorcery XIV:77

gjǫrsamliga *adv.* particularly XXIV:36

gjǫrsimi = **gersemi**

gjǫrst *adv. sup.* most accurately, most intimately XIV:51

gjǫrt, gjǫrvir *see* **gera**

glaðr (*f.* **glǫð** *Gr* 3.3.8.1 ex.3) *adj.* glad, cheerful VI:309 (with **hann**, *subject of* **rauð**); happy XXII:23/4 (*acc. sg. m.* 'the happy Gauka-Þórir'); *wk. form as nickname* III:15, 19

Glaðstýrandi *m.* (*pres. part.*) horse-steersman *or* -captain (in apposition to **Gunnarr**) XXVI A:95. Glaðr is the name of a mythical horse (see *SnE, Skáldskaparmál* 90/2 and 463), **Glaðr kjalar slóða** 'horse of the keel's path, i.e. of the sea' *is a kenning for* ship, whose steersman is a seafarer, meaning Gunnarr

glam *n.* din, clash XXII:38/3 (**randa glam** *probably a kenning* for battle)

glaumr *m.* merriment, revelry XXV:63

gleði *f.* joy *Gr* 3.1.7.4 (4), XII 86; happiness, entertainment? XXII:3/4

gleðimark *n.* sign of cheerfulness, indication of cheerfulness XXIII:50

gleðja (*past* **gladdi**, *pp.* **gladdr**) *wv.* gladden *Gr* 3.6.9.1 (7)

glepja (*past* **glapða**, *pp.* **glapðr**) *wv.* **1.** confuse, confound. **2.** -**sk** *form pres. for pass.* **glepsk** will be disturbed, destroyed VI:366

gleyma (*past* **gleymði**, *pp.* **gleymðr**) *wv. with dat.* forget XII:39 (*imp.*)

gleypa (*past* **gleypti**, *pp.* **gleypt**) *wv.* swallow I:91

glíkligr (= **líkligr**) *adj.* likely, probable; *n. as substantive* **glíkligs** (*gen. object of* **geta**) what is likely VI:349

glita (*past* **glitaði**, *pp.* **glitaðr**) *wv.* glitter XXI:173

glófi *m.* glove VI:37

glotta (*past* **glotti**) *sv.* grin (**at** at it) XXVI B:96

gluggr *m.* window (opening) III:4 (*acc. pl. with suffixed def. art.*); **ok gluggar** and (there were) windows XXVI A:24

Glúmr Geirason *m.* poet, father of Þórðr Ingunnarson XV:34

glý *n.* joy XXV:27

glýstamr *adj.* 'joy-hindered', joyless XXV:2

glæsiligr *adj.* splendid; *n.* **ok mjǫg glæsiligt** and (it was) a very splendid one (*see Gr* 3.9.2) VI:62

glœpr *m.* misdeed, crime XIV:99

glǫð *see* **glaðr**

glǫggr *adj.* clear-sighted, perceptive XXIII:19

Gná *f. name of a* goddess; *in kennings for* woman (= Steingerðr; cf. *SnE, Skáldskaparmál* ch. 31): **Gná steina** (*object of* **meina**) IV:55; **Gná borða** (*object of* **varða**) IV:57

gnauð *f.* noise, din XXII:56/1; **hjǫrva gnauð** 'din of swords' *may be a kenning for* battle

gnaustan *f.* clashing; **malma gnaustan** *is a kenning for* battle VI:352

gnísta (*past* **gnísti**, *pp.* **gníst**) *wv. with dat.* gnash XII:57

gnógr *adj.* enough; *n. as substantive* **gnógt** enough XXVI A:53

gnóttir *f.* abundance, plenty (**alls** of everything; cf. *Gr* 3.9.8.2 and XXI:18, 32 and note 3) XXI:161

gnýstœrandi *pres. part.* increaser of the clash (of battle), warrior XXVI A:95, *textual note*

goð *n.* (heathen) god, *see* **guð**

goðbarn *n.* divinely descended child *or* offspring XXV:77

goðborinn *adj. (pp.) as substantive* one born of gods, descended from a god XXV:58

goðgá *f.* 'barking at gods', blasphemy VIII:99

goði *m.* one of 36–39 priest-chieftains in pre-Christian Iceland VII A:167, VIII:11; *as title* XV:35, 41, XXVI A:4

góðmannliga *adv.* like a good man, conscientiously XIV:19

Goðmundr Þorgeirssonr *m.* lawspeaker 1123–1134 VIII:171

góðr (*n.* **gott** *Gr* 3.3.8.4 (3b)) *adj.* good (*Gr* 3.3.8.3, 3.3.9 ex. 21, 24) V:59, VI:89, 365 (*with* **grams**), VIII:68, XI:46, XV:24, XIX:98, XXI:51, XXII:37/1, XXIV:67, XXV:108, XXVI B:102; *n.* **gott kostum** with good qualities XXI:177; *acc. sg. m.* **góðan** XIX:77; *wk. dat. sg. m.* **góða** XXII:16/2; *acc. sg. f.* **góða** XIV:38 (cf. *Gr* 3.9.2); *gen. sg. f.*

góðrar satisfactory XXIV:23; *acc. m. pl.* **góða** XIV:15; fine V:56, XVI:3, 188; happy XV:80; noble-minded I:133; kind (*complement of* **yrði mér**) IV:96; *wk. form* **góði** XI:69; *n.* **gott** *as substantive* **svá (mikit) gott** such (great) goodness, such a (great) favour *or* kindness XVI:151, 184

góðsiðugr *adj.* well-conducted, well-bred XXIII:8

Golaþingslǫg *n. pl.* the early law of the assembly at Gola (Gula), western Norway VIII:39

gólf *n.* the unboarded floor down the middle of a medieval hall, the ground X:76; *with suffixed def. art.* **um þvert gólfit** *i.e.* across the room I:35, **við gólfit** close to the floor III:7

Gotar *m. pl.* Goths; *gen. pl.* **Gotna** XXV:84, 106, *partitive gen.* (*Gr* 3.2.6 (20)) XXV:81, = Gothic XXV:13; *gen. pl.* **gota** Goths, men, horses (uncertain which) XXV:64 (*see note*)

gotnar *m. pl. poetical word for* men VI:348 (*subject of* **þykkjat mér**, *Gr* 3.9.4), VII B:21 (*dat. with* **vill bjóða**)

gott *see* **góðr**

gráðr *m.* greed, hunger VII A:25 (a battle sates the hunger of carrion birds)

gráðugr *adj.* greedy XXIII:13, 62, 88, 90, XXV:104

grafa (*pres.* **grefr**, *past* **gróf**, *past pl.* **grófu**, *pp.* **grafinn**) *sv.* dig *Gr* 3.6.5.2

grafir *see* **grǫf**

Grágás *f.* 'grey (wild) goose', the name given to the Icelandic Law-Book under the Commonwealth XXVIII:*title*

grammatica *f.* (Latin word) grammar, *i.e.* the Latin language XIV:21, 154, 186

gramr *m.* hostile, fierce one; ruler; = Óláfr Tryggvason VI:282, 330, 343, 364, *acc. after* **hygg ek** *with inf.* **misstu** (*Gr* 3.9.4) VI:156; **lofða gramr** *is a kenning for* king (here King Óláfr) VI:335; = Óláfr helgi XXII:1/3, 13/4, 22/1, 27/4, 34/2; **himna gramr** = God XXII:51/4

grand *n.* injury; *dat. object of* **hœtir** IV:23; injury XXII:59/2

granda (*past* **grandaði**, *pp.* **grandat**) *wv. with dat.* injure, damage XIII:21, 26, XXII:52/4

Grani Gunnarsson *m.* son of Gunnarr of Hlíðarendi XXVI B:12, 50, 110

Grani *m.* a horse X:69, *see note*

granni *m.* neighbour *Gr* 3.1.7.1

grannr *adj.* thin *Gr* 3.3.8.1

grár *adj.* grey *Gr* 3.3.8.5 (3, 4), 3.3.9 (5, 15, 20), XXV:13

gras *n.* herb XII:17; *pl.* **grǫs** plants, herbage, pasture XXI:59

Grásteinn inn mikli ('Greystone the Great') *m.* a rock in Hítardalr V:79, 97

gráta (*pres.* **grætr** (*Gr* 3.6.5.2), *past* **grét**, *pp.* **grátinn**) *sv.* weep (*Gr* 3.6.6) II:107, XI:31; bewail, weep for XI:8, 71, XXV:38; **hvat grætr þú** what are you weeping for XI:33; *imp.* **grát þú** XXV:36; *pres. part.* **grátandi** X:137, XII:45

grátligr *adj.* tearful XXIII:71

grátr *m.* weeping; **at gráti** so as to cause you to weep, to your sorrow XXV:35

greddir *m.* feeder; **úlfa greddir** feeder of wolves, warrior (who provides corpses for the wolves to eat), *i.e.* Óláfr Tryggvason VII A:15

Gregóríus septimus *m.* Gregory VII (pope 1073–85) VIII:189

greiða (*past* **greiddi**, *pp.* **greiddr**) *wv.* prepare, put in order; **greiða fyrir um** keep in repair XIV:135

greiðr *adj.* smooth, clear of obstacles; *n. as adv.* **gekk þat greitt** it went smoothly XV:76

grein *f.* branch; type; **með ǫllum greinum** in every way XIII:42; disagreement IV:103

greina (*past* **greindi**, *pp.* **greindr**) *wv.* describe, give details V:105; specify XXII:22/3

greip *see* **grípa**

greni *n.* lair, hole (of a fox) XXVI B:68

greru *see* **gróa**

grét *see* **gráta**

grey *n.* (female) dog IX:20 (*dat. pl.* for his dogs); bitch, cur VIII:102; *pl.* **grey norna** bitches of the Norns, she-wolves XXV:104

grið *n. pl.* truce, quarter II:90, III:16, 17, 67, 70, 82, 96, VI:298; *with suffixed def. art.* VI:299; **ganga til griða** be given quarter III:118

griðamark *n.* symbol of truce II:92

griðungr *m.* bull VII A:157, XXI:119

Gríma *f.* Hebridean woman, wife of Kotkell XV:37, 38, 135

Grímhildr *f.* wife of Atli, sister of Gunnarr and half-sister of Hǫgni XI:2, 5, 13, 17, 19, 22, 23, 28, 30, 42, 52, 71

grimmðarnáttúra *f.* fierce nature, fierceness XIII:36

grimmr *adj.* fierce XII:57, XXIII:5, 23

Grímr *m.* Þórðr Kolbeinsson's farmhand V:128

Grímr geitskǫr *m.* 10th-century Icelander VIII:41

Grímr Njálsson *m.* XXVI B:2, 16, 18, 24, 35, 96, 193

Grímsnes *n.* area in southern Iceland XXVI A:115

grind *f.* fence; *pl.* pen, fold I:114

grípa (*past* **greip**, *past pl.* **gripu**, *pp.* **gripinn**) *sv.* grasp II:29, V:126; seize in the jaws, bite XXVI A:17

gripakaup *n.* the purchase of an ornament XV:20; *pl.* the buying of ornaments XVI:15

gripr *m.* precious object, precious possession II:40 (**í** in them), III:33, VI:113; (domestic) animal *Gr* 3.1.8 ex.; *pl.* fine ornaments XV:10

grjót *n.* rock, stones (collective) XXII:35/4, 44/4; *with suffixed def. art.* II:32, XXI:152

gróa (*pres.* **grœr**, *past* **greri**, *pp.* **gróit**) *sv.* grow; heal XV:122

Gróa Álfsdóttir *f.* (*acc., gen., dat.* **Gró**; *Gr* 3.1.7.5 (2)) died in the fire at Flugumýrr III:7, 12, 21 (*gen.*), 25, 29, 30 (*dat.*, **henni Gró**), 34 (*dat.*), 39, 40, 42, 47 (*acc.*)

gróf *f.* pit XXVI B:230

gruna (*past* **grunaði**, *pp.* **grunat**) *wv. impers. with acc. of person and acc. of thing* suspect, guess; be suspicious about XXVI B:228; **mik grunar** I suspect, I feel sure XVI:103; **grunaði þá** they guessed VI:124

grund *f.* ground XXII:60/3

Grund *f. see* **Hrund**

grunsemðarfullr *adj.* suspicious XXIII:71

grýta (*past* **grýtti**, *pp.* **grýtt**) *wv.* **throw stones** (**á** at); *imp. pl.* **grýtið ér á** stone XXV:92

grænn *see* **grœnn**

grætr *see* **gráta**

grœða (*past* **grœddi**, *pp.* **grœddr**) *wv.* heal XI:40

Grœnland *n.* Greenland VIII:64, 67, 74; XVI:10, 63, XXI:14, 38, 208

Grœnlenzkr *adj.* Greenlandic, of Greenland; **Grœnlenzkir menn** Greenlanders, people of Greenland XI:18

Grœnlendingar *m. pl.* Greenlanders, Norse settlers in Greenland VIII:71

grœnn/grænn *adj.* green XI:5, XXII:38/4

grœti *n. pl.* weeping XXV:2

grǫf (*pl.* **grafir**) *f.* pit, trench XXI:92, 93

grǫftr *m.* burial XIX:79

grǫn *f.* moustache; lip XXVI B:95; *as nickname* III:15, 49
guð, goð *n. and m.* (heathen) god XIV:81; *m. sg.* XXIV:36, cf. **fleiri**
  guð en einn XXIV:44; *m. pl.* **guðar** XXIV:41, **guða** XXIV:35; *n.*
  pl. IV:95 (*subject of* **yrði góð mér**), XXIV:42, *with suffixed def. art.*
  II:88, 91
Guð *m.* God III:10, VII A:64, 66, XIII:7, 8, 12, 13, 14, 20, 23, 25, 35, 39,
  43, XIV:2, 3, 11, 14, 65, 73, 117, 118, 123, 125, 177, 190, XVI:118,
  XIX:111, XXI:63, 81, XXII:26/4, 50/4, XXIV:16, 18, 33, 34, 40,
  52, XXVI B:104, 124; **Guði á hendi** into God's hand XXVI B:182
guðdómr *m.* divinity, theology; **er til guðdómsins er** which relate to
  theology XXIV:28 (cf. note 2 and *Gr* 3.9.8.2)
Guðlaugr piltr (boy, lad) *m.* died in the fire at Flugumýrr III:76
guðligr/guðlegr *adj.* godly, divine XIV:97, XXIV:33, 43
Guðmundr Fálkason *m.* III:118
Guðmundr (ofsi) *m.* a relative and follower of Gizurr Þorvaldsson
  III:35; **hann Guðmundr** the aforementioned Guðmundr III:91
Guðmundr *m.* son of Þorveig IV:2, 66
Guðríðr Þorbjarnardóttir *f.* XXI, *note* 22
Guðrún Gjúkadóttir *f.* XXV:8, 21, 35, 38
Guðrún Ósvífrsdóttir *f.* XV:3, 6, 7, 8, 13, 14, 16, 18, 20, 22, 25, 29,
  30, 31, 46, 48, 52, 55, 58, 59, 60, 67, 77, 78, 80, 93
guðvefr *m.* costly fabric; *pl.* clothing made of this XXV:58
guldu *see* **gjalda**
gull *n.* gold II:82 (*with suffixed def. art.*), IX:14, X:37, 69, XII:19, 30;
  an object made of gold X:126, XVI:148; *dat. sg. with suffixed def.*
  art. II:79; **gull eitt** nothing but gold, pure gold VI:111; *pl.* pieces of
  gold (jewellery or rings) III:24
gullauðigr *adj.* rich in gold II:78
gullband *n.* golden band or collar IX:20
gullhringr *m.* gold (arm-)ring VII A:122, X:78, XXVI A:52
gullhyrndr *adj. (pp.)* golden-horned, with gilded horns IX:89
Gullinhjalti *m.* 'Goldenhilted', name of a sword I:130, 148
gullinn *adj.* golden VI:240; *n.* **gullit** XXV:73
gulllauf *n.* gold leaf XII:31 (*pl., with suffixed def. art.*)
gullmalinn *pp. (of* **mala**) ground in a golden mill? XII:17
gullsmiðr *m.* goldsmith XII:2
gullu *see* **gjalla**
gulr *adj.* yellow XXIII:6, 26

gumi *m.* man XXV:101

gumnar *m. pl.* men XXII:23/3; *acc. pl.* **gumna** the men XXV:92

Gunnarr *m.* 10th-century Icelander VIII:50

Gunnarr *m.* brother of Grímhildr XI:28, 31, 45, 53, 74; son of Gjúki XXV:27

Gunarr Hámundarson *m.* at Hlíðarendi XXVI A:2, 6, 21, 22, 24, 25, 27, 29, 34, 37, 39, 41, 44, 49, 62, 63, 65, 69, 71, 73, 75, 76, 85, 88, 89, 96, 116, 118, B:60, 62

Gunnarr Lambason *m.* XXVI B:12

Gunnarr Úlfljótsson *m.* 10th-century Icelander VIII:37

Gunnarr enn spaki (Þorgrímsson) *m.* lawspeaker 1063–65 and 1075 VIII:169

gunnheilagr (-helgi) *adj.* inviolable in battle, i.e. he against whom one should not fight (because he is one's brother) *or* inviolate, invincible XXV:101

Gunnhildr *f.* daughter of **Búrizleifr** VI:2, 5

Gunnhildr *f.* daughter of Sigurðr sýr, King Haraldr's father VII B:7

Gunnlaugr Leifsson *m.* monk at Þingeyrar XIV:26, *note*, 167

Gunnlǫð *f.* a giantess II:116, 150

gunnr *f.* battle; *acc.* **gunni** VI:156, *dat.* **gunni** VI:308

Gunnr *f. a name for a* valkyrie; *in kennings for* woman (= Steingerðr; *cf. SnE, Skáldskaparmál* ch. 31): **Gunnr herkis sunds** IV:28; **þeiri Gunni sǫlva** that woman (*dat. object of* **unna**) IV:61

Gyða *f.* queen of **Óláfr Tryggvason** VII A:69, 73, 79, 84, 88, 94, 96, 107

Gyða *f.* mother of **Þorsteinn** XVI:191

gylltr *adj. pp.* gilded XII:8; *acc. sg. m.* **gylltan** VI:287; *n.* **gyllt** VI:99

gæfa[1] *f.* luck, good fortune; *dat. sg. with suffixed def. art.* V:62; success I:146. Cf. **gipta**[2]

gæfa[2], **gæfir** *see* **gefa**

gæfumaðr *m.* person of good luck, a successful person XVI:40, 190

gær, í gær *adv.* yesterday XXV:5; some other day XXV:108

gæra *f.* (sheep)skin (with the fleece on it) III:3, 59, 60 (*dat. sg. with suffixed def. art.*)

gæta (*past* **gætti**, *pp.* **gætt**) *wv. with gen.* look after, take care of, pay attention to II:159; watch XV:84, look after XV:101; **gæta sín** take care of him XXII:50/4; **gæta sín við** guard oneself from XIV:92; **gættu eigi annars** regarded it no differently, took no more care VI:257

gæzla *f.* keeping, guardianship; **til gæzlu sjálfum sér** as protection for himself XIV:63; **þar til gæzlu** in charge of it II:116

gœði *n.* well-being, good fortune VI:364 (*dat. object of* **brá**)

gǫfga (*past* **gǫfgaði,** *pp.* **gǫfgaðr**) *wv.* worship XXIV:40

gǫfugligr *adj.* magnificent, splendid II:11; *comp.* nobler in appearance VII A:36

gǫfugr *adj.* noble XIV:127, 132, XVI:151, XXIV:79; *sup.* **gǫfgastr** *Gr* 3.3.9 ex. 28

gǫgnum *adv. and prep. with acc.* through II:145, 147; **í gǫgnum** *postposition* (*Gr* 3.7) X:17

gǫmul *see* **gamall**

gǫngum *see* **ganga**[1]

gǫngur *see* **ganga**[2]

gǫr, gǫrða, gǫrðumz *see* **gera**

gǫrla *adv.* clearly V:81, XXIV:12. Cf. **gerla**

gǫrr, gǫrt, gǫrva, gǫrvar, gǫrvir, gǫrzk *pp. see* **gera**

gør, gøra, gørask, gørða, gørði(r), gørðisk, gørðu, gørðusk, gørið, gørir, gørva *see* **gera**

gørr (= **gerr**[1]) *adv. comp.* more extensively, more fully; **einna miklugi gørr** XXVII 32 *see* **einna**; cf. **gerla**

gørsimi *see* **gersemi**

há[1] *interrog. interjection* = **hvat** XXIV:9

há[2] *see* **hár**[1]

haf[1] *n.* sea VI:167, XVI:154, XXIV:37; open sea XIX:44, 71, 80; *with suffixed def. art.* **á hafet, í hafit** out to sea VI:121, VII A:10; ocean VII A:164

haf[2] *see* **hafa**

hafa (*pres.* **hefr/hefir,** *past* **hafði,** *past pl.* **hǫfðu/hafðu,** *past subj.* **hefði,** *pp.* **haft**) *wv.* have (*Gr* 3.6.7) I:30 (2), 69, 118, II:79, 88, 136 (it, *i.e.* the mead, *understood as object*), III:17, 54, VI:19, 20, 49, 118, VII A:61, IX:40, 41, X:58 (it, *i.e.* the missing ring, *understood as object*; *Gr* 3.9.5.1), XI:35, XIV:178, XV:31, XVI:13, XXI:10, 103, XXII:3/1, XXIII:80, XXV:32, XXVI A:85, B:56, XXVII:5; put, place III:111; take VII A:52, X:10, XIX:43; receive XXVII:37; get II:67; meet (a certain kind of weather) XXI:198; bring V:116; carry, bear XXIII:45; wear, have on V:28, 56, 159 (**á sér** on himself), XXI:44; use II:6, VII A:37, XV:82, 83, 130, XXI:16; keep VI:2, VII B:3, 31, VIII:3, XXVII:45; accept VIII:6; hold II:51, VIII:46, 59, 62, 170, XXVII:43; maintain I:34; carry on VIII:128 (*pp.* **haft**); keep to XIV:60; behave, act I:22; *pres.* **hefr** it has I:76 (1; *Gr* 3.9.5); **hefir þú** do you have IX:36; **hǫfum vér** we have II:81; **hǫfum allir**

let us all have VIII:134; **hafi þit** you have (*Gr* 3.6.9.1 (14)) I:52, 54; *past pl.* **hafðu** VI:58, 146, 304; *imp.* **haf sǫðlat hesta tvá** have two horses saddled XV:95; *pres. subj.* **at ek hafa** that I should have III:68; **hafir** may have XVI:53; **hafi** had I:74, may have I:135, has VI:85, may gain, win VIII:134; **hafi hann** let him have IX:60; **hafi ekki** should not have (*or* should have no, *see* **ekki¹**, **ekki²**) XXIV:46; **hafi á sér** have in them XXIII:33; *past subj.* **ef ek hefða** if I had XXI:134, **hefðir þú** you would have XXV:96, **þú hefðir** you had XXV:96, **þó at hann hefði** even if he got VI:4; **hafa af** inherit from VII B:8, 9; **hafa menn at** have people employed XIV:133; **hafa fyrir** receive in return for, exchange for XXI:78, 115; **hafði fyrir þeim** put before them, presented to them XXVI B:126; **hafa í** include in XIV:140; **hafa með sér** take away with one XIX:87, XXI:201, bring with her II:40; **hafði haft með sér** had brought with him III:2; **hǫfðu með sér** had brought with them XXI:57, kept with them XXI:95; **hafa þar með sér** take along with one III:25; **hafa til** have available, have for it I:118, use as a pretext, bring as a charge for VIII:100, use for XXII:37/2 (cf. *Gr* 3.9.5.1), *with at and inf.* XXVI A:58; **hafa um** use, say about it XXIV:9; **hafa kyrrt um sik** keep quiet I:110; **hafa út** bring out VIII:35, **hafði út** had brought out XI:17; **hafa þaðan** take away from there, get to go along VII A:68; *impers.* **hafði nær** it came close VIII:110; *pp. forming pass.* **var hafðr** was brought, was presented VII B:52; *as aux. with supine forming present or past perfect* (*Gr* 3.9.7.1) I:4, 15, 16, 17, 18, 25, 29, 30 (1), 31, 46 (*pres. subj.*), 48 (*past subj.*), 53, 55, 65, 76 (2), 111, 113 (*pres. subj.*), 115 (*past subj.*), 129, 140, 141, 142, 145, II:15, 39, 75, 86, 100, III:10, 104, 114, 119, IV:8, 48, V:15 (**hafi** *pres. subj.*), 57, 77, 96, 116, 125, 132, 159, VI:3, 33, 42 (*past pl.* **hafðu**), 72, 281, 304 (**hafðu**), VIII:29, IX:128, X:132, XI:23, XV:24, 26, *note*, 114 (*past subj.*), XVI:4, XIX:16, 27, 39, XXI:5, 9, 177, XXII:4/1, 13/1, 30/3, XXIV:59, XXV:6, 106, XXVI A:47, 50, 63, XXVII:10, 18, **þér hafið** you have XXIV:23, **hafi þar eptir verit** remained behind there XXI:162, **ok hafi eigi farit lengra** and that they did not travel further XXI:163 (*similarly* XXI:164, 165), **hefir þat** that has (never) V:15, **hefr haft** has had (held) XXVII:43, **hafði haft** had held VII B:4, had been holding XXVI B:151, **hǫfðu haft** had used VII B:78, **hefði veitt** had given XXVI A:116; *with pp. in agreement with the direct object* (*Gr* 3.9.7.1) IV:97, V:19, 63, VI:48, 55, IX:26, 27, XXII:29/1, XXV:69; *as aux. with inf.* **hafa at vinna** will have to overcome IV:80

hafin, hafizk *see* **hefja**
Hafliði Másson *m.* died 1130 VIII:172
hafna¹ (*past* **hafnaði,** *pp.* **hafnat**) *wv. with dat.* forsake, renounce IV:83
hafna² *see* **hǫfn**
háflœðr *f.* high tide XXI:89
hafr (*pl.* **hafrar**) *m.* (billy) goat IX:81
Hafra-Fasti *m.* robber XXII:23/4
haft *see* **hafa**
hafuð *see* **hǫfuð**
hafviti *m.* beacon of the sea, *kenning for* gold VI:281
hagi *m.* pasture VIII:55
hagleikr *m.* skill XII:8, 25, 47, 63
hagliga *adv.* neatly, nicely IX:64; skilfully XII:23, 59
hagligr *adj.* skilful, skilfully made (**at** in respect of) XII:10; *sup.* XII:30
hagr¹ *m.* state, situation VIII:124; **í hag** *with dat.* in someone's favour XXVII:10; *pl.* condition, nature I:135
hagr² *adj.* skilful; *sup.* **hagastr** most skilful XIV:16; **hagastr maðr** the most skilful of men X:14; *n. as adv.* **sem ek hagast kunna** as skilfully as I knew how X:92
haka *f.* chin XXIII:64; *acc.* **hǫku** XXIII:65
Haki *m.* a Scot, Scotsman XXI:39
Hákon Ívarsson *m.* 11th-century Norwegian (great-grandson of Hákon Hlaðajarl) VII B:81, 82
Hákon Sigurðarson Hlaðajarl *m.* the Great (*inn ríki*), ruler in Norway *c.*970–95 VI:42, VII A:125, 127, 169, B:5, 8
Hákonarson/-sunr *m.* son of Hákon Hlaðajarl VI:41, 192, VIII:148
halda (*pres.* **heldr,** *past* **helt,** *past pl.* **heldu,** *pp.* **haldinn,** *n.* **haldit**) *sv.* (*Gr* 3.6.9.1 (3, 10) **1.** last VIII:131 (*intransitive*); *with dat.* hold I:32, VII B:88 (*i.e.* fight; **eigi** *goes with this verb too*), XII:37, 49, XV:12 (*i.e.* not lose), XXVI B:150 (*imp. pl.*); keep hold of, hold on to XVI:143, 149, 177 (*subj.*); maintain, keep up VI:225; hold a course: **heldu skipunum** steered the ships, sailed XXI:35; *with acc.* hold, uphold XXII:2/1; keep, preserve VIII:176; maintain XIII:22; **halda tal af** depend on the words of, value what is said by (*or* hold conversations with?) XXI:15; **halda á** hold on to I:130, III:12, V:99; **helt á** was holding XIX:33; **halda á brottu** paddle away XXI:142; (*subj.*) **haldi sér þó aptr** and yet (if he) holds himself (leaning) backwards (i.e. with legs sloping backwards, body sloping forwards?) XXIII:102; **halda at** make one's way towards I:116 (could also be **heldr¹**); **halda**

eptir make one's way in pursuit of V:60, *with dat.* keep VII A:75 (**eptir** *is adv. here*); **halda inn með** sail in along XXI:55; **helt þar saman** there held it together there XXI:46; **halda til** make one's way to, lay one's course for VII A:2, 3, XV:131; **helt til** was the reason XV:80; **halda undan** get away XXI:130, retreat XXI:132; *past subj.* **heldi undan** made off VI:310; **halda upp** *with dat.* maintain, discharge XXIV:72, **halda upp svǫrum** be spokesman VII B:25. **2.** -sk *form* **haldizk** remained in force, remained valid, continued to be observed XIV:57; **haldask við (viðr)** stand firm VI:210, hold out VI:268

háleitliga *adv.* loftily; fervently III:9 (**á marga vega** *i.e.* showing many kinds of devotion or eloquence)

háleyskr *adj.* of Hálogaland (in northern Norway) XXII:10/3

hálfa *f.* region, part; **af Guðs hálfu** on behalf of God XIV:3

Hálfdan enn svarti (Goðrøðarson) *m.* 9th-century Norwegian king *Gr* 3.1.8 ex., VIII:8

hálfljóst *adv.* half-light, twilight (in the morning) III:131

hálfr *adj.* half III:79, VIII:32; XVI:52, XXI:94; **hálft eitt** only half XVI:65; **hálfar allar** half of all XXVII:38; *dat. sg. n. with comp.* **hálfu ríkari** twice as powerful XI:39; **hálfu fremr** twice as far off (in time) XXV:7

hálfsextøgr *adj.* 55 years old; **vetri miðr en hálfsextøgr** 54 years old VIII:192

hali *m.* tail; **hala sínum** with his tail XII:61

háll *adj.* slippery *Gr* 3.3.8.4 (1)

hallandi *m.* (*pres. part.*) one who causes something to sink, waster; *in kenning for* (generous) man (Eiríkr jarl), *gen. sg.* **hallands hafvita** distributor of gold VI:282 (*gen. with* **skeiðum**; *anomalous strong declension*)

hallar *see* **hǫll**

Hallbjǫrn slíkisteinsauga *m.* son of Kotkell XV:39, 138

Halldórr *m.* Irish slave XIX:37

Halldórr Guðmundarson *m.* III:81, *see note*

Halldórr Heðinsson Garpsdalsgoði *m.* XV:2

Halldórr ókristni, úkristni ('unchristian') *m.* Icelandic poet, early eleventh century VI:49, 229, 276

Hallfreðarstaðir *m. pl.* farm in eastern Iceland *Gr* 3.1.8 ex.

Hallfreðr/Hallfrøðr vandræðaskáld ('troublesome poet') *m.* Icelandic poet (died *c.*1007) VI:153, 172, 258, 304, 322, 324, VII A:10

Hallfreðr *m.* father of Hrafnkell *Gr* 3.1.8 ex.

Hallfríðr Garðafylja *f.* III:128

Hallgerðr Hǫskuldsdóttir *f.* wife of Gunnarr at Hlíðarendi XXVI A:26, 78

hallir *see* **hǫll**

Hallr Gizurarson *m.* the bridegroom, who died from wounds the morning after the fire III:51, 53, 55, 59, 60, 61, 64, 131

Hallr Órœkjusonr *m.* VIII:51

Hallr (Þórarinsson) *m.* of Haukadalr (995–1089) VIII:184

Hallr Þorsteinsson *m.* of Síða (Síðu-Hallr), *c.*950–1020 VIII:78, 116

Hallsteinn goði *m.* XV:35, 41, 127, 129

Hallsteinsnes *n.* farm in north-western Iceland XV:35

Hallveig Fróðadóttir *f.* XIX:107

hallvitjandi *m.* hall-visitor; *dat. pl.* **hallvitjǫndum** *poss. dat. in generic sense referring to* Kormakr (*i.e.* it was his shield) IV:19

hálmþúst *n.* flail (**hálmr** *m.* straw); **sem í hálmþústum** like with flails, like the sound of flails XXI:97

halr *m.* man XXII:62/2, XXV:51, 63, 65

háls *m.* **1.** neck II:130, III:85 (*with suffixed def. art.*), X:25, XXIII:74; **á hálsinn Helga** on Helgi's neck XXVI B:153; **ok hendr um háls** and (laid) his arms round her neck XII:82. **2.** ridge XV:86

Hamall Þormóðarson *m.* XIX:114

hamarr *m.* hammer IX:2, 12, 26, 41, 56, 71, 120, 124, 130; *dat. sg.* **hamri** (*see Gr* 3.1.7.5 (1)) IX:8, 131, *instrumental* X:98; crag: *gen. pl.* **hamra** XXI:130; hammer? back of an axe? crag, precipice? XXIII:12

hamarsgnípa *f.* peak of a crag XXI:67

Hamðir *m.* son of Guðrún and King Jónakr XXV:20, 75, 85, 94, *textual note,* 96, 111

Hamðismál *n. pl.* 'speeches of Hamðir' XXV:112

hamfarir *f. pl.* travelling in a changed shape VII A:146 (**í** by means of)

hamingja *f.* good fortune VII A:47

hamla *f.* oar-thong, thole-strap, a loop to hold the oar in position against the rowlock when rowing; **síga á hǫmlur** pull against the oar-thongs, *i.e.* draw backwards, row astern VI:214

hamr *m.* shape, form VII A:141

Hámundr Bjarnarson *m.* XIV:129, 130

hana *pron. acc.* her, it (*Gr* 3.2.1) I:16, II:69, XV:21

hand- *see* **hǫnd**

handleggr *m.* arm V:99, 100

hand-Viðrir *m.* Viðrir is a name for Óðinn; 'Viðrir of the hand', 'hand-god' means Týr, the god whose hand was bitten off by the wolf Fenrir (*SnE, Gylfaginning* ch. 34); his **grand**, 'injury', is the loss of a hand, which is what Kormakr thinks he is being threatened with IV:23

hanga (*past* **hekk,** *past pl.* **hengu,** *pp.* **hanginn**) *sv.* hang (*Gr* 3.6.9.3) V:157, XXIII:59

hann, hans *pron.* (*Gr* 3.2.1, 3.3.9 ex. 15) he, him, it, his, its *etc.* I:4, 5, 13, 22, 24, 87, 88, 90, 91, 92, 98, 102, 104, 149, II:1, 3, III:91 (*see* **Guðmundr** (ofsi)), IV:10 (= it, the scythe-blade), VI:5, VII A:30 (2; *in apposition to* **Óláfr**), VIII:14 (i.e. Edmund's), IX:1, 5, 29 (it, i.e. the hammer), 34, 42, 107, XI:25, 38 (*in apposition to* **Attila konung**), XV:2, 26, 36, 38, XIX:10, XXI:7, 66 (*in apposition to* **Þorhall**), XXII:5/1, XXV:32, XXVI A:8, 17 (*in apposition to* **Þorkel**), 19, 35, B:46, 156, XXVII:5, 22; **hann Auðunn** this Auðunn XVI:6; = Ormr enn langi VI:265; = King Óláfr VI:331; the aforementioned VIII:120; **hans** of his XXII:30/2, 44/3; **til hans** to him XXIV:17, 41; **var . . . hans** it was . . . of him XXII:29/3

hannyrðir *f. pl.* handwork, needlework, embroidery XIV:189

hánum = **honum**

happ *n.* good luck XXI:143

hár[1] (*f.* **há,** *n.* **hátt,** *pl.* **hávir** *Gr* 3.3.9 ex. 29) *adj.* high *Gr* 3.3.8.5 (3), X:54 (with **viðr**), XXV:82; tall X:170, XXVI B:149; long XXII:61/4; *acc. sg. f.* **háva** I:17; *n. as adv.* **hátt** high II:32, VI:114, XXIII:101, high up VI:290, XXIII:44, 52, loud(ly) I:14, II:71, 107, XXI:120, 206, XXVI A:18, noisily I:22, in a loud voice VI:169; **hátt upp** out loud XXI:124

hár[2] *n.* hair XII:20 (*with suffixed def. art.*), XXI:103, XXII:61/3, XXIII:4, 22 (*pl.*), 78, 80 (*with suffixed def. art.*), XXVI A:78; **hárit** his hair XXVI B:222

Haraldr Gormsson *m.* king of Denmark (died *c.*986) VI:2, 33, VII A:124, 125, 126, 139, 146

Haraldr (Sigurðarson) harðráði ('harsh-ruler') *m.* king of Norway 1046–66 VII B:3, 7, 11, 12, 34, 36, 86, XVI:16, 32, 71, 156, 157, 160, 166, XXII:14/3, 15/2

Haraldr hárfagri Hálfdanarson *m.* Norwegian king *c.*885–935 *Gr* 3.1.8 ex., VIII:7, 16, 26, 29, 60, 75, XIX:47

Haraldsson *m.* son of Haraldr bluetooth Gormsson (died *c*.986) VIII:146

harðhugaðr *adj. (pp.)* tough-minded IX:124

harðla *adv.* very, extremely VI:209, XXII:14/1, XXIII:89, absolutely XXII:7/2

harðr (*f.* **hǫrð**) *adj.* (*Gr* 3.3.8.1, 3.3.9 (2)) hard XXII:35/4 (*dat. sg. n.* **hǫrðu**); fierce (of battles) VI:195, 212, 254, 285, XXI:125; firm (ones) XXIII:94; violent I:43; strong XXI:131; harsh XIV:99, XXII:36/4; tough XXII:42/4, XXV:52; resistant XXII:30/1, 56/2; **í harða** (i.e. **raun**?) into a hard (time), into a harsh trial VI:230; *comp.* **harðari** *Gr* 3.3.9 (18); *sup.* **harðastr** V:137 (*Gr* 3.3.9 (12, 17)); *n. as adv.* **hart** hard V:117, *i.e.* fast V:66, 166, XXI:189, violently VI:271, XXII:39/1; *sup.* **sem harðast** as hard as we can VI:78

harðsnúinn *adj. (pp.)* 'hard-twisted', powerful, virulent XV:143; well-knit, staunch XXVI B:57

Hárekr ór Þjóttu Eyvindarson *m.* XXII:8/1, 36/1

hárfagri *adj.* finehaired, *nickname* VIII:7, 16, 61, 75, XIX:48

hárferð *f.* the hairstyle XXIII:6

hárgeirr *m.* 'hair-spear', *kenning for* comb IV:32

harka (*past* **harkaði**, *pp.* **harkat**) *wv. impers.* it goes badly (**um** with something), something goes badly V:7

harma (*past* **harmaði**, *pp.* **harmat**) *wv.* grieve for, sorrow over XIV:107; *impers. with acc. of person and acc. of thing* cause (someone) to sorrow, grieve (someone) XI:7, 34

harmdauði *m.* sorrowful death; **mǫrgum mǫnnum harmdauði** lamented by many XXVI A:120

harmr *m.* grief III:131, VI:324, XII:36, XXVI B:187; sorrow XII:39, 84, 88; injury, wrong(s) X:132

harmþrunginn *adj. (pp.)* weighed down by grief XIV:111

hárr *adj.* hoary, grey II:43

hart *see* **harðr**

háski *m.* danger I:84

háss *adj.* hoarse III:129

Hásteinn *m.* son of **Atli enn mjóvi** XIX:7, 24. Cf. *Landnámabók, ÍF* I 371–76 and *Flóamanna saga, ÍF* XIII 232–37, where he is called Hallsteinn

hásæti *n.* high seat, throne XI:53; *pl.* II:7, XI:57

hátíð *f.* festival XIV:139

hátt *see* **hár**[1]

hatta *see* **hǫttr**

hátta (*past* **háttaði,** *pp.* **háttat**) *wv.* arrange, fashion; **at mér muni svá háttat** that I am of that nature I:134

Hattar *see* **Hǫttr**

Hattargriði *m.* Hǫttr's protector I:59

hattr *m.* hood XXI:45

háttr *m.* manner, way (of doing something) XIII:30, XXIII:70; *dat. sg.* **með sama hætti** in the same way XII:21, **með hverjum hætti** in what way, by what means, how XIV:90, *note*; custom XIV:158; nature XXIII:35; measure, moderation; **um fram hátt** beyond measure XXIII:62; *pl.* behaviour, way of life XIV:48, 60

hauðrmen *n.* necklace of the land, *kenning for* sea (**hauðr** is a poetical word for land, see *SnE, Skáldskaparmál* 303)

haufuð *see* **hǫfuð**

haugr *m.* (grave-)mound IX:19, XV:154

Haugsnes *n.* headland on Skálmarnes XV:155

Haukadalr *m.* in south-west Iceland VIII:184 (north of Geysir)

haust *n.* autumn I:76 (*acc. of time*), V:52, VII A:70 (*with suffixed def. art.*), XXI:196, XXVI A:2 (*with suffixed def. art.*)

háva, hávir *see* **hár**

hávaðamaðr *m.* noisy, rowdy, assertive person IV:3

heðan *adv.* from here XXVI B:176; from this country (Iceland) VIII:65, 88, XVI:8, (from Denmark) XVI:126

Heðinn *m.* legendary king, whose shirt is a coat of mail VI:262

hefi, hefir, hefða, hefði *see* **hafa**

hefja (*pres.* **hefr,** *past* **hóf,** *past pl.* **hófu,** *pp.* **hafinn/hafit**) *sv.* (*Gr* 3.6.9.1 (5)) **1.** begin (*cf. Gr* 3.9.3 (a)) II:16; **hefja upp** begin VIII:123, XIV:1. **2.** lift, raise XXII:7/4, **hefja upp** XXIII:70; **hefja í sundr** open III:11. **3. -sk** *form (refl.)* originate II:86 (*pp.* **hafizk**); **hófsk** lifted himself X:136, 173

hefna (*past* **hefndi,** *pp.* **hefndr**) *wv. with gen.* avenge II:62, V:98, 115, VI:36 (**á** on), 94, VII A:132, B:72, X:132, XXV:9, 42, XXVI B:113, 139, 160; **hefna mín** avenge me XXVI B:218; *imp.* **hefndu vár en vér þín** you avenge us and we (shall avenge) you XXVI B:80; *with acc.* punish XXII:4/4, 23/1, **hefndi** punished it XXII:5/4; *with dat. and acc.* punish someone for something XXII:14/4

hefr *see* **hafa** *and* **hefja**

heiðinn (heiðn-) *adj.* heathen (*Gr* 3.3.8.5 (1), 3.3.9 (20)) VI:8, VIII:22, 109, 114, 119, XIV:80, XIX:109, XXIV:35

heiðni *f.* heathen practice(s) VIII:143, XXII:5/3

heiðr[1] *f.* (*Gr* 3.1.7.4 (2), 3.1.8 (17)) heath, moor V:151, VIII:54; **fyrir neðan heiði** below the the heath (i.e west of Mosfellsheiði and Hellisheiði in south-west Iceland); **ofan um heiði** down over Hellisheiði XIX:94

heiðr[2] *m.* honour XXII:9/4, 45/3; glory XXII:64/1; **haldr heiðr** *with dat.* hold someone in honour XXII:2/1

heilagr (helg-) *adj.* (*Gr* 3.3.8.4 (3c), 3.3.8.2–5 ex. 4, 3.3.9 ex. 24) holy, blessed XIII:22, 48, XIV:5, 30; saintly XXII:61/3; sacred XIV:35; *acc. sg. m.* **helgan** XXII:62/1, *f.* **heilug** XIV:73, **heilǫg** XXIV:46, *acc. sg. f.* **helga** XXII:25/1; *dat. sg. m.* **helgum** divine VII A:48, XXIV:27; *pl.* **helgir menn** saints: **heilagra manna sǫgur** lives of saints XIV:189; **helgir dagar** holy days XIV:58; **helgir fiskar** halibut XXI:93; *strong form as title* blessed XIV:120; *wk. form* **inn helgi Jón** St John XIV:17; *acc. sg. m.* **inn helga** (the) Saint V:57, **enn helga** VIII:12, *gen. sg.* **hins helga** XIII:11; *sup.* **helgasta hans** his most holy XIV:100

heili *m.* brain; *with suffixed def. art.* its brain XXVI A:18

heill[1] *adj.* whole, healed, recovered VII A:55; healthy, thriving X:148; safe, unharmed I:114, XIII:5, 35; at least, good, complete VIII:166; united, undivided X:72; **verða heill** recover VII A:55; **far heill** farewell XVI:153; *as greeting* **sittu heill** 'sit in health', hail as you sit XI:23; **eigi heil** pregnant, with child XXI:137

heill[2] *f.* (good) fortune *Gr* 3.1.8 ex.; *pl.* omens, auspices XIX:41

heilsa *f.* (restoration to) health XXII:57/4

heim[1] *adv.* home II:38, 52, 115, IV:67, XI:72, XII:3, 79, XV:12, 30, 110, XXVI B:18; in (to the dwelling) IX:81, to the buildings XIV:150; to the house XXVI A:28, B:84; back I:78, 93, 110, VII A:105, X:10, XII:70 (*i.e.* to the shieling XV:910, XXI:71 (i.e. to the camp); back home XXVI B:4, 24; **koma heim** get back home XIX:8, visit, pay a call I:115, *i.e.* to Valhǫll or Hel, to death V:23; **heim á bœinn (at bœnum)** up to the farm (i.e. to Gunnarr's farm) XXVI A:9, 14, (i.e. to Njáll's farm) B:44; **sœkja heim** attack (someone) in their home XXVI B:63

heim[2] *see* **heimr**

heima *adv.* at home II:51, IV:50, X:72, XV:135, XXVI A:27, 34, 109, 118; in the house V:27, in his house XXVI A:3; when at home VII B:31; in the precinct XIV:25

heimakona *f.* female household servant III:128

heimamaðr *m.* member of a household, servant, workman XXVI B:46

heimamannligr *adj.* human (domestic servant's, member of household's?) XXIII:37

heiman *adv.* from home, out (into the world) II:16, 123, from the house IV:63; **fara heiman** set out (from home) V:112; **hafði heiman haft** had brought with him from home V:116; **heim ok heiman** to and from his home XII:79

heimboð *n.* invitation to stay; **at heimboði** as a guest II:95

Heimdallr *m.* a god (one of the Æsir) II:9, IX:57

heimili *n.* home XXVII:5

heimkynni *n.* home, household XIV:148

heimr *m.* world II:94, XII:12, XIII:40, XIX:49, XXII:3/2, XXIV:37; *pl.* i.e. where someone dwells IX:18, 32; **norðr í heima** into northern lands XXII:64/4; **þessa heims ok annars** in this world and the next XXVI B:125

heimska *f.* foolishness XXIII:41, 45, 69

heimskligr *adj.* foolish XXII:7/3

heimskr *adj.* foolish XXIII:9, 92

heimta (*past* **heimti,** *pp.* **heimt**) *wv.* get back, recover IX:29, 71 (**þér** for yourself); **heimta at** claim from, recover from VI:18; draw, pull (*i.e.* row) VI:122

hein *f.* whetstone II:125; *with suffixed def. art.* II:126, 128

heipt *f.* fury (in battle), hostility (*gen. with* **nýta**) VI:277

heit *n.* vow promise XIX:10

heita[1] (*pres.* **heitr,** *past* **hét,** *past pl.* **hétu,** *pp.* **heitit**) *sv.* (*Gr* 3.6.9.3) *with dat. of person and dat. of thing* **1.** threaten; *impers. pass.* (*Gr* 3.9.3) II:46. **2.** promise VII A:122, VIII:89, XV:90, XVI:41 (*with two datives*), 156, XXII:36/2 (*with two datives*), XXVI B:171 (*with two datives*), 180; **heita góðu** make fair promises I:86; *with acc.* (!) vow XXV:80; *pp.* **því heitit honum** promised him this XXVI B:163. **3. heita á** call upon (to do something), command VI:115, 277; pray to XXI:63

heita[2] (*pres.* **heitir,** *past* **hét,** *past pl.* **hétu,** *pp.* **heitit**) *sv.* (*Gr* 3.6.9.3) be called I:9, 59, 147 (*subj.*), 147 (*inf.*), II:77, 89, 92, 97, 102, 115, 130, III:83, 128, IV:1, 107, V:128, VI:29, VII A:10, 94, 123, 129, 137, VIII:51, X:2, 87; XIII:1, XIV:16, 185, XV:2, 53, XVI:2, 45, XIX:36, XXI:39, 203, XXII:27/2, 37/1, XXVI A:114; be named I:148, VIII:15, 36, 65; **hét** was called XXVI A:8; **. . . hét maðr,**

maðr hét . . . there was a man called . . . XV:38, XIX:2, XXI:7; **hét kona hans** his wife was called XV:38; **ok hét maðr** and one was a man called III:78; **hétu** were the names of XIX:72; **heitir** has been called, is known as XV:33, 152, 155; **þar heitir** the place is called XIX:84, the place has been called XIX:86; **þar sem heitir/heita** in a place called II:115, XIX:82; **þar er nú heitir** in the place now called XIX:54; *pp.* **var um heitin** was called XXV:10

heiti *n.* name II:122; *pl.* your names XXII:22/2

Heiti *m.* a sea-king, legendary viking VI:325

heitr *adj.* hot XXV:89; *comp. acc. sg. m. (or n. as adv.?)* **heitara** hotter XXVI B:111 ('you will not need it hotter for baking')

heitstrenging *f.* vowing XIX:11

Hekja *f.* Scottish woman XXI:39

helda, heldi *see* **halda**

heldr[1] *adv. (comp.)* (*Gr* 3.5.2) rather, somewhat *Gr* 3.5.1–3 ex. 6 (d), I:8, 71, 116 (could also be **heldr**[2]; cf. *ÍF* XIII 350), III:19, 27, V:7, VI:230, VII B:2. XV:13, XVI:80, 91, XXI:11, 137, XXII:58/2; rather XIV:45, XXVI A:12; but rather XXIII:52, XXIV:78; most X:99; instead, rather I:81, 142, VIII:6, XXII:25/1, XXIV:9, 10; **enn heldr** still more XXIV:4; **eigi heldr** not either I:93; **heldr mega einn** it would be easier for one (rather than two) III:92; **heldr vildu** they would rather XXVI B:63; **heldr . . . þar** it was rather that XXVI B:226; **heldr en** rather than I:64 (*emphasising the comp.* **nær**), III:13, *with* **betr** V:161, XVI:111, XXIV:15, 58; any more than VI:8; **heldr . . . en** rather than, instead of VIII:163, XXIV:32, 51, any more . . . than XIII:37; **fyrir því at heldr þótt** any the more because of this that, even though VII B:55; **eigi at eins . . . heldr ok** not only . . . but also XIV:191

heldr[2] *pres. of* **halda**

heldu, heldusk *see* **halda**

Helga Arnardóttir (daughter of Ǫrn) *f.* sister of Ingólfr XIX:4, 11, 39

Helga Njálsdóttir *f.* wife of Kári XXVI B:148

helga, helgan, helgastr, helgi, helgir, helgum *see* **heilagr**

heljask (*past* **heljaðisk**) *wv.* **-sk** *form* work oneself to death (**á** at) XV:94

Helgi Njálsson *m.* XXVI B:2, 15, 24, 35, 72, 96, 138, 143, 146, 149, 151, 153

hella *f.* flat stone, slab of rock XXI:23

hellir *m.* cave *Gr* 3.1.9 ex. 14, XXI:204

Hellisdalr *m.* valley to the north-west of Hítardalr V:75

Helluland *n.* 'land of flat rocks' XXI:25

hellusteinn *m.* flat stone XXI:139

helmingr *m.* half XV:31; **helmingr alls** half of everything, half their total assets XV:9

helt *see* **halda**

helvíti *n.* Hell XIII:25

helzt *adv. sup.* (*Gr* 3.5.2) most; best XXVII:34; exceedingly I:105; most of all XXI:113; **allra helzt** especially XIV:142

henda (*past* **hendi**¹) *wv.* **1.** catch in the hand II:129. **2.** befall, happen to (**at** in it, in this) XXIV:5; **lát þek þat henda** let that happen to you XXIV:12

hendi², **hendr** *see* **hǫnd**

hennar, henni *pron.* her, it, *etc.* (*Gr* 3.2.1), XI:17, XIV:188, XV:47, XXI:138, 143, XXVI B:142, 150; **henni** to her XI:9, *poss. dat.* XIII:3

hepta (*past* **hepti**, *pp.* **hept**) *wv.* obstruct XVI:70

hér *adv.* here I:10, 80, 144, V:59, VI:69, VII B:37, 82, XI:29, XV:64, XVI:76, XXV:39, XXVI A:104, 110, B:61, 117; (i.e. at the Alþingi) XXVII:39, 40; in this country VIII:21, 22, 83, 85, XVI:122; to this country (Iceland) XIX:104; in this book, as follows X:15; **á landi hér**, **hér á landi** in this country VIII:43, 151; in this I:52; **... er hér** it is (I am) . . . III:67; **hér at** to this I:54, beside this IX:89; **hér til** up to now V:77, for this XV:27; **hér um** about this I:50, 86; **hér ... þar er Hǫttr er** here where Hǫttr is, *i.e.* out of Hǫttr I:146

herað *n.* district XIV:142 (sc. Skagafjǫrðr?), XIX:98, XXVI B:14 (*with suffixed def. art.*); **í heraði** in one's own district *or* area XV:65

heraðflótta *adj.* (*Gr* 3.3.8.5 (6)) fleeing the district, exiled from the district IV:73

heraðsmaðr *m.* person from the district, local inhabitant (here of Skagafjǫrðr) III:1

herbergi *n.* lodgings, quarters VII A:105, B:77 (*sg.*), XVI:16; building, house XII:52, XIII:34; chamber XIV:63

herða (*past* **herði**, *pp.* **hert**) *wv.* harden, temper; *with suffixed pron.* X:93; give power to, carry out forcefully (*or* multiply, promote) XXII:12/4

herðar *f. pl.* shoulders, XXIII:81; **sér miðil herða** between his shoulders XI:35; **mikil um herðar** broad across the shoulders XXVI B:149

herðimeiðr *m.* 'promoting tree'; **herðimeiðar hríðar mána viðar**
hauðrmens trees that promote battle, *kenning for* warriors (Gunnarr's
attackers) XXVI A:99 (object of **vann sára**)

herfang *n.* booty XIX:44

herferð *f.* military expedition, raid VII A:109

herfiligr *adj.*, wretched, horrible, shameful XXVI B:31

herja (*past* **herjaði,** *pp.* **herjat**) *wv.* raid, make raids (on) VII A:2, 3,
126, 128, XIX:32, XXII:10/2

herkir *m. poetical term for* fire; **sunds herkir** *is a kenning for* gold
(*see SnE, Skáldskaparmál* ch. 33) IV:29

herklæðask (*past* **herklæddisk**) *wv. refl.* arm oneself, put on armour;
3rd person subj. as imp. ('let men arm themselves') VI:170

herlið *n.* troops XXII:36/1

herma (*past* **hermdi,** *pp.* **hermdr**) *wv.* repeat XXIV:13

hernaðr *m.* warfare, raiding VII A:1, 27; raiding expedition(s), viking
raid(s) XIX:6, 14

herr *m.* host VI:58, 86, 194, 349; men V:35 (*gen. with* **víti**), VII B:15;
army VI:211, VII A:20, 127; *with suffixed def. art.* XXII:33/1

herra *m.* lord XIV:171; *used in address to a king or earl (vocative)*
I:140, VI:79, 88, 166, XVI:23, 28, 36, my lord XXIV:10

hersir *m.* lord, a man of high rank in early Norway *Gr* 3.1.7.3–5 ex. 4;
cf. 3.1.7.5 (1)

herskip *n.* warship VI:152

Hersteinn *m.* son of **Atli enn mjóvi** XIX:7, 18, 20, 22

hertryggð *f.* warlike confidence VI:177 (*gen. with* **hnekkir**)

hervápn *n. pl.* weapons of war, armour II:61

hervegr *m.* military road, high road XXV:12

Hervǫr *f.* a valkyrie X:9, 73

Hestlœkr *m.* stream in southern Iceland XXVI A:115

hestr *m.* horse (*Gr* 3.1.8 (1)) I:2, XI:10, XV:44, 95, XXIII:60, XXVI
B:43; *with suffixed def. art.* XV:101; **af hesti** from horseback X:170;
steed XXII:41/2 (to prepare food for a giantess's steed (wolf) is to
kill men in battle)

hét, hétu *see* **heita¹, heita²**

hetja *f.* hero XV:3

hey *n.* hay II:124

heygja (*past* **heygði,** *pp.* **heygðr**) *wv.* bury (in a **haugr**); **ok sé hér**
heygðir and that they be buried here XXVI A:104

heyja (*past* **háði,** *pp.* **hát/háit**) *wv.* perform, conduct *Gr* 3.6.9.3; hold, fight (a battle) XXII:33/2, 54/2

heyra/høyra/hœyra (*past* **heyrði/høyrði/hœyrði,** *pp.* **heyrt**) *wv.* hear (*Gr* 3.6.6) I:4, II: 22, III:9, 10, 37, 104, VII A:43, B:68, XIII:23, XIV:45, XXVI B:128; hear of (it) XIII:7, XVI:33; **høyri ek** do I hear XXIV:20; *imp. with suffixed pron.* **heyrðu/ høyrðu** hear IX:6, XXIV:19, listen XXI:190; *imp. pl.* **høyrið** XXIV:20; *past pl.* **hœyrðu** VI:117; **at heyra** to be heard XIV:162; **vildi eigi hœyra at hann myndi hafa** would not hear of his having VI:319; **heyra til** listen XIV:20, hear (anything) from/of XXV:64; *impers.* **hefir heyrt til hans** there has been heard from him XXVI B:200

heyverk *n. pl.* haymaking XXVI A:3

higat = **hingat**

Hildibrandr *m.* son of Reginbaldr and foster-father of Þiðrekr af Bern XI:56, 65, 75

hildíngr *m.* king XXII:62/1

Hildr *f.* a nun XIV:129

hilmir *m.* lord, ruler VII B:43, XXII:3/3, 9/3, 33/1, 51/3; **dagleygjar hilmir** = God (*or* Óðinn; *see note*) V:22 (*gen. with* **Ilmr**)

himinn (*pl.* **himnar** *Gr* 3.1.7.3–5 ex. 4) *m.* the sky II:74; heaven XXII:63/4; *pl.* heaven XIV:56; *gen. pl.* **himna** skies XXII:2/2, 25/2, 51/4

himintungl *n. pl.* heavenly bodies XIV:36

himnaríki *n.* the kingdom of heaven, the heavens XXIV:36

hindrvitni *f.* superstition XIV:79

hingat, higat *adv.* here, to this place I:76, IV:97, V:65, XI:28; this way XXVI B:205; to this country (Iceland) VIII:25, 28, 36; **higat/ hingat til lands** into this country VII A:91 (England), VIII:190 (Iceland); **hingat í Nóreg** here to Norway XVI:172

hinn[1] *pron.* (*Gr* 3.2.2) the other man I:69; *dat. sg. f.* **hinni** the other V:101; *m. pl.* **hinir** those (others) XIV:146, the others XXI:102; *n. pl.* **ok hin** with the others II:41; **hinn er, hin er** that one who V:151, IX:115, the one who VI:334 (with **árr**), XXIV:71; **hinn annarr** the other, the second (choice) XXVI B:103; *n.* **hitt** that IV:22, VI:325; this other thing, this on the contrary XVI:119, this on the other hand XXVI A:35; but this XV:55, XXV:20, 78; the others (sc. **fólk**, the man and the two women) XXI:200; *dat. sg. n.* **hinu** but it was this that XXVI B:171

hinn² *def. art.* = **inn²** (*Gr* 3.3.5) the I:136, IV:2 (*with comp.*), XIII:11, XIV:156 (*with sup.*), XXI:77, 170, 175, XXVI A:115; *with ordinal numerals* XXI:194, XXIV:36–38; **hins verra** (for) what was worse XXI:13; **hinum er** to him that XXIV:83; *f.* **hin** XXIII:57; *n.* **hit** II:63, XIV:143 (*with sup.*), XXI:165, 196; **hit ýtra** on the outer (seaward) side VI:59; *dat. sg. n.* **hinu** XXI:66, XXIV:82; *acc. pl.* **hin** VI:217, 220 (**hin skipin,** *Gr* 3.3.5); *dat. pl.* **hinum** I:2, XIV:44, 104

hirð *f.* following of a king or earl; *with suffixed def. art.* XVI:95, 102, 109

hirða (*past* **hirði,** *pp.* **hirt**) *wv.* keep, put for safe keeping II:115; look after; **at hirða** looking after XIV:135; mind, care about XXVI A:83

hirðir *m.* shepherd *Gr* 3.1.7.5 (1)

hirðmaðr *m.* king's man, courtier I:47, *with suffixed def. art.* I:48; **fyrir hirðmann minn** for my follower I:60; *pl.* **hirðmenn** I:34, 59, 105, 117, *with suffixed def. art.* I:44, XVI:100

hirta (*past* **hirti,** *pp.* **hirtr**) *wv.* chastise XIV:2, discipline XIV:163

hirting *f.* chastisement XIV:41

hirtingasamr *adj.* severe, strict in discipline XIV:49

Hísargafl *m.* (part of an) island off the coast of Norway XIX:15

hit *see* **hinn²**

Hítará *f.* river in Hítardalr (western Iceland) V:43

Hítdœlakappi *m.* champion of the men of Hítardalr (western Iceland) V:*title*

hiti *m.* heat III:13, 53, XIII:19, 22

hitt¹ *pron. n., see* **hinn¹**

hitta (*past* **hitti,** *pp.* **hitt²**) *wv.* **1.** meet *Gr* 3.6.9.1 (7), 3.6.9.3 ex. 4, XV:87, XVI:99, 102; see, visit IX:44; come upon, find IX:12; reach, arrive at XXI:198; meet in battle VI:82, 130. **2. -sk** *form reciprocal* meet each other VII B:58; *supine* **hizt á** had an encounter, come into collision VI:293

hizt *see* **hitta**

hjá *prep. with dat.* (*Gr* 3.7.3) by, with II:151, XII:5, 71, XXVI B:172; next to I:2, 26, III:7, VII B:85; by, near X:7, XIII:2, XXI:140, XXVI A:25; **(í) hjá** by the side of VI:290, XI:31, XII:45, situated close to VIII:103; *as adv.* **þar hjá** nearby III:99

hjaldrvitjuðr *m.* battle-frequenter, warrior (*here* King Haraldr; *gen. with* **herr**) VII B:16

hjaldrþorinn *adj.* bold in battle VI:310 (*with* **Þorketill**)

hjalli *m.* ledge (on a hillside) V:89 (*with suffixed def. art., i.e.*

Hvítingshjalli); *second element of compound separated* V:171, *see* **Hvítingshjalli**; *dat. pl. with suffixed def. art.* **hjǫllunum** V:45

hjalmfaldinn *adj. (pp.)* helmeted (of a valkyrie, Ilmr) V:24

hjálmr/hjalmr *m.* helmet II:61, V:171, VI:206, 236, 287, XI:20, 26; **und hjálmum** wearing helmets XXV:67

hjálp *f.* help; healing XXII:57/2

hjálpa, *earlier* **hjalpa** (*past* **halp/hjalp,** *past pl.* **hulpu,** *pp.* **hólpinn/ holpinn**) *sv. with dat.* help I:28; **at hjálpa** helping XIV:98; benefit, bring salvation to VII A:50

hjálpræði *n.* helping advice; **leggja til hjálpræði með sér** plan with her a way to save her VI:15

hjalt *n.* hilt (*usually pl.*, **hjǫlt**) III:99 (*with suffixed def. art.*), V:40

Hjalti¹ *m.* 'Hilted', name given to Hǫttr I:147; *as nickname* VIII:62

Hjalti² *m.* priest at Hólar XIV:131

Hjalti Skeggjasonr *m.* Icelander, 10th–11th century VIII:79, 88, 98, 107, 111

hjarðhundr *m.* shepherd's dog, herdsman's dog VII A:115

hjarta *n.* heart *Gr* 3.1.7.1, XIII:21; *with suffixed def. art.* its heart I:98, the heart XII:16

hjó, hjoggu *see* **hǫggva**

hjón *n. pl.* household XXVI B:19, 21

hjónskapliga *adv.* in conjugal fashion XII:74

hjú *n. pl.* married couple, household, family X:72

hjǫllum *see* **hjalli**

hjǫlt *see* **hjalt**

hjǫrð *f.* herd *Gr* 3.1.7.3; animals generally XXII:53/1

hjǫrr *m.* sword XXII:56/1

Hjǫrleifr *m.* = **Leifr Hróðmarsson** XIX:35, 38, 42, 43, 54, 59, 62, 63, 65, 67, 74, 75, 76, 79

Hjǫrleifshǫfði *m.* headland on south coast of Iceland XIX:60, 73, 76, 88

hlað *n.* pavement (in front of the homestead) XXVI B:47 (*with suffixed def. art.*)

hlaða (*pres.* **hleðr,** *past* **hlóð,** *past pl.* **hlóðu,** *pp.* **hlaðinn**) *sv.* **1.** load. **2.** *with dat.* lay down; lower (sails); *pres. pl.* **laða** VI:104, *past pl.* **lóðu** VI:125, 135

Hlaðguðr *f.* a valkyrie X:8, 73

hlaupa/laupa (*pres.* **hleypr/leypr,** *past* **hljóp/ljóp,** *past pl.* **hljópu/ ljópu/hlupu,** *pp.* **hlaupinn,** *n.* **hlaupit**) *sv.* (*Gr* 3.6.5.2, 3.6.6) **1.** run,

jump, leap III:49, 54, IV:62, V:127, VI:294 (*past* **ljóp**), 298 (*past pl.*
ljópu), VII A:116, B:67, 68, XV:110, XIX:70, 84, XXI:43, 49, 119,
120, 142, 179, 180, XXVI A:16, 38, 68, B:89, 203, 206, 221; flee
XIX:81; *imp.* **hlauptu út** you jump out XXVI B:203, 210; **hlaupa
fram** charge XXII:38/1; **hlaupa fyrir** jump over XIX:85; **hlaupa
út** rush out, (try to) escape III:27; jump out III:45, 64. **2.** *pp.* **-sk**
form **lœypizk** run off, escape VI:10

hlaut *see* **hljóta**

hleði *m.* shutter XXV:78

Hleiðargarðr *m.* palace of the Danish kings; modern Lejre in Denmark I:1

Hlér *m. alternative name for* **Ægir** II:1

Hlésey *f.* 'Hlér's island', = Læsø in the Kattegat off Denmark II:2

hleypa (*past* **hleypti,** *pp.* **hleypt**) *wv. transitive with dat.* cause to run;
   hleypa ofan í thrust down into III:98

hleypr *see* **hlaupa**

hlið *f.* side XI:55, XXI:45; *with suffixed def. art.* **á hliðina** onto his
   side XV:106; **á hlið** at his side V:29

hlíð *f.* slope, hillside *Gr* 3.1.8 (13)

Hlíðarendi *m.* 'end of the slope', Gunnarr's home in southern Iceland
   XXVI A:1, 10, 13, 21, XXVI B:60

hlíf *f.* shield XXII:18/4, 40/4

hlífa (*past* **hlífði,** *pp.* **hlíft**) *wv. with dat.* protect I:17, XIII:23

Hlín *f. name of* a goddess; **Hlín línu** *is a kenning for* a woman (=
   Steingerðr; cf. *SnE, Skáldskaparmál* ch. 31) IV:89 (*the nom. phrase
   is used to address her*)

hljóð *n.* silence; sound; **koma á hljóð** become aware, hear it rumoured,
   find out XIV:88; **af hljóði** in silence, on the quiet (secretly) XXII:58/2

hljóðlyndr *adj.* taciturn, uncommunicative XXI:12

hljóðr *adj.* quiet, silent I:83

hljóp, hljópu *see* **hlaupa**

hljóta (*past* **hlaut,** *past pl.* **hlutu,** *pp.* **hlotinn**) *sv.* (3.6.6 ex. 4) get,
   suffer V:154, IX:129; **hljóta at** *with inf.* get as one's lot XXVI A:112,
   have to, be forced to XXII:54/3

hló, hlógu *see* **hlæja**

Hlórriði *m.* a name for Þórr IX:26, 27, 56, 123

hlupu *see* **hlaupa**

hluta (*past* **hlutaði,** *pp.* **hlutat**) *wv.* cast lots XXVI A:112; *impers.*
   skal þá hluta lots are then to be drawn (as to, to decide) XXVII:9

hluti *m.* part, share XVI:6

hlutr/lutr *m.* **1.** thing II:4 (**váru** 'were' *is understood in this sentence*), II:93, VII A:98, XIII:47, XIV:13, 59, 82, 115, XVI:167; **í mǫrgum góðum hlutum** in many good ways XIV:4; **sjá einn var svá hlutrinn at** that alone was the thing (i.e. reason) such that XVI:126; *nom. pl.* **hlutir** XXIV:43; *acc. pl.* **hluti** XXIV:28, events (*object of* **sagði fyrir**) VII A:31, 60, 64, **þá luti aðra** the other things XXIV:49. **2.** part; **sá hlutr** that part (of something) XXIII:96; (**enn**) **meiri hlutr manna** the majority of people VIII:177, XXVII:27, *similarly* XXVII:46; **mestr lutr manna** the greatest portion of men, the majority of people VI:319; share II:160; **eiga hlut í** be involved in something IV:101. **3.** lot; the lot XXVII:10

hlýða (*past* **hlýddi**) *wv.* listen; **er til hlýddu** who were listening to him XIV:34, 37; *with dat.* listen to, hear XIV:43, 151; *impers.* **hlýðir** it will do; **þar mundi hlýða** it would work VIII:91

hlýðinn *adj. with dat.* obedient to, compliant to VIII:155

hlýðni *f.* obedience XIV:119

hlýri *m.* brother XXII:14/1

hlæja (*pres.* **hlær,** *past* **hló,** *past pl.* **hlógu,** *pp.* **hleginn**) *sv.* (*Gr* 3.6.9.3) laugh II:72, XVI:109, 111; *past* **hló** IX:123, XXV:70, **ló við** laughed (at it) VI:76; *past pl.* **hlógu** XXV:23; *pres. part.* **hlæjandi** laughing X:136, 173

hlœgja (*past* **hlœgði**) *wv.* cause to laugh, make laugh II:69; **þat hlœgir mik** that gladdens me XXVI B:217

Hlǫðvér *m.* legendary king (= Louis, Ludwig) X:8, 58, 73 (*dat.*)

hnakki *m.* nape of the neck XII:20 (*with suffixed def. art.*)

hné *see* **hníga**

hneigjask (*past* **hneigðisk**) *wv.* -**sk** *form* bend XXIII:21

hneit *see* **hníta**

Hneitir *m.* 'cutter', St Óláfr's sword XXII:37/1, 48/1

hnekkir *m.* one who halts or checks, puts an end to; **hertryggðar hnekkir** *i.e.* successful battle-leader (who destroys the enemy's confidence; *subject of* **baðat hyggja**) VI:178

hníga (*past* **hné,** *past pl.* **hnigu,** *pp.* **hniginn**) *sv.* (*Gr* 3.6.9.3 ex. 1) sink down, *i.e.* fall (in battle) V:171, VI:362, XXII:37/4, 45/3, XXV:56, 111

hníta (*past* **hneit,** *past pl.* **hnitu,** *pp.* **hnitinn**) *sv.* strike (**við** against) IV:18; **hníta saman** strike against each other (*i.e.* in battle) VI:231

Hnitbjǫrg *n. pl.* a mountain II:116, 120

hnot (*pl.* **hnøtr/hnetr**) *f.* nut (*Gr* 3.1.7.2) II:51, 54 (*with suffixed def. art.*)

hnykkja (*pres.* **hnykkir**, *past* **hnykkti**, *pp.* **hnykkt**) *wv. with dat.* pull, snatch I:13

hoddlestir *m.* 'hoard-harmer' *i.e.* 'hoard diminisher' *means* 'generous man', *here* Þorsteinn Kuggason (*gen. with* **sveit seggja**) V:53

hof *n.* (heathen) temple VIII:43

Hof *n.* farm in southern Iceland XXVI A:5

hóf¹ *see* **hefja**

hóf² *n.* moderation; what is reasonable II:127 (*object of* **gefa**); reason, restraint (**at** in it) XV:21; **ætla hóf fyrir sér** know what is sensible for oneself, keep within one's capabilities VI:168; **at sama hófi** to the same degree, just as good X:12; **á sitt hóf** in respect of herself *or* to the same extent, equally *or* proportionately? XV:61

hófsk *see* **hefja**

hógliga *adv.* gently; *sup.* **sem hógligast** as gently as he could III:111

hola *f.* hollow, hole XXI:204

Hólabyskup *m.* bishop of Hólar in Hjaltadalr XIV:177

Hólakirkja *f.* the church at Hólar in Hjaltadalr XIV:176

Hólar¹ *m. pl.* bishop's see in Hjaltadalr, inland from Skagafjǫrðr, northern Iceland VIII:192, XIV:5, 12, 143, 166, 184

Hólar² *m. pl.* = Álfhólar, farm on Eyjar (Landeyjar) XXVI B:3, 4

hold *n.* flesh X:53, XII:20 (*with suffixed def. art.*)

holdgan *f.* incarnation XIX:49

holdgróinn *adj. (pp.)* rooted in the (same) flesh XXV:48

hóll *m.* hill VII A:149

Hóll *m.* farm in Saurbœr, western Iceland XV:44

hólmganga *f.* duel, a fight to settle a dispute VII A:98, 99

hólmgǫngumaðr *m.* fighter of duels VII A:77

hólmi *m.* islet, small island VI:28, 29; *with suffixed def. art.* VI:60, 123, 124, 125, 133, 135, 136

hólmr *m.* = **hólmi** X:86, 179, 181; *acc. sg. with suffixed def. art.* **hólmenn** VI:121

Hólmr *m.* Bjǫrn Hítdœlakappi's farm in Hítardalr, western Iceland V:74, 87, 158

Hólmsteinn *m.* son of **Atli enn mjóvi** XIX:7, 10, 13, 16, 18

hólmsǫk *f.* a cause for duelling, a reason for holding a duel V:115

holr *adj.* hollow, cupped I:41

Hólsmenn *m. pl.* the people of **Hóll** XV:82

holt *n.* wood X:77; ?stony hill XXV:16; low hill *or* ridge XXI:91

hon/hún *f. pron.* she, it (*Gr* 3.2.1) I:17, 18, 19, IX:105, 129, X:3, 59, 75, XI:8, 31, XIII:5, 24, XV:26, XXI:13 (it, i.e. Christianity), 136, XXVI A:80, 105, B:23; **hún** it XIV:12

honum/hánum *pron. dat. sg.* (*Gr* 3.2.1) (to) him I:27, 32, 37, 66, 68, 74, 92, 94, 113, VIII:26, XI:31, XV:25, XIX:34, XXI:15, XXIV:68, XXVI A:11, 33, B:74, XXVII:32; **hánum** VI:97, 187, 243 (*dat. with* **fylgja**, = Eiríkr jarl), IX:43, 61, X:40, 183, 184, XXIV:81, it VI:115; **honum Auðuni** him, Auðunn XVI:107; **firir honum Þóri** for this Þórir XVI:5; *poss. dat.* **í andlit honum** into his face VII A:86, **í smáþarma honum** into his guts XXI:175, **ór hǫndum honum** from his hands VII A:103, **tenn hánum** his teeth X:81

Hóp *n.* 'lagoon'; *place-name formed with prep.* (*Gr* 3.1.8 ex.) XXI:90, 164, 193

horfa (*past* **horfði,** *pp.* **horft**) *wv.* **1.** face (in a certain direction) XII:21, XV:105, XIX:60; gaze XXI:67; **horfa á** look at I:119, look at something, look ahead III:54; **horfa til** tend towards XIV:90, *note,* refer to XXIV:3, 4, 83; **horfa upp** be turned upwards XV:151. **2.** **-sk** *form with reciprocal sense* **horfðusk þeir at** they faced each other III:8 (*Gr* 3.9.8.3)

horfit, horfinn *see* **hverfa**

horn *n.* corner I:5 (*with suffixed def. art.*); horn (musical instrument) XXV:65

hornungr *m.* bastard XXV:52

hósti *m.* cough XXVI B:200

hosur *f. pl.* hose, drawers, trousers V:56

hót[1] *n. pl.* threats (*with dat.,* against someone) XXII:7/3

hót[2] *n.* a little, somewhat; *dat. as adv. with comp.* XXII:32/2

hrafn *m.* raven (*Gr* 3.1.7.4) V:164, 165

Hrafn *m.* father of Bergþórr VIII:170

Hrafn Hœngsson *m.* lawspeaker 930–49 VIII:58, 62

Hrafna-Flóki *m.* Flóki Vilgerðarson XIX:27. He was one of the first viking explorers of Iceland (see *ÍF* I 36–39), and used ravens to help him find it.

Hrafnkell (*dat.* **Hrafnkatli**) **Hallfreðarson** *m. Gr* 3.1.8 ex.

hráki *m.* spittle II:91

Hrani (Koðránsson) *m.* III:107, *see note*

hrapalliga *adv.* hurriedly, headlong, in a hurry III:66

hrata (*past* **hrataði,** *pp.* **hratat**) *wv.* fall; **hrata ofan** tumble down XXVI A:31

hrauð *see* **hrjóða**

hraustgeðr *adj.* bold-minded; **enn hraustgeði** the bold-minded one (Þorsteinn Kuggason) V:52

hraustleikr *m.* valour, vigour, courage, manliness XV:146

hraustligr *adj.* valiant, brave-sounding, encouraging; *comp.* XXVI B:126

hraustr *adj.* tough, bold, valiant I:117, 123, 133, V:114. XXII:11/3; *pl. as substantive* **raustir** valiant ones VI:293

hraut *see* **hrjóta**

hreðjar *f. pl.* scrotum, testicles II:70

hreimr *m.* cry, noise, shriek; *as nickname* III:44

hreinferðugr *adj.* pure, chaste XIV:185

hreinliga *adv.* purely, absolutely XXIII:29; **svá hreinliga sem** as pure a life as XIX:112

hreinn[1] *m.* reindeer; *acc. pl.* (*with* **hafði krafða**) *in kenning for* ships, **húnlagar hreina** VI:54

hreinn[2] *adj.* pure Gr 3.3.9 (3), XIII:28, 41; *comp.* **hreinni** Gr 3.3.8.4 (1), 3.3.9 (20); *sup.* **hreinstr** Gr 3.3.9 (20)

Hreinn Styrmisson *m.* abbot at Þingeyrar from 1166 (died 1171) XIV:151

hremma (*past* **hrem(m)di,** *pp.* **hrem(m)dr**) *wv.* clutch, hold firmly XXII:35/3

hressask (*past* **hresstisk**) *wv. refl.* recover III:130

hreysti *f.* toughness, courage, boldness I:128; valour XI:50

hríð/ríð *f.* **1.** (period of) time, while: **um hríð** for a while IV:103, V:44, XVI:77, XIX:17, 71, XXVI A:40, B:194, for a time, once XXVI B:139; *acc. in adv. phrase* **nǫkk(u)ra hríð, skamma hríð, litla hríð** for a short time I:4, III:104, XV:54, for a while XXVI A:111, for a certain period XIV:166. **2.** storm XV:144; **hjalms hríð** (*object of* **vann**), **geira hríð, odda hríð** *are kennings for* battle VI:237, VII A:25, XXII:55/1; *also* **hríð mána viðar hauðrmens** storm of shields XXVI A:99 (*gen. with* **herðimeiða**). **3.** attack, onset, assault XXVI A:43; *gen.* (*object of* **væntir mek**) **þeirar ríðar at** such a battle that VI:91

hrinda (*past* **hratt,** *past pl.* **hrundu,** *pp.* **hrundit**) *sv.* push; *past subj.* **hryndi** III:47

hringja (*past* **hringði,** *pp.* **hringt**) *wv.* (cause to) ring *(with dat.)* XII:46 *(pres. part.)*; **hringja til tíða** ring (a bell) for divine services XIV:160

hringr *m.* ring, circle V:109, XXIII:32 (i.e. iris?); (gold) ring IX:116, 130, XVI:146, 182; *with suffixed def. art.* XVI:150, 183

hrís *n.* brushwood X:54 (*instrumental dat.*)

hrista (*past* **hristi,** *pp.* **hrist**) *wv.* (*transitive*) shake IX:3

hrjóða (*pres.* **hrýðr,** *past* **hrauð,** *past pl.* **hruðu,** *pp.* **hroðinn/roðinn,** *n.* **hroðit/roðit**) *sv.* strip, clear (of men, by killing them); *pp.* **roðinn,** *n.* **roðit** VI:217, 227, 275; **váru roðin** had been cleared VI:305; *impers.* **hrauð af** splinters *or* sparks flew off? XXII:48/2; **-sk** *form for pass.* **ruðusk** were stripped VI:219, 223

hrjóta[1] (*pres.* **hrýtr,** *past* **hraut,** *past pl.* **hrutu,** *pp.* **hrotinn**) *sv.* fly, be flung II:146, splash III:86

hrjóta[2] (*pres.* **hrýtr,** *past* **hraut,** *past pl.* **hrutu,** *pp.* **hrotinn**) *sv.* roar, growl (**við** in response) XXV:90; *past subj.* **sem bjǫrn hryti** as a bear would have roared (growled) XXV:91

Hróaldr Geirsson *m.* XXVI A:114, 116

Hróaldr Hrómundarson *m.* Icelandic settler XIX:2, 5

Hróaldr Ǫzurarson *m.* of Breiðá XXVI B:88, 91

Hróðmarr Hróaldsson *m.* XIX:5

hróðrglaðr *adj.* glad of fame XXV:78 (see note 22)

Hrólfr kraki *m.* legendary Danish king I:28, 45, 50, 106, 132

Hrómundr Gripsson *m.* XIX:2. He is the subject of a *fornaldarsaga*

hrópa (*past* **hrópaði,** *pp.* **hrópat**) *wv.* slander, defame falsely XII:42, 62, 89

hrósa (*past* **hrósaði,** *pp.* **hrósat**) *wv. with dat.* praise, glory in X:122; boast of XXVI A:116, 117

hross *n.* horse V:6, VIII:55, XXV:13; *acc. pl. with suffixed def. art.* V:45, 46, 67, 91; *gen. pl. with suffixed def. art.* **hrossanna** V:28; *dat. pl. with suffixed def. art.* V:89

hrossakjǫt *n.* horseflesh VIII:141

(h)rossæta *f.* horse-eater, one who eats horseflesh; *acc. pl.with suffixed def. art.* VI:188

hrotti *m.* sword; *dat. as instrumental* **hrotta** with my sword XXII:15/1

hrukku *see* **hrøkkva**

Hrund *f. name of a* valkyrie IV:88; *written* **Grund** XVIII:122rb11

Hrungnir *m.* a giant IV:18

hrygð *f.* sorrow XII:36

hryggiliga *adv.* sadly, unhappily XIII:33

hryggr *adj.* sad XII:87; mournful XXIII:20, 71

hrynja (*past* **hrundi**, *pp.* **hrunit**) *wv.* jangle IX:61

hryndi *see* **hrinda**

hræ *n.* corpse; *in pl.* (*with suffixed def. art.*) the remains of the body VIII:52

hræðask (*past* **hræddisk**) *wv.* be afraid of, fear I:105 (*subj.*), 107, XXVI B:75; **ræddusk** were afraid VI:321; **ræddisk við** was in fear of VI:131

hræddr *adj. pp.* frightened, afraid I:26, 36, 90, II:47; fearful XXIII:93; **ræddr** VI:77

hræðiligr *adj.* dreadful, fearful XXII:56/1

hrædýr *n.* carrion animal XXIII:35 (*gen. pl. with* **hátt**)

hræra *see* **hrœra**

hræzla *f.* fear XIV:115

hrœra (**hræra**) (*past* **hrœrði**, *pp.* **hrœrt**) *wv.* move (transitive), wield XXII:12/3; **-sk** *form* move (intransitive) XXI:173, XXIII:34, XXVI B:176

hrœriligr *adj.* movable, changeable XXIII:42

hrøkkva/røkkva (*past* **hrøkk**, *past pl.* **hrukku**, *pp.* **hrokkinn**) *sv.* fall back; **hrøkkva frá** withdraw, draw back XXVI A:41; **røkkva undan** draw back, give way, retreat VI:272; swing, be wielded V:41; curl (of hair) XXIII:5

húð *f.* hide (of an animal) XXVI B:179 (*with suffixed def. art.*)

húðkeipr *m.* skin boat (i.e. canoe), boat made of animal hide XXI:96, 110

hugða, hugði, hugðu *see* **hyggja**

hugframr *adj.* valiant at heart VI:311 (*with* **Þórketill**)

hugfullr *adj.* full of courage, brave XXIII:80, 106, valiant XXV:65

hugga (*past* **huggaði**, *pp.* **huggat**) *wv.* comfort, console XIV:111

huggan *f.* comfort, consolation XII:86, 87, XIV:112

huggóðr *adj.* kind-hearted XIV:198

hugleiða (*past* **hugleiddi**, *pp.* **hugleiddr**) *wv.* consider, bear in mind XXIV:76

hugléttr *adj.* light of heart; *comp. n. as adv.* **henni mundi hugléttara** she would be happier, comforted II:107

hugna (*past* **hugnaði**, *pp.* **hugnat**) *wv. with dat.* please VII B:15

hugprýði *f.* courage, valour V:131, 152

hugr *m.* thought, mind IX:123, XIII:41, XIV:93, XXIII:2, 5, 15, 26 (*with suffixed def. art.*), 30, 59, 61 (*pl.,* thoughts?); attitude XXIII:22;

heart, courage I:118, XXV:96; **í hug (honum)** in his mind III:13, 27; **kom honum þat í hug at** it occurred to him that XIX:81, **kemr mér í hug** has come into my mind XXVI B:116; **erum hugr á** my mind is on IV:28; **eigi er honum hugr at** he has no mind to, no desire to XII:72

hugreifr *adj.* glad of mind VI:278 (*with* **þengill**)

hugsa (*past* **hugsaði,** *pp.* **hugsat**) *wv.* think, consider XXIII:36; think about, ponder XXII:32/1; plan XXIII:74

hugsunarmikill *adj.* thoughtful XXIII:2

hugumstórr *adj.* great of heart, courageous XXV:20, 85

hugvit *n.* intelligence, understanding, good sense XXIII:4, 89, 109

hugvitr *adj.* clever, intelligent XXIII:30

hulði, huldr/hulit/hult *see* **hylja**

hún = **hon**

Húnaland *n.* the land of the Huns XI:38, 70

hunang *n.* honey II:98

hundr *m.* dog VII A:115 (*with suffixed def. art.*), 116 (*with suffixed def. art.*), 119, 123, XXVI A:9 (*with suffixed def. art.*); *poss. dat.* XXVI A:18 (*with suffixed def. art.*); *as nickname* XXII:8/3, 42/1

Hundr *m.* = Þórir hundr XXII:30/1, 45/2

hundrað *n.* (*Gr* 3.4.1, 2 (5, 6)) hundred VIII:13, 148 (*see* **tegr**), XIV:139; **hundrað heilt** a good hundred, *or perhaps* a full hundred, i.e. 120? VIII:166; **fjorir tigir annars hundraðs** 140 (*Gr* 3.4.2 (9)) XXI:19; *pl.* **hundruð** VII A:116, VII B:33, X:48, XI:11, XIV:140, XIX:50; = 120 XXV:81, XXVII:37

hungrdœyfir *m.* 'hunger-allayer'; he who allays the hunger of carrion birds is a successful warrior who provides dead bodies for them to eat (here = King Óláfr) VI:326 (*object of* **skal ek lœyfa**)

húnlenzkr *adj.* Hunnish, from Hunland XXV:42

húnlǫgr *m.* mast-top liquid, *kenning for* the sea; *gen. with* **hreina** VI:54 (**húnn**[1] *m.* was a four-sided structure fixed to the top of a mast, crow's-nest)

húnn[2] *m.* cub; young boy X:114, 148, 158; one of the pieces used in a board-game IV:33

hurð *f.* door XV:103, *with suffixed def. art.* XV:104

hurfu *see* **hverfa**

hús *n.* building XI:61, XII:14, XIV:15, 26, 157, XXVI A:58 (*pl.*); *with suffixed def. art.* room IV:35, 36; house X:5, XIV:152 (*pl.*), XV:102, XX1:204, home V:10; *acc. of what is travelled over* (*with*

rennda ek) IV:34; *pl. with suffixed def. art*. III:5, 35, 88; *pl.* buildings, farmstead XXVI A:15, B:61, *with suffixed def. art*. XXVI A:37, 38, B:87, 88, 118

húsbak *n.* back of the building XXV:111

húsfreyja *f.* mistress of the house, housekeeper XIV:127; *in address* lady XXVI B:161

húsganga *f.* (people going on a) visit V:3

húskarl *m.* farmhand V:2, 26, 128; servant, workman XXVI B:134; *in Norway*, member of a king's or jarl's bodyguard or following VII B:44

hvaðan, hvaðan af *adv.* (*Gr* 3.8.2.3) where from, from what origin I:128, II:86, VII A:63; **hvaðan af sem** *as conj.* from wherever VII A:61

hválf *n.* vault XII:10; vaulted room XII:64

Hvalfjǫrðr *m.* 'whale-fjord', fjord in western Iceland XIX:97

hválfhús *n.* vaulted building *or* chamber XII:7, 67, 80

hváll *m.* hillock, knoll; *with suffixed def. art*. (i.e. Bergþórshváll) XXVI B:42

hvalr *m.* whale XXI:73, 74 (see **hvat**); *dat. pl.* **hvǫlum** XXI:75

hvalslíki *n.* the form of a whale VII A:147

Hvammsdalr *m.* valley in western Iceland above Saurbœr XV:82

hvar[1] *adv. conj.* where (*Gr* 3.8.2.1, 3) II:54, 156, III:97, VI:120, 126, IX:99, X:67, XXVI B:175; as to where XII:78, as to what VIII:40; **hvar sem** wherever XXII:19/4

hvar[2] *adv.* in each place, everywhere; **sex eru hvar saman** they are all in groups of six V:81

hvarf[1] *n.* disappearance II:43

hvarf[2] *see* **hverfa**

hvarfa (*past* **hvarfaði,** *pp.* **hvarfat**) *wv. intransitive* turn round, wave about XXV:73

hvárgi *pron.* neither *Gr* 3.2.4, XXVI B:102; *n.* **lagði hvártki til** supported neither side (in the dispute), contributed nothing on either side V:162; *n. as adv.* **hvárki/hvórki . . . né** neither . . . nor XII:76, XIV:75, XXII:3/4, 53/3, XXIII:51, XXIV:8–9, XXVI A:77, B:85; **hvárki . . . ok eigi** XXIV:52; **svá . . . at . . . hvárki** without either VI:9

hvárr *pron.* each (of two) (*Gr* 3.2.5, 3.8.2.3) III:16, XI:46; **hvárr okkar** each of us XXVI B:216; **sitt skip hvárr** each his own ship XIX:43; *pl.* **hvárir** which (side) XXVI B:54, each (side) VII A:100, VIII:114, XXVII:14; **hvárr sem** whichever III:17; **at hváru** according to both, in either case VI:330; **ykru hváru** to each of you XXV:34

hvárt *interrog. adv. (Gr* 3.8.2.3) whether I:48, 112, 114, VI:325, XXVI
   A:27, 84; *introducing a direct question (Gr* 3.9.1) XI:23, XV:64,
   XXVI B:109, 224, **hvárt launaði hann** did he reward XVI:179,
   hvárt er (þat) can it be XV:49, XVI:32, is . . .? XXVI A:34, B:128;
   hvárt sem, hvárt er *as conj.* whether VIII:154, XIV:45, XV:9, XXVI
   B:176, XXVII:11
hvártki = **hvárki**, *n. of* **hvárgi**
hvártveggja *pron.* each of the two; *n.* **hvárttveggja** II:71, III:116,
   both (*i.e.* that he is dead and alive) VI:332 (*object of* **sannliga segja**),
   XVI:186; *acc. sg.* **í hvárntveggja flokkenn** on each side, in each force
   VI:220; *gen. sg.* **til hvárstveggja** for each of these two things XIV:29;
   dat. sg. n. **hvárutveggja** XXI:83; *nom. pl.* **hvárirtveggju** each side,
   both sides II:90, VIII:134, 137; *dat. pl.* **af hvárumtveggja** from each
   of the two sides, from both sides VI:212; *n. as adv.* **hvártveggja** both
   XXIV:72, **hvárttveggja** on both sides VI:293, in each case XV:63
hvass (*f.* **hvǫss**) *adj.* sharp *Gr* 3.3.9 (4); keen, bold (of the heart or
   mind) XXII:19/3; *comp.* **hvassari** *Gr* 3.3.9 (20); *comp. n. as adv.*
   hvassara more keenly IX:99; *sup.* **hvassastr** *Gr* 3.3.8.5 (2), 3.3.9
   (20), 3.3.9 ex. 26
hvat *pron.* what (*Gr* 3.2.5, 3.8.2.3); I:10, 111, 112, 135, 140, II:44,
   IV:29, V:11, 16, VII A:45, IX:6, 23, X:148, XII:78, XV:59, XVI:80,
   168, XXI:99, XXIV:11, XXVI B:45; what for XI:33; to what extent,
   how VIII:155, XXV:47; *with gen.* **hvat ráðs** what plan XXVI B:48,
   hvat manna what (kind of) people XV:88, **hvat hvala** what kind of
   whale XXI:74; **hvat sem** whatever XXI:136; **hvat er** whatever is
   XXIII:35; *as interjection* what? XXIV:9
hvatr *adj.* quick; *n. as adv.* **hvatt** vigorously, swiftly X:99
hvatki *pron.* whatever *Gr* 3.2.5; **hvatki es** *as conj.* VIII:5
hvatti *see* **hvetja**
hvé *adv.* how (*Gr* 3.8.2.3) V:80, VIII:112, IX:56, XVI:72, XXV:44.
   XXVI A:93
hveiti *n.* wheat XXI:50
hveitiakr (*gen.* **-akrs**) *m.* wheat-field XXI:90
hvelfa (*past* **hvelfði**) *wv. impers. with dat.* overturn, capsize II:104
hvelpr *m.* whelp, puppy; *as nickname* XV:81
hvenær *adv.* when *Gr* 3.8.2.3
hverfa (*past* **hvarf**, *past pl.* **hurfu**, *pp.* **horfinn/horfit**) *sv.* turn III:38,
   39 (*i.e.* in the narrative), V:78, XXI:181; fall XXVII:9; **hverfa at**

attend VIII:47; **hverfa braut/á brott/á brutt** go away IV:27, go off, disappear XIX:100, XXI:65; **hverfa frá** turn away, leave off, give up XXVI A:48, B:64, 103; **hverfa saman** gather together VIII:109; *pp.* **horfinn** disappeared, gone XIX:82; *with dat.* surrounded by, blessed with XXI:14; **horfinn frá** turned away from, turned against XXII:9/3

hverft *adv.* changeably, unpredictably, suddenly XXVI B:36

hvergi *adv.* nowhere, not at all V:10, 110, VIII:160, XIII:6, XXII:3/3, XXVI B:176; in no way XV:123, *after a neg.* anywhere at all IX:7

hvernig, hvernug *adv. (Gr* 3.8.2.3) how II:122, III:107; as to how VII A:46

hverr (*n.* **hvert**) *pron.* **1.** who, which, what (*Gr* 3.2.5) I:7, 56, 121, III:65, VI:106, 181, XV:114, XVI:59, 106, XXIV:14, XXVII:6, 18; **hverr maðr** what kind of person, who VII A:86; *f.* **hver** what XXVI B:8; *acc. sg. m.* **hvern** which IV:88 (*with* **skapfrǫmuð**), VII A:78; *as rel.* which XIV:26, *note*, whom XIV:169, **í hvern** into which XXVII:9, **hvern er** whoever, anyone who XIV:187, **hvern veg** how V:84; *dat. sg. m.* **hverjum** (to) whom V:135, what XIV:90, *note*; *n.* **hvert** what V:105; **hvert nafn . . . var** what the name . . . was VII A:90; *gen. sg. n.* **hvers** of what II:76, XXVI A:28, for what XXV:35; *dat. sg. n.* **hverju** what I:74, V:8, *with* **gegna** II:22, with what, how XV:26, XVI:161; *m. pl.* **hverir** who VI:186, 190, X:64, XXVII:42; *f. pl.* **hverjar** what (kind of) I:60; **hverr er** whoever II:99, 160, XXIV:18. **2.** each V:23, VI:162, VIII:27, 31, 43, XIV:63, XIX:84, XXVI B:20, XXVII:34; every XI:48, 49, XII:76, XVI:43, XXI:91, 112, XXIV:17, 29, XXVII:26; every, any II:140, V:4; all (the) XXV:4; each one/person XXV:30; everyone XXVI A:85; **hverr maðr annarra** any other man VIII:150; **hverr maðr . . . er** anyone who XXVII:35, 41; **hverjum** to each, to everyone XIX:78; **hverjum manni** to every person XXVI B:212; *n.* **hvert** each VII A:134, XXVII:37, each one (ship) VI:217, every XI:61, XII:86, **hvert þat** every single XIII:34; *acc. sg. m.* **mann hvern er** everyone who XXV:97; **duga hvern** each one to be valiant I:117 (*after* **bað**, *parallel to* **hirðmenn vera hrausta**), **hvern dag** every day XIV:61; **hverr . . . annan (ǫðrum)** each other II:44, 129, VII B:71; **hverr við annan** with each other VI:149; **hverr at ǫðrum** one after the other (did so) XXI:150; **hvern at ǫðrum** one after another XI:9; **hverjum at ǫðrum** (with) each ones (group, rank) after the other(s) XI:58; **hverjum sem einum** each and every

XIII:42; **á þremr sumrum hverjum** over every three summers; **hverr . . . sína (sitt)** each his own, *i.e.* in turn II:80, III:106; **sér hvern** each one separately VII A:84

hversdagligr *adj.* daily, everyday XIV:60, usually XXI:12

hversu *adv.* how *Gr* 3.8.2.3, XI:7, 18, 66, XV:76, 85, XVI:39, 65, 132, XXIV:27, XXVI A:6, B:55, 175; **hversu . . . sem** however XV:17

hvert[1] *adv.* (*Gr* 3.8.2.3) whither, to what place V:165, XV:119

hvert[2] *see* **hverr**

hvessa (*past* **hves(s)ti,** *pp.* **hves(s)t**) *wv.* sharpen X:92; stir up, excite: **hvessa darra él** (i.e. battle) *is* to fight energetically XXII:41/4

hvetja (*pres.* **hvetr,** *past* **hvatti,** *pp.* **hvattr**) *wv.* whet, sharpen IV:39; urge, incite, goad XXV:8; *with suffixed pron.* **hvǫttumk at** incited me to it XXV:100

hví *adv. conj.* (*Gr* 3.2.5, 3.8.2.3) why V:143, IX:24, 108, XVI:38, XXIV:26, 55, XXVI A:66, B:36

hvíla[1] *f.* bed III:24 (*with suffixed def. art.*), XXVI B:167, 174 (*with suffixed def. art.*)

hvíla[2] (*past* **hvíldi**) *wv.* rest, lie quiet VIII:120; **hvíla sik = hvílask** rest oneself XXVI B:230; **-sk** *form* **hvílask** have a rest X:19, 141

hvíld *f.* rest XXVI A:40

hvílugólf *n.* bed closet, bed space XV:93

Hvítingshjalli *m.* a ledge on a hillside in Hítardalr, western Iceland V:5, 42, 45; **hjalli Hvítings** V:172

hvítr *adj.* white VI:104, X:25, XII:34, XXI:101, 205, XXIII:88, 106, 108, XXV:12; shining V:37, XI:4, 19, XXII:20/4, XXV:72; *sup.* IX:57; *wk. form as nickname* ('white-haired') VIII:80, XXVI A:4, 42

Hvítramannaland *n.* the land of the white men XXI:206

hvórki *see* **hvárgi**

hvǫlum *see* **hvalr**

hvǫss *see* **hvass**

hvǫt *f.* incitement, bait XXV:62

hvǫttumk *see* **hvetja**

hyggja[1] (*past* **hugði,** *past pl.* **hugðu,** *pp.* **hugðr,** *n.* **hugat**) *wv.* think (*Gr* 3.6.9.2 (3)) I:54, II:19, 33, 68, III:122, V:63, VI:154, 183, 297, X:58, XII:59, 74, XIV:7, XXIV:44; **hygg (hugða) ek** *with acc. and pp.* (*adj.*) (*verb to be understood*) I think (thought) VI:360, X:70, XXV:102; *1st sg. pres. with suffixed pron.* **-k** *and suffixed neg.* **-at,** **hykkat** I do not think (*with acc. and inf.*) VI:246; *subj.* **hyggi** may think (that) I:109; **hyggja á** think of VI:171; **baðat hyggja á** told (them) not to think of VI:177; **hyggja at** pay attention, watch III:61, observe XXVI B:48, consider XVI:72 (*imp.*)

hyggja² *f.* thought XXII:19/3; mind, wit XXV:32

hyggjandi *f.* intellect, forethought XXV:96

hykkat *see* **hyggja**

hylja (*past* **hulði,** *pp.* **huldr/hulit/hult**) *wv. transitive* hide III:100; *pp.* **huldr** hidden, covered XXII:59/1, **hult** covered XXIII:78, 79

hylli *f.* favour IX:118

hyrna *f.* point, horn, corner of an axe-blade; *with suffixed def. art.* **hyrnan sú in fremri** the foremost (i.e. upper) point of the axe-blade XXVI B:91

hýrr *adj.* gentle, friendly X:77

hýski *n.* household, family XXIV:64

hæðiligr *adj.* disgraceful XIV:84

hægri *see* **hœgri**

hæll *m.* heel; **á hæla** *with dat.* on someone's heels VII B:43, XXVI B:206

hæra *adv. (n. adj.) comp.* (*Gr* 3.3.8.5 (3)) higher VII A:160

hæri *adj. comp.* higher XXIV:16

hæstr *adj. sup.* highest VI:224, XXIII:89, noblest? XXII:51/3

hætta¹ *f.* danger V:63

hætta² (*past* **hætti,** *pp.* **hættr¹**) *wv. with dat.* leave off, stop V:141, XXVI B:196

hætta³ (*past* **hætti,** *pp.* **hættr²**) *wv. with dat.* risk, endanger XXI:192

hætti *see* **háttr**

hættr³ *adj.* dangerous XVI:138 (*with dat.* for); *n. as adv. with dat. and* **við** one (is) in danger of something; **við engu mun mér þá hætt** I shall then be in no danger VII B:63; **hætt er** it is problematical, doubtful, unreliable, uncertain VI:331

hœfa (*past* **hœfði,** *pp.* **hœft**) *wv. with dat.* **1.** befall, happen (to someone) I:94. **2.** suit, be suitable for XXIII:61; befit (be proper to?) XXIII:63

hœfiligr *adj.* proper, fit XXIII:53, 87

hœgr *adj.* gentle (*with dat.* to) XIV:49, mild, easy? XXIII:8

hœgri/hægri *adj. comp.* right (as opposed to left) III:57, 86, XII:28, XV:108, XXII:63/3; **á hœgra veg sér** on his right hand side XI:53; *sup. n. as adv.* **hœgst** most suitable X:93

Hœngr *m.* = Ketill hœngr, Icelandic settler VIII:58

Hœnir *m.* a god (one of the Æsir) II:9, 17

hœta (*past* **hœtti,** *pp.* **hœtt**) *wv. with dat. of person and thing* threaten someone with something IV:22 (*the subject is understood*: Narfi or Þorkell)

hœve(r)skr *adj.* courtly, well-bred, polite XXIV:58

hœyra = **heyra**

hǫfðaskip *n.* ship with figurehead(s) at prow and/or stern; dragon-ship VI:68

hǫfði[1] *m.* headland; *with suffixed def. art.* XIX:61, 80

hǫfði[2] *see* **hǫfuð**

hǫfðingi (*acc. sg., gen. sg., acc. pl., gen. pl.* **hǫfðingja**) *m.* chief, leader VI:181 (**fyrir** over), VII B:72 (*gen. sg.*); ruler, prince VI:35, 162 (*gen. pl.*), 317, XXIV:67; *nom. pl.* **hǫfðingjar** rulers, leaders VI:29, 58, 91, 198, XXIV:64; chieftains, leading men VIII:46, 81, 183, XXVI B:63; *with suffixed def. art.* VI:59; **þeir hǫfðingjarnir** the chieftains VI:126 (*Gr* 3.3.5)

hǫfðu *see* **hafa**; **hǫfðum** *see* **hǫfuð**

hǫfn *f.* **1.** harbour (*Gr* 3.1.7.1, 2) VI:58, VII A:70, XVI:138. **2.** grazing, feed VIII:55

hǫfuð (*dat. sg.* **hǫfði**) *n.* head II:110 (**henni** *poss. dat.*), V:147, 148, 157, IX:64, XII:46, XVIII:9, **haufuð** his (Jǫrmunrekkr's) head XXV:98; *acc. pl.* **hǫfuð** X:114, 158, **hafuð** figureheads VI:76; *with suffixed def. art.* his head III:7, VII A:160, XXVI B:154; **á hǫfði** on his head III:28, V:29, on their heads XXI:104, *with gen.* on the head of XXIII:6; **á hǫfuð/hǫfði sér** on his/her head XI:20, XII:25; **at hǫfði Helga** on (round/over) Helgi's head XXVI B:146; **í hǫfuð** in my head X:145; **í hǫfuð honum** at his head III:56, V:102, in his head XXI:139; **í hǫfuð hundinum** on/into the dog's head XXVI A:18; **um hǫfuð sér** round their heads XXI:116; **yfir hafuð sér** above his head VI:295; **yfir hǫfuð þeim** over their heads XIII:3; **til hǫfuðs þér** to kill you IV:38; *dat. pl.* **hǫfðum** figureheads VI:77, *with suffixed def. art.* **hǫfðunum** with their heads (*i.e.* they were lying head to head) III:8

hǫfuðdúkr *m.* head-cloth (-scarf) *or* hood XXVI B:144

hǫfuðsmátt *f.* opening for the head, neck (of a garment) XV:28, 62

hǫfugr *adj.* heavy; *f. pl.* **hǫfgar** X:62; *n.* **œrit hǫfugt** hard enough XIV:92

hǫfum¹ *see* **hafa**
hǫfum² *see* **haf**
hǫgg *n.* blow I:17, 18, 33, III:106, V:98, IX:130, XXII:42/3; **annat hǫgg** with a second blow VII A:103; *dat. sg.* (*Gr* 3.1.7.3–5 ex. 4) **í ǫðru hǫggvi** with the second blow V:147; *gen. pl.* **hǫggva** V:146; *with suffixed def. art.* II:30, V:100
hǫggfœri *n.* striking distance, range (of a sword) I:139
hǫggormr *m.* poisonous snake, viper XXIII:66
hǫggva¹ (*pres.* **høggr**, *past* **hjó**, *past pl.* **hjoggu**, *pp.* **hǫggvit/hǫggit**) *sv.* (*Gr* 3.6.5.2, 3.6.9.3) strike III:56, 57, 72, 106, V:116, 122, 124, 125, 129, 147, VII A:24, XXVI A:17; strike with the edge of a weapon VII B:67, XXII:15/1, cut XXVI A:68; *with dat. of the weapon* VII A:102; cut, cut down V:27; **hǫggva á** strike (a blow) on XXVI B:153; **hǫggva af** cut off XXVI B:90; **hǫggva frá, hǫggva í frá** cut free, cut away (cf. line 169) VI:217, 227; **hjó í** hacked at XXI:151; **høggr með** with it strikes XXI:150; **hǫggva til** strike at I:138, III:85, V:98, 145, XXII:44/1; **hǫggva til manns** struck at a man XXVI B:152
hǫggva², hǫggvi *see* **hǫgg**
Hǫgni *m.* son of Gjúki, (half-)brother of Gunnarr XI:19, 23, 25, 37, 46, 50, 55, 66, 69, 75, XXV:21
hǫku *see* **haka**
hǫll (*gen.* **hallar**) *f.* hall I:3, IV:30 (*object of* **merkir**), XI:48; **himna hǫll** heaven XXII:2/2; *with suffixed def. art.* (*Gr* 3.1.9) I:79; *acc. sg. with suffixed def. art.* **hǫllina** II:5, XI:17, XVI:96, *gen. sg. with suffixed def. art.* **hallarinnar** I:46, *dat. sg.* **hǫllu** XXV:63; *dat. sg. with suffixed def. art.* **hǫllinni** I:23, 70, 89, XI:47, **hǫllunni** (*Gr* 3.1.7.4 (3)) I:28, *pl. with suffixed def. art.* **hallirnar** XI:14; **innan hallar** within your hall, *i.e.* in your household X:155
hǫnd (*gen. sg.* **handar,** *dat. sg.* **hendi,** *nom. pl.* **hendr,** *gen. pl.* **handa**) *f.* hand (*Gr* 3.1.7.2 (3)) I:6 (*with suffixed def. art.*), XII:28, 54, XIV:191 (*with suffixed def. art.*), XXII:35/3, XXIII:87, XXV:48, XXVI A:69; hand or arm XXII:15/3, XXV:88; arm XV:108 (*with suffixed def. art.*), XXII:50/2, XXVI A:52; **leggja hǫnd sína yfir** lay one's arm over (someone's shoulders) XI:47; **sú hǫndin** the one arm XV:123; **hendi** with his hand XXV:70, **hinni hendinni** in the other hand (cf. *Gr* 3.3.5) V:101; **Várar hendi** by the hand of Vár IX:122; **þinnar handar** on your part XVI:73; **hægri hǫnd** right hand (side) XXII:63/3; *pl.* **hendr** II:31 (*understand* **váru fastar**),

II:33 (= arms; *subject of* **munu slitna**), VII B:71 (*see* **fallask**); *dat. pl.* **hǫndum** arms (object of **orpit**) XXV:88, in her arms IV:65; **taka hǫndum** seize, take hold of XXVI A:11, capture X:15; **á hendi** on my arm XVI:182; **á hendi** *with dat.* into someone's hands *or* care XIV:174; **á hendi þeim Guði** into the hands of that God XIX:111; **ganga á hǫnd** *with dat.* submit to someone, join someone's band XXII:10/1; **á hendr** against XV:81; **sér á hǫndum** on his hands (arms) X:62; **af hendi sér** from his arm XVI:146; **þér af hǫndum** from your hands IX:116; **af hendi** *with gen.* on someone's part II:72; **henni í hǫnd** into her hand III:31; **tók í hǫnd honum** took him by the hand XVI:106; **í hǫnd þegar** on the spot XIV:118; **í hǫnd sér** in his hand XXVI B:219; **sér í hendi** in his/her hand XII:49, XXV:73; **í hendr** against *or* from XXI:195; **í hendi** (he had) in his/her hand III:29, 54, 95, V:29, VII A:160, XXI:50; **ór hendi** from, *i.e.* while held in, my hand V:40; **ór hǫndum honum** from his hands VII A:103; **komsk ór hǫndum þeim** escaped them XXVI A:91; **til handa henni** for her XV:10; **Guði til handa** into God's hands XXII:26/4; **undir hendi sér** under his arm XXVI B:152; **undir hennar hendi** in her hands, under her care XIV:188

hǫrð, hǫrðu, hǫrðum *see* **harðr**

Hǫrða-Kárason *m.* son of Hǫrða-Kári VIII:39

Hǫrða-Kári *m.* ninth-century Norwegian XIX:17

Hǫrn *f. a name for the goddess* Freyja; **Hǫrn húns** *is a kenning for* woman (= Steingerðr; playing board-games being conceived as one of the activities proper to a woman, cf. *SnE, Skáldskaparmál* ch. 31); *object of* **erum fúsir at finna** IV:33

hǫttr *m.* hat, hood (*Gr* 3.1.7.1 ex. 5, 3.1.7.2 (2)) V:29

Hǫttr (*gen.* **Hattar**) *m.* a farmer's son visiting Hleiðargarðr I:9, 11, 13, 21, 26, 29, 35, 36, 38, 73, 81, 87, 90, 99, 100, 107, 108, 123, 127, 129, 130, 134, 141, 146, 147; **vit Hǫttr** Hǫttr and I I:64; **þeir Hǫttr** he and Hǫttr I:70

hǫggr *see* **hǫggva**

høyra *see* **heyra**

í *prep.* (*Gr* 3.7.4) *with dat.* in, on I:7, 53, 69, 70, 94, 96, 98, 114, 125, II:1, III:74 (*with* **skálanum**), VI:290, 311, VIII:5, 14, IX:123, X:2, XI:2, XIX:3, 18, XXI:16, 104, XXII:3/2, 18/4, XXIII:2, XXIV:17, XXV:16, XXVI A:3, 22, B:68, XXVII:40; **í því** in this, as a result of this VI:220, at that moment XXVI A:16; dressed in III:28; of, from (a place) IV:107, VIII:184, XI:11; *with acc.* into I:32, 45, 84, 92, 139, II:5, 18, 39, 42 (*understand* **flýgr**), VI:256, IX:24, 84, X:5, XI:17, XV:9, XXI:169 (2), XXII:26/3 (*with* **skírnarbrunn**), 27/4, 49/4, 51/1, XXV:58, 89, XXVI A:15, B:230, XXVII:9, 15 (1), 18; to I:3, IV:3, V:158, VIII:92, IX:47, XI:3, 14, XV:50 (2), XVI:129, XXI:83, 88, 169; in, on II:7, 22, IX:121, X:85, XXII:62/2, XXVII:22; on I:29, V:89, XIX:6; onto XIX:71 (1), XXI:61; *of time*, at, on II:20, III:120, VIII:8, 16, 20, XII:38, XV:35; *as adv.* into it II:91, in it III:99, IV:11 (*Gr* 3.7.7), in them XV:50 (1), inside X:103, in the affair IV:101, in this matter V:135; **ok í** and in them XXI:156; **þar í** into it XIX:33; **er . . . í** in which II:40, IV:35, XIII:16, XXVII:5; **í brott** *see* **brott**; **í burt** *see* **burt**; **í frá** *see* **frá**, **ífrá**; **í gegn** *see* **gegn**²; **í gǫgnum** *see* **gǫgnum**; **í hjá** *see* **hjá**; **í mót, í móti** *see* **mót**²; **í meðal** *see* **meðal**; **í nánd** *see* **nánd**; **í sundr** *see* **sundr**

íð *f.* deed XXV:1

Iði *m.* a giant II:81

iðinn *adj.* diligent (**at því** in this) XIV:95

iðja¹ (*past* **iðjaði,** *pp.* **iðjat**) *wv.* do, be busy with I:111

iðja² *f.* activity, business XIV:135

iðjufullr *adj.* active, hard-working XXIII:2

iðna (*past* **iðnaði,** *pp.* **iðnat**) *wv.* work, do; **eigi væri nǫkkut iðnat í** some work was not done in, was not used for some work XIV:157

iðuliga *adv.* constantly XIII:46

Iðunn *f.* a goddess, one of the **Ásynjur**, wife of **Bragi** II:10, 50; *acc.* **Iðunni** II:38, 42; *gen.* **Iðunnar** II:43, 45, 52; *dat.* **Iðunni** II:35, 48

ifa (*past* **ifaði,** *pp.* **ifat**) *wv.* doubt, have doubts (**um** about) VII A:51 (*subj.*)

ifi *m.* doubt (**at hann væri eigi** as to whether he was not, *i.e.* of his being) VII A:44

ífrá, í frá *adv.* = **frá**; **segja ífrá** tell, narrate XIV:88; **vísa ífrá** *with dat.* refuse XXIV:54; **falla (í)frá** die XXIV:67, 71

íhuga (*past* **íhugaði,** *pp.* **íhugat**) *wv.* consider, wonder XVI:59; think about XII:87, XXI:145

íhugi *m.* concern; **var þeim inn mesti íhugi á honum** they were greatly worried by him I:72

il *f.* sole of the foot XXI:23

illa¹ *adv.* (*Gr* 3.5.2) badly *Gr* 3.5.3 (1), III:68 (*see* **líka**), VII A:97 (*see* **líka**), VII B:13 (*see* **duga**), XV:70 (*see* **líka**), XVI:147 (*see* **verða**);

badly, badly affected (**við** by) II:43, 107; **illa at þola** be badly affected XXVI B:121; **láta illa yfir** express disapproval of something IV:77, be dismayed by XIX:75; **mælask illa fyrir** be spoken ill of, be condemned XXVI A:119; wickedly XXVI A:87; with difficulty XXVI B:58, 60

illa² *see* **illr** (*Gr* 3.3.5 ex. 5)

illgerðir/illgjǫrðir *f. pl.* evil doings, deeds XXIII:27, 45, 73, 85

illgirni *f.* ill-nature, malice XXIII:49

illgjarn *adj.* malicious, ill-natured XXIII:73, 85, 104; *m. acc. sg.* an ill-natured person XXIII:91, 100

illiliga *adv.* horribly, hideously XXI:128

illiligr *adj.* evil-looking XXI:103

illmæli *n.* slander I:124 (**þat at** in which)

illr (*n.* **illt**) *adj.* (*Gr* 3.3.5 ex. 5, 3.3.8.3) bad I:52; evil XIV:82, XXIII:26 (*acc. pl. m.*); **þá er vár fǫr ill** then our journey will have turned out poorly (will have been wasted) XXVI B:50; **enn illi** the evil/wicked XXII:8/4; **þykkja illar** be displeased with (something) V:3 (*f. acc. pl.*); *n.* **illt** I:30 (dismal, dismayed), II:131 (poor), V:59, nasty, ugly (with **hár**) XXI:103; *n. as substantive* **illt** evil, harm I:31, IV:12, XXIII:74; **til ills** for poor reward, to poor advantage XIX:98; *n. as adv.* **illt er** it is bad IX:25, XXV:51; **vera illt til** *with gen.* something is difficult to obtain II:17, difficult to find XVI:138; **gjǫrðisk illt til matarins** food became difficult to find XXI:60; **varð ǫllum illt af** it made them all ill XXI:76

illúð *f.* evil intent X:103, 113

ilmr *m.* smell, scent XII:13, 19

Ilmr *f. name of a goddess used in kennings for females; in kenning for* valkyrie, **hjalmfaldin armleggjar orma Ilmr** helmeted lady of arm-rings V:22; *acc.* **Ilmi** *as a half-kenning (i.e. there is lacking the usual genitive of an attribute of a human being) for* Steingerðr IV:20

imbrudagahald *n.* the observance of Ember Days XXVII:29

ímóti *see* **mót²** (*Gr* 3.7, 3.7.3)

ímun/ímǫn *f.* battle XXII:33/2

in¹ *adv. with comp.* the (more) IX:100, 101, XV:55

in² *see* **inn²**

ina *see* **inn²**

Ingibjǫrg Sturludóttir *f.* III:21, 39, 40 (*dat.*, for Ingibjǫrg), 49

Ingólfr *m.* Icelandic settler VIII:15, 45, XIX:4, 18, 31, 38, 39, 42, 44, 47, 52, 54, 72, 74, 75, 79, 80, 83, 84, 87, 88, 94, 96, 100, 102, 104, 107

Ingólfsfell *n.* mountain in the south-west of Iceland VIII:19, XIX:91
Ingólfshǫfði *m.* headland in the south-east of Iceland VIII:17, XIX:54
Ingunn *f.* XIV:185
Ingunn Þórólfsdóttir *f.* mother of Þórðr XV:33, 124, 130, 133
Ingunnarstaðir *f. pl.* farm in Króksfjǫrðr, western Iceland; **á Inngunnar-stǫðum** (cf. *Gr* 3.1.8 ex.) XV:33
inir *see* **inn²**
inn¹ *adv.* in I:3, II:5, 56, 148, IV:20, VII A:150, B:64, IX:114, 120, X:33, 75, XI:17, XII:58, XXI:89, XXVI B:59, 81, 135; *i.e.* into the hall XVI:100, 102, 109; *i.e.* towards the shore VI:135, 136, VIII:97, XXI:52, 169, i.e. away from the open sea XXI:55, 83; inland XIX:60; inside XXVI B:165; **inn í** inside into XXVI B:215; **þar inn** into it (the **lopt**) XXVI B:117; **sem inn var gengit** where one went in, *i.e.* at the entrance XII:52
inn², enn *def. art.* = **hinn** (*Gr* 3.3.5) the *with following adj.* V:37, 52, 57, VI:270, VII B:37, 48, X:44, 55, XXII:20/4, 50/2, XXV:20, 45, 90, 99, XXVI B:19, XXVII:20; *with comp.* **inn fyrra** the first XXVII:44, **inn meiri** the greater XXVII:46; *with sup.* I:72, VII B:10, XI:58, 73; *with ordinal num.* VI:161, X:27, 28; **enn illi** the Wicked XXII:8/4, **inn mikli** the Great V:79, **enn langi** the Long VI:64, 66; **enn helgi** the Saint(ly) VIII:12, XIV:11, **enn digri** the Stout VIII:31, **enn hárfargi** the Fine-haired VIII:61; **flokk enn svarta** your black flock V:166; **kóngsins skáld it fríða** the handsome poet of the king XXII:19/2; *gen. sg. m.* **ens** VIII:7, 8, **ens mjóva** XIX:7, **ens gamla** XIX:107; *dat. sg. m.* **inum** II:152, III:86, **enum** VIII 74; *f.* **in** IX:102, 114, X:24, XXV:19, **en** X:9, XXVI B:92; *acc. sg. f.* **ina** IX:127, XXVI A:43, B:13; *dat. sg. f.* **inni** XXV:82; *n.* **it, et** I:81, II:28 (*with sup.*), IV:31, 63, VI:127, VIII:3, IX:60, XI:20, XXII:42/2, 62/3, XXIII:89 (*with sup.*), XXVII:5, 44; *dat. sg. n.* **inu** IX:73; *m. pl.* **enir** VIII:109; **inir mestu** very great XV:40; *acc. pl. m.* **ena** XXI:42, **enu** XXI:42, *textual note* (cf. C–V under *hinn*); *f. pl.* **inar** XXV:24; *n. pl.* **en** VI:190, **in** XI:7, XXV:2, 112, XXVII:33; *dat. pl.* III:51; **þetta it** this XI:5, **þetta et mikla skip** the large ship (*Gr* 3.3.5) VI:104, 125, **þat it mikla men** IX:50; **þræll minn inn bezti** my best servant (*Gr* 3.3.5) X:175; **ormi þeim inum f021 fup fránaga** to (those of) the glittering serpent X:83; **mæki þann enn snarpa** this sharp sword here XXII:15/4; *used in addressing an insult to someone* **in vánda kerling** you evil old woman IV:75
inna (*past* **innti**, *pp.* **innt**) *wv.* tell XXII:22/2; speak XXII:46/4; **þér**

innið you mean (or *imp.* speak: 'go a little further in your speech'?) XXII:32/2

innan *adv.* inside XIV:9; from inside, *i.e.* out (from behind the island) VI:136; *as prep. with gen.* (*Gr* 3.7.2) within X:155, XIV:142; inside XXV:87, **þar innan borðs** on board that ship VI:82; *of time* within VII A:55; **innan at** *with dat.* on the inner shore of, on the side (of the island) facing the mainland VI:58; **fyr/fyrir innan** *with acc.* inside II:60, IX:18, **fyrir innan fjǫrðu** round by the heads of the fjords XV:133, *see* **fyr innan**, **fyrir innan**

innar *adv. comp.* further in (away from the door) I:70, III:35

inni *adv.* inside, indoors III:14, IV:41, XXVI A:53, B:120; in his house VIII:50, XXVI A:55, B:64; in the house XXVI B:74; in their house XXVI B:104; **þar inni** inside it XII:14

innri *adv. comp.* inner; **et innra hús** the inside of the house IV:31

inu, inum *see* **inn²**

Írar *m. pl.* the Irish VII A:22 (along with **eyverskan her**, the object of **lét deyja**)

Írland *n.* Ireland VII A:6, 74, 91, 108, 109, XII:52, XIX:32, 35

írskr *adj.* Irish VIII:23, 24

Ísland *n.* Iceland VII A:132, 134, 146, VIII:7, 16, 20, 33, 35, 42, 56, 64, 73, 76, 144, 157, 158, 159, 168, XIV:8, XVI:119, 122, 123, 177, 190, XIX:27, 42, 47, 51, 52, 114

Íslandsferð *f.* journey to Iceland XVI:189, XIX:31, 43

Ísleifr Gizurarson¹ *m.* son of **Gizurr Þorvaldsson**; died in the fire at Flugumýrr III:74

Ísleifr Gizurarson² *m.* son of **Gizurr hvíti**, bishop 1056–80 VIII:9

Ísleifr Grímsson *m.* XIV:182

Ísleifr Hallsson *m.* XIV:169

Íslendingabók *f.* Book of the Icelanders VIII:1

Íslendingar *m. pl.* Icelanders VII A:133

íslenzkr *adj.* Icelandic (*Gr* 3.3.9 ex. 2) VII A:135, XVI:17, 62

Ísodd *f.* wife of Tristram XII:71, 75,

ístra *f.* paunch; *acc. with suffixed def. art.* **ístruna** my paunch XXI:177

Ísǫnd *f.* wife of King Markis, beloved of Tristram XII:22, 36, 38, 50, 51, 81, 86

it¹ *see* **inn²**

it² *pron. dual 2nd person* Gr 3.2.1, X:109, XVI:51 (i.e. Auðunn and the bear), 53; **it Vǫlundr** you and Vǫlundr X:179

Ívarr *m.* son of **Ragnarr Loðbrók** VIII:12

íviðgjarn *adj.* malicious (*with* **harma**?) X:133

íþrótt *f.* craft, art, skill II:86, XIV:20

íþróttamaðr *m.* skilled person XIV:22

já *adv.* yes I:127

jafn/jamn *adj.* equal, the same *Gr* 3.1.7.3, 3.3.8.4 (1); *acc. sg. m.* **jamnan** *with dat.* equal to XXIV:83; *n.* **jafnt viðr sik** justly proportioned? XXIII:52; *n. as adv.* **jafnt sem** just as IV:76

jafna (*past* **jafnaði**, *pp.* **jafnat**) *wv.* trim, cut to an even length IX:21

jafnan/jamnan *adv.* always XI:35, XII:80, XV:49, XXI:13, XXIV:29; constantly XXI:154; continually, repeatedly *Gr* 3.5.3 (2), I:53, XV:58; all the time XV:60, 85, XXII:4/3; generally I:76, XXVI A:58

jafnberr *adj.* so exposed (*i.e.* as now) I:33

jafnfjáðr *adj.* of equal means, of the same means XV:11

jafnfríðr *adj.* as beautiful, as fine; *n.* **jafnfrítt** VI:112

jafngóðr *adj.* as good; *acc. sg. m.* one (an emerald) as good XII:28

jafningi *m.* equal I:145

jafnlangt *adv.* as far XXIII:83

jafnmargr *adj.* equally many, the same number II:80, VII A:117; *pl.* **jafnmargir** of equal number, equal in number XXVII:14; *acc. pl. m.* **jafnmarga sér** the same number as themselves XIX:69

jafnmenni *n.* equal (in rank *or* status) XV:6

jafnmikit *adj. n. as subst.* as much, the same amount XXI:118

jafnsítt *adv. with dat.* as low as, at the same level as XII:16

jafnskjótt *adv.* immediately, at once VII B:67; **jafnskjótt sem** as soon as XXVI B:193

jafnskoruliga *adv.* as outstandingly, prominently, splendidly, boldly (**sem** as) XXVI B:101

jalda *f.* mare VII A:144 (*gen. with* **líki**)

jammaki (jafnmaki) *m.* equal XXIV:84

jamnan *see* jafnan *and* jafn

jamvel (jafnvel) *adv.* as well (**sem** as) XXIV:71

jarða (*past* **jarðaði**, *pp.* **jarðaðr**) *wv.* bury VII B:85

jarðar *see* jǫrð

jarðhús *n.* underground chamber XIX:32

jarknasteinn *m.* precious stone X:118, 162

jarl *m.* (in England) earl VII A:75, 92; (in Norway) ruler next in rank to a king VI:198, VII B:44 (*poss. dat. with* **á hæla**), VIII:147; =

Eiríkr jarl VI:55 (*subject of* **hafði um krafða**; *see note*), 236, 248;
ok jarl enn þriðja (*with* **vá við**, *parallel to* **jǫfra tvá**) and a jarl
(who was) the third VI:161; viceroy, subject ruler VI:34; *as title*
VI:24, 33, 40, 65, 103, 163, 217, 269, 275, 302, VII A:125, 169,
B:5, 8, XIX:6, 15; *with suffixed def. art.* **jarlenn** VI:73, 96, 100,
271, 272, 273, **jarlsins** XIX:10, **jarlenum** VI:298
járn *n.* iron; *pl.* weapons XXV:93
Járnbarðinn *m.* name of a ship (with an iron strengthening or
projection on the prow for ramming) VI:192, 228
járnstafr *m.* iron pole, iron staff VII A:160, XII:54
jarpr *adj.* brown, dark-brown, reddish brown XXV:72
jarpskammr *adj.* (*as subst.*) short (reddish) brown(-haired) one XXV:44
jartegn *f. or n.* sign, token VIII:155; miracle XIII:7 (*pl.*), 20
játa/játta (*past* **játti/játaði**) *wv. with dat. or acc.* agree (to something)
II:27, 125, III:20, VII A:66, B:20, VIII:137, XVI:36
Jóan (Jón) Qgmundarsonr *m.* bishop at Hólar 1106–1121 VIII:191
jóð *n.* child X:155
Johannes *m. Latin form of* **Jón** XIV:120
jók *see* **auka**
jól *n. pl.* **1.** feast; the wolf's feast is the carrion resulting from a battle;
'at the wolf's feast' *means therefore* 'in battle' V:51. **2.** Yule,
midwinter feast later identified with Christmas I:73
jólaaptann *m.* Yule-Eve, Christmas Eve I:82
Jóm *n.* a district in present-day Poland VI:24
Jón af Bakka *m.* one of the incendiaries at Flugumýrr, subsequently
(late January 1254) killed on his own farm III:2
Jón prestr Halldórsson *m.* III:93, 95
Jón svarti *m.* XIV:183
Jón Qgmundarson *m.* bishop at Hólar 1106–21 XIV:1, 5, 11, 13, 24,
47, 57, 140, 153, 169, 174; cf. **Johannes** XIV:120
Jónakr *m.* father of Hamðir and Sǫrli XXV:93
jór *m.* horse XV:12
jungfrú *f.* young lady, maiden XIV:185
júngr (= ungr) *adj.* young XXII:14/1
Júnii (Latin) *gen.* of June VIII:197
junkherra *m.* young lord, prince XI:54
jurtakyn *n. pl.* varieties of aromatic herbs XII:14
jǫfurr *m.* prince, ruler; *acc. sg.* (*object of* **vann**) VI:247, XXII:34/4;

dat. sg. **jǫfri** XXII:17/2; *nom. pl.* **jǫfrar** X:64; *acc. pl.* **jǫfra** kings VI:158

Jǫkulsdalr *m.* valley in eastern Iceland *Gr* 3.1.8 ex.

jǫldu *see* **jalda**

jǫrð *f.* earth, ground III:99, 100 (*with suffixed def. art.*), IX:28, 83, XXI:200; the earth XXIV:37; land VII A:23, XXII:53/3, *dat. sg.* **jǫrðu** XXII:37/4; a piece of ground XXVI A:104; *adv. gen. sg.* **jarðar** on earth IX:7; **til jarðar** to the ground I:98, V:96; *as second part of compound* **fjǫrðjǫrð** 'land of fjords', *i.e.* Norway, *separated by tmesis* VI:248

Jǫrð *f.* a goddess, personification of the earth, mother of Þórr IX:4

Jǫrmunrekkr *m.* (Ermanaric, Ostro-Gothic king, d. AD 375) XXV:11, 66, 70, 86, 89

Jǫtunheimar *m. pl.* giantland, the world of giants II:48, 49, IX:24, 47, 52, 80, 84, 105, 113

jǫtunn *m.* giant; *with suffixed def. art.* XII:6, 53; *as title* II:41, 50, 59, 61; *gen. sg.* IX:103, 126; *dat. sg.* **jǫtni** II:102, *dat. of respect* for the giant IX:90; *nom. pl.* **jǫtnar** VII A:161, IX:70, 86; *acc. pl.* IX:94 *gen. pl.* **jǫtna** II:82, 84, IX:18, 114

-k/-g *suffixed 1st person pron. with verbs* V:153, VIII:2, 4, XVI:63, 64; *duplicating* **ek** IX:12, X:93, 159, 183, 184, XVI:69; *duplicating* **ek** *and with suffixed neg.* VI:138, 246, IX:100, X:95, 97, 124, **vilkat ek** I do not want XXV:33

kaf *n.* plunge, dive; *with suffixed def. art.* **í kafit** under water VI:296

kafna (*past* **kafnaði,** *past pl.* **kǫfnuðu,** *pp.* **kafnat**) *wv.* become choked, suffocate II:100, III:78

kala (*pres.* **kell,** *past* **kól,** *past pl.* **kólu,** *pp.* **kalinn**) *sv. impers. with acc.* one gets very cold (frozen, frostbitten) III:62, X:145

kaldr *adj.* cold XXII:51/2; *f.* **kǫld** X:145; *n.* **kalt var** it was cold III:103; **svá var honum kalt orðit** he had become so cold III:126

kalendas *f. pl.* (Latin word) kalends, the first day of a month VIII:197

kálfr *m.* calf; *as nickname* VII B:7

Kálfr Árnason *m.* XXII:8/4, 9/1, 29/1, 52/1 (see note 2; but at 52/1 it may be **Kálfr Arnfinnsson** that is referred to, see *ÍF* XXVII 385, note 2)

Kálfr Brandsson *m.* III:129

Kálfr illviti (the Ill-willed) *m.* enemy of Bjǫrn Hítdœlakappi V:60, 85, 93, 105, 129, 158, 162

kalla (*past* **kallaði,** *past pl.* **kǫlluðu/kallaðu,** *pp.* **kallaðr/kallat** *Gr* 3.3.8.4 (2)) *wv.* (*Gr* 3.6.6) **1.** call I:59, II:82, 86, 95, VI:126, VII A:37, VIII:21, IX:66, XXI:28 (2), 45, call him XXII:18/2 (*Gr* 3.9.5.1); call out II:33, X:66, XI:43; shout XI:132; declare XIV:91; **kallaðu svá at** they claimed that XXIV:35; **sem er at kalla** such as to call it (a day) XIV:81; **kalla á** call out to X:110, XXVI B:155, call on, invoke XXIV:45; declare (something *or* someone to be) I:88, II:131, VII A:136, XIX:56; *pres. 1st pl.* **kǫllum** II:83, 116, 160; *past 3rd pl.* **ok kǫlluðu** and they called it/them (*Gr* 3.9.5.1) XXI:24, 28 (1), 34, **kǫlluðu þar** called that place XXI:33; *imp. pl.* **kallið** summon I:55; *pp.* **er/es/var/ váru kallaðr/kǫlluð/kallat** is/was known as II:2, III:128, IV:107, VIII:18, 30, 37, 49, 52, XV:153, is called XIV:90; **svá verit kallaða** been called that XV:54; **þetta er kǫlluð** this is called XXV:112 (*verb in agreement with complement; see Gr* 3.9.8.2); **ok þá var kallat** and (which) then (thereafter) was called XIX:27; **er síðan kǫlluð** has since been called XXVI B:230; **síðan var hann kallaðr** after that he was known as XIX:35; **Þórhallr var kallaðr** a certain Þórhallr was known as XXI:9; **kallaðar, kallaðr** said to be XXIII:94, XXVI A:57; *impers.* **kalla má** one may say XXVI B:13. **2. -sk** *form* **kallask** is called XXIII:96; **kallaðisk** claimed that she, declared that she VI:19

kann *see* **kunna**

kanna (*past* **kannaði**) *wv.* investigate, explore VIII:42, XXI:22

kappi *m.* man of valour, fighting man VII A:76; warrior, champion I:29, 45, 77, 146

kappmæli *n. pl.* dispute; **þreyta kappmæli** enter into a dispute, start to argue VII B:28

kappsamligr *adj.* provocative, rash V:160

kapulánn *m.* chaplain XIV:155

Káragróf *f.* 'Kári's pit *or* hollow' XXVI B:231

Kári Sǫlmundarson *m.* Njáll's son-in-law XXVI B:46, 76, 78, 81, 85, 92, 96, 193, 202, 208, 213, 219, 221, 228

karl *m.* (old) fellow, churl IV:41; man, male XIV:145, XV:60

Karli *m.* slave XIX:72, 92, 98, 103

karlkona *f.* masculine woman XV:70

karlmaðr *m.* man V:114; male XIV:84, XV:61, XI:39, XXIII:1

karlmannligr *adj.* manly; **karlmannligt mark** a sign of manliness XXIII:52

Karlsefni *n.* = Þorfinnr (*m.*) karlsefni Þórðarson XXI:2, 3, 17, 41, 50,

66, 74, 86, 98, 114, 119, 126, 129, 143, 163, 166, 172, 190, 197, 199; **af Karlsefni** of Karlsefni's troop XXI:144. The name, originally a nickname, means 'the makings of a man', a promising lad

Karlshafuð *n.* (Eiríksson), one of Óláfr Tryggvason's followers VI:300

kasta (*past* **kastaði,** *past pl.* **kǫstuðu,** *pp.* **kastat**) *wv. with dat.* throw (*Gr* 3.6.9.1 (7)) I:35, 43, 92, II:74 (*understand* them, the eyes *as object* (*Gr* 3.9.5.1)), II:128, XIX:58, XXI:80, 152, XXII:35/4 (*impers. pass.*), XXVI A:70, B:144, 220; cast (anchor) XXI:47; throw overboard XV:147; put aside, reject, apostatise from VII A:125; cast off (*imp.*) XXII:25/3; throw off XXVI B:151; lay aside XVI:97; **kasta sér** throw oneself XXVI B:229

kastali *m.* castle, fortress I:46 (*with suffixed def. art.*), XII:70

katlar *see* **ketill**

Katli *see* **Ketill**

kátr *adj.* cheerful, merry, full of good cheer XI:60, 69

kaup *n.* bargain, agreement II:140; payment, reward (**til** for it) I:121; wages, salary XIV:18 (*with suffixed def. art.*), 29; **sér til kaups** as his payment II:134

kaupa (*past* **keypti,** *pp.* **keypt**) *wv.* (*Gr* 3.6.9.3) buy II:127, XV:10, XVI:11, XXI:113; **keyptak** I bought XVI:64; **sem þú keyptir** as you bought it for XVI:22; **kaupa at** make a bargain with VIII:118

kaupmaðr (*pl.* **kaupmenn**) *m.* merchant *Gr* 3.1.9 ex.14

kaupstefna *f.* market, trading XXI:113

kaus *see* **kjósa**

keiplabrot *n. pl.* pieces of (small) boats VIII:69

keipr *m.* small boat, canoe; = **húðkeipr** XXI:120 (*with suffixed def. art.*)

kell *see* **kala**

kem, kemr, kemsk *see* **koma**

kenna (*past* **ken(n)di,** *pp.* **ken(n)dr**) *wv.* **1.** *with acc. and dat.* teach II:94, XIV:20, 26, 154, 186, XXI:201, XXV:51; preach VIII:78; **kennir** (he *or* it) teaches, shows XIV:90, *note.* **2.** perceive, feel III:112; *impers. with gen.* **þar sem holta kenndi** where ridges could be seen XXI:91. **3.** recognise I:136, V:85, VI:79, 289, VII A:113 (*understand* them *as object, Gr* 3.9.5.1), 119, XVI:105, XXI:75; know XVI:59, XXI:74; **-sk** *form* **kendiz ei** there was not found XXII:40/3. **4.** *with acc. and dat.* impute to, accuse of, blame on XII:89. **5.** denote, refer to (**þá** them; **með** by) XXIV:74; **kenndr** called, known as XXII:43/3; **kenna við** name after VIII:52, XIX:86, 101, XXII:19/1

kennimaðr *m.* teacher XIV:175; *pl.* **kennimenn** clerics, clergymen VIII:179, XIV:165, 182

kenning *f.* teaching, preaching; *pl.* XIV:31, 35, 36, 39, 151

kennir *m.* one who knows, experiences, deals in (*with gen.*), *in kenning for* man (here = the poet, Hallfrøðr) **kennir auðar** VI:351 (*dat. with* **segir**)

keppa (*past* **keppti**, *pp.* **keppt**) *wv.* contend, compete; **-sk** *form in reciprocal sense* contend with each other VII A:98

ker *n.* vat II:90, 97, 157, III:99; *with suffixed def. art.* III:101, 109; **þar í kerit** into that cask III:102; *pl. with suffixed def. art.* **kerin** II:97, 158; cup, goblet XII:49, 50 (*with suffixed def. art.*), XXV:73

kerling *f.* old woman (*Gr* 3.1.8 (14)) IV:75

Ketilbjǫrn (Gizurarson) *m.* son of Gizurr Þorvaldsson; died in the fire at Flugumýrr III:74

Ketilbjǫrn (Ketilsson) *m.* Icelandic settler VIII:80

ketill (*pl.* **katlar**) *m.* pot (*Gr* 3.1.7.2 ex. 4, 3.1.8 (3)) II:97

Ketill kálfr *m.* of Hringunes (modern Ringnes) in Norway VII B:7

Ketill ór Mǫrk *m.* son-in-law of Njáll and one of the burners; son of Sigfúss Sighvatsson, brother of Þráinn Sigfússon XXVI B:184, 186

Ketill sútari (cobbler) *m.* died in the fire at Flugumýrr III:76

Ketill (*dat.* **Katli**) **Þorsteinsson** *m.* 1074/75–1145, bishop at Hólar 1122–45; married to Gróa, daughter of Bishop Gizurr Ísleifsson VIII:1, XIV:177

keyptak, keypti *see* **kaupa**

keyra (*past* **keyrði**, *pp.* **keyrt**) *wv.* drive; *impers.* **keyrir skipit** the ship was driven XV:145

Kíarr *m.* legendary king (perhaps = Caesar) X:9, 74

kinnhestr *m.* blow *or* slap on the cheek XV:21, XXVI A:83 (*with suffixed def. art.*)

kinn (*pl.* **kinnr**) *f.* cheek XXI:104 (*with suffixed def. art.*), XXIII:22, 48

kippa (*past* **kippti**, *pp.* **kippt**) *wv. with dat.* snatch, pull quickly I:69, III:60, XXVI B:184

kirkja *f.* church XIII:1, XIV:6, 61; **til kirkju** to the church III:46, 50, 122, to church XVI:94; *with suffixed def. art.* III:83, 84, 86 (*i.e.* the wall of the church), XIII:4; *gen. sg. with suffixed def. art.* III:61

kirkjudyrr *m. pl.* church-entrance XIV:25

kirkjugarðr *m.* churchyard XIV:152

kirkjugjǫrð *f.* building of a church XIV:14

kirkjuskot *n.* recess in the side of a church XVI:93

kista *f.* chest, box X:102, 112

kjafal *m.* a kind of tunic (cf. Old Irish *cabhail* 'body of a shirt') or hooded cloak (Old Irish *cochall*) XXI:45 (see note)

Kjalarey *f.* island in Breiðafjǫrðr XV:153

Kjalarnes[1] *n.* promontory north of Reykjavík in the south-west of Iceland VIII:45, XIX:108

Kjalarnes[2] *n.* promontory in North America XXI:33, 167

kjósa (*pres.* **kýss,** *past* **kaus/køri,** *past pl.* **køru,** *pp.* **kørit/kosit**) *sv.* (*Gr* 3.6.9.3 and ex. 11) choose (**sér** for oneself) II:63, 64 (**at** by), II:66, III:19, VII A:80, 88, XXVI A:12; **kjósa yðr mat** choose food for yourselves XXVI B:20; *inf. with* **myndir þú** IV:91 (**þér** for yourself; **at** as); **kaustu** you have chosen IV:97; **mundum sízt til kjósa** would least have chosen (to be killed) XXVI B:99; *past subj.* **køri** might choose III:42; *pp.* **undarliga kosit** a strange thing to choose, a strange choice XVI:120

kjǫlr *m.* keel XXI:33, XXVI A:94; *with suffixed def. art.* XV:151, 152

Kjǫlr *m.* area in central Iceland XXVI A:96

kjǫt *n.* flesh; *dat. sg.* with flesh XXIII:79

kjǫtmikill *adj.* fleshy; *f. pl.* **kjǫtmiklar** fleshy ones (cheeks) XIII:93

kjǫtsfullr *adj.* full of meat, meaty, fleshy XXIII:54, 94

kjør *n.* choice (**af** from what was available) VII A:78

klakklaust *adv.* without harm, unscathed XVI:35

klámhǫgg *n.* obscene blow, shaming blow, a blow in the rear; *dat. sg. (instrumental)* **klámhǫggvi** V:126 (*see note*)

klefi *m.* small room, closet (often apparently a partitioned-off alcove of a larger room, used for sleeping or storage; here presumably the same as the **lopt**) III:76 (*with suffixed def. art.*)

klerkr *m.* cleric, scholar XIV:27, 175

Klifsandr *m.* an area of sand in Hítardalr west of Hítará V:78, 163, 168

Klifsdalr *m.* valley between Hellisdalr and Hítardalr V:75

Klifsjǫrvi *m.* a sandbank in Hítardalr west of Hítará V:78

kló *f.* claw; *dat. pl.* **klóm** II:51

klofna (*past* **klofnaði,** *pp.* **klofnaðr**) *wv. intransitive* split XXVI A:74

klókr *adj.* clever, skilful XXII:40/3

klóra (*past* **klóraði,** *pp.* **klóraðr**) *wv. with dat.* scratch XXI:68

klyfjaðr *adj. (pp.)* pack-saddled *Gr* 3.3.9 ex. 19

klýpa (*past* **klýpti,** *pp.* **klýpt**), *wv.* pinch XXI:68

klæða (*past* **klæddi,** *pp.* **klæddr**) *wv.* dress; *pp.* **klæddr** clothed, clad XII:24, 30; **-sk** *form* **klæddiz** clothed himself XXII:30/1

klæði *n.* cloth XXI:113; article of clothing XXI:44; *in pl.* clothes III:127, VII A:81, XVI:113, XXI:205; **klæðin ǫll á Kára** all the clothes Kári had on XXVI B:221

klækiligr *adj.* lewd, indecent XIV:84

klækishǫgg *n.* shameful blow, base blow V:123

Klœngr Þorsteinsson *m.* bishop at Skálaholt 1152–76 XIV:88, 173

kná (*past* **knátti**) *wv.* can; *past subj.* **knætta** could XXV:74

knappr *m.* button XXI:46

knarrasmiðr *m.* 'ship-builder', nickname (*see* **knǫrr**) XXII:43/3

kné *n.* knee (*Gr* 3.1.7.5 (2), (3), 3.1.8 (29)) II:71, III:57, IX:62, XXII:21/1; *acc., object of* **sníða** XXII:49/1; *dat. sg. with suffixed def. art.* **knénu** XXIII:97; *pl.* lap IX:121; *gen. pl.* **knjá** XIX:83; *dat. pl.* **í knjám henni** on her lap XIII:3; **hann stóð á knjám** he was down on his knees V:130, **svá at hann stóð á knjám** while still down on his knees V:142

kneppa (*past* **kneppti,** *pp.* **kneppt**) *wv.* fasten, button; *pp.* **ok kneppt** and it was buttoned XXI:46

knésfótr *m.* the back of the knee X:86

knoða (*past* **knoðaði,** *pp.* **knoðat**) *wv.* knead XIX:56

knúði *see* **knýja**

knúta *f.* knuckle-bone I:39; *with suffixed def. art.* I:42

Knútr *m.* brother of Auðr XV:81

knýja (*past* **knúði,** *pp.* **knúinn**) *sv.* drive forward, force onward XV:99

knætta *see* **kná**

knǫrr *m.* (merchant) ship XVI:172

knǫttr *m.* ball XXI:127

kóðu *see* **kveða**

kol *n.* coal, charcoal; cinders, ashes XXI:111

kól *see* **kala**

Kolbeinn grǫn (moustache) **Dufgusson** *m.* died January, 1254 III:15, 16, 20, 40, 42, 49, 70, 71, 107

Kolbjǫrn *m.* Óláfr Tryggvason's marshal VI:291, 295

Kolbjǫrn (veljungr) *m.* died in the fire at Flugumýrr III:75

Kolbrún *f.* = Þorbjǫrg kolbrún Glúmsdóttir XXII:19/1. She lived in the Western Fjords of Iceland. Her nickname **kolbrún** ('coal-brow') is from her black hair and eyebrows

Kolli inn prúði (the Splendid, the Elegant) *m.* supposed to be son of Bjǫrn Hítdœlakappi's enemy Þórðr Kolbeinsson V:86, 93, 103, 133, 134, 139, 141

kollóttr *adj.* bald XVI:91

Kolr *m.* a slave in 10th-century Iceland VIII:51

Kolr Þorsteinsson *m.* one of the burners XXVI B:114

Kolsgjá *f.* 'Kol's Rift', a ravine or small gorge, possibly at Þingvǫllr VIII:52 (see Björn Þorsteinsson, *Thingvellir. Iceland's National Shrine*, tr. Peter Foote (1987), 37)

koma (*pres.* **kemr/kømr,** *past* **kom,** *past pl.* **kómu/kvámu,** *pp.* **kominn,** *n.* **komit,** *m. pl.* **komnir** *Gr* 3.3.9 (7)) *sv.* **1.** come (*Gr* 3.6.9.3 and ex. 12) I:1, 6, 74, 78, 115, 139, II:18, 38, 41, 52, III:21, IV:6, V:119, VI:5, 14 (*pp. f.* **komin**), 230, VIII:18, 88, 95 (**kvámu** they used to come), 103, IX:17, 18, X:40, XI:17, 43, XIII:4, XV:9, 25, XVI:14, XIX:57, XXI:14, XXII:27/1, 43/4, XXV:19, 95, XXVI A:52, B:5, 24, XXVII:28; *of time*, arrive I:82; *imp.* **kom** come XVI:39; *imp. pl.* **komið** come X:106; *pres. subj.* **komir** come XI:72; *past* **kom** it went XXVI A:18; *2nd sg. past* **komst** I:144; *past subj.* **kœmi/kvæmi** came III:114, VI:45, VIII:73, XVI:87, XIX:54, should come XIV:142, should go V:158; *pp.* **em kominn** have come XVI:62, **var komit** was come, had arrived XVI:17, **sé kominn** is come I:46, **mun kominn** must be come XXVI B:15; *pp. m. pl.* **komnir** come, reached V:163, arrived XXV:68; **koma á** hit, strike V:96, 99, land on I:18 (*supine*), get on to VI:272; **kom á** it struck XXVI A:49, it struck/hit him on III:85, XV:108; **ei fær tǫlu á komit** one cannot put a number on them, they cannot be numbered XI:12; **koma á, koma á leið** *with dat.* bring about, arrange IV:72, VII B:58 (*impers. pass., Gr* 3.9.3), XII:69; **koma á flótta** take to flight VI:155; **koma á óvart** *with dat.* take someone by surprise XXVI A:7; **kvámu áðr** had already come VIII:108; **koma af** abolish XIV:87; **því hafði eigi orðit af komit með ǫllu** that had not been entirely abolished XIV:78; **koma aptr** come back XXI:43, **kvámu eigi aptr** did not return X:12; **koma at** reach, get hold of II:122, IX:131, arrive, come up III:2, IV:11, come to IV:52, approach, come up to XIX:17, get up to, reach XXI:141; get to IV:10, V:93, VI:274 (**var komnir**: *vb. sg. in agreement with first part of a subject placed after the vb., see Gr* 3.9.8.2), XIX:83, get into I:128 (*pp. f.* **komin**); **vér kómum at** we came here XXVI B:10; **er þeir kómu/kvámu at** when they got there (to Gunnarr's home) XXVI A:26, where they came ashore XXI:31; **þá kom Flosi at** then Flosi came up XXVI B:153; **komnar at** come there XXVI B:5; **kæmi** (*past subj.*)

hlíf at gagni that his shield was of use, was any help (to him)
XXII:40/4; **kom at þeim ǫrunum** got at them with arrows XXVI
A:39; **koma eptir** follow VII A:111; **komnir frá** descended from
VIII:38; **var kominn frá** was descended from XVI:191; **koma fram**
come about, happen XXVI B:79; **ok vera eigi fram komna** and
that they have not (yet) taken place, not yet happened, not yet
brought into effect XXIII:26; **koma því fram at** bring it about that
VIII:156; **koma fyrir/firir** come before, reach I:45; come into the
presence of XVI:18; **koma skildi fyrir sik** bring one's shield in
front of one XXVI A:72; **koma heim** approach the house XXVI
B:87, get back home XIX:8; **koma í** arrive at VII A:9, 28, X:5, get
into III:61, hit XXVI B:152; **koma í stað** take his place XXIV:70;
koma með *with acc.* bring V:53, XXII:54/1; **koma niðr** *with dat.*
put down XXI:55; **þar er niðr kom** where it came down XXI:128;
koma nær *with dat.* approach XIII:17; **koma ofan** land III:45; **kom
ofan í** came down onto (i.e. the top of his shield) XXVI B:91; **koma
ór** escape from VI:338, 348 (*inf. with* **myndi**), **vera kominn ór** to
have escaped from VI:338, **eða [frá hánum] brott of komnum**
(*pp. dat. sg. m.*) **ór** or about him having escaped from, or that he
had escaped from VI:354, **komit ór** (which had) flowed from
XXV:84; **koma saman viðr** meet near (*or* meet with?) XXIII:18;
komnir saman assembled VI:28; **koma til** arrive, come up V:113,
be born XXI:196, reach VI:11, XIX:73, attend VII A:72, be required
by, concern XIV:116; **kvámu til** came for it, prescribed (i.e. in
accordance with his instructions) VIII:185; **ok til þess er kominn
at** and (who) has reached a position where he deserves to, and (who)
deserves to XXIV:61; **vel kominn** welcome XI:9, 70, XVI:107; **ek
kem boganum við** I can make use of my bow against them XXVI
A:82; **sér við koma** employ himself for, involve himself in XIV:31;
koma þar arrive there XXVI B:41. **2.** *impers.* **þar kom at, kom
þar at** it came to this that, the outcome was that IV:101, XXVI
A:91, it reached the point where VI:213; **honum fyrir allt eitt koma**
it would all come to the same thing for him V:106; **kom svá** it came
about, it turned out, came to the point (that) VII B:13, 28, 58; **var
komit** it was come (*or* [people] had arrived) IX:93; **of kvæmi við**
with dat. were brought concerning it, it was prosecuted using
(witnesses) VIII:142. **3.** *with dat.* bring II:35, VII A:128, introduce
VIII:76, lead VII A:50, get (someone somewhere) III:63; *pp.
(impers. pass.)* **komit** would be brought VIII:124; **honum var svá**

nær komit it was such a close thing for him, it so nearly happened for him II:158; **koma sér** get oneself VI:296. **4. -sk** *form* manage to come, get I:34, III:24 (**fram** out, *i.e.* towards the door), V:79, 110 (*pres. subj.*), XVI:34, 148, XXVI B:85 (*pres. subj.*), 204; **komisk vel út** may easily get out XXVI B:208; **er komask mátti** that it was possible to take VII A:130; **komsk eigi** could not get V:97; **komask at** *with dat.* get up to, get at XXVI A:64, gain possession of, win VI:248; **komask fyrir** reach, be revealed to, become known to I:50; **komask í** manage to get into III:87, 101; **komask inn í** get into XXI:89; **komsk ór hǫndum þeim** escaped them XXVI A:90; **komask til** (manage to) reach III:46, manage to get to IV:65; **kvæmisk** (*past subj.*) **til leiðar** should be able to come about, should be brought about XVI:49; **komsk undan** got away XXI:200; **komask við** be touched *or* moved XIV:37; *pp.* **komizk** got V:97; **fá eigi komizk** do not manage to get XVI:34

kompása (*past* **kompásaði**, *pp.* **kompásaðr**) *wv.* accomplish, complete XII:3

kómu *see* **koma**

kona (*gen. pl.* **kvenna**) *f.* woman III:127, IV:1, VII A:90, 95, VIII:33, IX:96, X:6, XIV:90, *note*, 145, XV:6, 11, 23, 59, 61, 133, XIX:11, XXIII:2, 61, XXVI B:141; wife II:103, 106, III:7, V:5, VI:2, VII B:77, X:119, XII:71, XV:38, 49; lady XI:49; female XIV:84, XXI:39; *with suffixed def. art.* VI:4; *pl.* **konur** women, wives XIX:70, 87, XXVI B:5, 114, 134; **ok tvær konur** and two were women XXI:199

konar *m. gen. sg. in phrase* **nakkvars konar** some kind of (*i.e.* some term for) II:118; **þess konar** of that kind, of the same kind VIII:70, that kind of XIV:22; **alls konar** all kinds of XI:60, XII:25, 32, XXI:57

kóngr *m.* = **konungr** XXII:1/1

konungaævi *n. pl.* lives of kings VIII:4

konungr *m.* king, the king I:1, 2, 47, 57, 60, 62, 66, 77, 82, 86, 112, 114, 116, 117, 119, 128, 135, 141, 144, VI:51, 105, 198, 264, VII A:35, 137, B:22 (*subject of* **vill bjóða**), 27, 51, 54, VIII:29, 32, X:2, XI:48, XVI:15, XIX:48, XXI:38, 202, XXIV:1; *as title* I:45, 50, 106, 132, V:57, VI:3, 6, 7, 15, 38, 142, 215, VII A:1, 146, B:3, 4, 7, 11, 12, 35, 85, 86, X:8, 14, 78, XI:14, XVI:14, XXI:37; *in address, as vocative* I:134; *with suffixed def. art.* I:80, VI:9, 45, 136 (*gen. pl.*), 289, 291, 292, 297, 323, VII B:66, VIII:26, 84, XXIV:6; *dat. sg.* **konungi** to the king XVI:50, for the king X:87

konungsdóttir *f.* king's daughter, princess VII A:91

konungsgarðr *m.* king's premises, residence, palace VII B:59, 78

konungsmenn *m. pl.* the king's men VII B:70

koparr *m.* copper XII:41, 59

Kormakr (Ǫgmundarson) *m.* IV:5, 6, 8, 10, 11, 14, 16, 26, 35, 38, 47, 49, 52, 62, 67, 68, 75, 76, 77, 87, 97, 99, 100, 101, 110

Kormakr bryti (steward, bailiff) *m.* died in the fire at Flugumýrr III:76

kóróna *f.* crown XII:25

kórr *m.* choir, chancel; **í kórinn** from in the chancel XIV:162

kosit *see* **kjósa**

kosta (*past* **kostaði,** *pp.* **kostat**) *wv.* put forth effort; **kosta rásar** run at great speed XXI:180

kostgæfi *f.* care, concern XIV:97

kostr *m.* opportunity, chance VI:90, XIV:45, XVI:185, XXVI B:212; choice, alternative XXVI B:102; **gera kost** *with dat.* give someone a choice XXVI A:11; charge, expense XIV:147; *pl.* qualities: **gott land kostum** a land with fine qualities XXI:177; terms (of marriage agreement) XV:5

Kotkell *m.* a Hebridean XV:37, 38, 126, 134, 139, 142; *dat.* **Kotkatli** XV:135

krafða *see* **krefja**

kraptlauss *adj.* lacking strength XXIII:29

kraptr *m.* strength, power XXIII:75, 107

krás *f.* delicacy, dainty IX:96

krefja (*past* **krafði,** *past pl.* **krǫfðu,** *pp.* **krafðr**) *wv.* (*Gr* 3.6.6) *with gen. and acc.* demand (something from someone/something) X:102,112; order, summon (ships to a rendezvous), *pp.* **um krafða** *in agreement with direct obj.* (**hreina,** *acc. pl.*) VI:55 (*Gr* 3.9.7.1)

krellr *m.* strength, spirit, valour I:124

kringlóttr *adj.* round, circular XXIII:14, 46

kristinn *adj.* Christian VII A:64, 71, XIV:60; *n.* **kristit** VII A:71; *m. pl.* **kristnir** VIII:21, 139; XIX:112, XXVI B:105; *wk. pl.* **kristnu** VIII:114, 116

kristna (*past* **kristnaði,** *pp.* **kristnat**) *wv.* convert (to Christianity) XXII:4/1

kristni *f.* Christianity VII A:126, VIII:73, 76, 78, 85, 144, XIV:2, 30, 74, 125, XIX:113, XXI:38; *with suffixed def. art.* VIII:90, 117, XIV:79, 176

Kristr *m.* Christ VIII:14, 149, XXI:78, XXII:62/3

Króksfjǫrðr *m.* fjord in north-western Iceland XV:33
kroppinskeggi *m.* a nickname, 'crop-beard'? 'crooked beard'? VIII:48, 49
kroppr *m.* body II:30 (*with suffixed def. art.*), II:31
kross *m.* cross, crucifix XIV:61
krǫfðu *see* **krefja**
kulði *m.* cold(ness) III:62, 114, 130
kumrskr *adj.* Cumbrian VII A:26
kunna (*pres.* **kann,** *past* **kunni**) *pret.-pres. vb.* know (*Gr* 3.6.7) II:93,
    X:154, XIV:68, XV:21 (**at** in it), 27, XXI:74; know to be VIII:9;
    know how to II:161, VII B:38, X:92, *with suffixed pron.* X:183; be
    able, can XI:34, XXIV:28, XXVI B:7, 53; respond: **kunna illa** be
    distressed II:106; feel XVI:75; **kunni** could XII:9; **hann betr kunni**
    he was wilier (than she) X:130; **kann vera at, vera kann at** maybe
    V:72, XXI:100; **kann þat vera at** it may be that XVI:40; **Nú kann
    svá til at bera at** If it should happen that XXIV:1; **ef svá kann til at
    verða at** if it should come about that XXIV:7; *subj.* **kunnim eigi**
    are not able V:104; **kynni** knew how to, was able II:101, might be
    able to VII A:147; **kann ek eigi margt at** I take little notice of (do
    not greatly understand? am not greatly bothered by?) VI:357; **kunna
    vel til** have good knowledge of, good understanding of VII B:26;
    kunna at *with inf.* be able to, can XII:11, 63, **kunnu sér at vera**
    knew how to be, were sensible enough to be XIV:163
kunnasta *f.* ability; *acc.* **kunnustu** (*Gr* 3.1.7.1) XVI:135
kunnigr *adj.* cunning X:119, 139, 163; knowledgeable, skilled in
    magic; *dat. sg. m.* **kunngum** VII A:146; familiar: **honum var víða
    kunnigt** he had knowledge of many places, he was widely experienced
    XXI:16
kunningi *m.* acquaintance; *acc. pl.* **kunningja** I:31
kunnr *adj.* (well) known, renowned X:74; *comp.* better known VIII:4
kurteiss *adj.* courtly XI:49
kvað *see* **kveða**
kvaddi *see* **kveðja**
kváðu *see* **kveða**
kváma *f.* coming, visit IV:3, XXV:86; **leggja kvámur sínar** direct
    one's visits IV:98
kvámu *see* **koma**
kván *f.* wife IX:43, 87, X:40, 139, 152, 154, 163
kvánfang *n.* marriage XVIII:122rb31

kvángaðr *adj. (pp.)* married XXI:196

kvánlauss *adj.* without a wife, unmarried XXI:195

kváran Irish surname; *cúarán* (*m.*) in Old Irish means a shoe or sock VII A:74

Kvasir *m.* a wise being created by the gods II:92, 100, 117

kvaz, kvazk *see* **kveða**

kveða (*pres.* **kveðr**, *past* **kvað**, *past pl.* **kváðu/kóðu**, *pp.* **kveðinn**) *sv.* **1.** cry out I:14. **2.** say, declare, speak, utter, express (especially in verse) I:91, IV:17, 26, 77, 87, V:16, 148, VI:137, 258, 341, 350, VII B:36, VIII:100, 121, 132, IX:5, 13, X:80, 90, 125, 134, XII:38, XIV:86, XXV:20; compose and deliver (a poem) XXII:*heading*; speak aloud, recite XXI:182; chant XV:143; *with acc. and inf.* (*Gr* 3.9.4) III:42, 92, 123, IV:5 (*inf. understood*), 11, 14, V:6, 9, 105, VI:337, VIII:67, 93, XV:21, 85, XXI:69, **kváðu þar engi hús** said there were no houses there XXI:204, **(menn) kváðu, kóðu** they said VI:176, 242, XXV:52, **kvað mik** (*inf. understood*) said I would be XVI:176, **kvað svá vera skyldu** said so it should be XXVI B:18, 81; **kveða á** give orders XXVI A:107; **var kveðit á** it was determined (to be), stipulated as, agreed to for XVI:7; **kveða af** summon from IV:12; **kveða svá at orði** utter this, express oneself thus XXIV:9; **er at oss kveðinn** has been allotted to us XXVI B:187; **kveða um** relate X:15; **kvað við** cried out (at it), howled at it XXVI A:18. **3.** *refl. pres.* **kvezk** says that he II:136, IV:68, XVI:21, 47, 116, XXI:70, *past* **kvazk, kvaz** said that he/she II:23, 47, 135, III:33, V:7, 8, 158, VII A:38, XV:6, 51, 115, XXV:45, said he was XV:113, XXVI B:129, 155; **eigi kvazk hann hafa** he said he had never III:10; **kváðusk** said that they II:127, said they were XXVI B:5; *reciprocal* **kveðask at** exchange verses, recite verses to each other XIV:83

kveðja[1] (*pres.* **kveðr**, *past* **kvaddi**, *past pl.* **kvǫddu**, *pp.* **kvatt**) *wv.* **1.** greet, salute I:57, XVI:18, 157, XXII:21/2. **2.** *with gen.* summon, convoke VII A:79 (*impers. pass.*, *Gr* 3.9.3)

kveðja[2] *f.* greeting, salutation XVI:19, 158

kveld *n.* evening XI:59, XV:25; *with suffixed def. art.* (*Gr* 3.1.9) II: 4, IV:52, XXVI B:43; **í kveld** this evening VI:115, XXVI B:20, 25; **um kveldit** in the evening XV:90, XVI:94, that evening XXVI B:4; *acc. of time* **hvert kveld** every night XIV:70, **ekki kveld** through no evening, not for one evening XXV:109

kvelda (*past* **kveldaði**, *pp.* **kveldat**) *wv. impers.* **kveldar** it becomes evening I:28

kveldsǫngr *m.* evensong XVI:98

kvelja (*past* **kvalði,** *pp.* **kvalit**) *wv.* kill? torment; *with neg. suffix* **at þú kveljat** (*imp. for subj.*) that you will not torment X:152

kvenna *see* **kona**

kvennafólk *n.* womenfolk XXVI B:121 (*with suffixed def. art.*)

kvennamaðr *m.* women's man, womaniser XXIII:28

kvennligr *adj.* womanly, feminine XXIII:61

kvenskikkja *f.* woman's cloak XXVI B:144

kvensligr (i.e. **kvenskligr**) *adj.* feminine XXIII:98

kvennváðir *f. pl.* women's clothes IX:62

kvernsteinn *m.* millstone II:110

kveykja/kveykva (*past* **kveykti,** *pp.* **kveykt**) *wv.* kindle; **kveykvið þér** you are lighting *or* are you lighting? XXVI B:109; arouse, awaken XXV:4; **kveykja upp til þess** inflame, arouse to it XIV:93; **kveykva við** kindle (the fire) with *or* set fire to it with XXVI B:117

kvezk *see* **kveða**

kviðlingr *m.* little poem VIII:100, XXI:182

kviðr[1] *m.* belly XXII:51/1, XXIII:77 (*with suffixed def. art.*); **fyrir kviði sér** in front of his belly III:111

kviðr[2] *m.* verdict, sentence, decree XXV:109

kvikligr *adj.* lifelike XII:23

kvikr *adj.* alive I:109, XII:12, 33; *acc. sg. m.* **kvikvan** *with* **hungrdœyfi,** *parallel to* **dauðan** VI:328

kvistr *m.* twig, branch XXV:17, 107

kvistskœðr *adj.* damaging to branches; *f. as subst.* **in kvistskœða** the branch-damaging girl XXV:19

kvæði *n.* poem *Gr* 3.1.7.5 (1), XIV:86, 94

kvæmi, kvæmisk *see* **koma**

kvæn *f.* wife IX:30

kvǫddu *see* **kveðja**[1]

kvǫl *f.* torment *Gr* 3.1.7.1

Kymraland *n.* Cumberland VII A:7

kyn *n.* family, origin II:76, XVI:2; kind: **alls kyns** all kinds of X:88, **margra kynja** of many kinds VIII:161; **engis kyns** no kind of XIII:36

kynligr *adj.* strange; wondrous XXI:187; **þótti henni kynligt hvar** was mystified about where XII:78

kynna (*past* **kynnti,** *pp.* **kynnt**) *wv.* make known (*pres. part.*) XIV:190

kynni *see* **kunna**

kýr *f.* cow *Gr* 3.1.7.2 and (3, 5), 3.1.8 (21); *pl.* VII A:112, IX:89

kyrr *adj.* quiet I:83; at rest XXIII:25; **hafa kyrrt um sik** keep quiet I:110; *n. pl.* **látum vera kyrr** let (something) be quiet, *i.e.* let us not speak of XI:37; *n. as adv.* **kyrrt** uneventful IV:103, XV:124; **er/var þó kyrrt** yet there was no trouble XV:14, 70

kyrtill *m.* tunic V:56, XI:18, XXVI A:29; *with suffixed def. art.* **kyrtillinn** his tunic XII:56

kýs *see* **kjósa**

kyssa (*past* **kyssti,** *pp.* **kysstr**) *wv.* kiss IX:106, XI:9, 30, XII:81, 86; *subj. after* **nema** VII B:47 (to kiss the mouth of the axe = be executed)

kæmi *see* **koma**

kærleikr *m.* intimacy XV:19 *(pl.)*

kærr *adj.* dear; **kærr með** friendly towards XII:72, highly valued by, close to, intimate with XXII:9/2

kœmi *see* **koma**

kœnliga *adv.* skilfully, ably; **svá fór hann kœnliga með því** he went about this so skilfully XIV:96

kǫld *see* **kaldr**

kǫlluð, kǫlluðu, kǫllum *see* **kalla**

kǫngurváfa *f.* spider XXIII:94

kǫnnuðu *see* **kanna**

kǫstuðu *see* **kasta**

kǫttr *m.* cat *Gr* 3.1.7.2 (3)

kømr *see* **koma**

køri *see* **kjósa**

lá *see* **liggja**

laða = **hlaða**

lag *n.* thrust (*gen. pl. with* **mildr**) XXII:42/3; **í ǫðru lagi** on the other hand V:1; **í mesta lagi** to the greatest degree, hardest of all V:104

Lagarfljót *n.* lake in eastern Iceland *Gr* 3.1.8 ex.

lagðar, lagði, lagðisk, lagit *see* **leggja**

lágr (*n.* **lágt**) *adj.* low *Gr* 3.3.8.2; low down XXIII:52

lagsmaðr *m.* companion, fellow; *gen. pl.* **lagsmanna** II:37

lagt *see* **leggja**

lágu *see* **liggja**

lamb *n.* lamb *Gr* 3.1.7.1 ex. 5

Lambadalr *m.* valley on the west side of Sælingsdalr XV:82, *textual note,* 83

lamði *see* **lemja**

land (*pl.* **lǫnd** *Gr* 3.1.7.1) *n.* land VII A:126, 169, VIII:48, 52, XIX:54
(2), XXI:22, 59, 177, XXII:5/2, 64/2, XXVI A:102; his land
XXII:34/4; estate XIV:134, XV:33; country VI:42, 86, VII A:7, 35,
B:46, VIII:64, X:70, XI:50, XVI:33, 138, XIX:27, XXII:4/1,
XXVII:2; *with suffixed def. art.* the country VII A:2, 72, 148, 156,
B:12, VIII:66, 67, XVI:15, XIX:28, 29 (2), 105, the land XIX:29
(1), XXI:24, 92; coast II:104, XXI:167; shore II:106; **á land** ashore
VII A:111, 150, VIII:18, XV:154, XVI:148, XIX:54, 59, XXI:43,
103; **upp á land** in from the sea XXI:128; **á landi** ashore, on dry
land VI:257, XV:147, 148; **er á var landinu** which was in the country
VII A:135; **á landi hér** in this country (Iceland) VIII:43, 125, 140,
164; **þar ... á landi** in that country (Greenland) VIII:69; **á landinu**
on the landward side? XXI:146; **af landi** from off the land XXI:169;
af landi ofan from inland to the shore XXI:49; **af hvárutveggja
landinu** from the land on both sides XXI:84; **kominn frá landi** put
out from the shore XV:139; **fyrir landi** off the coast X:87; **fyrir
land (fram)** along the coast II:104, XIX:55, XXI:86; **í landi** in the
country (*with* **allar þjóðár**) IV:84, *i.e.* from in the country VII A:143;
með landi along the coast VII A:168, XVI:42; **með endilǫngu landi**
along the whole length of the coast VII A:162; **millim landanna**
between the (two) countries VII A:164; **ór landi** abroad VI:20, out
of the country, so as to make him leave the country VI:142; **til lands**
to the shore XXI:33; **til síns lands** to their own country XXI:155;
higat til lands into this country VII A:92; *pl.* **lǫnd** estates VIII:154
landauðn *f.* depopulation VIII:26
landaurar *m. pl.* 'land-ounces', land dues VIII:30
landhallt *adv.* keeping close to the shore VI:122
landherðr *f.* 'land-shoulder', mountain; *gen. with* **lýða** VI:345
landi *m.* countryman VIII:87
landnámamaðr/landnámsmaðr *m.* settler VIII:45, 58, XIX:104, 105
landnorðr *adv.* north-east; **landnorðr frá** to the north-east of V:168
landskostir *m. pl.* qualities of the land, resources XXI:43; **landskostir
góðir** good land XXI:51, 153
landsmenn *m. pl.* people (inhabitants) of the country (Iceland) VIII:44,
53, 150; the people of those countries (Norway and Denmark)
VIII:129
landsnytjar *f. pl.* produce of the land XXI:57
landsréttr *m.* the law of the land VII B:29

landsuðr *n.* south-east; **í landsuðr** to the south-east XXI:27

landtaka *f.* reaching land, making the shore XV:148

landvéttr/landvættr *f.* guardian spirit of a country VII A:149 (*see note*), 158

langorf *n.* a long (scythe-)handle; **í langorfi** on a long handle IV:9

langskip *n.* long ship, viking ship VI:112, VII A:165, VII B:33

langr (*f. sg. and n. pl.* **lǫng**) *adj.* long (*Gr* 3.3.8.1, 2) VIII:129, IX:37, X:52, XXI:32, XXIII:14, 22, 64; *wk. form in name* **enn langi** VI:64, 66; *f.* **lǫng** VI:212; **mjǫk langir** very long ones XXIII:99; *n.* **langt** a long time VI:98, XIV:184, XXV:6, XXVI B:124, a long way (in time) VIII:10, over a long distance, from far away XXVI B:5; **stíga langt** take long strides XXIII:101; **langt var at** it took a long time to XXI:34; **lángt af** (by) far, by a long way XXII:13/4; *dat. pl. as adv.* **lǫngum** for long periods XIV:122, XV:19, 58

las *see* **lesa**

láskat *see* **liggja**

lasta (*past* **lastaði**, *pp.* **lastat**) *wv.* blame, criticise, find fault with XXII:23/2

láta (*pres.* **lætr**, *past* **lét**, *past pl.* **létu**, *pp.* **látinn**) *sv.* (*Gr* 3.6.9.1 (10), 3.6.9.3 ex. 7) **1.** lose III:72, XXII:49/3; loose, let go (of); *imp.* **láttu þér af hǫndum** hand over IX:116; put, let go XXI:42; put aside XI:16; put, keep XXI:31; **láta einn** leave on one's own XV:74; **láta á** put (them, *i.e.* the rings) on X:49; **láta af** leave off, keep back X:50; **láta eptir** leave behind VIII:23, (*intransitive*) give way, allow oneself to be drawn back II:70; **láta í haf** put out to sea XVI:154 (1). **2.** *with inf.* let, allow II:91, V:13, 26, VI:88 (*imp.* **lát**), 109, VII B:54, VIII:132, XI:37, XIV:86, XVI:71; *imp. pl.* **látið yðr** let yourself XXIV:11; *2nd person sg. past* **lézt** XVI:186; **láta verða** be allowed to happen VIII:126; *imp.* **lát þek þat henda** let that happen to you XXIV:12; cause (something to be done), have (something done) I:47, II:5, 96, VI:6, 13, 104, 113, 214, 217, 227, VII A:169, B:55, 60, 84, VIII:86, 158, 165, 194, IX:74, X:107, XII:1, 64, XIV:6, 188, XV:131, 141, XVI:154 (2), XIX:62, 79 (**lét búa . . . ok sjá fyrir**), 102, 108; **látum** let us make IX:61; **ok léti hann** and made him XXVI A:8; **lét sik bera** had himself carried XIX:110; **láta drepa** have (someone) killed VIII:12; **oss brenna láta** have us burned XXVI B:125; **fé lætr dœma** has money awarded him by judgment XXVII:41; **lét gjǫra honum laug** had a bath prepared for him XVI:113; **lét taka**

hann hǫndum had him captured X:15; cause, make (someone *or* something do something) I:87, 102, 103, VII A:19, 64, XIX:64, XXII:6/3, 18/3, 37/3, 39/3, XXV:56, 73; **lætr byrja ferð** has an expedition mounted XXII:12/1; **láta hanga** let something hang (*Gr* 3.9.5.1) V:157; **láta falla** drop II:110; **láta sjá sik** let oneself be seen XVI:94; **láta svæla mik** let myself be suffocated XXVI B:67; **láta vera** have accepted, have followed, have done VII B:14; *with inf. understood* let there be: **láta hǫggva á milli** leave (space) between blows, pause between blows V:146; *with* **-sk** *inf.* let oneself do something II:27, 56, 71; **læt bindask** let myself be tied IX:67; **lét skírask** had himself baptised VIII:79; **láta vígjask** let oneself be ordained VIII:184. **3.** behave; utter; **láta herfiligum látum** behave in a shameful way, utter shameful sounds XXVI B:31; **láta sem** act as if I:36; *impers.* sound **lét í sem** it sounded like XXI:97; **láta við** answer, respond to, grant (a prayer) XXI:64; **lét illiliga við** it made a horrible noise XXI:128; **láta vel yfir** express satisfaction about it XV:121; **láta illa yfir** express disapproval of something IV:77, be dismayed by XIX:75; **láta at** give as one's opinion that VI:320; **láta sem** declare that, give as one's opinion that, speak as if I:124; **sem létu** as they said they would XXVI B:101. **4.** *with acc. and inf.* (*Gr* 3.9.4) say, declare II:142, VI:121; **lét vera** declared there was VI:96; **-sk** *form* **látask** say that one V:159, **lézk** said that he XVI:47; *with impers. vb.* **lætr sér hafa vel sofnat** said he had fallen asleep easily XI:66; *with inf. understood* declare it to be VIII:85, declare there to be VIII:90. **5. -sk** *form* (*cf.* **4** *above*) lose, be defeated VI:293; be lost, die, perish, *past* **lézk** III:77, 79, XIX:85, *past pl.* **létusk** III:76, *past subj.* **létisk** VI:226 (**fyrir hánum** on his side)

latínubók *f.* book written in Latin XIV:188

latínusaga *f.* saga written in Latin XIV:26, *note (with suffixed def. art.)*

latti *see* **letja**

látum[1] *see* **læti**

látum[2] *see* **láta**

lauf *n.* leaf XII:32, XXV:18; thin plate of metal XII:27

Laufey *f.* a goddess (perhaps), mother of Loki IX:68, 78

laug *f.* bath *Gr* 3.1.8 (11), XVI:113

Laugamenn *m. pl.* the people of Laugar XV:83

Laugar *f. pl.* 'hot springs', Ósvífr's farm in western Iceland XV:30, 46, 77, 79, 85, 87, 101, 120

Laugardalr *m.* valley about 20 km east of Þingvǫllr (and outside the Assembly boundaries) VIII:98

lauk *see* **lúka**

laun[1] *f.* secrecy; **á laun** in secret VIII:141

laun[2] *n. pl.* reward XVI:5

launa (*past* **launaði,** *pp.* **launat**) *wv. with dat. of the person and of the payment* repay, reward IV:73, XVI:163; **því launar þú mér . . . er** that is how you reward me . . . for XXVI B:112; *with acc.* repay, give reward for: **ok launa bjarndýrit** in reward for the wild bear XVI:134; *with dat. of the person and acc. of what the repayment is for* XVI:40, 151, 185; *with acc. of what is being paid for and dat. of payment* XV:26; *with dat. of person and of the payment and acc. of what the payment is for* XVI:161; **launa í hǫnd þegar** repay out of hand, on the spot XIV:118

laundyrr *f. pl.* secret doorway XXVI B:88

laungetinn *adj. (pp.)* 'secretly begotten', illegitimate XXVI A:114

lausaaurar *m. pl.* movable property, chattels VIII:154

lausafé *n.* movable property, chattels XV:132, XIX:70

lausamaðr *m.* unattached person, a man without legal domicile III:77

lauss *adj.* free II:35, 36; quit, free of obligation XVI:179; **lauss frá** quit of, free from XXVII:45; *with gen.* without, deprived of, lacking X:61, 143; **lausir aurar** movable property VIII:161; **verða lauss** *with dat.* 'become loose for someone': **Þorgrími varð lauss skjǫldrinn** Þorgrímr dropped his shield XXVI A:31

laust *see* **ljósta**

lausung *f.* looseness (of living), lying, unreliability XXIII:11

laut *see* **lúta**

lax *m.* salmon IX:95

Laxárdalr *m.* valley in eastern Iceland *Gr* 3.1.8 ex.

leðrhosa *f.* leather bag *or* purse XVI:141, 176

léðu *see* **ljá**

leggbiti *m.* 'leg-biter', name for a sword (*gen. with* **sennu**) VI:243

leggja (*past* **lagði,** *past pl.* **lǫgðu,** *pp.* **lagiðr/lagðr/lagit/lagt**) *wv.* (*Gr* 3.6.9.3) **1.** put III:4, 7, X:115; *with suffixed pron.* X:159; place VI:216; lay IX:121, XI:46, XII:82, XXII:5/3, 62/2, XXVI B:147; thrust, stab I:97, III:109, V:103 (*past subj.* **legði** stabbed), VII B:67, XXII:51/1; *metaphorically* lay (*see* **liðr**): *1st person pl. referring to the speaker* IV:24 ('I shall not lay'); appoint, make, arrange (an appointment) II:89, VII A:99; land, come ashore VI:12; put (a ship; *in dat. if expressed*), sail VI:133, 162, 210, XXI:52, 169, *with acc.* position VI:235; direct: *pp. f. pl.* **lagðar** (*in agreement with direct object*) IV:98; lay down (**á þat** about this) VIII:158; **á lǫgð** laid down about it VIII:157; **leggja á** place on, impose X:64; put into it XXII:34/3; **leggja á at hjálpa** devote to helping XIV:98; **leggja á hendr** *with dat.* impose on someone XIV:98; **leggja eigu sína á** take possession of VIII:19; **leggja at** (*with dat.*) thrust, stab at XV:107, attack VI:218, 255; **leggjum at** let us attack VI:78; **lagit at velli** laid to the ground, felled XXVI A:101; **leggja fyr** put in trust for XVI:6; **leggja fyrir** urge (someone to do something), lay down (something as someone's duty) V:136; **leggja ofan** pull down XIV:6; *imp.* (*or 3rd person pl. subj.*?) **leggi saman** (let them) position side by side VI:169; **leggja til** contribute, give (*or* support) an opinion V:162, contribute to, endow (with) VIII:160, XIV:9, set apart for, devote to VIII:53, put forward, offer VI:15, XXVI A:57, lay *or* place upon XVI:117, 118, 170, lay down, provide XVI:123, sail to, put out to XIX:44, advance (ships) to, engage in (sea battle) VI:81 (*pres. subj.* **leggim**; *see note*), 84, 198, XIX:15, approach, make for, attack (in ships) VI:103, thrust, lay on XV:109, **leggja til hans** (*with dat.*) thrust at him (with a weapon) XXVI A:71, B:89; *pres. part.* **vel til leggjandi** properly to be offered XXIV:74; **leggja undir sik** subjugate, conquer VI:33; **leggja upp** put away, swallow II:28; **leggja út** thrust out XXVI A:30, *with weapon in dat.* XXVI B:96; **leggja ríkt við** *see* **ríkr. 2.** *impers.* is being blown XXVI B:205. **3.** **-sk** *form* **leggjask** make one's way, set off VII A:152; position itself, be positioned VI:228; **leggjask niðr** lie down III:6, VIII:120; **lítit lagðisk fyrir góðan dreng** it didn't take much to finish a fine fellow off (i.e. he came to a shameful end) XIX:77

leggr *m.* bone (of arm or leg; *collective*) I:27; *with suffixed def. art.* I:42; stem XII:30

leið[1] *f.* way XVI:38, XXVI B:13; **á leið til** away towards III:60; **á þá leið sem** in the same way as V:8; **alla leið** all the way XI:47; *dat. sg.* **leiðu** path X:69; **leið sína** on one's way I:1, VII B:76; **sína leið fara** go his own way XXVI B:216; **fara leiðar sinnar** go on one's way XXI:52; **koma á leið** *with dat.* bring something about XII:69 (cf. **koma 3**); **komask til leiðar** manage to come about XVI:49

leið[2] *see* **líða**

leiða (*past* **leiddi,** *pp.* **leiddr,** *n.* **leitt**) *wv.* lead, bring I:2, 25, XXIV:48; **leiða eptir sér** pull behind oneself, take with one XVI:15; **leiðir hann eptir sér inn** takes him in with him XVI:108; **í lǫg leitt** made law VIII:153; conduct, escort VII A:105; *pp.* **leiddr** brought XXV:37; **var leiddr** was being helped III:122

leiðask (*past* **leiddisk**) *wv.* **-sk** *form impers. with dat. and acc.* one gets tired of something II:111

leiði *n.* tomb VII B:85; grave XXII:60/4

leiðrétta (*past* **leiðrétti,** *pp.* **leiðréttr**) *wv.* correct; *pp. acc. sg. m.* **leiðréttan** XIV:97 (*Gr* 3.9.7.1)

leifa (*past* **leifði,** *pp.* **leift**) *wv.* leave behind XI:26

Leifr Eiríksson *m.* XXI:37, 39, 41

Leifr Hróðmarsson *m.* Icelandic settler XIX:5, 6, 12, 16, 17, 20, 21, 25, 31 34. See **Hjǫrleifr**

leiga[1] *f.* hire, wages II:138

leiga[2] (*past* **leigði,** *pp.* **leigt**) *wv.* rent XVI:16

leika (*past* **lék,** *past pl.* **léku,** *pp.* **leikinn**) *sv.* play *Gr* 3.6.5.2, 3.6.6; swing to and fro, rock back and forth XXV:50; *transitive* treat XXVI A:22

leikmaðr *m.* layman XIV:131

leikr *m.* game XIV:83; bout, attempt; **á nýja leik** for a fresh attempt, 'for a new go' VIII:90; **málma leikr** *kenning for* battle XXII:55/4

leit *see* **líta**

leita (*past* **leitaði,** *pp.* **leitat**) *wv.* search III:108, 116; investigate, find out, discover XXI:43; *with gen.* look for, try to find III:43, IV:112 (**sér** for themselves), V:167, X:13, XIX:26, 67, 73, 82, XXI:2, 65, 166; seek XIX:41; **leita sér** seek out for oneself XXI:57; **leita sér lífs** try to preserve one's life XXVI B:212; *impers. with gen.* **hvar beina okkarra er at leita** where our bones are to be sought (for burial) XXVI B:177; **leita á** attack, assault I:55; seek to go: **leita innar** make one's way further in III:35; **leita til** make one's way to III:96; **leita undan** try to get away XI:180; **leita út** try to get out III:13, 37; *impers. with gen.* **mundi eigi út leitat** would not be sought outside XXVI A:53

leitt *see* **leiða**

lék *see* **leika**

lemja (*past* **lamði,** *pp.* **lamiðr**) *wv.* batter IX:126

lendr maðr *m.* 'landed man', one who held land in fief from the king, and acted as his local lieutenant, military leader and counsellor; next in rank to a **jarl** in Norway; *pl.* **lendir menn** landowners VII B:2 (*see note*), 87

lengi *adv.* for a long time (*Gr* 3.5.2) I:18, 102, 104, IV:62, VI:239, 123, XIV:175, XV:56, 122, XIX:102, XXI:9, XXVI A:43, 91, B:168; *i.e.* for ever VI:266 (*with* **vanr man**, *line* 263), XXVI A:86, 87; a long way XXI:87, 168; **mjǫk lengi** for a very long time V:142, VII A:67; **svá lengi** for such a long time X:60

lengr *adv. comp.* (any) longer, further (*Gr* 3.5.2) I:20, 147, III:14, 126, XXI:164, XXVII:46; **lengr eða skemr** for a longer or shorter time XXVI A:84; **eigi lengr** not any longer XXI:192

lengri *adj. comp.* (*Gr* 3.3.8.2, 3.3.9 ex. 6; *cf.* **langr**) longer, lasting for a longer time XV:10; **eiga lengra til** have further to go to, be further off from V:82; greater in length XXIII:77, 84; *n. as adv.* **lengra** (*Gr* 3.5.3 (10)) further V:90, XXI:163, XXIII:85; *dat. pl. as adv.* **at lengrum** the longer (because of this) V:18

lengst *adv.* longest (*Gr* 3.5.2) VI:268; for a very long time XXI:70 (**svá lengst** for such a very long time?)

lengstr *adj. sup.* longest XXIII:83 (*weak nom. pl. m., see Gr* 3.3.2)

león *n.* lion XII:59

leppr *m.* lock (of hair) XXVI A:78

lesa (*pres.* **les(s)**, *past* **las**, *past pl.* **lásu**, *pp.* **lesinn**) *sv.* gather; read *Gr* 3.6.9.1 (11), XIV:90, *note*, 91; **las** was reading XIV:90; **hon lét lesa fyrir sér** she had them read to her XIV:188

lét, léti, létisk *see* **láta**

leti *f.* laziness, sloth XXIII:47

letja (*past* **latti**, *pp.* **lattr**) *wv.* **1.** (try to) dissuade (someone from doing something), urge someone not to do something V:26; hinder, stop XVI:137. **2.** *refl.* be dissuaded; **láta ekki letjask** not let oneself be dissuaded V:26

létta (*past* **létti**, *pp.* **létt**) *wv. with dat.* lighten XIV:102

léttbærr *adj.* easy to bear (*with dat.* for someone) XIV:39

léttleiki *m.* irresponsibility, lack of seriousness, lack of earnestness XXIII:51

léttr *adj.* light; friendly *or* cheerful XXIII:70; *sup.* **léttasti** *Gr* 3.3.8.1

létu, létusk *see* **láta**

leyfa/lœyfa (*past* **leyfði**, *pp.* **leyfðr**) *wv.* **1.** praise VI:326, XXV:21. **2.** *with dat.* permit; *impers. pass.* **þeim ǫllum er leyft er** all those to whom it is permitted XXVI B:136

leyna (*past* **leyndi,** *pp.* **leynt**) *wv.* **1.** conceal XXVI B:8; **leyndi** hid it (**fyrir** from) XII:75; *pp.* **leyndr** hidden (i.e. from men) XIII:13, XIV:11; *n. as adv.* **leynt** secretly; **fór hann leynt með** he kept it secret XII:73. **2. -sk** *form* hide oneself; **leynask í burt** steal away I:87

leyniliga *adv.* secretly; **lœyniliga** VI:14

leynistígr *m.* secret path XII:79

leypr *see* **hlaupa**

leysa (*past* **leysti,** *pp.* **leystr**) *wv.* (*Gr* 3.6.9.1 (7)) **1.** make free, unfasten V:111; open XXV:94; solve XXII:26/2; free, release, redeem, deliver XIII:8, XXVI A:12; discharge, carry out XIV:18. **2. -sk** *form* **leysask því undan** get oneself out of it in this way VIII:117

leysingr *m.* freedman VIII:48

lézk *see* **láta**

lið *n.* help, support IV:51, 65 (**með** of, for), VII B:27; following, companionship V:34, VII B:33, 34; people, (members of a) house-hold, (work)men XXVI A:3, B:142; troop, band V:55, VI:265, 274, 275, VII B:44 (*subject of* **drífr**), XXI:128, 129, 146, XXVI B:55; troops, army, force VI:20, 40, 44, 152, 153, 163, 164, 166, 167, 182, 184, 195, 214, VII A:53, 57, 128 (*with suffixed def. art.*), 132, 168, B:35, 56, XXII:28/4; fleet, sea-force VI:136; men VI:115, 221 (*with suffixed def. art.*), 223, 225 (*with suffixed def. art.*), 294, VII B:61, 63 (*with suffixed def. art.*), 75; **liði sínu** members of their expedition XXI:192; **mikit lið** a large number of men VI:213; **annat lið hans/þeira** the rest of his troops VII B:60, the other members of their party XXI:86; **liðit** the (remainder of the) expedition XXI:166

líð *n.* strong drink; *the strong drink of giants is* poetry (*see* II:88–163) VI:344 (*dat. with* **ek fer meðr**)

líða (*pres.* **líðr,** *past* **leið,** *past pl.* **liðu,** *pp.* **liðinn**) *sv.* **1.** pass (of time) II:21, IV:110, XVI:78, 135, XXI:30, 44, 122; *impers.* **líðr á** *with acc.* something draws to a close XVI:128; **til þess er mjǫk leið á kveldit** until it was nearly dark XXVI B:43; **leið at** it came close to, approached I:73; *pp.* **liðit/liðnir** passed XXI:49, XXV:6; **var liðit** had passed (*Gr* 3.9.8.2) XIX:48. **2.** travel XXV:41; *pres. part.* **líðandi** gliding, travelling on skis X:52

liðr *m.* limb; joint I:27 (*collective*); *metaphorical phrase* **leggja fyr lið** put aside, abandon IV:24

liðveizla *f.* help, support VI:23

líf *n.* life III:31, 72, XIV:120, XVI:186, XXII:48/4, XXVI A:12, 56, 81, B:212; *gen. sg. as adv.* alive III:118

lifa (*past* **lifði,** *pp.* **lifat**) *wv.* live I:31, V:124, VIII:131, XIII:48, XIV:120, XIX:112, XXI:70, XXV:109, XXVI B:160, be alive VI:335, VII B:4, XXIV:70, XXV:15, *i.e.* are not forgotten VI:179; **lifði** (*subj.*) were alive XXV:98; **lifa eptir** survive, be still alive VI:299, XXVI B:80, 173; *pres. part.* **lifandi** alive XII:23, 34, 60, 82; **at sér lifanda** with himself living, while he was still living VIII:195 (*Gr* 3.9.7.3)

lifnaðr *m.* (conduct of) life, way of life XIII:28

lífsgrið *n. pl.* quarter, sparing of one's life II:113

liggja (*pres.* **liggr,** *past* **lá,** *past pl.* **lágu,** *pp.* **legit**) *sv.* (*Gr* 3.6.9.3) **1.** lie I:6, 92, 99, 100, II:151, III:8, 59, 68, V:169, XII:44, XXII:48/3, XXIII:47, XXV:59, 84; lie at anchor *or* beached VI:58, 86, VII A:30, 70; lie, *i.e.* be positioned VI:182, 186, 191; be situated XIX:80; **þeir lágu** they (i.e. their ships) lay, were lying XXI:47, 174; be placed XXIII:32; lie in bed XV:122; sleep XXI:204; **liggr** is lying XXVI A:44, **lá** was lying XXI:140, XXVI A:15, 52, B:179, **lágu** were lying XXVI A:58; **liggja á** lie upon them, oppress them, trouble them XXI:154; **lét hann liggja fyrir sér** he placed in front of himself XIV:32; **er Þórðr lá í** which Þórðr was lying in XV:104; **liggja til** lead to V:42, be appropriate XVI:69; **liggja viðr/við** lie (be positioned) close by VI:215, lie (at anchor) on XXI:170; **liggja við** be at stake, depend on it XXVI A:81; **liggr þér nǫkkut við** does anything depend on it for you, is it important to you XXVI A:80; *subj.* **liggi við** were at stake, depended on it XXVI A:56; *impers.* **mǫrgum lá við bana** many were at the point of death XXVI A:89; *pres. part. as noun* **liggjandi** one who is lying down IX:39. **2.** **-sk** *form past with suffixed neg.* **-at: láskat . . . at** (line 153) it did not fail (to happen) that V:149

lík *n.* corpse VII B:84 (*pl.*), XV:153, 154, XXII:58/1

líka[1] (*past* **líkaði,** *pp.* **líkat**) *wv. with dat.* please I:68, VIII:179, XII:68; *impers. with dat.* **líkar** it pleases someone, someone is pleased VIII:2, XII:1; **líkar illa** *with dat.* someone is displeased *or* annoyed VII A:97, XV:70; **mér líkar eigi illa** I am not displeased III:68

líka[2] *see* **líkr**

líkami, líkamr *m.* body XII:11, XIII:22, 41, XXII:59/3, 61/1; his body XXII:63/2, XXIII:38, 75, 83; *with suffixed def. art.* his body XXIII:103

líkamligr *adj.* bodily *Gr* 3.3.9 ex. 25, XIV:147; fleshly, physical XIV:92, 115

líkamslosti *m.* carnal relations XII:72

líki *n.* likeness, appearance, form II:51, 149, VII A:145 (*dat. with* í)

líkindi *n. pl.* likelihood, signs (**til** of this) I:115

líking *f.* likeness, form XII:41, 53

líkligr (= **glíkligr**) *adj.* likely, to be expected VI:292, XV:86, XXI:134

líkna (*past* **líknaði,** *pp.* **líknat**) *wv. with dat.* show mercy *or* compassion to XIV:104

líkneski *n.,* **líkneskja** *f.* image, statue XII:10, 77, 84, XIII:2, 5, 10, 14; *with suffixed def. art.* XII:87, XIII:8, 15 *(poss. dat.),* 20; **ein líkneskja eptir** a statue of XII:47

líknsýnir *f. pl.* merciful appearance, compassionate glances IV:90

líkr *adj.* like *(with dat.)* XII:22; *f.* **lík** XXIII:69; *acc. pl. m.* **líka** (to be) like XXIII:66; *nom. pl. f.* **líkar** (*with dat.*: 'like those of a spider'?) XXIII:95; *n. as adv.* **því líkt sem** looking as if XII:44; *sup. n.* **líkast** most likely IV:72; **lét því líkast í sem** it sounded just like XXI:97; *sup. n. as adv.* **því líkast sem** looking just as if XII:43

limr *m.* limb XII:12

lín *n.* linen, linen garment; **brúðar lín** bridal head-dress (made of linen) IX:46 (*dat.* = with, in); flax, linen thread X:7, 20

lína[1] *f.* (a woman's) headdress IV:89, IX:106

lína[2] *f.* line, rope XXI:205, *textual note*

lindbaugr *m.* serpentine arm-ring X:38

lindi *m.* belt V:29, X:91; **af linda sér** from his belt V:112

línklæði *n. pl.* linen underclothes, shirt and breeches III:28, 45 (*with suffixed def. art.*), 102

linnr[1] *m. poetical word for* snake IV:81; **linnr Loddu lǫgðis** *is a kenning for* sword (snake of blood *or* snake of the shield; cf. *SnE, Háttatal* st. 6)

linnr[2] *m. poetical word for* fire; **linnr ǫlstafns** *is a kenning for* a (golden) ornament on an ale-cup IV:85

linr *adj.* gentle, mild XIV:39

list *f.* art, artifice XII:15

líta (*pres.* **lítr,** *past* **leit,** *past pl.* **litu,** *pp.* **litinn**) *sv.* **1.** look I:5; see XXI:110; **litu** they saw XXII:53/3; **líta á þat/þetta** consider this XVI:52, 55; **líta í** look inside X:113; **líta sem** look like XXII:20/2; **líta til** look in that direction II:23, look for XXIV:29; **líta við** look at XXVI A:33. **2. -sk** *form* **mér lízk svá sem** it seems to me that XXVI B:48; **hversu lízk** (*impers.*) **þér á** how do you like XVI:132; *past subj.* **litisk** seemed VIII:175

litarapt *n.* complexion, colour XV:24

litask (*past* **litaðisk**) *wv. refl.* **litask um** look around IV:16 (see I:15, *note*; *Gr* 3.9.8.3), XXI:96; **fagrt var þar um at litask** it was beautiful to look around one there, i.e. there were beautiful views there XXI:58

lítill (*n.* **lítit**) *adj.* small (*Gr* 3.3.8.3, 3.3.8.4 (3a)) III:113, V:54, XV:52, little V:121, XII:45, XXIII:10, 14, 45; *acc. sg. m.* **lítinn** gentle, not strong VI:26, 122; *acc. sg. f.* **litla** short (of time) XV:54; *dat. sg. m.* **litlum** XXIII:58; *pl.* **litlir** XXIII:91, 92; **ok eigi lítill** and no small one (*litotes*) II:24; *n.* **lítit** small, little V:34, VI:11, 152, a small one III:99; *n. as substantive* little VI:19, VII B:61 (?—*see* **op**), a mean thing XIX:77, **of lítit** too little XV:121, **lítit til** not much to be had in the way of XXI:62; *dat. sg. n. as substantive* **fyrir litlu** a short while before XV:38; **litlu, lítlu** *as adv. of degree with comp.* a little III:51, IV:68, V:172, XXI:73, 179, XXIII:85; *gen. sg. as adv.* (*with* **meira**) little IV:25

lítillátliga *adv.* humbly XIV:100

lítillátr *adj.* humble XXIII:84

lítillæti *n.* humility XIV:33; insignificance, lack of power? XXIII:75

litlastofa *f.* (both parts of this compound inflect, the first part as a weak adjective (*Gr* 3.3.4)) the small room (which might be used as a living room or for audience or reception) III:36, 77, 88

litr[1] *m.* colour V:46; **at lit** in colour XXI:127; **ǫllum litum** with all colours (in them) XII:26; **með alls konar litum fjaðranna** with all kinds of colours in the feathers, with feathers of all colours XII:32

litr[2] *adj.* coloured; **lítt litr** having little colour XXIII:91, *textual note*

lítt *adv.* little, not much (*Gr* 3.5.2) III:54, VI:199, *i.e.* not at all V:35, VI:252, XV:14, XVI:139, 144, XXI:13, 14, XXIII:91, *textual note*, XXV:21, XXVI B:94, 159

líttat *adv.* just a little XXIII:89

litu *see* **líta**

lízk *see* **líta**

ljá (*past* **léði**, *pp.* **léðr**, *n.* **lét**) *wv.* (*Gr* 3.6.9.3) *with dat. of person and gen. of thing* lend II:48, IX:11, XV:44

ljár *m.* scythe II:125 (*probably acc. pl.*); *with suffixed def. art.* II:129; scythe-blade IV:9, 10 (*with suffixed def. art.*)

ljóði *m.* prince X:57

ljóp, ljópu = **hljóp, hljópu**, *see* **hlaupa**

ljóri *m.* skylight, hole in the roof for smoke to escape VII B:61 (*with suffixed def. art.*)

ljós *n.* light, lamp II:6, III:108, XIV:55; *metaphorically* joy, hope, encouragement IV:91 (*object of* **lúka mér**)

ljóss *adj.* light, bright, X:22; fair X:39, XXIII:7; *n. as adv.* **ljóst** clearly V:167

ljósta (*pres.* **lýstr,** *past* **laust,** *past pl.* **lustu,** *pp.* **lostinn**) *sv.* (*Gr* 3.6.9.1 (10)) hit I:38; strike VII A:102, XV:150; *impers. (with dat.)* **laust á** came down XV:144; **laust eldinum í** (something) caught fire II:58; *(with acc.)* something was struck XIII:4, 33; *supine* **lostit** VI:37

ljótr *adj.* ugly II:66; evil XIV:95

ljúfr *adj.* beloved, dear (*with dat.,* to someone) XI:38; *n. as adv.* **þeim var ljúft at** it was pleasant for them to, they were happy to XXII:10/2

ljúga (*pres.* **lýgr,** *past* **laug,** *past pl.* **lugu,** *pp.* **logit**) *wv.* lie, tell a lie; **logit vera** be untrue, be false VI:321

ló = **hló,** *see* **hlæja**

loða (*past* **loddi,** *pp.* **loðat**) *wv.* stick, lodge XIV:21

loðbrók *f.* nickname, 'shaggy breeches' VIII:12

Lodda *f.* a river-name (the Lud) or the name of an island IV:80; **Lodda lǫgðis** *is then a kenning either for* blood (liquid of the sword) *or for* shield (island of the sword, that on which the sword rests)

loði *m.* fur (*or* coarse wollen) cloak XXV:57

loðinn *adj.* shaggy, hairy XII:56 (*cf. Gr* 3.9.2)

loðkápa *f.* shaggy cape VII A:82

lóðu *see* **hlaða**

lofa[1] (*past* **lofaði,** *pp.* **lofat**) *wv. with dat.* allow II:151, XII:3; *with acc. and dat.* permit something to someone XXVI B:130; **sá er lofat er** to whom it is permitted XXVI B:137

lofa[2] (*past* **lofaði,** *pp.* **lofat**) *wv.* praise XIII:7, XXI:143

lofðar *m. pl. poetical word for* men, warriors VI:335

lofðúngr *m.* ruler, king XXII:13/3

lófi *m.* palm (of the hand); *with suffixed def. art. acc. sg.* **lófann** his palm I:41, *acc. pl.* **lófana** his palms III:111, *dat. pl.* **lófunum** III:112

loga (*past* **logaði,** *pp.* **logat**) *wv.* flame, be in flames III:45, XXVI B:120, 127, 221; blaze III:50, 88; *pres. part* **loganda** burning, flaming XXVI B:219

lóga (*past* **lógaði,** *pp.* **lógat**) *wv. with dat.* part with XVI:184

logi *m.* flame; *dat. sg.* **loga** with fire IX:83

logit *see* **ljúga**

lok[1] *n.* end; **und lok** *i.e.* to death VI:363

lok² *n.* lid XII:49

loka *f.* bolt XV:105 *(with suffixed def. art.)*

lokarspánn *m.* wood-shaving (from a plane) II:55; *acc. pl.* **-spánu** II:57

lokit *see* **lúka**

Loki *m.* a god (one of the Æsir) II:9, 16, 29, 34, 36, 38, 46, 51, 53, 69, 71, IX:6, 16, 31, 68, 78

lokkr *m.* lock (of hair) XIII:6

lokrekkja *f.* bed-closet, enclosed bed, private bedroom XV:104, *with suffixed def. art.* XV:105

Lón *n.* area on the south-east coast of Iceland VIII:41

lopt *n.* **1.** sky XXIV:38; **at lopti, í lopt** into the air II:128, X:136, 173; **í lopt upp** upwards (to the sky) XV:105, XXI:67; **á lopti** (while still) in the air V:95, IX:37, XXVI B:195. **2.** loft, upper room (a small room standing on the cross-beams of the building) III:73 *(with suffixed def. art.)* XXVI A:25, B:116

Loptr enn gamli *m.* son of Ormr Fróðason XIX:107

loptsvalir *f. pl.* balcony VII B:35

lostasemi *f.* lustfulness XIII:22 *(gen. sg.)*

lostinn, lostit *see* **ljósta**

lúka (*pres.* **lýkr** *Gr* 3.6.5.2, *past* **lauk,** *past pl.* **luku,** *pp.* **lokinn**) *sv.* **1.** shut IV:13; **lokit um** *with dat.* closed something round, surrounded with VI:284 *(supine with* **hǫfðu**). **2.** *with dat.* bring to an end VIII:137, finish XII:70, XIV:72; **at lúka** finishing XXVI A:3. **3.** *impers with dat.* something ends IV:65; **orrostunni var lokit** the battle was over VI:302; **er lokit** is finished, used up XVI:123; **lokit mun** will be over XXII:47/4; **því lauk svá** the outcome of it was XXI:3; **skal nú yfir lúka með oss** things must now come to an end between us, our dealings are going to come to a final issue XXVI B:133. **4.** *with acc. and dat.* impart something to someone IV:90; *subj. (optative)* **lúki** let (men) repay XXII:36/3. **5. -sk** *form* **lúkask upp** open, **lúkask aptr** close XXIII:40

lukði *see* **lykja**

lukla *see* **lykill**

lukt *see* **lykja**

lund *f.* manner; **á þá lund** in this way, as follows II:90, VI:172; **á nǫkkura lund** in some way XIV:97; mind, temper, feelings XXII:33/3

lundaðr *adj. (pp.)* disposed, inclined XII:75

lúta (*pres.* **lýtr,** *past* **laut,** *past pl.* **lutu,** *pp.* **lotinn**) *sv.* (*Gr* 3.6.9.2 (1))
bend down IX:106; *with dat.* bow down to VII B:19, XXII:61/2;
lúta niðr lean forward XXIII:102

lutr = **hlutr**

lutskipti (= **hlutskipti**) *n.* share of booty VI:148

lýðr *m.* people XXVI B:136; *dat. sg.* **lýð** to/for people XXII:53/4; *pl.*
men VI:265, XXII:61/1, folk XXII:31/4, troops XXII:13/3 (*acc. pl.*),
24/4; **lýðir landherðar** *is a kenning for* (mountain) giants VI:344

lygi *f.* lie IX:39 (*acc. sg., object of* **bellir**)

lyginn *adj.* lying, mendacious XXIII:73

lykð/lykt *f.* end, conclusion XXII:26/1; **at lykðum** eventually, in the
end VII B:28; **til lykða** finally; **vega at honum til lykða** deal him
the final blow V:111

lykill *m.* key *Gr* 3.1.7.2 (1), 4 (1); *acc. pl.* **lukla** IX:61, *(with suffixed
def. art.)* **lyklana** (**at** to) XII:67; *gen. pl.* **lukla** X:102, 112

lykja (*past* **lukði/lukti,** *pp.* **lukðr/luktr**) *wv.* close XXIII:42, join the
ends of X:38

lýkr *see* **lúka**

lyng/lýng *m.* heather; ground 48/3

lypta (*past* **lypti,** *pp.* **lypt**) *wv. with dat.* lift XI:18; raise XXII:47/3

lypting *f.* poop, the raised after-deck of a viking ship VI:290; *with
suffixed def. art.* VI:275, 286, 289

lýsa (*past* **lýsti,** *pp.* **lýstr**) *wv. with dat.* proclaim, announce V:158
(*past subj.*), declare publicly VI:322, XIII:7; publish XXVII:7; *subj.*
lýsi ljós yðart let your light shine XIV:55; *impers.* **lýsti** it shone II:6,
XIX:33

lýsigrund *f.* 'shining ground' IV:84; **lýsigrund** (*vocative*) **linns ǫlstafns**
is a kenning for woman (the one who carries the ornamented ale-
cup, cf. *SnE, Skáldskaparmál* ch. 31, = Steingerðr)

lysta (*past* **lysti**) *wv. impers. with acc. (understood)* one desires IX:106

lystiliga *adv.* pleasantly, gracefully I:57

lystr *adj.* (*pp.*) desirous, inclined XXII:8/3, 52/3

lýtalauss *adj.* without fault *or* blemish XXIII:15

lýtr *see* **lúta**

lægð *f.* hollow, low ground XXI:91

lægri *adj. comp.* lower *Gr* 3.3.8.2, 3.3.9 ex. 15, XXII:47/3; *with dat.
of comparison* **engum þessum var hon lægri** to none of these was
she inferior XIV:186

lægstr *adj. sup.* lowest VI:267

lær *n.* thigh, ham II:28; **á lærum sér** on her thighs III:127

læra (*past* **lærði.** *pp.* **lærðr**) *wv.* teach; *pp.* **lærðr** taught XIV:180; *cf.* **lærðr**

Læradalr *m.* Lærdal, an inland valley in western Norway VII A:130

lærdómsmaðr *m.* man of learning XIV:156

lærifaðir (*pl.* **-feðr**) *m.* (religious) teacher, theologian XXIV:28

lærðr *adj.* (*pp., cf.* **læra**) learned; **lærðir menn** clerics VII A:68

læring *f.* instruction XIV:153

lærisveinn *m.* disciple XIV:53; pupil, student XIV:168, 172, 178

læstyggr *adj.* shunning injury or deceit VI:336 (*with* **burar**)

læt, lætr *see* **láta**

læti (*dat.* **látum**) *n. pl.* behaviour; noise XXVI B:31

lœkr *m.* stream XXI:91, XXVI B:228

lœyfa = leyfa

lœyniliga = leyniliga

lœypizk *see* **hlaupa**

lǫg *n. pl.* law, laws VIII:94, 116, 141; the law XXVII:3; *gen.* **laga** VII B:26; **hafa í lǫgum** make law, adopt into the laws VII A:133; constitution VIII:36, 124, 134, 135; **úr lǫgum við** 'out of the laws with', not under the same laws as VIII:114

Lǫgberg/Lǫgbergi *n.* Law Rock VIII:100, 111, 115, 122, XV:68, XXVII:22, 23, 27, 49

lǫgðir *m. sword-name,* 'thruster, stabber' IV:80

lǫgð, lǫgðu *see* **leggja**

lǫgmaðr *m.* man learned in the law, legal expert XXVII:33

lǫgmál *n. pl.* legal prescriptions, laws XXII:6/1

lǫgr *m.* liquid II:118, 120; sea, water XXII:53/3

lǫgrétta *f.* legislature, legislative assembly; Law Council (see *HOIC* 63–66; *Laws* II 384 and references there; *cf.* also Text XXVII) VIII:176, XXVII:18; session of the Law Council XXVII:21

lǫgréttufé *n. pl.* Law Council funds XXVII:38 (see note)

lǫgréttumaðr *m.* member of the Law Council XXVII:8, 46

lǫgréttuseta *f.* seat on the Law Council XXVII:14

lǫgsaga *f.* lawspeaking, the office of lawspeaker in the medieval Icelandic commonwealth VIII:58, 62, 169; lawspeakership XXVII:9, 43

lǫgsǫgumaðr *m.* lawspeaker, the president of the Alþingi VIII:46, 118, 152, XIX:109, XXVII:3, 43

lǫgsǫgumannsþáttr *m.* the Lawspeaker's section (of the law) XXVII:1
lǫgþáttr *m.* section of the law; *acc. pl.* **lǫgþáttu alla** all sections of
the law XXVII:25
lǫmb *see* **lamb**
lǫnd *see* **land**
lǫng, lǫngum *see* **langr**
lǫstr *m.* vice XIV:95
má *see* **mega**
maðr (*pl.* **menn**) *m.* (*Gr* 3.1.7.1; cf. 3.1.7.4 (5)) man, person I:27, 29,
46, 55, 111, 137, II:1, 13, III:79, V:30, 144, VI:165, VIII:15, 32, 35,
43, IX:29, X:14, 88, 170, XII:11, XV:2, 36, XVI:2, XIX:2, 102,
XXI:7, XXII:27/1, XXVII:19, 35; a man XIX:33, XXV:109; **sá maðr
nokkurr er** some man who XXVII:2; **sem þú ert maðr til** as a man
like you would XXVI B:112; *as indefinite subject* **maðr** someone
XV:106, one XIV:68, XXIV:15, i.e. (blind) people XXII:58/3; *with
suffixed def. art.* **maðrinn** the man VII B:52, XXIII:82, a man, a
person XIV:64; follower I:62, 63; *acc.* **mann** man XVI:70, XIX:34,
XXI:138, husband II:63, VI:8, VII A:80, person II:92, XV:97,
someone III:19, 42, XXVII:4, *with suffixed def. art.* the man I:47,
51, VII B:54, 56; **øngvan mann** no one XXVI B:37; *gen.* **manns**
I:123, II:64, VII A:33, VIII:9, XXII:61/3; *partitive gen.* (*Gr* 3.2.6
(20)) XXII:29/1; *dat.* **manni** VI:167, VII A:42, *with suffixed def.
art.* VII B:53, XXVI B:153; **þeim manni** for, by that person I:132;
pl. **menn** people, men I:28, 52, 73, 83, 109, 114, 124, 136, III:74,
IV:53, 54 (*subject of* **sitja ok meina**), 78, 101, VI:6, 42, 117, 244,
318, 339, VIII:21, 22, 33, 67 (*object of* **fýsa**), X:14, XI:64, XIII:45,
XIV:90, *note*, XV:12, 39, XIX:24, XXI:2, XXII:15/3, 53/1, XXIII:3,
XXV:81, XXVI A:16, 75, B:25, XXVII:6, 18, persons XXI:23, 38,
40, followers I:85, XXVI B:88; **menn kváðu** they said VI:174; **segja
menn** it is said VII B:36; **allir menn** everyone VI:289; *with suffixed
def. art.* **mennirnir, menninir** VI:219, 267, 268; *gen. pl.* **manna**
I:3, II:134, VI:357 (*with* **veifanar orði**), XI:11 (*Gr* 3.4.2 (5)),
XXII:57/1, XXV:3, XXVI B:55, *partitive gen.* (*Gr* 3.2.6 (20))
XXVII:12, 27, *with a numeral* (*Gr* 3.4.2 (5)) XXI:18, *emphasising
a sup.* I:137 (see **njóta**), **manna bezt vígr** a very good fighter V:31;
dat. pl. **mǫnnum** people I:70, 71, II:94, 161, VII A:32, XI:10, XIX:12,
XXVI A:119, B:131, XXVII:3, men XXV:69, followers I:84, VII
A:33, XXII:7/4; **mannum** VI:194, in his men VI:97

magn *n.* strength, power X:84 (*dat. of respect, see* **sníða**); **af magni** with strength, powerfully XXII:40/2

Magnús biskup (Gizurarson) *m.* bishop of Skál(a)holt 1216–37 III:32

Magnús (Óláfsson) *m.* the Good, king of Norway 1035–46 VII B:4, 85

magr (*acc. sg. m.* **magran**) *adj.* thin XVI:89

mágr *m.* relative by marriage; son-in-law XXI:7; brother-in-law XI:14, 54, XIX:43, in address XXVI B:76, 217; father-in-law XXVI B:185; **þeir mágar** the brothers-in-law (Þorkell hvelpr, Knútr, Þórðr Ingunnarson) XV:44

maki *m.* match, equal XIV:110

makligr *adj.* fitting, deserving XVI:73

mál *n.* **1.** speech II:22, 83, VIII:137, XXI:201 (i.e. to speak), XXVII:24; words VI:173, IX:103, X:168, XXII:32/1, XXV:33; **mál mitt** what I say XXVI B:128; discussion IX:54; talk XXVII:35; information, account VI:339 (*dat. with* **ferri**), XIV:72, 130; narrative XXVI B:2. **2.** business, affair, matter IV:66, VII A:95, 99, XV:128; subject, question XXIV:26; proposal, argument VII B:14; suit XV:4, 78; case VIII:134; affairs: **snúa sínu máli til Guðs miskunnar** submit one's fate to God's mercy, put oneself in God's hands XXI:81; *pl.* lawsuit: **fara málum á hendr** bring a lawsuit against XV:81; **miðla mál** make a compromise VIII:133; **máli skipta** make a difference, be of importance VII B:55

máldagi *m.* terms of (marriage) settlement XV:8

málgan *see* **málugr**

malmr/málmr *m.* metal; *in pl.* = weapons, *in kennings for* battle, **malma gnaustan** VI:352, **málma leikr** XXII:55/4

malmþing *n.* 'metal-assembly', parliament of weapons, *kenning for* battle VI:206

málóði *adj.* (*Gr* 3.3.8.5 (6)) furious in speech, using violent language IV:12

málspeki *f.* wisdom in speech, eloquence XXIV:38

málstofa *f.* council-chamber VII B:59, 66

málugr *adj.* talkative XXIII:88

man¹, mankat *see* **munu**

man² *see* **muna**

mánaðr/mánuðr *m.* month; **hálfan mánuð** for a fortnight XXI:94; *acc. pl.* **mánuðr tólf** XXII:59/4, **tvá mánuðu** XXI:165; **á tólf mánuðum** in twelve months, i.e. every year XIV:143

Manar *see* **Mǫn**

máni *m.* moon X:44; *as nickname* VIII:46; **máni viðar hauðrmens** 'moon of the ship', *kenning for* shield XXVI A:98

mann, manna, manni, mannum *see* **maðr**

mannamál *n.* people's talk, people talking III:37, 104

mannfátt *adj. n. as adv.* short of men; **er oss eigi mannfátt** we are not short of men V:108

mannfjǫlði *m.* multitude of men XIII:27

manngi *pron.* no one (*Gr* 3.2.4) VIII:180

mannliga *adv.* like a man XVI:124

mannraun *f.* trial (of manhood) III:131

manns *see* **maðr**

mannshǫnd *f.* person's hand I:6

mannskaði *m.* manslaughter, losses XXVI B:98, 140

mannskœðr *adj.* dangerous to men, causing many casualties, bloody VI:209

mannsmót *n.* sign of manliness (**at** in) VII A:85

mannspjall *n.* loss of men, destruction of men VI:220

mannsverk *n.* the labour performed by a single man; **níu mannsverk** the work of nine men II:138

manntal *n.* number of men; **at manntali** in number of men VI:226

mannvit *n.* (human) intelligence II:100, XXIV:38; common sense (*gen. with* **vant**) XXV:97

manskæri *n. pl.* mane-shears, shears for cutting horses' manes V:28, 112

mansǫngr *m.* love-song XIV:86; **mansǫngr mikill** a good deal of love-poetry XIV:90

mant, mantu *see* **munu**

mánuðr, mánuðu *see* **mánaðr**

Már *m.* father of **Hafliði** VIII:173

Már Hamalsson *m.* XIX:114

margdýrr *adj.* very splendid VI:347 (*with* **stýrir**)

margfalda (*past* **margfaldaði,** *pp.* **margfaldaðr**) *wv.* multiply; use a plural in XXIV:2 (*subj.*), 42 (*subj.*); use in the plural XXIV:55; *pp.* **margfaldaðu** plural XXIV:86; **-sk** *form* **en margfaldaz** rather than be used in the plural XXIV:51

margfaldr *adj.* manifold XXIV:73; plural XXIV:52, 58, 74

margr (*f.* **mǫrg,** *n.* **mart/margt**) *adj.* many (*Gr* 3.3.8.3, 3.3.8.4 (3b))

II:4, III:9, IV:101, VI:28, 90, 155 (*with* **drótt**), 320, VII A:161, VIII:81, 125, XIV:145, 168, XVI:148, XXI:10, 23, XXIV:34; plentiful, numerous XXI:24, 54; much XV:19; many a XI:3, 4, XXII:24/2, 37/3 (*with* **þegn**); **margr maðr** many a man XXII:54/3; **margr maðr þar** many a man who was there VI:131; **er sá nú margr er** there is now many a one who XXVI B:100; **margs manns þeira er** of many a man who VI:303; **mǫrgum manni** to many a man XVI:166; *n.* **mart, margt** much, a great deal of IV:12, VI:196, XV:77, a great many XXVI B:142, 148; *as substantive* IV:86, VIII:178, many things VII A:62; *with partitive gen.* **seggja mart** many warriors XXII:39/3; *as adv.* much (**at** with regard to) VI:357, a lot XXI:3; *pl.* **margir** many people XIV:187, XXVI B:53, many of them XXVI B:99, **þeir margir** many of them III:123, **hans margir** many of his XXII:30/2; *acc. pl. m.* **marga** many people XXIV:66; *n. pl.* **mǫrg** many III:113, V:132, VI:72 (*understand* **skip**), XI:11, numerous XXIII:23; *dat. pl.* **mǫrgum** II:14, VII A:32, XII:83, XXVI A:89, 119, B:96, (to) many people XIV:186, XXII:36/2, **með mǫrgum** along with (among) *or* for many (other) people XXIV:72
margreifi *m.* marquis XI:56
margspakr (*f.* **margspǫk**) *adj.* wise about many things VIII:11
María *f.* St Mary the Virgin XIII:2, 5, 43; Medieval Latin *gen.* **Marie** (= Classical Latin *Mariae*) XIII:14, 30
mark *n.* mark, token, sign VII A:52, XIV:66, XXIII:11, 45, 53, 60; symbol, image, figure XIV:63; *pl.* **til merkja** as proof XXVI B:24
marka (*past* **markaði,** *pp.* **markaðr**) *wv.* mark; *pp. n. pl.* **mǫrkuð** VII A:118
markir *see* **mǫrk**
Markis *m.* king in England XII:52, 62
Markland *n.* 'forest land' (cf. **mǫrk**[1]) XXI:29, 198
Markús (**Skeggjason**) *m.* lawspeaker from 1084 to 1107 (when he died) VIII:152, 169
Marnar *see* **Mǫrn**
marr *m.* horse IX:21 (*poss. dat.*), X:151, XXV:39, 42, 50
mart *see* **margr**
mat[1] *see* **meta**
mat[2] *see* **matr**
matask (*past* **mataðisk**) *wv. refl.* take food, eat a meal V:2 (breakfast), XVI:97

matfǫng *n. pl.* supply of food; **lítit til matfanga** not much food to be found XXI:62; **nǫkkut til matfanga** something to eat XXI:63

mátkum *see* **máttugr**

matmál *n.* mealtime XXVI B:41

matr *m.* food XXVI B:20, 27, 29 (*with suffixed def. art.*); *acc.* sg. **mat** I:37, 66, VI:9, XIV:67, **at mat** eating XIX:83; *gen. sg.* **matar** II:17, V:167 (*object of* **leita**), XVI:43, 91, *with suffixed def. art.* XXI:60

matsveinn *m.* cook XXI:75

máttak, mátti, máttu *see* **mega**

máttr (*dat. sg.* **mætti**) *m.* might, strength *Gr* 3.1.7.2 ex. 4, XXII:24/1 ('our strength'), XXIII:15

máttugr *adj.* mighty; *dat. pl.* **mátkum** XXV:69

máttuligr *adj.* **1.** mighty. **2.** possible XXIII:36? **3.** = **mátuligr** XXIII:36?

mátuliga *adv.* properly, fittingly, appropriately XXIII:8, 67

mátuligr *adj.* proper, appropriate, suitable XXIII:16

með, meðr *prep.* (*Gr* 3.7.4) **1.** *with dat.* with I:43, 87, II:4, 12, 45, III:35, 85, IV:50, V:94, VI:9, 34, 37, VIII:107, IX:25, 52, 79, XI:26, XIV:26, *note*, 93 (**meðr**), XIX:6, XXI:7, 72, XXII:9/1, XXIII:16, 17, 108, 109, XXV:76, XXVI A:9, 17, B:74; together with VI:274 (**meðr**), 278, VIII:152, XIII:22, XXII:49/3, along with XIV:127, XXIII:78, **með mǫrgum** along with many others XXIV:72; **vera með** stay with, live with IV:109, XVI:116, XXVI A:117, be in someone's employment VII B:53; **var með** was staying with XXI:37; among XI:70, XXIV:59; amid, along XXVI B:222; between XIX:7, XXVI B:213, XXVII:13; (made) out of XIII:14, 19; **hvat er með** what's up with IX:23; **með sér** with him XVI:13, XXVI A:15, along with himself III:19, to go with herself III:42, between themselves II:89, VII A:99, with them X:10, XIV:146, as well XXIV:78, **hafa með sér** take with one XIX:87, have with one XXI:156; along VII A:162, 168, XXI:55, 130, along the shore of VI:136; **með landi/landinu** along the coast XVI:42, XXI:31; **með sjó** along the coast XIX:72, 90; alongside III:6; among II:82, XI:70; **með þeim Haraldi (Áka)** between him and Haraldr (Áki) VII B:3, XVI:66; as a result of XIII:13; by XIII:24, 25; by means of, using II:122, XXII:5/4, XXIV:10; **með henni** by (*or* in?) her XIII:23 (*see* **tendra**); **með vápnum** carrying arms, armed V:70; **með valdi** by force VII B:56; **með ǫllu** altogether, entirely I:93, XIV:76; **með því at** according as VIII:2, since, it being the case that XXIV:22, 29, 72. **2.** *with acc.*

carrying II:36, 54, VI:265 (**meðr**), taking V:34, 166 (*i.e.* in, consisting of?), VI:163, 270 (**meðr**), 285 (**meðr**), VII A:130, B:34, XVI:33, XIX:70, XXI:5; bringing V:55, VII B:60, XXII:54/1, having with us VI:86; together with VIII:98; as well as XXVI A:14; wearing VI:291 (**meðr**). **3.** *as adv.* (*Gr* 3.7.7) with (her) II:42, with it XXI:140, 150, XXII:31/4, along them XXI:35; **til at festa með** for securing . . . with XXVI A:58; **þar með** along with it I:42, and in addition XIV:44, **er . . . með** with whom XXVII:15

meðal/miðil, á meðal, í meðal *prep. with gen.* among, between *Gr* 3.7.2, XI:35, XXVI A:73; **okkar í meðal** between us (i.e. between our deaths) XXVI A:23; **á meðal þeirra** between them XXVI B:147; *as adv.* **þar meðal** between them (the eyebrows) XXIII:20

meðallag *n.* average; **til meðallags** so so, not too well XI:68; *dat. sg. as adv.* **meðallagi** moderately, not very XV:36

meðalskinnslitr *m.* middling, average skin-colour XXIII:108

meðan *adv.* meanwhile III:19; *as conj.* (*Gr* 3.8.2.1) while II:6, III:18, V:111, XIV:75, XVI:97, XXIV:70; as long as V:124, VI:225, VII B:4, VIII:131, 158, XXVI A:82, 102, B:172, 212

meðr = með

mega (*pres.* **má**, *past* **mátti**, *past subj.* **mætti**, *pp.* **mátt**) *pret.-pres. vb.* be able, can (*Gr* 3.6.7, 3.6.10) I:91, II:57, 68, 142 (*pres. subj.* **megi**), III:11, 92, 101, IV:86, 106, V:80 (2), 92, 143, XI:60, XIII:24, 45, XXII:28/2, XXV:81, XXVI B:23, 79, XXVII:12, 34; have the power to X:184 (*with suffixed pron.*); *inf.* might XVI:182, could XXVI B:129; **ekki vera mega** could not be true III:123; **má** can XXIII:36, is able XXIV:48; **þat er hann má** as much as he can XII:1; **má ek** may I XXVI B:74; **vel má ek** I am content to XXVI B:74; **eigi má ek þat vita** I cannot see, I am not sure V:80; *with suffixed 2nd person pron.* **máttu** you can I:125, VII A:52, you may/ must XV:87, XVI:52, you will be able XXVI B:177; **vér megum** we shall be able VI:82; **megum vér/vit** we can XXI:177, XXIV:47; **eigi megum vera** we cannot stay XXVI A:109; **megu þér** (*Gr* 3.6.9.1 (14)) you will be able VI:130; **megu þér vel** you may well XXVI B:197, **megum vit vel** we might as well XXIV:48; **megu eigi** cannot XXVI B:65; **mátti/máttu** could XII:73, XIII:23, XIV:30, XXI:23, has been able XIV:167; **varla mátti hann sjá** he could scarcely bear to look at XIV:108; *pres. subj.* **megi** can XXVI B:128, could XXV:47, may XXIV:52, (*impers.*) one may XXII:22/4; *past subj.*

mætta/mætti might XIV:124, XVI:49, XXIV:44, could XXVI B:31, was able VII A:113, would be able XV:11, **mættim** could V:79, **eigi mætti** should not be able XIII:21, **þér mættið** you could XXI:134, *with suffixed pron.* **mættak** I might IX:13; *impers. (Gr* 3.9.3 (c)) **má** can one I:135, one can VIII:70, it may XVI:143, **kalla má** one might say XXVI B:13, **vera má** it could be, maybe I:143, **þat er nú má sjá** that which now can be seen VI:118, **mátti** one could VIII:23, XII:8, 13, XXI:55, **mátti ekki** one could not XXII:55/3, **mátti eigi** it was not possible XXI:88, **er komask mátti** which could be taken VII A:131

megin *adv.*; **ǫðru(m) megin** on one side III:6, XII:52, on the other side XXI:205, on one side . . . on the other side IV:9; *with gen.* on the other side of XII:47, 58; **inum hœgra megin** on the right hand side III:86; **ǫllum megin** on all sides V:81

meginland *n.* mainland VIII:97, *with suffixed def. art.* XXI:84, (as opposed to the sandbanks, *line* 88) XXI:107

megn *n.* 'main', strength XXII:24/1; might XXII:34/3

meiða (*past* **meiddi**) *wv.* maim VIII:86

meiðmar *f. pl.* treasures IX:91

meiðr *m.* tree; gallows XXV:60; **ǫrva meiðr** *kenning for* warrior, person XXII:2/3; **meiðr morðvandar** *is also a kenning for* man *or* warrior V:154, *but since here the phrase is dependent on* **beiði**, *it must be a kenning for* shield, wood of the slaying-wand; *in kenning for* seafarer, King Óláfr **mætr meiðr unnviggs** VI:53

mein *n.* harm, injury VI:40; **vera til meins** *with dat.* cause harm to someone XIV:109

meina (*past* **meinaði**, *pp.* **meinat**) *wv.* prohibit; *with dat. and acc.* deny someone access to someone IV:54, deny someone the sight of someone IV:78

meinlæti *n.* punishment, self-chastisement, self-denial XIV:102

meiri *adj. comp.* more (*Gr* 3.3.8.3) IV:25, IX:101, X:71, XV:32; greater XIV:14, XXII:55/3, XXIV:84, XXVII:27, 46, stronger VI:27; larger VI:74, VII A:36, VIII:176, XXIII:57; **ekki meira skip** no greater ship VI:118; *n.* **meira** *as substantive* VII A:37, VIII:31, XVI:155, more XXI:118, XXIV:9; *n. as adv.* faster *Gr* 3.5.1–3 ex. 6 (e); more highly, as more important XXVI B:113; **því meira . . . er meira** the more . . . the more IV:58–59; **in meira** the more XV:55

meir(r) *adv. comp.* more (*Gr* 3.5.2) VIII:57 (i.e. more settlement),

196, X:168, XIV:114; more so V:133; **meir skammir en** shorter than XXIII:87; **þess at meir** all the more VII A:43; *in place of substantive or adj.* VIII:162

meistari (*dat. pl.* **meistǫrum**) *m.* master XIV:164, *of a classical authority* XXIII:66, *as title* XIV:90, *note*, lord XI:56, 75; scholar XIV:154 (*acc. pl.*); teacher XIV:168 (*gen. pl.*)

mek = mik

mektugr *adj.* mighty, splendid, important XIV:182

melrakki *m.* (arctic) fox XXI:24, XXVI B:67

men (*gen. pl.* **menja**) *n.* (ornamental) neck-ring (of precious metal), torque V:159, IX:50, 60, 73; *in pl.* treasures, jewellery IX:91, X:104

menmyrðir *m.* 'neck-ring murderer', 'neck-ring destroyer', giver of neck-rings, generous man; *here* = the speaker, Bjǫrn Hítdœlakappi V:36

menn, menninir, mennirnir *see* **maðr**

menntr *adj. (pp.)* educated, accomplished XIV:187

ment *f.* skill, accomplishment XXII:3/1

mér *pron. 1st person dat.* me, to me (*Gr* 3.2.1) I:15, 17, 21, 60, 130, 134, IV:96 (*with* **góð**), VI:332, 348, VIII:4, IX:11, 30, 92, 109, X:93, 149, XI:23, XV:23, XVI:27, XXI:79, 134, XXII:22/2, 65/3, XXIV:23, 30, XXVI A:78, B:28; (for) myself I:11, to me, for me I:53, IX:87, X:145, XXVI A:79; from me (*with* **fjarri**) X:94; *poss. dat.* (*Gr* 3.9.6.2) XVI:75, 119

merki *n.* **1.** significance, something remarkable (**at** in it) II:77 (*pl.*). **2.** miracle; *pl. with suffixed def. art.* **fyr merkin slík** as a result of miracles like these XXII:58/3. **3.** standard, banner VII B:74, 88, XXII:38/2 (*with suffixed def. art.*). **4.** remains, traces XIV:26

merkiligr *adj.* noteworthy, important XIV:179

merkja¹ (*past* **merkti,** *pp.* **merktr**) *wv.* mark; sign XIV:66; mark out, distinguish, make remarkable IV:29; show, signify XXIII:46; *pp.* (*in agreement with object, Gr* 3.9.7.1) marked out for, assigned to *i.e.* filled with? XXII:29/2; signify, symbolise XII:35; (they) mean, indicate (that) XXIII:18, 26, 27, 42; **merkir** (it) denotes, indicates XXIII:22, 23, 97

merkja² *see* **mark**

merkr *adj.* noteworthy, significant XXII:16/1; outstanding XXII:17/4;

mest¹ *adv. sup.* most, mostly (*Gr* 3.5.2) VI:23, VIII:133, XI:34, XIV:33; mainly VI:254, very much XXII:31/2, most of all VI:316, XIII:47, XXVI B:20; to the greatest extent, principal VII B:24; **þat var mest til**

at this was the main reason why VI:46; **mest um vera** it was at its greatest, most significant V:9; **fellu Danir mest** the Danes had the most losses VI:209; **sem mest** as hard as possible, as fast as possible II:52

mestr (*n.* **mest**²) *adj. sup.* greatest (*Gr* 3.3.8.3, 3.3.9 ex. 11, 17) I:72, 81, V:25, 104, VI:41, 319, XXII:3/2; the greatest, very great XXII:57/2; largest VI:193, VII A:34; **mest** (*sc.* **lið**) the largest number VI:213; **mestr hluti** the major part XVI:6; **inn mesti** a most V:131, a very great XIV:22, 156, 176, XVI:190; **einna mestir** greatest of all I:78; **inir mestu** very great XV:40; **miklu mest** by far the greatest VI:98, 110; **hafði mest gǫr verit** was the biggest to have been built XIV:8

meta (*past* **mat,** *past pl.* **mátu,** *pp.* **metinn**) *sv.* value, put a price on something II:126; *pp.* **metnar** priced XV:17; adjudge, adjudicate XVI:57; **-sk** *form* **metask** be valued, be deemed XXVII:17

mettr *pp.* fed, finished one's meal XXVI B:25

mey, meyjar, meyjum *see* **mær**

Michael *m.* Latin form (*gen.* **Michaelis**) of a Hebrew name, St Michael the Archangel XIII:11

Michial *m.* = Michael XIII:29; *cf.* **Mikjáll**

Miðfjǫrðr *m.* a fjord (and the valley leading into it) in Húnavatnssýsla, north-western Iceland IV:2

miði *see* **mjǫðr**

miðil *see* **meðal**

miðja *f.* middle XXVI B:202

miðla (*past* **miðlaði**) *wv.* mediate; **miðlum** let us mediate VIII:133

miðli *see* **milli**

miðr¹ (*n.* **mitt,** *dat.* **miðjum**) *adj.* mid, middle (of) (*Gr* 3.3.8.2–5 ex. 4) IX:34, XII:10; **á hann miðjan** at his middle XXVI A:30; **þat kom á Þorvald miðjan** it struck Þorvaldr in the middle V:96; **í mitt þing** in the middle of the Assembly, halfway through the Assembly XXVII:40; **um mitt skipit** amidships VI:267

miðr² *adv. comp.* less XXIII:64; **vetri miðr en** one year short of VIII:192

miðskipa *adv.* amidships VI:269

miðvikudagr *m.* Wednesday; *acc. of time* on the Wednesday XXVII:40

mik/mek *pron. 1st person sg. acc.* (*Gr* 3.2.1) me I:18, 59, VI:91, 114, IX:51, X:65, 168, XI:7, XV:24, XVI:103, XXIV:19, XXVI A:81, B:67, 70; myself IV:94; **við mik/mek** to(wards) me XXIV:21, with me XXIV:26

mikilhugaðr *adj.* high-spirited, of great courage XXIII:16, 23, 57; ambitious, aiming high XXIII:101

mikill (*n.* **mikit**) *adj.* big, large, great (*Gr* 3.3.8.3, 3.3.8.4 (3a), 3.3.8.2–5 ex. 4, 3.3.9 (9), ex. 3, 24) I:6, 75, 146, III:86, V:28, 86, 113, VI:1, 20, 30, 35, 36, 131, 274, VII A:151, 154, 157, B:33, VIII:25, 155, XI:61, XV:15, 108, XVI:17, XIX:22, 26, 32, XXIII:9, 17, 44, 63, XXIV:68, XXVI A:50, B:98; much, a great deal of III:5, V:131, VI:22, XIV:36, XV:127, XVI:53, 85, 151, XIX:34, 36; extensive XXI:27, 59; very (great) IV:3, XIV:42; broad XXVI B:149; strong XXI:53; hard XXI:60; great (in abstract sense) XXVI A:101; **inn mikli** the Great V:79; *with dat.* **mikill vexti** of great size III:22, V:30, XXI:11; **mikill fyrir sér** mighty, of great importance or power, a great person II:75; *acc. sg. m.* **mikinn** I:77, VII A:115, XI:25, XXI:122; *dat. sg. m.* **myklum** (*Gr* 3.3.8.4 (3 a)) I:44, **miklum** VI:356; *acc. sg. f.* **mikla** II:29, VII A:102, XVI:11, 34, XXII:54/3, XXVI B:187; *dat. pl.* **miklum** XXVI A:19; *nom. sg. n. wk.* **mikla** VI:104, IX:50; *n.* **mikit** V:98, 100 (heavy, powerful), 130, VI:61, 68, 85, 112, 220, VII A:163, 164, XXVI B:55, **mikit lið** a large number of men VI:213; **mikit** *as substantive or adv.* a great deal I:129, 141, much III:34, IV:86, V:72, VI:322, XVI:109, XXVI B:30, great pains, great importance VI:318; *gen. sg. n. as substantive* **mikils** much, a great deal XXV:97 (*with* **vant**), XXVI A:106; *dat. sg. n.* **miklu** XIX:41, a great deal of XXIII:78, 79; *dat. sg. n. as substantive* **miklu** XV:23; *dat. sg. n. as adv. with comp.* **myklu** (*Gr* 3.3.8.4 (3 a)) much II:126, **miklu** VI:74, VII B:31, X:128, XXVI B:23, 172, **miklugi** very much XXVII:32 (*see* **-gi**), *with sup.* by far VI:98, 110

mikillátr *adj.* proud *Gr* 3.3.5 ex. 7

mikilleikr *m.* size XII:22, XXIII:16

mikilúðligr *adj.* imposing in appearance, of great demeanour I:46

Mikjáll *m.* St Michael the Archangel XIII:1 (*see* **Michael**)

mildi *f.* kindness, generosity XXIII:79

milding(r) *m.* generous man, king XXII:3/1, 53/2

mildr *adj.* gracious *Gr* 3.3.9 ex. 30; kind *or* generous XIV:109, XXII:11/1, 16/1; *with gen.* liberal with, profuse with XXII:42/3; good, pure, free from sin? XXI:59/3

milli/miðli, á milli/miðli, í milli, millim, í millum *prep. with gen.* (*Gr* 3.7.2) between IV:103, V:97, 147 (2), VI:216, VII A:163, B:30, 57, VIII:20, 32, 127 (among), 129 (2), XIV:159, XV:86, 93, XIX:96,

XXI:46, 55; **á milli/miðli sín, sín á milli/millum** between themselves
II:21, VI:147, VII A:96, between each other VIII:129, with each
other XXI:113; **í millum sín** between them XXVI B:181; **í milli . .
. landa þessa** between these (two) countries XVI:33; **láta hǫggva á
milli** leave a pause between blows V:147; **milli ok** between him and
XI:31, between it (Brynjudalsá) and XIX:97; **á miðli** *as adv.* between
VIII:110; **sendask á miðli** send each other, exchange VIII:131

mín[1] *pron. 1st person gen.*(3.2.1) my, me XXVI B:218; **til mín** to me
I:56, XXIV:11, to see me XVI:39

mín[2], **mína, mínar, mínir, minn, minna, minnar, minni, míns, mínu,
mínum** *poss. adj.* my (*Gr* 3.3.9 (21)) I:16, 60, 62, 84, 85, VIII:9, 10,
IX:12, 117, X:96, 132, 144, 148, 153, 175, XI:6, XXI:78, XXII:15/3,
XXIV:11, 18, 19, 22, XXV:15, XXVI A:79, B:21, 70, 74; *n.* **mitt,
mítt** V:37 (*with* **sverð**), XVI:186, XXVI A:56, 81

minda, mindi, mindu *see* **munu**

minna[1] (*past* **minnti,** *pp.* **minnt**) *wv.* remind; **-sk** *form* **minnask,
minnask á** call to mind, remember XI:7, XII:85, 88; *with gen.* remember to say XIV:69

minna[2] *see* **mín**[2]

minni[1] *adj. comp.* less, smaller *Gr* 3.3.8.3, XXIII:53, XXIV:69 (**en**
than); **eigi minni ván** not less expectation, more than likely V:62,
VI:96; fewer, smaller VII B:42 (*with* **húskarla lið**); **eigi minna** no
fewer (**lið**, men) VI:222; lesser, lower in rank XXIV:85; **minni firi
sér** of less consequence XXIV:75; *n. as substantive* VIII:31

minni[2] *see* **mín**[2]

minning *f.* memory, remembrance XII:39

minnka (*past* **minnkaði,** *pp.* **minnkat**) *wv.* lessen; **er minnka tók**
when (the cloth) began to run short XXI:116

minnr, minnst *adv. comp., sup.* less, least *Gr* 3.5.2; *sup.* very little,
hardly at all X:144

minnstr *adj. sup.* smallest *Gr* 3.3.8.3

míns, mínu, mínum *see* **mín**[2]

minþak *n.* gruel XIX:57, *with suffixed def. art.* XIX:58 (Old Irish
menadach 'gruel made with meal and water, or occasionally butter')

Minþakseyrr *f.* a small tongue of land on the south coast of Iceland
(now unidentifiable) VIII:18, XIX:59

misbjóða (*cf.* **bjóða**) *sv. with dat.* offend; *impers. pass.* (*Gr* 3.9.3) **sér
mun þykkja misboðit** will feel themselves offended, will feel
resentment XV:66

miskunn *f.* mercy, grace XIII:25, XXI:81; *with gen.* for XXII:62/4
miskunna (*past* **miskunnaði,** *pp.* **miskunnat**) *wv.* have mercy on
(*imp.*) XXIV:19
miskunnsamliga (**mys-**) *adv.* mercifully XIV:104; sympathetically
XIV:137
miskunnsamr *adj.* merciful, sympathetic XXIII:3, XXVI B:124
mislíka (*past* **mislíkaði,** *pp.* **mislíkat**) *wv.* displease XVI:125
mismælt *pp.* (*cf.* **mæla**); **verðr mismælt** *with dat.* someone makes a
slip of the tongue V:125
missa[1] (*past* **missti,** *pp.* **misst**) *wv. with gen.* miss, fail to catch II:58;
fail to hit II:150; lack, be short of VI:1, feel the lack of VII B:81;
lose XXIV:69, *with acc.* I:85; *pp.* **mikils misst** lost much, suffered a
great loss XXVI A:107; *past inf.* (*Gr* 3.9.4) **misstu** felt the lack of
(**þar til** for that (battle)) VI:154; *impers. with gen.* **eins manns missi**
one man is missed, lost XXIV:67, **missir við** (someone) dies (while
in office) XXVII:4
missa[2] *f.* loss XXIV:68
missagt *pp.* (*cf.* **segja**) wrongly told VIII:5
misseri *n.* season, a period of six months; *pl.* **þau misseri** that year XIX:91
misseristal *n.* calendar (*object of* **upp at segja**) XXVII:28
mitt[1] *see* **miðr**[1]
mitt[2], **mítt** *see* **mín**[2]
mjór (*n.* **mjótt**) *adj.* narrow XXIII:13; thin, slender; *weak form as
nickname* **enn mjóvi** XIX:7; *n. as adv.* **nǫkkut mjótt meðal** rather
a thin space between XXIII:20
mjǫðm *f.* hip XXIII:84 (*with suffixed def. art.*)
mjǫðr (*gen.* **mjaðar**) *m.* mead II:12, 98, 119, IX:97, 101; *dat. sg.*
miði II:122, 135 (*Gr* 3.1.8 (4)); *with suffixed def. art.* II:114, 115,
dat. sg. **miðinum** II:135, 141
mjǫk *adv.* very (*Gr* 3.5.2) I:7, II:2, 78, III:52, 129, IV:1, V:8, 142,
VI:61, 96, VII A:67, B:4, VIII:25, 86, XII:78, XV:40, XVI:85,
XXIII:9, 13, 21, 41, XXV:52; much VI:340 (*with* **verr**), VII B:86;
very much, a great deal II:13, III:50, VI:3, 39, 154, VII B:28, XIV:37,
XXI:195, XXIII:5, XXVI B:36, 202; to a great extent VI:194,
XXIII:79; nearly, almost III:82, 100, XV:50, XXIII:42, 83; very far
XXVI B:43; hard, vehemently VII B:79; strongly VIII:186; very
frequently, generally VII A:32; continually (*or* very *with* **réttan**)
XXIII:76; **eygðr mjǫk** with very large eyes XXI:104; **hon rétti mjǫk
latínubœkr** she spent a lot of time correcting Latin books XIV:188

mjǫl *n.* meal, flour XIX:56

Mjǫllnir *m.* the name of Þórr's hammer ('masher, grinder') IX:121

mó *see* **mór**

móðir (*acc.* **móður**) *f.* mother (*Gr* 3.1.7.2 (7)) V:136, VI:37, XIII:23, XV:124, 132, XVI:6, 122, XXI:202, XXV:33, XXVI A:26, 47, 79, 114; *gen. sg.* **móður** XIII:14; *dat. sg.* **mœðr** X:128, **móður** XIV:174; XXVI B:3

móðr *adj.* weary (**af** from, as a result of) III:53

móðurfrændr *m. pl.* kinsmen on the mother's side, mother's family VII B:8

mold *f.* soil, earth XXV:56

mon, monum = **mun, munum,** *see* **munu**

mór *m. poetical word for* horse, *once a proper name* (*see SnE, Skáldskaparmál* 88, 89) VII A:138; **mór Marnar** *is a kenning for* ship

morð *n.* killing, slaughter VI:358 (*with* **er sannfregit**), VII A:14, XXV:28, 42; murder VIII:47; **at morði** *i.e.* in battle VI:52

morðkunnr *adj.* famed for slaying VII A:139

morðvǫndr *m.* 'slaying wand', *kenning for* sword V:153

morginn/morgunn *m.* morning V:2; **of/um morgin** in the morning X:6, XXV:3; **einn morgin** one morning XXI:96, 172; *with suffixed def. art.* **um morguninn** in the morning, next day I:112, **of morguninn eptir** the next morning VIII:121

morgna (*past* **morgnaði,** *pp.* **morgnat**) *wv.* become morning, dawn XI:64

Mosfell *n.* in Grímsnes, south-west Iceland VIII:81, XXVI A:118

mosi *m.* moss I:92 (*with suffixed def. art.*)

mót[1] *n.* manner; degree; **með mestu móti** most forcefully V:25; **með ǫllu móti** of every shape and kind XXI:94

mót[2]: **móti, á mót, í mot, í móti, ímóti, á móti** *prep. with dat.,* **til móts við** *with acc.* towards (*Gr* 3.7.3, 4) V:44, 47, 163, VI:136, VII A:154, 157, 159; against VI:194, VII B:13, XV:29, XXII:7/1, 12/2; to oppose, to attack VI:70; to meet I:94, 122, VIII:104, 108, XI:8; **honum í móti** against him XIV:113; **oss í móti** against us XXII:32/4; **taka í móti** meet, take hold of XXVI B:184; **at móti** *as adv.* against him, in opposition to him XV:129; **í mót** *as adv.* towards them, to meet them XXI:101, 102, 124; **í móti** *as adv.* in return XVI:188, **þar í móti** in return for that XVI:50; **mæla ekki í móti** make no objection XV:78; **til móts við** to meet XXVI B:16, to oppose VI:205, to go against, to attack XIX:15

mót³ *n.* meeting V:121, VII B:51; gathering XXII:57/1; *with suffixed def. art.* VII B:51, 52, 56

muðr/munnr (*acc.* **munn**) *m.* mouth (*Gr* 3.1.7.4 (5)) III:11, XXIII:61, *with suffixed def. art.* XII:13, 21; **øxar muðr** the biting edge of the axe VII B:48; *dat. sg.* **munni** XXI:68, XXIII:58, 59 (*with suffixed def. art.*), XXIV:66

múgr/múgi *m.* crowd, mob XXII:12/2; **múgi manns** a crowd of men XXII:29/1; *with suffixed def. art.* **múginn** XXII:34/1

mun *see* **munu**

muna (*pres.* **man,** *past* **munði/mundi,** *past subj.* **mynði/myndi,** *pp.* **munat**) *pret.-pres. vb.* remember (*Gr* 3.6.7) III:70, VIII:10, XIV:167, XV:150; **muna þér** hold against you, remember against you, i.e. take vengeance on you for XXVI A:83

munaðsemi *f.* lustfulness XIV:90, *note*

munda *see* **munu**

mundjǫkull *m.* 'ice of the hand', *kenning for* silver (or gold), the shining metal of rings worn on the hand; *or* 'icicle of the hand', *kenning for* sword VI:346 (*gen. with* **stýrir**)

mundriði *m.* hand-grip V:99 (*dat. sg. with suffixed def. art.*)

mundu *see* **munu**

munhugð *f.* lustfulness XXIII:55

munklífi *n.* monastery XIII:1; *with suffixed def. art.* XIII:2, 29

munkr *m.* monk III:58, XIII:6, 12; *with suffixed def. art.* III:62

munn, munni *see* **muðr**

munnfyllr *f.* mouthful II:80

munnnám *n.* taking in the mouth, use of the mouth; **með orðum munnnáms** verbally, orally XIV:191

munnr *see* **muðr**

munntal *n.* 'mouth-count', 'mouth-tale' II:82

munr¹ *m.* desire, delight; **at mun** *with dat.* to the delight of XXV:54

munr² *m.* difference, importance; **fyrir øngan mun** by no means, under no circumstances XXVI B:162

munu (*pres.* **man/mun/mon,** *past* **mundi/mindi**) *pret.-pres. vb.* (*Gr* 3.6.7) will (*expressing belief or probability*) II:19, 22, 25, 33, 40, 77, V:8, 46, 90, 136, VI:72, 114, VII B:45, IX:66, 70, XVI:52, XXVI A:81, B:15, 24 (2); will be I:39, II:66, VII B:63; (*expressing intention*) *1st person sg.* **mun ek, ek mun** I shall I:107, 127, III:67, IV:50, V:78, 89, IX:79, XVI:51, XXVI B:21, 206, I shall do so XXVI B:210,

ek man, man ek VI:88, 129; *with suffixed pron. and neg.* **mankat** I shall not VI:138; *2nd person sg.* **munt** will (*in a prophecy*) VII A:49, 52, *2nd person sg. with suffixed pron.* **mantu/muntu** you will I:20, IV:75, V:124, VII A:50, XI:71, will you IX:11; **attu mun** that you will XXVI B:218; *3rd person sg.* **man/mun** it must be VI:69, will VI:86, 118, XIV:130, XXII:23/2, XXV:44, XXVI B:23, 72, it will XXIV:79, must XXI:146, XXVI B:199, will be VI:263, XXVI A:87, 102, B:24, it will be XXVI B:33, 69, must be VI:330; XXVI B:15; **mun þat** that will be XVI:24; **mun þá at** there must be in it XV:52; **man/mun vera** must be VI:93, can be VI:112, it will be XXVI B:123, **þeim man vera** it will be for them, they will find it is VI:188; **eigi man hafa** will not have VI:89; **mon/mun (nú) verða** will turn out to be VIII:135, will now take place XXVI B:213; **eigi man þetta vera** that will not be VI:71; **hvat mun** what can XXI:99; **hví mun eigi þat til** why should that not be possible XVI:38; **svá mun enn** it will be so still V:77; **mun ætlat** will be intended I:39; *pres. pl.* **munum** we shall XXV:39, **vér monum** we will VIII:135; **vit munum** we shall XXVI B:214; **munu vit** (*Gr* 3.6.9.1 (13)) we shall I:63, **munu vér** we will XXVI B:101, we shall XXVI B:40, 52; **þér munuð** you will XXVI B:69; **eigi munu** they (the eyes) will not XXIII:36; *past* **munda/mundi** would I:91, VIII:85, XXI:135, XXVI A:27 (1), 105, should XXVI A:27 (2), was likely XXVI A:2, might III:19, XIX:81 (must?), might have II:158, **þar mundi** there would be there XXI:153; **mundum** would have XXVI B:99; **mundu** would XXIV:28, XXVI A:7, 11, would be XXVI B:4, must have been XXI:157; *past pl. with suffixed neg.* **mundut verða skǫp** it could not have been fated VI:342; *impers. past* **mundi** it would VIII:91, it would be II:107 (**henni** for her), XIV:92, **þar mundi** there would there XXI:61; *pres. subj.* **myni** would be XXV:80, **muni** will I:37, must be I:55; **þú munir** you will XVI:33; **muni vera** (that) it must be I:109, can be, will be I:125; **sá muni vera maðrinn** that must be the man *or* there must be such a man XVI:103; *impers.* (that) it will I:89, (that) it will be I:134; **þeim muni illa sœkjask** it will be hard work for them XXVI B:58; **mynim** should XXV:103, **vér munim** we shall XXVI B:49; *past subj.* **mynda, mindi, myndi, mundi, myndir** would IV:88, V:5, VI:13, VII B:54, IX:14, XV:5, XVI:125, XXV:76; it would VI:97; might, could XVI:59; must VI:319, 321, VII A:60, 119, should VI:346, VIII:110; **myndir þú þá** must you then have XXV:21; **minda hafa** would have XVI:163; **launa mindi hann** he will have rewarded you XVI:171; *with suffixed 1st person pron.* **at myndak** that I should V:153 *(followed by* **verða**); *past subj. pl.* **mundi**, **myndi** would I:144, III:2, must VI:124, should XXVI A:65, **myndu hafa** must have VI:134; *past inf.* **mindu, myndu, mundu** (*Gr* 3.9.4) *after* **kvað, kváðu, kvaz, kvazk, kvezk, lézk** would II:47, 136, III:42 (**eigi mundu** should not be), VIII:67, XV:116, 122 (would have), XVI:47, 116, XXV:45

munúð *f.* lust XIV:92

mús (*pl.* **mýss**) *f.* mouse *Gr* 3.1.7.2, 4 (1)

musteri *n.* minster, monastic church XIII:2 *(with suffixed def. art.)*

mygla (*past* **myglaði**, *pp.* **myglat**) *wv.* go mouldy XIX:58

mykiskán *f.* sheet of dung XXI:160

mykl- *see* **mikill**

mynda, myndi¹, myndir, myndu *see* **munu**

myndi² *see* **muna**

myni/mynim *see* **munu**

mynni *n.* mouth (of a river), estuary VI:207

Mýrar *f. pl.* district between Hítardalr and Borgarfjǫrðr V:39

myrða (*past* **myrði**, *pp.* **myrðr**) *wv.* (*Gr* 3.6.9.3 ex. 4) murder VIII:51, XIX:69, 88

myrðir *m.* slaughterer VI:283, VII A:140; the 'slaughterers of the Wends' are Óláfr Tryggvason and Haraldr Gormsson

myrkr¹ *adj.* dark, obscure; *acc. m. sg.* **myrkvan** X:29; *n. as predicative adj. or adv.* **myrkt** II:121 ('so as to be obscure'), dark XIX:33; **myrkt er** it is dark VII B:66

myrkr² *n.* darkness XXII:53/1

myrkviðr *m.* dark forest X:17; cf. X:29

myskunnsamliga *see* **miskunnsamliga**

mýss *see* **mús**

mæfingr *adj.* slender-fingered (one) XXV:79

mækir *m.* sword X:94, 151, XXII:15/4, XXV:54

mæla (*past* **mælti**, *pp.* **mælt**) *wv.* **1.** speak, say I:14, 20, 21, 38, 60, 62, 79, 82, 100, 104, 123, 128, 130, 132, 135, 139, 144, II:21, 24, 65, 75, 85, 121, III:70, IV:37, V:10, 58, 105, VI:63, 76, IX:6, XI:5, 69, XIV:52, XV:21, 64, XVI:22, XIX:76, XXI:77, 98, 176, XXIV:1, 11 (*Norwegian form* **þér mæltur** you spoke), XXVI A:22, 33, 66, 78, B:47; utter, give vent to (*imp. pl.*) XXVI B:123; announce XXVII:30;

with suffixed neg. **mæltira þú** you could not have spoken X:168; *pp.* **mælt** expressed II:12; **mæla málum sínum** make their speeches XXVII:23; **mæla firir/fyrir** argue to, propose to XVI:56, make a pronouncement, announce XIX:53; **mæla (í) gegn** oppose VIII:82, 177, 179; **mæla (ekki/eigi) í móti** speak against, oppose VII B:13, raise (no) objection XV:29, 78; **mæla svá** mean as follows XIV:55; **mæla til** stipulate, demand as II:134, **mæltu til samfara með sér** arranged between themselves to go out together XIX:8; **mæla mikit um** make a big thing of something IV:86 (*imp.* **mæl**); **mæla við** say to VII B:62, XI:28, XII:85, XVI:78, XXV:79, XXVI B:76, speak to, address V:88, VI:127, 128, 165; *inf. in acc. and inf. construction after* **kváðu** (*Gr* 3.9.4), **mæla við** spoke to VI:173; *impers. pass.* **vera mælt til** to address XXIV:57, **sem við er mælt** who are being addressed XXIV:60, **ef til höfðingja verðr mælt** if rulers are addressed XXIV:79; **vel er mælt, vel var þat mælt** that is (was) well spoken XVI:124, 171; **vas þat mælt í lögum** it had been declared in the laws VIII:94, it was declared (made) law VIII:139; **er mælt** (it) is prescribed: XXVII:2, 25; **mæla skal** are to be spoken (addressed) XXIV:15. **2. -sk** *form* **mælask illa fyrir** be ill spoken of, be condemned XXVI A:119; *with reciprocal sense* **þat við mælzk at** made this compact together that III:16

mæling *f.* measuring (**at** of) II:79

mær *f.* maiden, girl X:22; virgin XIII:41; *acc.* **mey** IX:101, young woman (i.e. Svanhildr) XXV:69, *with suffixed def. art.* **meyna** X:176; *gen.* **meyjar** IX:121; *nom. pl.* **meyjar** X:17, 29; *dat. pl.* **meyjum** to maids, female servants X:108

mærr *adj.* eminent, splendid one XXV:50

mæta *see* **mœta**

mæti *n. pl.* treasure, valuables X:71

mætr *adj.* glorious, worthy VI:52 (*with* **meiðr**); excellent XXII:50/2, 58/4

mætta, mætti[1], mættið, mættim *see* **mega**

mætti[2] *see* **máttr**

mœða (*past* **mœddi**, *pp.* **mœddr**) *wv.* weary, exhaust *(transitive)* XIV:171, XV:112

mœði *f.* exhaustion, weariness XXVI A:90

mœðr *see* **móðir**

Mœrr *f.* district in Norway (Norðmœrr–Raumsdalr–Sunnmœrr; modern Møre and Romsdal) XVI:9

mœta/mæta (*past* **mœtti/mætti,** *pp.* **mœtt**) *wv. with dat.* meet VII
A:52, 56, IX:34; strike against IV:10 (**hann** = **ljáinn**), XXII:44/4;
-sk *form* **mœtask** meet (each other) XII:20; **þar sem landit mœttisk**
ok flóðit gekk efst where the land and the tide (when it) flowed
highest met XXI:92

mœtir *m.* meeter, one who encounters or attends; *in kenning for* warrior
(Óláfr Tryggvason) **mœtir malmþings** VI:205

Mǫðruvellir *m. pl.* farm in Hǫrgárdalr, northern Iceland III:84

mǫgr *m.* boy, young man X:104, XXV:56, 79; son XXII:18/1

mǫn *f.* (*Gr* 3.1.8.12) mane (*collective*) V:6, IX:21 (*with poss. dat. pl.,*
i.e. for)

Mǫn *f.* (Isle of) Man VII A:5, 18

mǫnnum *see* **maðr**

Mǫrðr Valgarðsson *m.* enemy of Gunarr XXVI A:2, 7, 55, 59, 64

mǫrg, mǫrgum, *see* **margr**

mǫrk¹ *f.* forest; *pl.* **markir** VII A:130

mǫrk² *f.* mark, 8 ounces of silver VIII:32, XXVII:35

Mǫrk *f.* farm in southern Iceland XXVI B:184

mǫrkuð *see* **marka**

Mǫrn *f.* name of a river (Marne?); *in a kenning for* ship VII A:138

mǫrum *see* **marr**

ná (*pres.* **náir,** *past* **náði,** *pp.* **nát**) *wv. with dat.* get hold of II:142,
158; **náðu eigi** could not (go) XVI:187; **ná til** get within range of
V:95; *with inf.* manage, be able I:33, XXII:46/2, *past subj.* **næði**
I:34; *impers.* **ef því um náir** if that can be done XXVII:28; **-sk** *form*
as meaningless aux. **náðuz at líta sem** did look like XXII:20/1

náborinn *adj.* (*pp.*) closely related XXV:37

náð *f.* grace, salvation (*often in pl.*) XXII:1/4, 51/4

naddfár *n.* 'spike-damage, spear-hatred', fighting with spears VI:260
(*gen. with* **bǫð**)

naddskúr *f.* 'point-shower', shower of pointed missiles (spears,
arrows), *i.e.* battle VII A:13

naðr (*gen.* **naðrs**) *m.* adder, serpent; = **Ormr enn langi** VI:259; **báðir**
Naðrar = **Ormr enn langi** and **Ormr enn skammi** VI:309 (*object*
of **sá fljóta auða,** *parallel to* **Tranu**); **unda naðr** *is a kenning for*
sword XXII:40/1 (*sg. for pl.*)

nafarr *m.* auger, tool for boring II:143, 144 (*with suffixed def. art.*),
II:145; *dat.* (*of instrument*) **nafrinum** (*with suffixed def. art.*) II:150

nafli *m.* navel XII:57

nafn *n.* name (*Gr* 3.1.7.1 ex. 3) VIII:66, 68, XV:55, XXI:24, XXIV:43, 45; *gen. sg.* **nafs** XXIV:33; *dat. sg.* **nafni**[1] I:58, VII A:37

nafni[2] *m.* namesake III:18

nagl (*pl.* **negl**) *m.* (finger-)nail XXII:61/3, XXIII:88, 90

nakinn *adj.* naked XII:57

nakkvarr/nokkurr/nokkverr/nokkvorr/nǫkkurr/nǫkkverr, nǫkkurn, nokkverra/nǫkkura, nǫkkuru, nokkurir/nǫkkurar/nǫkkurir, nǫkkurum; *n.* **nakkvat/nokkut/nǫkkut/nǫkkvot** *pron. adj.* (*Gr* 3.2.3) some, (a) certain I:5, 23, II:18, 39, 70, VII A:31, XIV:166, XV:113, XVI:151, 184, XXI:130, XXIV:1, XXVI A:16, B:230; a little I:4; any I:84, XXVII:8, 16, XXVI B:87, 130 (2); (a) rather XXVI B:7; a kind of XXI:172; **sá maðr nokkurr er** some man who XXVII:2; **nǫkkura hríð** for a while XXVI A:111; **ǫðrum . . . nokkurum** some other XXVII:12; *n.* **nǫkkut** something XIV:157, XXI:69, XXVI A:85, anything XXVI A:80; **nǫkkut af** a bit of I:103, XXI:61; **nǫkkut til** something for XXI:63; **nakkvat** something, some part VIII:134; **nokkut** some kind of III:92; *pl.* some V:164, VI:124, 134, VII A:5, XVI:45, 78, a few V:106, VII B:49, XIV:172, several VI:73, VII B:30; any VII A:84; **eru nokkurir** if there are any XXVII:16; **nǫkkurir . . . nǫkkurir** some of them . . . some others XXIII:31–32; *n. as adv.* **nǫkkut** somewhat, rather V:4, XIV:102, XXIII:5, 11, 20, 71, 105; a little, in passing XXIV:82; at all, in any way I:113, XXVI B:130; **nǫkkut svá** a little bit XXIII:59, somewhat, rather XXIII:67; **á nǫkkut brúnu** to a brownish colour XXIII:109; **nǫkkvot eptir sem** somewhat in accordance with what XVI:55; *dat. sg. n. as adv.* **nǫkkuru** a little XV:97, *with comp.* somewhat XIV:140, by a small amount XXIII:57

nálgask (*past* **nálgaðisk**) *wv.* -**sk** *form* gain IV:90, *note*

náliga *adv.* nearly, almost XI:10, 61 (*with* **hvert**); **náliga engi, engi náliga** almost no one XIV:96, 113; **ekki náliga** hardly any XIV:157

nám *n.* learning XIV:23; study: **þá er náms varð í milli** between periods of study, in the intervals of study XIV:159; **til náms** at study, being educated XIV:166

nam, námu *see* **nema**[2]

nánd *f.* neighbourhood; **í nánd** nearby I:23; *as prep. with dat.* round about VI:152

Nanna *f.* a goddess, one of the **Ásynjur**, wife of **Baldr** II:11

Narfi *m.* a member of Þorkell of Tunga's household IV:9, 50, 62

nári *m.* groin; *with suffixed def. art.* his groin XXVI A:17

nasir *see* **nǫs**

nátt *see* **nótt** (*Gr* 3.1.7.2 (6))

náttserkr *m.* nightshirt III:21, 29

náttstaðr *m.* night's lodging II:130

náttúra *f.* nature, constitution XXIII:107

náttúrligr *adj.* natural, innate XXIII:1

nauð/nauðr *f.* need, necessity, distress X:28, XXII:56/3, 59/2; *pl.* difficulties, harm I:40; constraints, bonds X:62; trouble, affliction XXII:53/4

nauðigr *adj.* against one's will, unwillingly, under compulsion I:88, XXVI A:9; *dat. sg. f.* **nauðgri** VI:6

nauðsyn *f.* necessity, need; **þó at nauðsyn eigi til** though they have need for it, though they are on urgent business XVI:35

nauðsynjalauss *adj.* unnecessary, lacking good reason; *n. as substantive* **at nauðsynjalausu** without legitimate excuse XXVII:50

nauðsynlegr *adj.* necessary XXIV:51

nautaflokkr *m.* herd of cattle VII A:115 (*acc. pl. with suffixed def. art.*)

naut *n. pl.* cattle VII A:116, 117

ne *neg. adv.* not IV:24, XXV:27, 92, *followed by suffixed neg.* **-t** *on the vb.* XXV:31, 35; **ne einn** = **neinn** no, (not) any; *after neg.* any at all XIV:93

né *neg. conj.* nor (*Gr* 3.8.1) X:169; and (did) not X:98; or *in a rhetorical question* XXV:48; *after a neg.* or I:37, VI:9, IX:8, 101, X:108, 153, 171, XII:63, 74, XXV:5, XXVI B:31; **ne ... né** not ... nor ... nor XXV:93; *after* **hvárki** XII:77, XIV:75, XXII:3/4, 53/3, XXIII:52, XXIV:9, XXVI A:77, B:85

neðan *adv.* from below X:171; *see also* **fyr neðan, fyrir neðan** (*Gr* 3.7.1)

neðri *adj. comp.* lower (one) XXIII:57

nef *n.* nose, beak VI:140, XXIII:51, *with suffixed def. art.* XXIII:18, 72; *as nickname* III:8; **fyrir nef hvert** for every nose, *i.e.* one for each person VII A:134

nefja *f.* upturned nose; *as nickname* VI:105, 300, 304

nefna (*past* **nefndi,** *pp.* **nefndr**) *wv.* name VI:138, VIII:113, XIV:172, XV:68, XXII:4/2; call XIX:56; **nefna sik** say one's name is, give one's name as VII A:86; **nefndu móður sína** said their mother's name was XXI:201; *pp.* II:1, 8, XIX:37; **es nefndr** is named as, (his) name is given as VIII:48; **er ... er nefnd** whose name was ... VII A:73, 76; **nefnt** called me/us XXII:23/3; *refl.* **nefndisk** said his name was II:133

negl *see* **nagl**

negla (*past* **negldi,** *pp.* **negldr**) *wv.* rivet; *pp.* X:43 (i.e. the rings on the chain mail were riveted)

neisa *f.* shame, disgrace VI:85

neita (*past* **neitti,** *pp.* **neitt**) *wv. with dat.* refuse I:63, VII A:89, VIII:82

nema¹ *conj.* unless (*Gr* 3.8.2.4) II:35, III:42, VII B:47, IX:30, 71, XVI:151, 184, XXVII:20; except I:132, III:88, VIII:33, X:88, 124, 133, XII:6, XXI:58, 89, XXVI A:8, 110, B:30; but VI:319, but that I:135; **nema eigi** except not, but not VI:223; **ekki nema** nothing but VII A:163, XIV:162; **nema því at eins at** except only if XXIV:70; **fátt nema** little but VII B:20

nema² (*past* **nam,** *past pl.* **námu,** *pp.* **numinn**) *sv.* take *Gr* 3.6.9.1 (6); appropriate, settle VIII:65, XIX:96; learn, receive instruction (in) VII A:68, XIV:187; hear, catch, understand, take in XXIV:8 (*subj.*); amount to VIII:26; *with acc. and dat.* deprive someone of something X:135; **af nema** take away VIII:40, abolish VIII:143; **nema stað/ staðar** stop XV:100, 109, XXVI A:14, B:47; *past subj.* **næmi frá** exempted VIII:33; *as aux.* **nema at** begin to IX:3, X:122, XXII:28/3; **nam (at)** did (*meaningless periphrasis*) X:21, XXII:6/1, 14/3, 16/3, 43/2

nenninn *adj.* eager, tireless, undaunted VI:360 (*with* **dróttin**)

nes *n.* ness, headland, peninsula XIX:97, XXI:31, 105 (*with suffixed def. art.*)

nestbaggi *m.* provision-bag *Gr* 3.1.9 ex. 4

neyzla *f.* use, benefit VIII:53

nezla *f.* buttonhole *or* loop for button XXI:47

Níarar *m. pl.* unidentified people X:41, 66, 142

níð *n.* insult, slander, insulting poem VII A:132, 137, 137 (*with suffixed def. art.*)

níða (*past* **níddi,** *pp.* **níddr**) *wv.* insult, slander; *supine* **nítt** lampooned VIII:84; *pp. agreeing with direct object* (*Gr* 3.9.7.1) **hǫfðu hann níddan** had slandered him with VII A:133

níðingligr *adj.* knavish, dastardly; **níðingligt var hans** it was dastardly of him XXII:29/3

níðingr *m.* villain, scoundrel; **á níðingi** on the scoundrel (*i.e.* he can be recognised by this feature) VI:141

niðr¹ *adv.* down I:70, 92, 98, 139, II:32, 56, III:6, 102, V:91, 101 (*i.e.*

to the ground), VI:257, 259, VIII:120, XII:57, XV:50, XVI:159,
XXI:128, 152, 200, XXIII:102, XXVI A:20, 28, B:167; on the ground
XXI:55; **niðr af** out below, underneath *or* away downwards?
XXIII:21; **niðr frá** down from XXIII:51, below XXIII:59; **setja
niðr** settle *(transitive)*, establish XV:41

niðr² *m.* kinsman, relative XXV:37 *(acc. pl.* **niðja)**

niðrbjúgr *adj.* bent downwards VI:140

niðri *adv.* below *(i.e.* below the town) VII B:59

niðrlútr *adj.* leaning down, bowed down (i.e. forwards?) XXIII:15

Níðuðr/Níðaðr *(gen.* **Níðaðar,** *dat.* **Níðaði)** *m.* legendary king X:2,
14, 16, 41, 66, 78, 91 *(dat. of respect),* 99 (for Níðuðr), 101, 117,
119, 135, 139, 142, 161, 163, 174, 180

níðvísa *f.* insulting or slanderous verse VII A:134

Niflungar *m. pl.* used of the royal family of Burgundians (and their
men), especially Gunnarr and his brothers XI:8, 15, 43, 64, 73, 76

Niflungaskattr *m.* the Niflungs' treasure XI:24

niflúngr *adj.* king XXII:20/1, 29/4

níta¹ *vb.* torment, afflict? X:169

níta² *(past* **nítaði/nítti,** *pp.* **nítat/nítt)** *wv./sv. with dat.* refuse, reject
XXVII:16

nítján *num.* nineteen *Gr* 3.4.1

nítt *see* **níða**

níu *num.* nine *(Gr* 3.4.1) II:124, 132, 134, 137, III:78, VII B:33,
VIII:170, XXI:96; **níu (hundruð)** i.e. 1080 VIII:167

níundi *ordinal num.* ninth *(Gr* 3.4.1) VIII:13, X:28

Njáll Þorgeirsson *m.* XXVI B:27, 36, 37, 39, 46, 55, 59, 69, 122, 127,
129, 135, 141, 155, 156, 157, 159, 163, 167, 173, 174, 179, 185

Njálssynir *m. pl.* the sons of Njáll XXVI B:85

Njarðar *see* **Njǫrðr**

njósn *f.* information (**af** about) XIX:21

njósna *(past* **njósnaði,** *pp.* **njósnat)** *wv.* spy (out), find out by spying
XV:95

njóta *(past* **naut,** *past pl.* **nutu,** *pp.* **notit)** *sv.* 1. *with gen.* have the use
of, benefit from; **megum vér varla njóta** it is not much benefit to
us XXI:178; *imp.* **njót manna bezt** use it best of anyone, *i.e.* better
than anyone else (the formula used when giving a gift) I:137; **lítt
nýtr þú þá þess** you will then have benefitted very little from this
XVI:144; enjoy the love of IV:74; *past subj.* **nyti** should enjoy III:33.
2. -sk *form* **njótask** enjoy each other's love IV:106

Njǫrðr *m.* a god, personification of the sea IX:88 (*gen.*); one of the **Vanir**, though here described as one of the **Æsir** II:8, 67

Nóatún *n. pl.* 'enclosure or field of ships', *kenning for* the sea, Njǫrðr's ocean home (**nór** *m.* is a poetical word for 'ship') II:67, IX:88

nokkurr = nakkvarr

nokkut = nakkvat *see* **nakkvarr**

nokkverra, nokkvorr *see* **nakkvarr**

norðan *adv.* from the north; **norðan af** from the northern side of III:73; **fyrir norðan** *with acc.* to the north of VII A:148

norðanveðr *n.* wind from the north (*adv. acc., see* **sigla**) XXI:21, 26

Norðimbraland *n.* Northumbria, province of England from the Humber to lowland Scotland VII A:3

Norðimbrar *m. pl.* Northumbrians VII A:14 (*gen. with* **morði**)

Norðlendingafjórðungr *m.* the Northern Quarter (of Iceland) XIV:74, 165

Norðlendingar *m. pl.* people of the north (of Iceland) VIII:164

Norðmenn *m. pl.* Norwegians VI:185, 195, VIII:21; *gen. pl.* **Norð-manna** VI:360 (*with* **dróttin**); *dat. pl.* **Norðmannum** VI:210

norðr *adv.* north, northwards II:49, VII A:3, 4, to the north XXI:180; in the north XXII:64/4; on the northerly side, to the north XIX:29; **norðr fyrir** northwards along (the coast) XXI:155, northwards past XXI:167

Norðrlǫnd *n. pl.* Northlands, Scandinavia and the Baltic countries; *dat. pl.* **Norðrlandum** VI:314

Nóregr *m.* Norway VI:15, 32, VII A:127, VIII:76, XVI:12, 63, 130, 154, 155, 173, XIX:30, 38, 48, XXII:1/2

Nóregskonungr *m.* king of Norway VI:149

norn *f.* Norn, one of the three Fates of northern mythology (*SnE, Gylfaginning* ch. 15) XXV:104, 109

Norvegr *m.* Norway VIII:7, 25, 32, 36, 128, 148

norrœnn/nórœnn *adj.* Norwegian (*Gr* 3.3.5 ex. 4) VIII:15

nótt/nátt (*gen. sg. and nom. acc. pl.* **nætr**) *f.* night (*Gr* 3.1.7.2 and (6)) VII A:55, 59, VIII:196; **í nótt** tonight I:83, in the night, *i.e.* last night V:16; **nú í nótt** last night V:25; **þá/þessa nótt** that night XI:62, 66; *acc. sg. with suffixed def. art.* **um nóttina** during the night I:87, 113, V:7, **nóttina eptir** the following night VIII:121; *pl.* (*with num., acc. of time*) **nætr** II:151, VI:8; **nætr ok daga** night and day XIV:121; **átta nóttum** for eight nights IX:104; **nóttum** by night X:43

nú *adv.* now I:15, 16, 20, 21, 34, 38, 39, 45, 55, 68, 76, 82, 83, 90, 95, 96, 101, 105, 110, 148, II:1, 82, III:70, 88, IV:29, 48, V:9, 25, VI:61, 63, 203, 355, 361, VIII:5, 30, IX:6, X:77, 96, XV:12, 23, XIX:54, XXI:145, 193, XXII:9/3, XXIV:22, 54, XXV:35, XXVI A:54, 83, B:13, 100; next V:145, X:66, XI:3 (2), 33, XVI:7, XXI:161; just now XVI:62 (2), XXI:78; lately XVI:62 (1); today XXV:5, 108; so XXI:107, 208, XXIV:40; **nú eigi** not this time V:107; **nú er** now he is XII:62/3, **nú . . . er** now that XXVI B:83; *as conj. followed by inverted vb.* + *subject and a main clause beginning with* **þá** *or* **ok** but if XXIV:1, XXVII:12, 16, 45

numin *see* **nema²**

nunna *f.* nun XIV:129

nýgenginn *pp.* newly gone, just gone III:58

nýhvattr *pp.* (*see* **hvetja**) freshly sharpened V:112

nýlunda *f.* strange thing XXVI B:7

nýmæli *n.* innovation, new pronouncement, new law (see *Laws* II 388 and references, 445–46) VIII:172, 174

nýr *adj.* new, fresh (*Gr* 3.3.8.5 (5)) VIII:90 (*acc. sg. m. wk.* **nýja**), XI:3

nyti *see* **njóta**

nýta (*past* **nýtti**, *pp.* **nýttr**) *wv.* make use of, eat, consume XXI:80

nýtr¹ *adj.* helpful, valuable (*with gen.*, in something), *acc. pl. with* **sína drengi** VI:277; **øngu nýtr** good for nothing, worthless XXI:152

nýtr² *see* **njóta**

nytsamligr *adj.* useful, beneficial XXIII:66

nytsemð *f.* usefulness; **til nytsemðar var** was of some use XIV:157

næði *see* **ná**

næmi *see* **nema²**

næmleikr *m.* quickness to learn XIV:22

næmr *adj.* quick at learning, attentive XIV:19

nær¹ *adv. pos. and comp.* close, near by II:59, 158, III:55, VI:139; **svá nær at** near enough to XXVI B:128; nearly III:57, 131; closely, accurately XXVI B:177; almost V:104, XXII:20/2; **hafði nær** it came close VIII:110; *as prep. with dat.* (*Gr* 3.7.3) close to V:122, VI:125, XIII:17, XXIII:47, XXV:37, nearly VII B:33, XXVI B:47, present at, involved in VI:42; **því nær . . . næstr** almost immediately after? *or* about that time . . . next after? VIII:58; *comp. with dat.* **nær** closer to I:64, XXI:107

nær² *conj.* when *Gr* 3.8.2.3

nærri *adv.* near XII:67; **þar nærri** nearby XIII:34

nærsta *see* **næsta**

næst *adv. sup.* closest; next XIV:170; **því næst** next I:90, V:119, VI:109, XI:43, XV:143, XXI:180; *as prep. with dat.* **næst** next to XIV:7, after *(in time)* XIV:130; **næst oss** closest to us VI:182

næsta/nærsta *adv.* **1.** nearly, almost V:143, XXII:29/3; **því var næsta** it was close to that, almost, practically so I:49. **2.** fairly, pretty, *i.e.* very, exceptionally I:123

næstr *adj. sup. with dat.* next VIII:189; next after VIII:58, 62, following XXVII:5; **in næstu dægr áðr** on the preceding day, during the preceding 24 hours XXVII:33; *wk. dat.* **næsta** the next, nearest XXVI A:8; **er þar var næstr** who was closest (to it) XXVI B:224; **et næsta (sumar) eptir** the following summer VIII:91, 176, 187; **þá . . . et næsta sumar áðr, áðr . . . et næsta sumar** the previous summer VIII:94, 99; closest to someone V:84, 145, VI:210, XI:9, next to someone II:13; **er þessu væri næstr** who was most involved in it, most responsible for it VI:148; **þar næstr** next to him XI:54

nætr *see* **nótt**

nœfr *adj.* clever; skilled in fighting, valiant (*with* **allvaldr**) VI:158

nœrir *m.* nourisher; **sá naddskúrar nœrir** 'that nourisher of battle' *is a kenning for* warrior, the king VII A:13

nǫfnum *see* **nafn**

nǫkkurn, nǫkkurar, nǫkkurir, nǫkkurr, nǫkkut, nǫkkverjar, nǫkkvot *see* **nakkvarr**

nǫs *f.* nostril XXI:68, XXIII:50; *pl. with suffixed def. art.* **nasirnar** his nostrils III:7

óáheyriligr *adj.* which ought not to be listened to, unacceptable XIV:85

óbrenndr *adj. pp.* unburned VII A:129

óbyggð *f.* wilderness, uninhabited area XXI:16

óbyggðr *adj (pp.)* unsettled, uninhabited; **at óbyggðu landi** when the land was uninhabited (*Gr* 3.9.7.3) XIX:105

óbœttr *adj. pp.* unatoned for (*understand* **verði** shall be) IV:73

óð *see* **vaða**

Oddbjǫrg Skjǫldólfsdóttir *f.* wife of Hrafnkell *Gr* 3.1.8 ex.

oddflagð *n.* 'point (of spear) giantess or troll-wife', *a kenning for* battle-axe VI:334

Oddi *m.* farm in southern Iceland XXVI A:113

oddr *m.* point (of a weapon) XXII:55/1

Oddr *m.* son of Þorveig IV:2, 3, 5, 66

óðfúss *adj.* madly eager (to go) IX:105

Óðinn *m.* a god, one of the Æsir II:5, 16, 73, 123, 130, 133, 156, 157, 161, 162, XIV:81 (**Óðins dagr** = Wednesday); Óðinn's son = Þórr IX:84, 131

óðr (*n.* **ótt**) *adj.* (*Gr* 3.3.8.4 (2)) eager, furious, fast; **óðr við** furious at XV:140; *n. as adv.* **ekki ótt** slowly, deliberately; **fara ekki ótt at** not to be in a hurry over it III:106; **eigi svá ótt** (he was) not (to be) in such a hurry (to go) III:84

Óðrerir, Óðreyrir *m.* name of a pot II:97, 118, 152

ódæll *adj.* hard to deal with XXI:11

ódælt *adv.* hard to deal with (**við**) I:71

ódœmi *n. pl.* lack of examples; **með ódœmum miklum vera** (to be) completely unparalleled XXVI A:19

of¹, uf *prep. with acc.* (*Gr* 3.7.1) over II:35, 56, XXI:189; covering VIII:3; concerning VIII:140, 141; because of, for VIII:47, 99; throughout VIII:168; across V:39; above V:170; *of time,* in III:63, X:6, on VIII:121, during VIII:173, 179, 190, XVI:4, 8, 12, 98, 115; *with dat.* above, by XXV:78 (MS **uf**)

of² *adv.* too V:72, VI:70, XV:121

of³ *meaningless adverbial particle often found with verbs in verse* (cf. **um²**); *with* **genginn** IV:21, **komnum** VI:354; **beðit** IX:128; *in prose* **of sá** VIII:110 (*see* **sjá¹**), **of kvæmi** VIII:142 (*see* **koma**)

ófagrligr *adj.* unpleasant, unattractive, unseemly XIV:83

ofan *adv.* (*Gr* 3.5.1–3 ex. 6 (c); cf. 3.7.1) down II:18, III:45, 73, 98, IV:10, XII:56, XXI:174, 186, XXVI B:10, 35; *i.e.* to the shore VII A:56, 111, 151, XVI:128, XXI:49, 87, 169; *i.e.* from the hillside V:163; above, on top III:100, XXVI B:120; *with preps.* **ofan á** up on XXV:107; **ofan af** down off XXVI A:31; **fyrir ofan** down over XXI:81, above XXI:172, XXVI B:118; **ofan í** down onto XXVI B:91; **þar í ofan** down into it XXVI B:229; **ofan um** down over XIX:94; **yfir ofan** up on the top XXIII:10

ofar *adv. comp.* higher up (the hillside; *i.e.* from here) V:172

ofdrykkja *f.* excessive drinking XXIII:48

ofkaldr *adj.* excessively cold, over cold XXIII:107

ofnar *see* **vefa**

óframi *m.* lack of forwardness, shyness XXIII:41

óframliga *adv.* not boldly, timidly I:8

óframr *adj.* not bold, timid; not forward XXIII:15; *as noun* a timid person XV:67

ofrefli *n.* something beyond one's strength; **kvað sér þat ekki ofrefli** said this was not too much for him to do IV:5; **ofrefli liðs** an overwhelming force VI:166

ófriðarmaðr *m.* hostile person, enemy VII A:56

ófriðr *m.* hostility, war VIII:128, XVI:33; fighting XXI:154

ofrlið *n.* overwhelming force; **urðu þeir ofrliði bornir** they (the vikings) were overpowered *or* outnumbered XXI:145

ófúss *adj. with gen.* not eager, reluctant (**þess at** for this, to) XXVI B:67

ofvægr *adj.* forceful (*literally* 'excessively weighty', overwhelming) VII A:12

ófǫlr *adj.* not pale, unfaded (untanned?) *or* without pale markings XXI:115

ógetit *pp. n.* (*cf.* **geta**) *in phrase* **gerði sér at þessu ógetit** was displeased at this XV:13

ógn *f.* threat, menace, hostility V:19

ógnblíðr *adj.* joyful in battle VII A:16

ógnharðr *adj.* strong in battle; *acc. sg. m. as substantive*, one strong in battle (King Óláfr *or* Eiríkr jarl?), *in acc. and inf. construction after* **hykkat** VI:249

ógrœðir *m.* one who does not increase the growth of something but gives it away, *in kenning for* (generous) man, **ógræðir armgrjóts** VI:306 (Þorkell nefja *or* Eiríkr jarl?)

ógurliga *adv.* horribly VII A:158

ógurligr *adj.* terrible, horrible I:75

ógæfa *f.* misfortune XXVI B:187

ógǫrla *adv.* unclearly, without certainty, not . . . with certainty V:7

óharðfœrliga *adv.* not harshly, gently; **talaði óharðfœrliga** did not make strong demands XV:6

óháttr *m.* evil practice, wicked behaviour XIV:77

óhreinn *adj.* impure, dirty XXIII:98

óhræddr *adj.* (*pp.*) unafraid I:93, fearless XXIII:4

óhætt *adj. n. as adv.* without danger; **sem honum var óhætt** where he was out of danger V:118

óhœfa *f.* enormity, wickedness; **hvat er af óhœfunni** whatever originates from wickedness XXIII:35

ok *conj.* and (*Gr* 3.8.1) I:3, 4, 6, 7, 8, 14, 16, 22, 83, II:4, 13, VI:50, 309,

VIII:1, IX:2, XI:2 (1), XV:26, XVI:4 (2), XIX:3, XXI:1, XXII:1/4, XXIII:2, XXIV:12, 50, XXV:36, XXVI A:4, XXVII:3, 6, 22; **ok svá** and also XI:11; **ok þat** and also XI:2; **ok ekki þik** nor of you, and (I shall) not (be afraid of) you (either) I:107; with II:41 (2), XV:27; (together) with (*Gr* 3.9.2) V:88, VIII:91, XXI:86 (1), as well as XXI:8, XXVI A:26; and who, and he I:146 (*Gr* 3.9.5), and who XXIV:84; and (went) XXI:105 (2), and they flowed XXI:53 (2); when, it being the case that XI:35; **ok á** and on it XXI:159; **slíka ok** the same as III:69; *introducing a main clause after a subordinate clause* (*cf.* **þá**[1]; *Gr* 3.9.9) II:21, XXI:38 (*or* = **at**[2]), XXVII:8, 13, 17, 43 (2); = **at**[2] XV:145; *as adv.* also I:103, II:12, 67, III:29, 62 (*twice*, 1 *and* 3), 68, 93, 124, VI:35, VII A:6 (2), 71 (2), VIII:56, 132, 136, 158, 181, IX:79, XI:11 (1), XII:75, 85, XIII:20, XIV:76, 79, 95 (1), 180, 181 (2), 185, XV:10, XVI:4 (1), XIX:112, XXI:7, 34, 126 (1), 149 (1), XXIV:43, 82, XXV:38, XXVI B:12 (1), 52 (1), 67, 213 (2), XXVII:25, 38, 45; as well VI:134, too XIV:18 (2); **þat er ok** it is also prescribed XXVII:31, 43, 48; **svá ok** likewise XIV:181; **svá er ok** that is right, too V:136

ók *see* **aka**

oka (*past* **okaði,** *pp.* **okat**) *wv.* subjugate; **oka undir** make subservient *or* obedient to XIV:119

ókátr *adj.* uneasy, gloomy I:73; unhappy, miserable X:174

okkar, ok(k)r *pron. 1st person dual* our, us (*Gr* 3.2.1) I:39 (1), V:67, 70, 76, 80, 82, IX:122, XII:39, XXV:38, 44, XXVI A:23, B:164, 213; **okkar** of us XXVI B:216; **ok(k)r** for us I:39 (2), XXV:102

okkarr *poss. adj. dual* our XXII:24/4, XXIV:49, XXV:99, XXVI B:177; *gen. sg. f.* **okkarrar** XXV:86, XXVI B:167; **okkarr Helga** between me and Helgi XXVI B:138

ókristinn, úkristinn *adj.* unchristian; *wk. form as nickname* VI:49, 229, 276

Óláfr gestr *m.* III:119 (*see note*)

Óláfr Haraldsson *m.* son of **Haraldr hárfagri** VIII:75

Óláfr inn helgi *m.* St Óláfr Haraldsson, king of Norway, died 1030, V:57, XXII:*heading*, 1/1, 65/3; called **Óláfr enn digri** VIII:31

Óláfr (Sigtryggsson) kváran *m.* king of the Scandinavian 'foreigners' in Dublin from *c.*938 to 980, when he was ejected; in Northumbria 941–44 and 949–52; died 980 VII A:74

Óláfr (enn) svænski/scenski Eiríksson *m.* king of the Swedes (died *c.*1022) VI:35, 37, 84, 128, 146, 163, 187, 213, VIII:146

Óláfr Tryggvason (Tryygvasunr) *m.* king of Norway, died 999/1000
VI:15, 18, 22, 25, 30, 31, 32, 36, 40, 41, 44, 46, 47, 48, 59, 77, 79,
82, 85, 89, 117, 133, 147, 151, 152, 165, 169, 181, 184, 186, 187,
190, 193, 199, 211, 215, 219, 276, 286, 294, 303, 305, 318, VII A:1,
2, 27, 29, 30, 32, 35, 38 (**Óli**), 43, 46, 56, 58, 59, 62, 65, 66, 69, 70,
81, 85, 86 (**Óli**), 96, 99, 101, 104, 105, 106, 107, 109, 112, 119, 122,
123, VIII:75, 84, 145, XXI:37; *acc.* **Óláf** *in acc. and inf. construction*
VI:338; *dat.* **Óláfi Tryggvasyni** for Óláfr Tryggvason VI:107; **af
Óláfi konungi** from King Óláfr's army, on King Óláfr's side VI:223;
með Óleifi along with Óláfr VI:278

Óláfskirkja *f.* St Óláfr's church in Trondheim (Niðaróss) VII B:85

óleiðari *adj. comp.* less reluctant; **vera óleiðari** *with dat.* someone is
less reluctant; **at Danum myndi eigi vera óleiðari** there would be
no less reluctance in the Danes VI:97

Óleifr *see* **Óláfr Tryggvason**

Óleifr hjalti *m.* 10th-century Icelander VIII:62

Óli *m. hypocoristic for* Óláfr VII A:38, 86

ólíkligr *adj.* unlikely, improbable XXVI B:66

óljúgfróðr *adj.* reliably well-informed VIII:11

olli *see* **valda**

ólœyfi *n. in phrase* **at ólœyfi hans** without his permission VI:31

ólǫg *n. pl.* injustice, breaking of the law VII B:29

ómakligr *adj.* undeserving; **þú brennr ómakligr inni** you do not
deserve to be burned in your house XXVI B:157 (*equivalent of adv.,
Gr* 3.9.8.1)

ómerkr *adj.* insignificant; silly; unreliable XXIII:87

ómildr *adj.* unkind, uncharitable, ungenerous XXIII:62

óminnigr *adj.* forgetful XXIII:10

ómjúkr *adj.* ungentle, harsh XXIII:62, 65

ónýtr *adj.* useless, unviable VIII:124

ónæmi *n.* slowness in learning XXIII:46

ónæmr *adj.* not quick at learning *or* insensitive? XXIII:7, 13, 79, 94

óorðinn *pp.* (*cf.* **verða**) not yet happened, future VII A:31, 64

op *n.* opening (**á** in it) VII B:61 (*with suffixed def. art.; or* **opit** *could
be n. of* **opinn** *adj.*, 'little of it was open')

óp *n.* crying, howling II:111

opinn (*n.* **opit**) *adj.* open *Gr* 3.3.8.4 (3a), 5 (1), XV:103; wide open
XXIII:41, 50; **ok opit** and it (the garment) was open XXI:45; cf. **op**

n. VII B:61; *at* X:103 *and* 113 *both the meanings* unlocked *and* manifest, evident *may be implied*; face upwards XII:44

opt *adv.* often (*Gr* 3.5.2) IV:97, V:8, 18, 50, 132, VI:18, 80, 196, VII B:42, IX:38, XIII:4, 32, XV:85, XXII:23/1, XXV:95; *comp.* **optar** more often XXIV:13; **sem optar** as on other occasions XXVI B:69

optliga *adv.* frequently, repeatedly XIV:59, XXIII:40

ór[1] *prep. with dat.* (= **úr**) from, out of (*Gr* 3.7.3) I:6, 3, 23, 97, II:27, 33, 45, III:24, IV:27, V:23, 32, VI:20, 42, 210, 271, 337 (*with* **kominn**), 349 (*with* **koma**), 354 (*with* **of komnum**), 356 (*with* **sannfregit**), VII A:103, B:46, IX:88, 109, X:45, 77, 137, XV:130, XVI:74, XXI:119, 141, 169, XXIII:36, XXV:40, 53, 84, 95, XXVI A:78, 91, B:10, 214, XXVII:4, 11; from, who lived at XIX:23, XXVI A:17, B:184; *postposition* **svefni ór** out of sleep XXV:22; (made) of IX:14, 15, X:118, 120, 162, 164; off XII:4; **ofan ór** down from XXVI B:198; **út ór** out of XI:47; *as adv.* **þar ór** out of it (*Gr* 3.7.7) II:92

ór[2] *see* **órr** VIII:172

órar = **várar**, *f. pl. of* **várr** *poss. adj.* our IV:60 (with reference to the speaker, Kormakr: 'authorial' we; the archaic form is required for the alliteration)

orð *n.* word (*Gr* 3.1.8 (25)) VIII:121, XII:37, 83, 85, XIV:38, 54, 72, 177, 190, XXV:34 (*gen.* **orðz**); remark VI:172; **gera orð á** comment on, make remarks about XXVI B:31; report VI:358 (*dat. with* **at**); message VIII:104, 122, 182; **senda orð** send word XXVI A:5; **taka til orðs** begin to speak, choose to speak XXIV:20; **í hinu fyrra orði** in my previous discourse XXIV:82; **kveða svá at orði** *see* **kveða**; **þeirra orð** their votes XXVII:17; *pl.* words (*subject of* **lifa**) VI:180, XXII:46/4, XXIV:1, 10 (2), 13, messages IV:103, XXVI A:2, instructions VII:185, an answer IX:103; **þat orða** this (in the way) of words IX:5; *gen. of respect* **þeira orða** with respect to those words IX:69

orðaskipti *n. pl.* exchange of words, conversation II:14

orðinn, orðit *see* **verða**

orðstírr *m.* glory, fame VI:212

orðtak *n.* saying, expression II:82; language II:83

óríkr *adj.* lacking power, humiliated, subordinated VII A:145

orka *f.* power, strength XXII:34/3

órlausn *f.* solution, answer II:93, XXIV:24

ormr *m.* snake, serpent II:149, VII A:152, X:83; *in kenning for* gold rings, **armleggjar ormar** snakes of the arm V:21; **Ormr enn langi** 'the long serpent', Óláfr Tryggvason's ship VI:64, 65, 69, 71, 94, 100, 102, 112, 114, 129, 189, 216, 224, 228, 233 (*subject of* **kom í harða**), 241, 253, 302, *also referred to simply as* **Ormr, Ormi** (*dat. with* **stýri**) VI:263; **Ormr enn skammi** 'the short serpent' VI:126, 216, 227; *with suffixed def. art.* the dragon-ship VI:121 (**Ormr enn skammi**), VI:255 (**Ormr enn langi**), VI:269 (**Ormr enn langi**), VI:287 (**Ormr enn langi**)

orpinn, orpit *see* **verpa**

órr = **várr** *poss. adj.* our VIII:1, 172, XXVII:2

orrosta *f.* battle VI:81, 149, 185, 195, 199, 209, 212, 254, 314, VII A:5, B:79, VIII:129, XIX:16; *with suffixed def. art.* VI:199, 302

ort, orta, orti *see* **yrkja**

óru *see* **órr**

órœkinn *adj. pp.* uncaring, *i.e.* vicious, savage IV:46 (*dat.with* **úlfi**)

Órœkjusonr *m.* son of Órœkja VIII:51

ósakaðr *adj. pp.* unharmed, unhurt I:114

ósárari *adj.* less painful *Gr* 3.3.9 ex. 7

ósiðamaðr *m.* immoral person XIV:49

óskaddr *adj. (pp.)* unscathed XIII:35

óskírðr *adj. (pp.)* unbaptised VIII:140

óskyldr *adj.* unnecessary, not required, uncalled for; *n.* **óskylt** V:160; *comp.* **óskyldari** less of an obligation, further from one's duty XXVI B:113

ósparr *adj.* unsparing; **var óspart** *with dat.* someone was generous, not mean XV:76

oss *pron. 1st person acc. and dat. pl.* (*Gr* 3.2.1) us, to us, for us II:82, VI:83, 182, 195, XI:70, XIII:8, 44, XV:23, XXII:32/4, XXVI A:42, 101, B:33, 58; **fyrir oss** for ourselves XXVI B:102; *referring to the author* VIII:34, 36, 55, 144; *referring to the king speaking of himself* VII B:47, XVI:22, 81, 159, XXII:25/4

ossir = **várir,** *poss. adj. nom. pl.* our VIII:87

óstaðfastr *adj.* unsteadfast, changeable, inconstant XXIII:25, 43

óstaðfesti *f.* unsteadfastness, changeability, unreliability XXIII:51

óstyrkr *adj.* weak XXIII:29, 59, 71, 99, 104

óstyrkt *f.* weakness, infirmity XXIII:107

óstǫðugr *adj.* unsteady, unstable, inconstant XXIII:38, 78

Ósvífr Helgason *m.* father of Guðrún XV:3, 5, 7, 78, 94, 112, 113, 115

Ósvífrssynir *m. pl.* the sons of Ósvífr Helgason (Óspakr, Helgi, Vandráðr, Torráðr, Þórólfr) XV:71

ósyndr *adj.* unable to swim II:105

ósælligr *adj.* wretched-looking XVI:92

ósætt *f.* disagreement, dispute; **hafa ósætt við** be at war with II:88

ósætti *n.* disturbance of the peace VIII:126

ótalðr *adj. (pp.)* uncounted VIII:167 (*cf.* **telja**)

ótrauðr *adj.* not reluctant, willing XXIII:37?; *see* **útrauðr**

ótt *see* **óðr**

óttafullr *adj.* fearful XXIII:40

óttagjarn *adj.* inclined to be fearful

óttask (*past* **óttaðisk,** *pp.* **óttazk**) *wv.* -sk *form* fear, be afraid (of *or* to) VI:184, 188, XIII:17, 35

ótti *m.* fear I:44, VI:131, XIV:41 (**at** of it), XXI:128, 154

óvarliga *adv.* incautiously IV:37

óvarr *adj.* unwary, careless V:11; **koma á óvart** *with dat.* take someone by surprise XXVI A:7

óvenja *f.* bad habit(s) XXIII:11, 76

Ovidius *m.* Latin poet, Publius Ovidius Naso (Ovid) 43 BC to AD 18 XIV:90 *and note*

óvígr *adj.* disabled, unable to fight IV:66, V:117; *acc. sg. m.* **óvígjan** invincible VI:86; *cf.* **úvígr**

óvinr/úvinr *m.* enemy XI:25, XVI:72; fiend, false god XXIV:53

óvirðing *f.* dishonour, something dishonourable I:53, IV:111

óvitr *adj.* ignorant XVI:32; ignorant (one) XXIII:10 (*understand* **sýnir mann**), 20; *acc. pl. m.* **óvitra** ignorant (*or* foolish) people XXIII:90

óvizka *f.* foolishness, lack of sense XXIII:45

Óvægir *m.* North American native XXI:202

óvænligr *adj.* unpromising (**til** for, as regards), looking unlikely (**til** to achieve), showing little hope (**til** of) I:146

óværr *adj.* uneasy, distressed; **gera óvært** *with dat.* cause someone distress XV:127

óvættr *m.* evil creature, monster I:118

ox- *see* **uxi**

óx *see* **vaxa**

Oxi Hjaltason *m.* XIV:7, 8

óþingfœrr *adj.* unable to attend the assembly VIII:182

óþokkaðr *adj. (pp.)* disliked (**af** as a consequence of) VII B:86

óþorstlátr *adj.* not causing thirst, that does not cause thirst XIX:56
óþrifnaðr *m.* slothfulness, idleness XXIII:54, 60
padda *f.* toad VII A:152
páfi *m.* pope VIII:189
páfuglafjaðrar *f. pl.* peacock-feathers XIII:19
Páll *m.*, **lausamaðr**; died in the fire at Flugumýrr III:77
pallr *m.* a platform, usually across one end of the room, used as a seat for the female members of the household IV:7. *Cf.* **bekkr**
papar *m. pl.* a name used for Irish hermits in Iceland VIII:21
páskar *m. pl.* Easter XIV:144, XVI:92
Pater Noster *m.* (Latin) 'Our Father', the Lord's prayer XIV:69, 71
penningr *m.* penny, one tenth of an **eyrir** VIII:43 (it is not certain whether a 'penny weighed' or a 'penny counted' is meant; cf. *Laws* II 389–90), XVI:43
piltr *m.* boy, lad; *as nickname* III:76
pín *f.* suffering XXII:54/3
písl *f.* torture II:47
Plato *m.* Greek philosopher XXIII:66
prédika (*past* **prédikaði,** *pp.* **prédikat**) *wv.* preach XIV:31; *pres. part.* XIV:176
prestlingr *m.* student priest XIV:20, 89
prestr *m.* priest III:93, 96, VII A:68, VIII:2, 77, 91, 145, XIV:59, 155
prettóttr *adj.* deceitful, tricky XXIII:68; *acc. sg. m.* a deceitful one XXIII:100
prýða (*past* **prýddi,** *pp.* **pryddr**) *wv.* ornament, adorn, ennoble XXII:24/2
prýði *f.* courtesy; **mest af prýði** with the greatest courtesy XXII:31/2
pungr *m.* pouch, purse III:24
purpurapell *n.* purple material, a costly material XII:35
purpuri *m.* a costly material XII:34
pǫddur *see* **padda**
quinto (Latin) *num.* fifth; i.e. **quinto die**, on the fifth day before (the fifth day before the kalends of June was Tuesday 28th May 1118) VIII:197
ráð *n.* control (*with gen.*, over something), say in the disposal (of something) II:135; **at ráðum** in authority, in charge XIV:131; advice VII A:41, direction VIII:39, 42, 44; **án ráði** *with gen.* without consultation with someone VI:16; plan, course of action IV:48, 104,

VI:214, XV:27 (**hér til** for this), XVI:83, XXV:68 (*pl.*?), XXVI A:57; **taka til ráða** take as our plan XXVI B:166; **hvat þeir taka ráðs** what course of action they adopt XXVI B:48; **gera þat ráð at** make a plan to, put forward the proposal that XIX:65; **tóku þat ráð at** took this course, that, decided to XIX:56; **gera annat ráð** make another plan XXVI B:102; stratagem XXVI B:116; what is advisable XXVI B:208; **kvað þat eitt ráð** said that was the only thing to do III:123; way of life XIV:52; **um sitt ráð** in their lives XIV:38; **yðart ráð** your affairs/lives XXVI B:71; **ráð fyrir honum at gjǫra** to look after him XXI:71; policy VIII:130; what is advisable VIII:132; **sjá þat at ráði** see fit XVI:71; solution IV:112; agreement VI:147; **við fleiri manna ráð** with the approval of more people XV:65; *pl.* counsels X:145, XXV:95, deliberations XXII:9/2; *dat.* **snótar ráðum** using, following a woman's counsels XXII:51/2; **með ráðum** *with gen.* with someone's advice, with someone's help VI:10; **bera ráðum** overrule, reject someone's advice XXVI B:69; **í ráðum** in council, involved in decision-making XIV:132

ráða (*pres.* **ræðr,** *past* **réð,** *past pl.* **réðu,** *pp.* **ráðinn,** *n.* **ráðit**) *sv.* (*Gr* 3.6.5.2) **1.** *with dat.* be the cause of something, be responsible for something II:23, VII A:13; advise XV:64, XVI:150; determine, direct V:13; control, be the one to determine IV:75; rule XXII:1/2; **ráða ríki** rule a realm, have great power VII A:92; decide XV:7, XXVII:18, 47; prevail, have one's way VIII:132, XXVII:15; **ráða með þeim** decide/prevail between them XXVII:13; **ráða á** attack XIX:66; **ráða á at** set about doing something XXII:49/1; **ráða af** get rid of I:118; **af hefir þú mik ráðit** you have made me leave off XV:24; **ráða fyrir** be responsible for the decision VII A:136, have charge of XV:8; **ráða ráðum** make plans, make arrangements IV:104 (*impers. pass.*); **ráða hversu** discuss how XXVI A:6; **ráða um** discuss, take counsel about IX:55; **ráða oss ór landi** cause us (*i.e.* me, the king) to leave the land, bring about my exile VII B:45; *with inf.* decide to VIII:138, proceed to IX:4; *as meaningless auxiliary* did XXII:22/1, 46/3. **2.** **-sk** *form* (*refl.*) **ráðask til** move to, go and live at XIV:150; **ráðask til ferðar** join an expedition XXI:4, 17; **ráðask til þessa** take this upon myself, undertake this I:127; **ráðask undir** move under, put oneself under XV:125

ráðagerð *f.* (making of) decision(s), deliberation(s) XXIV:78, 81
ráðahagr *m.* marriage IV:112

raddar *see* **rǫdd**

ráðgjafi *m.* counsellor; **ok hans eru ráðgjafar** and are his counsellors, advisers XXIV:81

Ragabróðir *m.* brother of Ragi, son of Óleifr hjalti, 10th-century Icelander VIII:61

Ragnarr *m.* **loðbrók** (Sigurðarson), a Viking of the ninth century VIII:12

rak *see* **reka**

rakki *m.* dog XII:45, *with suffixed def. art.* XXVI A:15

ramliga *adv.* mightily, greatly XXII:52/3

rammligr *adj.* strong, well-built XXVI B:61

ramr *adj.* mighty, harsh VI:311 (*dat. with* **bǫð**)

rán *f.* plunder, robbery V:154, XXI:5/1

randa *see* **rǫnd**

Rangá *f.* 'crooked river', in the east of Iceland *Gr* 3.1.8 ex.

Rangárhverfi *n.* the district between the Rang rivers in south-western Iceland VIII:59

rangr/rángr *adj.* wrong, wrongful XIV:93, XXII:4/4

rangsœlis *adv.* against the course of the sun, widdershins XXI:123

Rangæingafjórðungr *m.* the Quarter of the people of the Rangá district of south-western Iceland VIII:166

rann *n.* house, building XXV:83

Rannveig Sigfússdottir *f.* Gunnarr's mother XXVI A:87, 103

rás *f.* running at speed XXI:188

Rati *m.* an auger (*cf.* **rata** *wv.* find one's way) II:143

rauð *see* **rjóða**

rauðr (*n.* **rautt**) *adj.* red (of gold rings) IX:116, X:37, 97, XXI:113, 124, XXIII:30, XXVI A:29; *wk. form as nickname* ('red-haired') VI:270, VIII:65, 74, XXI:*title*, 7, 175, 208

rauðskeggjaðr *adj. pp.* with a red beard V:31; **hinn rauðskeggjaði** the red-bearded one (i.e. Þórr) XXI:77

rauf *f.* hole (*with gen.*, made by something) II:145, 149

raufa (*past* **raufaði,** *pp.* **raufat**) *wv.* break open, uncover II:19, 20

raun *f.* trial, test, experience, proof (*á* of something); **sem hǫfðu raunir á orðit** as had been demonstrated V:132. *Cf.* **harðr**

raunillr *adj.* truly bad, very bad V:15

rausn *f.* magnificence; **mikil rausn er at** it is very splendid to, it is (a sign of) great magnificence to VI:113

raustir = **hraustir**

rautt *see* **rauðr**

réð, réðu *see* **ráða**

refsa (*past* **refsti,** *pp.* **refstr**) *wv. with dat.* punish XXII:5/1

reginkunnigr *adj.* divinely descended, of divine descent (= **goðborinn**) XXV:90

reginn *m.* ruler, wielder; *or the name of a* dwarf *or* god, *in kenning for* warrior (Eiríkr jarl), **brynflagðs reginn** *subject of* **lagði** VI:235

regluligr *adj.* regular, bound by a (monastic) rule XIII:27

regn *n.* rain XIX:57; **randa regn** shields' storm, *kenning for* battle XXII:46/1

reið[1] *see* **ríða**

reið[2] *see* **reiðr**

reið[3] *f.* riding XV:99 *(with suffixed def. art.)*

reið[4] *f.* (clap of) thunder XIII:4

reiða (*past* **reiddi,** *pp.* **reiddr**) *wv.* swing II:29; carry XII:54; pay XIV:17, 28

reiðarþruma *f.* peal of thunder XIII:32

reiðask (*past* **reiddisk**) *wv. refl. with dat.* be angry at VII B:28; *imp.* **reiðzt þú ei** do not be angry XXII:65/1

reiðfara *adj. indeclinable, in the phrase* **verða vel reiðfara** have a good passage XVI:12

reiði *f.* anger, wrath *Gr* 3.1.8 (24), X:138, XXII:52/3, 60/2

reiðr *adj.* angry II:29, VI:96, VIII:86, IX:1, 48, XII:88, XXII:45/1, XXIII:15 (*or* **reiðr** *adj.* ready?), XXIII:64; *sup.* **reiðasti** *Gr* 3.3.3 ex. 5

reis *see* **rísa**

reisa (*past* **reisti,** *pp.* **reistr**) *wv.* raise, set up VII B:88, XII:10, start XXII:38/3; **reisum** let us lift I:108

reka (*past* **rak,** *past pl.* **ráku,** *pp.* **rekinn**) *sv.* (*Gr* 3.6.6) drive II:29, V:102, 127, VII A:111, 116, 117, XV:77; **ok rekr** and drives it XXVI A:70; *imp. with suffixed pron.* **rektu af þér** clear yourself of I:124; *impers. with acc.* be driven XIX:55, be washed up (ashore) XV:152, 153, XIX:59, **skyldi reka** were to be driven XV:132; *pp. pl.* **reknir** driven IX:81

reki *m.* something drifted ashore (such as a dead whale) XXI:62

rekkja *f.* bed XV:9, XXVI B:191

rekkr *m.* warrior X:135, XXII:7/1; *acc. pl.* (*with* **baðat hyggja**) **sína rekka** VI:178

remma (*past* **rem(m)di,** *pp.* **rem(m)dr**) *wv.* strengthen, make fierce; *pp. f.* **remd** fought fiercely XXII:35/1

renna¹/rinna (*pres.* **renn/rennr,** *past* **rann,** *past pl.* **runnu,** *pp.* **runnit**) *sv.* run IX:82, XXII:11/4, XXIII:72; *of the eyes,* move from side to side, look in different directions XXIII:25; **renna at** hurry to join XXII:28/1 (*see note*); **renna undan** run away from XXI:133; **rinna upp** flow upwards, uphill IV:85 (the archaic form is required for the rhyme); **láta renna** pour II:96; *pp.* **hvergi var runnit á** it (the fire) did not at all run over *or* affect (*i.e.* burn, discolour) XIII:6

renna² (*past* **renndi,** *pp.* **renndr**) *wv. with dat.* (cause to) run (*with acc.* over something); *of the eyes,* cast over IV:31 (**at** for, in search of); *intransitive* move quickly, pass, run XXVI A:72

reri, reru *see* **róa**

rétta (*past* **rétti,** *pp.* **réttr¹**) *wv.* (*Gr* 3.6.9.1 (7)) right, set upright II:105; correct, amend XIV:188

réttamaðr *m.* person attending a sheep-gathering meeting, a sheep-gatherer V:73

réttlátr *adj.* righteous, just XXIII:30

réttliga *adv.* rightly, properly XXIV:45

réttr² *adj.* correct, true VII A:68, XXIV:52, 53; right XXIV:46; straight XXIII:52, 76; erect XXIII:82; *dat. sg. n. as substantive* **með réttu** rightly, by rights VI:19; *comp. n.* **réttara** fairer XVI:25; *n. as adv.* **rétt** correctly VII A:119, VIII:153; directly, straight I:43

réttr³ *m.* justice XV:128; what is right XXII:47/1 (*or* **rétt** *adv.* rightly); law, claim, rights; **á mót ræsi ok rétti sǫnnum** against the king and his lawful commands XXII:7/2

rex (Latin) *m.* king = **konungr** VIII:75

Reykjanes *n.* peninsula in south-west Iceland VII A:159

Reykjarvík *f.* a small bay in south-western Iceland, the site of modern Reykjavík VIII:17, XIX:95

reykjarþefr *m.* smell of smoke XIII:37

reykr *m.* smoke III:5, 11, 129, XIII:19, XXVI B:176, 205, 223; *pl.* plumes of smoke XIX:103

reyna (*past* **reyndi,** *pp.* **reynt**) *wv.* **1.** test VII A:33. **2.** experience I:31 **3. -sk** *form* turn out to be, prove to be VIII:6

reyrstafr *m.* reed-stem, reed-stalk; hollow stick, pipe XII:19

ríð *see* **hríð**

ríða (*past* **reið,** *past pl.* **riðu,** *pp.* **riðinn**) *sv.* (*Gr* 3.6.5.2, 3.6.9.1 (10)) ride III:120, 121, V:162, 163, VIII:108, XI:3, XII:70, 79, XV:12,

46, 47, XXVI A:3, B:40; **sá ríða** saw riding XXVI B:10; *pres. part.*
ríðandi riding VIII:107
ríðar = **hríðar** VI:91
riddari *m.* knight XI:65, XXII:24/2
ríki *n.* rule, power, kingship (*or* earldom) VI:43 (*with suffixed def. art.*), VII A:46, 76 (*with suffixed def. art.*); area of rule, realm (kingdom *or* earldom) I:80, VI:21, 32, VII A:76, 92, 93 (*with suffixed def. art.*), 127, XXII:10/4 (*with suffixed def. art.*); diocese XIV:1
Ríkini *m.* a French (*or* Frankish) priest XIV:155
ríkismaðr *m.* ruler XXIV:15, 55
ríkja (*past* **ríkti,** *pp.* **ríkt**) *wv.* reign XIII:48
ríklundaðr *adj.* imperious, arbitrary, despotic VII B:12
ríkr *adj.* powerful VII A:75, mighty IX:55, XXII:11/1, 64/1; wealthy? XI:39, XV:36; *pl.* **ríkir** powerful ones XXV:68; *n. as substantive* **leggja ríkt við** place great emphasis on, impose great sanctions on XIV:57; *sup.* **ríkastr** VII B:2
ríma *f.* stanzaic narrative poem with end-rhyme XXII:*heading*
Rín *f.* the Rhine (river) X:70
ringabrynja = **hringabrynja** *f.* coat of ring-mail VI:287
rinna = **renna**[1]
rísa (*past* **reis,** *past pl.* **risu,** *pp.* **risinn**) *sv.* rise XV:149; arise, grow, derive XIV:82; **rísa í móti** resist, oppose, fight against XIV:77; *imp.* **upp rístu** get up! X:175
risi *m.* giant XXII:20/2
rísta (*past* **reist,** *past pl.* **ristum,** *pp.* **ristinn**) *sv.* cleave XXII:38/4
rita (*past* **ritaði,** *pp.* **ritat**) *wv.* write VII B:5, XV:35; inscribe XII:37; copy (manuscripts) XIV:159; *pres. part.* XIV:178
ríta (*past* **reit,** *pp.* **ritit**) *sv.* write VIII:14
rjóða (*pres.* **rýðr,** *past* **rauð,** *past pl.* **ruðu,** *pp.* **roðinn**) *sv.* redden (with blood; to redden the sword or spear or shield is to fight valiantly) VI:52, 308, XXII:4/3, 16/4; *pp.* **roðinn** reddened (with blood, in valiant fight) VI:208 (*with* **sárlauk**)
rjóðandi *m.* (*pres. part.*) reddener; *with* **randa bliks** *forms a kenning for* warrior, who reddens swords with blood in battle; here refers to Einarr þambarskelfir VII B:45
rjóðr[1] *n.* clearing (in a forest) XXI:172
rjóðr[2] *adj.* red, ruddy XXIII:89, 106
rjúfa (*pres.* **rýfr,** *past* **rauf,** *past pl.* **rufu,** *pp.* **rofit**) *sv.* break; *supine* I:16
ro = **eru,** *see* **vera**

róa (*pres.* **rœr,** *past* **reri/røri,** *pp.* **róinn**) *sv.* row, paddle (*Gr* 3.6.7)
    II:50, 103, 106, VI:103, 124, VII B:75, 82, XXI:22, 81, 102
Roðingeirr *m.* marquis in the land of the Huns XI:56
roðinn[1]**, roðit** = **hroðinn, hroðit,** *see* **hrjóða**
roðinn[2] *see* **rjóða**
roðna (*past* **roðnaði,** *pp.* **roðnat**) *wv.* redden, go red XIX:12
rofit *see* **rjúfa**
róg *n.* strife; **nær rógi** close to strife (*understatement*) i.e. to death XXV:37
rólítill *adj.* restless XXIII:38
róma *f.* battle XXII:35/1 (*with suffixed def. art.*), 39/2
Rómaborg *f.* the city of Rome XVI:88
roskinn *adj. pp.* full-grown, adult IV:107, V:28
ross- *see* **hross-**
rót (*pl.* **rœtr**) *f.* root *Gr* 3.1.7.2 ex. 4, XIV:82
ruðusk *see* **hrjóða**
rúm *n.* space, room XXIV:46; **rúm þat er** enough space so that III:101;
    place, seat I:25, 62, 68, XXVII:22; bed XV:93, XXVI B:181 (*with
    suffixed def. art.*)
Rúmferill *m.* pilgrim to Rome XVI:86, 97
rún *f.* secret; *pl.* secret language, hidden lore II:83, 85
rúnameistari *m.* rune-master, expert in runic writing (writing in the
    runic alphabet) XIV:17, *note*
runnit *see* **renna**[1]
runnr *m.* bush; tree, *in kennings for* man **runnr ægis dýrs** ship-tree
    V:38; *acc. pl.* **danska dolgs runna** Danish hostility-trees, *i.e.*
    warriors VI:245, *parallel to* **svænska menn** *in acc. and inf. con-
    struction after* **kváðu**
Rúnólfr Þorláksson *m.* 11th-century Icelander VIII:183
ryðja (*past* **ruddi,** *pp.* **ruddr**) *wv.* clear, empty *Gr* 3.6.9.3 ex. 5
ræðismaðr *m.* steward XII:61, 90
ræddisk, ræddusk = **hræddisk, hræddusk,** *see* **hræðask; ræddr** =
    hræddr
ræfr *n.* roof; *with suffixed def. art.* XXVI A:60, B:198
rækr *adj.* outcast (*with dat.,* by someone) VII A:143 (*understand* **varð**
    from line 140)
ræna (*past* ** rænti,** *pp.* **ræntr**) *wv.* plunder XXVI A:107
ræsir *m.* ruler, king XXII:7/1, 46/2
rœða[1] (*past* **rœddi,** *pp.* **rœddr**) *wv.* **1.** talk X:177; speak XII:83

(**mǫrgum ... orðum** using many ... words); **þarf at ræða** needs to speak *or* be spoken XXIV:75; **ræða um ráð** deliberate, take counsel (about what to do) XXV:68; **ræða viðr** speak to, address XXIV:84; *imp.* **ræð allt vingjarnliga til** speak (refer) in every way friendlily about (*or* to) XV:88; *supine* **rætt** spoken I:54. **2. -sk** *form* (*reciprocal*) **ræðask við** discuss with each other V:111 (*Gr* 3.9.8.3)

ræða² *f.* speech, talk XXIV:30, 75; discussion XXIV:49; **þessi ræða** what I have said XXIV:48

rægja (*past* **rægði**, *pp.* **rægt**) *wv.* slander XII:42, 62

rækta (*past* **rækti**, *pp.* **ræktaðr**) *wv.* take care of, perform diligently XXII:5/2

rœr *see* **róa**

rœtask (*past* **rœttisk**) *wv. refl.* take root; result, come about; *impers.* **mun rœtast á** it will cause, result in VII A:53

rœtr *see* **rót**

rœyr = reyr *n.* reed; *in kenning for* swords **rœyr drœyra** (*subject of* **hnitu saman**) VI:231

rǫdd (*gen.* **raddar**) *f.* voice *Gr* 3.1.7.1 ex. 5, XXIII:69, 70, 72 (1), *with suffixed def. art.* XXIII:72 (2); *dat.* **rǫddu** X:76

Rǫgnvaldr Brúsason *m.* XXII:16/1

rǫnd *f.* edge, border, rim (of a shield or of the boss of a shield) X:150; *by synecdoche for the* shield *itself* VII B:46, XXII:38/3, 46/1; *collective sg.* XXII:4/3, 15/1

rǫst *f.* a measure of distance, a league (perhaps about 12 km); *adv. dat. pl. with* **fyr ... neðan** IX:28

røkkva = hrøkkva

røri *see* **róa**

sá¹ *demonstrative pron.* (*Gr* 3.2.2) that I:29, II:98, 119, III:83, VIII:131, X:48, 94 (*with* **mækir**), XIV:83, XXII:18/1; he II:92, XXVII:11, this man XXII:19/3, 43/3, that person XXVII:3, it II:97; *i.e.* that little boy V:122, 125; *i.e.* that valley XV:83; **sá kom náliga engi ... at** there was almost no one came ... who, so that XIV:96; **sá er/es/ sem** who XXIV:63, to whom XXVI B:137, that/the one who II:23, XXII:43/1, he who II:127, VIII:49, XIV:105 (**... hann**), one who VII A:31, VIII:27, 32, 36, 48, XXIII:102, 103, who XIV:88, 142 (*with* **hverr maðr**), which XV:150; **sá ... er/es/sem** (*Gr* 3.8.2.1) he ... who VIII:51, 73, that one who X:77, XVI:103, that/the ... which XXIII:61, 76, 96, one ... in respect of whom III:68; **en sá ...**

er and that one is . . . whom XXVI B:99; **sá . . . at** such . . . that
XXVI B:213; **sá þeira er** the one of them who VI:147; **sá maðr er**
the man who VI:322; **sá maðr nokkur er** some man who XXVII:2;
sá annarr the first XXVI B:102; **sá annarr er** some other person
who, someone else who XXIV:70; **er sá nú margr er** there is now
many a one who XXVI B:100; **Kálfr . . . sá** this Kálfr XXII:9/1

sá² *see* **sjá¹**

sá³ (*past* **seri/søri,** *pp.* **sát/sáinn**) *sv.* sow (corn) XIX:64; **sem kolum**
væri sáit as if ashes/cinders had been strewn XXI:111

saddr *adj. (pp.)* full, sated, filled (*with dat.* with something) XIV:147

safna (*past* **safnaði,** *pp.* **safnat**) *wv. with dat.* gather, muster XXII:13/1

safnaðr *m.* gathering, mobilisation XXII:11/2

saga *f.* story (*Gr* 3.1.7.1, 3.1.8 (23)) II:123 (**til** explaining the origin
of), X:14; **at sǫgu** according to the account VIII:145, according to
the dictation VIII:173; **í sǫgu hans** in the saga about him, in his bio-
graphy (i.e. Edmund's) VIII:14; *pl.* **sǫgur** tales, accounts, speech IX:38;
heilagra manna sǫgur lives of saints XIV:190

sagðan, sagði, sagðr, sagðra, sagðu, sagt *see* **segja**

sagnir *see* **sǫgn**

sáka *see* **sjá**

sakar, sakir *see* **sǫk**

sakask (*past* **sakaðisk**) *wv.* **-sk** *form* blame one another (**um¹** about it,
for it) *or* injure one another (**um²**) XXV:103

saklauss *adj.* innocent, guiltless I:52; without cause I:48

sakna (*past* **saknaði,** *pp.* **saknat**) *wv. with gen.* miss, find (something,
someone) gone II:52, IX:2, X:57

sál *f.* soul XVI:112, XXII:32/3, 51/3

sáld *n.* a liquid measure, a cask IX:97

salgarðr *m.* wall of (*or* round) the building X:141

salr *m.* room IV:27; hall IX:49, 107; building X:45, 46, 75, 140,
XXV:110; *pl.* (apartments of a) dwelling X:32

salþjóðir *f. pl.* house-servants, domestics X:108

sám *see* **sjá¹**

saman *adv.* together II:41 (**ok** with), III:60, VI:231, (i.e. in marriage)
IX:122, X:179, 181, XII:3, XIX:56, XXIII:5, 18, XXVI A:79; close,
next to each other VI:169; **allt saman** altogether, all included
XIV:145, the whole XXIII:54, the whole business XVI:57; **einn**
saman on his own XXVI A:50, **einir saman** on their own XXIV:78;

fimm saman five in all, in a group of five XXVI B:13; **sex eru hvar saman** they are all in groups of six V:82; **saman eiga** share XXVI B:188; **saman komnir** assembled VI:28; **saman setja** compile, compose XIV:26, *note*; **af einu saman** just from XIV:36

samfagna (*past* **samfagnaði,** *pp.* **samfagnat**) *wv. with dat.* rejoice with people in something XIV:107

samfast *adv.* continuously, running XXVII:20

samfelldr *adj. (pp.)* joined together XXIII:90

samflot *n.* sailing together; **hafa samflot** keep together (at sea) XIX:50

samfǫr *f.* companionship, going together XIX:8 (*pl.*); living together, marriage, wedded life XV:9 (*pl.*), 80

samharma (*past* **samharmaði,** *pp.* **samharmat**) *wv. with dat.* have compassion on XIV:101

samhljóða (*past* **samhljóðaði,** *pp.* **samhljóðat**) *wv. with dat.* sound together with; **nefit samhljóði rǫddinni** the voice resounds in the nose XXIII:72

samit *see* **semja**

samkvæði *n.* assent (**á** to it) XXVII:19

sammœðr *adj.* born of the same mother XXV:87

samr *adj.* **1.** same I:34, 136, VIII:3, 88, 145, X:129, XII:20, XIV:102, XV:25, XXI:165, XXVI B:13; **inn sami** the same person XXVII:20; *acc. f. sg.* **þá sǫmu** this same VI:38; *wk. n. as adv.* **slíkt sama** similarly II:10, XIII:38; **slíkt it sama** likewise XI:20; **í samt** *as adv.* together, in succession I:75, XXI:66, 121. **2.** seemly, fitting, acting properly VI:333

Sámr *m.* ('dark') Gunnarr's Irish dog XXVI A:9, 22

samþykkja (*past* **samþykkti,** *pp.* **samþykkt**) *wv. with dat.* agree with, be concordant with XXIII:6

samþykkr *adj.* in agreement, on good terms XIV:159

sanctus *adj.* (Latin word) saint, holy; *nom. sg. f.* **sancta** XIII:43; Medieval Latin *gen. sg. f.* **sancte** (= Classical Latin *sanctae*) XIII:30

sandr *m.* sand XXII:59/4; *in pl.* VII A:163, XXI:32; **yfir sanda** across the sands (sandy areas near rivers) XXVI A:5

sannfregit *pp. n.* truly learned, truly reported (*with* **morð**; *cf.* **fregna**) VI:355

sannindi *n. pl.* truth I:50

sannliga *adv.* truly XXII:39/3, correctly VIII:15; **segja sannliga** assert the truth of, tell as a fact VI:329 (*or* 'truly they tell'?)

sannligr *adj.* right, correct, just, fair XVI:72; probable, reasonable XXIV:50; true XIV:34

sannr (*n.* **satt**) *adj.* true, righteous V:155; accurate VI:339 (*dat. sg. n.* sǫnnu *Gr* 3.3.8.1 ex. 3), VII A:61; correct XXII:7/2; true, real VII A:61, XIV:41, 110, XXII:45/3; *n.* **satt** true VIII:135, X:178, 180, XV:49, XVI:67; *as substantive* the truth VI:100, XXII:22/4; **allt it sanna** the whole truth XXVI B:186; **með sǫnnu** in truth, truly (*with* **gæta**?) XXII:50/3; *comp. n.* **sannara** (*Gr* 3.3.3 ex. 5) more correct VIII:6

sannsǫgull *adj.* truthful XXIII:39

sár *n.* wound V:130, VII A:53, 54, 55, XXI:179, XXVI A:50, 117; *pl.* III:62, 113, V:132, XI:7, 35, 37, 40, XV:114, XXVI A:76, 77; **í sárum** with his wounds XV:122

sárafar *n.* nature of wounds, extent of wounds V:105

sárbeitr *adj.* wound-cutting XXV:31

sárlaukr *m.* 'wound-leek', *kenning for* sword (*collective, unless the first person pl. means* I, *the speaker*) VI:208 (*object of* **bárum**)

sárliga *adv.* bitterly XI:32

sárr *adj.* wounded VI:260 (*nom. pl. with* **verkendr sukku**), 299 (*understand* were *or* being?), 330, VII A:58, XV:108, XXVI B:99; i.e. dead? XXV:60; bitter, angry (full of rage) XXII:34/2; painful XXII:39/4; **vinna [menn] sára** cause (men) to be wounded XXVI A:97; **frá sárum tyggja** *i.e.* about the ruler that he was wounded VI:353; *n. as adv.* **sárt** sorely XXVI A:22

sásk *see* **sjá**

sat *see* **sitja**

satt *see* **sannr**

sáttmál *n.* words or offers of reconciliation VII B:57

sáttr *adj.* agreed, in agreement; **verða sáttir á** reach agreement on, agree on XXVII:7, 11; **verða eigi á sáttir** do not reach agreement on it, do not agree on it XXVII:13

sáttu *see* **sjá**

sátu, sátuð *see* **sitja**

sauma (*past* **saumaði**, *pp.* **saumat**) *wv.* sew XIV:189

sáu *see* **sjá**[1]

Saurbœr *m.* settlement in western Iceland XV:43, 44, 75

saurlífi *n.* unclean behaviour, lechery XIV:90, *note*

sax *n.* a short, one-edged sword XV:107, 109 (*with suffixed def. art.*); *pl.* **sǫx** shears; *dat. pl. with suffixed def. art.* = **manskæri** V:103

Saxland *n.* Saxony *or* Germany XVI:129
saztu *see* **sitja**
sé¹ *see* **sjá¹**
sé² *see* **vera**
seðja (*past* **saddi**, *pp.* **saddr**) *wv.* feed, fill; *imp.* XXII:31/4
sefr *see* **sofa**
seggr *m.* man V:150 (= Bjǫrn), VI:332 (*subject of* **sannliga segja**), 353 (*subject of* **segir**), X:48 (= Vǫlundr), XXI:183, XXII:6/2, 22/3, XXV:67; warrior X:43; **seggr** the warrior (i.e. Bjǫrn) XXII:45/4; *gen. pl.* **seggja** *with* **sveit** V:54, *with* **áttar** VI:56, *with* **miskunn** XXII:62/4; **seggja mart** many a warrior XXII:39/3
segja (*pres.* **segir**, *past* **sagði**, *past pl.* **sǫgðu**, *pp.* **sagt**) *wv.* (*Gr* 3.6.9.2 (5)) **1.** say, tell I:12, 49, 51, 66, 74, 81, 88, 108, 116, 134, 141, 143, II:14, 34, 39, 78, 99, 106, III:25, 110, 121, IV:92, 97, VI:32, 49, 329, 351, VII A:10, VIII:33, 36, X:124, XI:25, 34, XV:5, 25, XVI:24, XIX:66, 67, XXI:50, 136, XXIV:9, XXVI A:35, 76, B:3; report VI:334, VII A:147, XXV:66, XXVII:3; declare (*with dat.* to someone) XIV:65; show, indicate XXIII:12; proclaim, bespeak XXIII:79, 89, **segja mann** proclaim a man to be XXXIII:105; **segja, sagði** i.e. wrote XXIII:1, 66; **segir** says, i.e. writes XIV:26, *note*, 166; **ek segi** I say XXVI B:26; **menn segja, segja menn** it is said, they say VI:323, VII B:36; *imp.* **seg (þú) mér** tell me V:16, X:147, XVI:39, **segðu** tell IX:37, **segiða** do not tell X:108; *past* **sagði** he said X:180, had said VI:211; *past pl.* **sǫgðu** they told X:178, **sǫgðu** said VI:94; *pp. n. and supine* **sagt** III:114, V:1, 125, 145, VIII:15, related VIII:5, *n. pl.* **sǫgð** II:37; (afore)said, aforementioned: *nom. sg. f.* **fyrr sǫgð** XIII:34, *acc. sg. m.* **sagðan** XIII:37, *dat. sg. m.* **sǫgðum** XIII:32, *gen. pl.* **sagðra** XIV:168, 172, *dat. pl.* **sǫgðum** XIV:186; **sagt er** there is told, there are stories VI:314; **svá er sagt** so it is said (reported) VIII:28, 112, XIII:27; **var sagt** *with dat.* someone was told VII B:53, XVI:16; **honum (hánum) var sagt** he was told I:113, VI:187; **kváðusk engi tíðendi segja** they said they had no tidings to tell XXVI B:6; **af segja** say about it XXVI B:23; **nú er at segja** now it must be told III:90; **segja frá** report, tell the story XXVI B:54; **þat er sagt ífrá** it is told XIV:88; **er nú var frá sagt** of whom an account has just been given XIV:46; **er langt er frá at segja** whom it takes a long time to enumerate XIV:184; **segja fyrir** foretell VII A:31, 46 (*past subj.* **segði**), 63; **segja skilit við** declare oneself divorced from XV:28 (*imp.*), 30, 64; **segja til** give

information about, tell about VI:160, report to (*with dat.*) XXVII:41, witness to XXIII:24; **segja upp** announce, pronounce, proclaim VIII:117, 118, 138, 176, XXVII:27, recite VIII:171, 181, XXVII:5, 25, 31, *subj.* **segi upp** XXVII:34; *with acc. and inf.* XV:117, *with inf. understood* **sagði mik** said I should be XVI:183; **þeir sǫgðu land þar** they said there was a land there XXI:204. **2.** **-sk** *form* say that one: **sagðisk vera** said he was VII A:39; **sǫgðusk** declared themselves (to be) VIII:114

segl *n.* sail VI:74, 104, 125, 135, 166 (*pl.*)

seiða (*past* **seiddi**, *pp.* **seiddr**) *wv.* cast a spell (**til at** so that) IV:105

seiðhjallr *m.* scaffold for performing magical rites, ritual platform XV:142

seiðmaðr *m.* sorcerer XV:40

seigr *adj.* stubborn *Gr* 3.3.9 ex. 30

seimr *m.* gold wire (as used in jewellery); gold, riches VII A:17, XXII:3/4

seinn *adj.* slow VI:70, XXI:137; **seinn til** (you are) late for V:121; *n. as adv.* **seint** slowly (*i.e.* not at all) III:1, IV:63, XXVI B:45; *i.e.* coldly: **svarar heldr seint** was rather slow to answer XVI:80; *sup.* **seinst** last *Gr* 3.5.1–3 ex. 6 (f)

sékka *see* **sjá**[1]

sekr *adj.* convicted; **verða sekr** be found guilty, be outlawed (**of** for) VIII:47, 99

sel *n.* shieling (a hut in the summer mountain pasture) XV:83, 88; *gen. pl. with suffixed def. art.* **seljanna** XV:86

selfǫr *f.* keeping of cattle in a shieling; **hafa selfǫr** use a shed in the mountain pasture for the milch cows (*or* sheep) XV:82

selja (*pres.* **selr**, *past* **seldi**, *pp.* **seldr**) *wv.* (*Gr* 3.6.9.3) give IX:15, X:117, XVI:141, XXII:63/2; sell (**sér** to them) II:128, XV:33, XVI:47; **selja við** sell for XVI:22

sem *conj.* (*Gr* 3.8.2.1, 4) as I:15, 19, 73, 79, 91, 118, III:125, IV:76, 97, V:8, 131, VI:49, 73, 153, 211, 228, 292 (1), VII B:12, 15, VIII:109, X:93, XI:35, XIII:23, 40, XV:35, 43, XVI:38, XXI:181, XXIV:24, 71, XXVI B:26, 61, 69, 72; like, as VI:195, VIII:143, IX:58, XIV:105, XV:70, XXII:20/2, XXIV:63, XXV:16, 46, 91, 104, 107, XXVI B:67, 112; in the way that XXIV:35; as well as, equal to, commensurate with IX:36; as if XII:33, 57, 82, XIII:17, 30, XVI:75, XXI:160, XXII:44/4, XXIV:67, 69, XXVI B:29, as if, that V:15,

XXI:135, XXVI B:49; as though I:37, 124; so that XXIII:102; when I:4, XII:70, 80, XIII:15; as soon as VI:217, as much as XVI:51, as long as XVI:88; which I:23, 25, 61, 68, 69, VI:148, VIII:138, XIII:34, XXIII:37, 40, XXIV:5, XXVI B:66; who I:43, 78, 133, XIII:47 (2), XIV:130, whom XXVII:10, 23; that which, what XIII:47 (1); **sú/þat . . . sem** a . . . which XXIII:70, 77; **sem gerðisk** however it might turn out (*or* if it happened?) IV:95; *with sup.* as . . . as possible II:52, 154, III:111, 112, V:14, VI:63, 78, 214, VII A:34, XIV:15, XXIV:12, XXVI B:84; **sem ek hagast kunna** as skilfully as I knew how X:92; **þar sem** in the place which, where II:115, VI:267, from where V:60, to where VII B:79, whereas III:93, when VI:292; **þar . . . sem** there . . . where, (in the place) where VIII:18, 52, **þar til . . . sem** towards the spot where XXIII:18; **þangat sem** to where I:99, 100, V:118; **þá er sem** then it will be as if IV:45; **sem er** such as XIV:81; **slíkt . . . sem** such as XIV:30; **því líkast sem** just as if XXI:97; **þat . . . sem** the . . . which XIII:18; **þær sem** which VII B:4, XI:15; **þá** *(acc. pl. m.)* **sem** whom XIV:166; **þat sem** (to) what VII B:21, which XV:33; **at því sem** in accordance with what VIII:38; **því . . . sem** the . . . the V:67 (*see* **því**); **hvat sem** whatever XXI:136, **hvar sem** wherever XXII:19/4, **hvárt sem** (cf. *Gr* 3.8.2.1) whether VIII:154, XXVII:11

sém *see* **vera**

semja (*past* **samði,** *pp.* **samit**) *wv.* arrange, agree on, settle VII A:95; arrange, order XIV:72

senda (*past* **sendi,** *pp.* **sendr**) *wv.* (*Gr* 3.6.9.1 (7)) **1.** send I:42, V:6, 95, VI:5, VII A:33, VIII:77, 182, X:119, 121, 161, 163, 165, XVI:18 XIX:24, 72, XXVI B:195; *subj.* XXI:63; expel II:159; **senda eptir** send for XXVI A:10. **2. -sk** *form* **sendusk á miðli** = **sendu á miðli sín** were sending each other VIII:130 (cf. *Gr* 3.9.8.3)

sendimaðr *m.* messenger VII A:39, 42

sénir *see* **sjá**

senn *adv.* together, at once VI:111; straightway IX:53, 81

senna *f.* quarrel; *in kennings for* battle **vápna senna** VI:174, **fráns leggbita senna** VI:244

septimus (Latin) *num. adj.* seventh VIII:189

sér[1] *refl. pron. dat.* (*Gr* 3.2.1) him, himself, herself, themselves *etc.* I:26, 28, 55, 87, 88, II:89, III:3, 94, VI:296, VIII:195, XIV:178, XV:13, 18, XVI:13, 116, XIX:9, XXI:68, XXII:50/1, XXIII:102, XXV:31, XXVI A:77, B:222; *poss. dat.* (*Gr* 3.9.6.2) II:51 ('in his claws'), 70, 125, V:157, VI:295, X:62, XI:20, 35, XVI:146; for himself XVI:91, XIX:42; for himself, his VI:16; her XV:126, for herself II:63, VII A:79; for themselves VIII:90, X:5; **en sér** but (death) for himself III:31; **eiga sér son** have a son XXVI A:113; **jafnmarga sér** the same number as themselves XIX:69; **á sér** on himself (*i.e.* on his neck) V:159, on one's person XVI:148, (that was) on him XXVI B:229, in them XXIII:33; **vel at sér** XXVI B:63 *see* **vel**; **firi sér einum ok** just for himself and for XXIV:63; **minni firi sér** of less consequence XXIV:69; **sér í hendi, í hǫnd sér** in his hand XXV:73, XXVI B:219; **undir hendi sér** under his arm XXVI B:152; **með sér** with himself XIV:126, with them XXI:72, XXVI A:9; **sér til liðs** for his troop XXII:28/4; **sér hvern mann** each man separately VII A:84. Cf. **sérhverr**

sér² *see* **sjá¹**

sér³, sért *see* **vera**

sérhverr *pron.* each one singly (separately) XIX:69

serkr *m.* shirt; *with suffixed def. art.* her shirt XXI:141; **Heðins baugs serkr** a shirt made of rings, mail-coat (as used by Heðinn) VI:262 (*gen. with* **verkendr**); *see under* **baugr**

sess *m.* seat X:131

sessi *m.* table-companion, friend; **þess sessa þjóðar** of this friend of the people (*i.e.* King Óláfr; *gen. with* **þróttar orð**) VI:179

sét *see* **sjá¹**

setgeirabrœkr *f. pl.* breeches with a gore in the seat XV:70

setgeiri *m.* gore (*i.e.* a triangular strip of cloth) in the seat (of a man's pair of breeches) XV:50

setit *see* **sitja**

setja (*pres.* **setr,** *past* **setti,** *pp.* **settr**) *wv.* (*Gr* 3.6.9.3) **1.** set, put, place I:26, 29, II:113, 116, 156, IV:8, 9, X:85 (*imp.*), XI:53, XII:17; establish II:89, XIV:24, XIX:108; set out, set up VIII:40; lay down XXII:6/1; **ok setr** and puts (it; *Gr* 3.9.5.1) XI:20; *with suffixed 1st person pron.* **ek settak þik** I had set you up to be XVI:69; *pp.* **sett** established, set up VIII:38, 44, XIX:108, in session VII A:73; **ok sett(r) með** and it was set (adorned, inlaid) with XII:26, 30; assigned XIV:138, *note*; *with verb* to be *understood,* **settr** he was put X:86; *pp. after aux.* **hafa** *in agreement with direct object* (*Gr* 3.9.7.1) **mik hafa settan** had put me V:63; **setja á** hurl at, aim at I:43; **setja at** attack XIX:69; **setja niðr** settle (*transitive*), establish XV:41; **setja**

saman compose XIV:26, *note*; **setja upp** raise VII B:74; **setja við** (*adv.*, *Gr* 3.7.7) place against, *i.e.* to meet (it), receive (it) upon I:41. **2. -sk** *form refl.* **setjask** sit down XXVII:22; **sezk** sits down I:4, alights II:27; **setjask niðr** sit down XXVI A:28; *imp.* **sezk niðr** sit down XVI:159; **setisk** sets (of the sun) VI:115 (*pres. subj.*); *past* **settisk, settusk** sat (down) I:70, II:7, III:102, V:91, alighted X:19, 141; **settisk þar** settled himself there XXVI A:113; **er þar settisk** *(subj.)* **í** who might attend there, who should come to stay there XIV:27; **settisk upp** sat up, got up VIII:122; *pp.* **sezt** settled himself, set himself up (as king) VI:32, 43

setning *f.* ordinance XIV:120

setstokkr *m.* a wooden plank or beam dividing the raised floor (**set**) along the sides(s) of the hall from the ground in the middle (**gólf**) III:6 (*with suffixed def. art.*), XXVI B:219

sett, settak, settir, settisk, settr *see* **setja**

sétti *num.* sixth *Gr* 3.4.1, XXIV:38; **við sétta mann** *i.e.* in a group of six, with five others V:93 (*Gr* 3.4.2 (8))

séu *see* **vera**

sex *num.* six (*Gr* 3.4.1) V:44, 47, 81, 94, 113, XIX:49; six (summers) VIII:170; **sex tigu** (*acc.*), **sex tegum** (*dat.*) sixty VI:21, VIII:56, 59

sextán *num.* sixteen (*Gr* 3.4.1) VIII:16, XXVI A:98

seyðir *m.* cooking XXVI B:109; cooking pit, earth oven II:19; *with suffixed def. art.* II:20, 23, 26 (a fire was lit in a pit and covered with earth or ashes, the meat put on top and the whole covered with earth)

sezk, sezt *see* **setja**

síbyrðr *adj.* broadside on (**viðr** to) VI:228; *n. as adv.* **síbyrðt** broadside on (**viðr** to the enemy?) VI:215

síð *adv.* late *Gr* 3.5.1–3 ex. 6 (d); **síð ok snemma** late and early, evening and morning XIV:61

síða *f.* side XXIII:93; **við síðu** by *or* against the side (of) VI:237 (*phrase belongs with* **reginn lagði**)

Síða *f.* an area in south-east Iceland VIII:79, 116

siðaðr *adj.* (*pp.*) behaved XIV:163; conducted (i.e. in conduct, in morals); **bezt siðaðr** highest in conduct, whose conduct is finest XIX:110, 113

síðan *adv.* later, afterwards III:83, 128, IV:66, 76, VII A:123, 169, VII B:84, VIII:19, 22, 43, 57, 147, XIV:173, 183, XV:30, 33, 75, XIX:66, XXVI A:103, B:230; since VIII:4, 66, XIV:13, 57, 75, XV:152, 155,

XIX:86, XXIV:59, XXV:6; then, next I:1, 3, 22, 25, 70, 120, 138,
V:75, VI:228, VII A:2, 56, 95, B:56, VIII:97, X:26, 85, XII:4, XV:7,
109, 135, XVI:19, 141, XXII:45/3; after that XIX:34, XXI:20, 63,
105, XXVI A:10, 32, 36, 108, B:119, 142, 228; **aldrigi/aldri síðan**
never again XVI:75, XXVI B:214; **lengi síðan** for a long time
afterwards XIV:175, for a long time to come XV:56; *as conj.* (*Gr*
3.8.2.4) **síðan, síðan er** after IV:104, VII A:27, 36, 92, XXIV:69,
since XVI:108, XXI:13
síðari *adj. comp.* latter *Gr* 3.3.5 ex. 6
síðar(r) *adv. comp.* later *Gr* 3.5.3 (11), III:51, IV:68, VIII:17, 193, 197,
XIV:130; **litlu síðar** a little later XXI:73, 179; **síðar fám vetrum** a
few years later VIII:142; behind VI:27
síðarst, síðast *adv. sup.* last II:44, 45; most recently XXVII:5; for the
last time XXVI B:21; **mæltu þat síðast** this was the last they spoke
XXVI B:183; last, in the rear III:121, VI:127
siðlátr *adj.* virtuous, of good life XIV:3, 150
siðlæti *n.* morality, morals XXIII:78
síðir *in* **of síðir, um síðir** in the end III:63, IV:101
siðr *m.* custom VII A:97; religion VIII:135; **sem siðr er til** as is the
custom for XVI:97; **til siðar tekit** established as a custom XXIV:77;
pl. conduct, moral life XIV:48, 73; morals XXIII:24, 109; behaviour,
practices XIV:94; activity (*subject or complement of* **er at segja**)
VI:161
síðr *adv. comp.* less; **eigi at síðr** none the less VI:212; *sup.* **sízt** least
XXVI B:99; **sem sízt** as little as possible III:112
siðvenja *f.* custom XXIV:59
Sif (*gen.* **Sifjar**) *f.* a goddess, wife of Þórr IX:97; *used as if a name for
a giantess or troll-wife in a kenning for* wolf, **Sifjar sóti** VI:252
sífella *f.* continuity; **í sífellu** continuously, constantly, all the time V:104
síga (*past* **seig**, *past pl.* **sigu**, *pp.* **sigit**) *sv.* sink down; draw along,
glide along; **síga á hǫmlur** pull against the oar-thongs, *i.e.* draw backwards, row astern VI:214; *refl.* **lætr sígask** lets himself drop II:27
Sigfússsynir *m. pl.* sons of Sigfúss Sighvatsson, Gunnarr's maternal
uncles (*Njáls saga* ch. 34, *ÍF* XII 87–88) XXVI A:110, B:10
sigla (*past* **sigldi**, *pp.* **siglt**) *wv.* sail VI:25, 60, 63, 75, 110, 120, VII
A:3, 70, XXI:20, 35, 89; sail by VI:88, 130; *with acc. of route* sail
along VI:87; *with acc. of wind* **sigla norðanveðr** sail with a wind
from the north XXI:20; **siglum** let us sail VI:167; *with dat.* sail with,
take VII A:132; **sigla fyrir** sail past VI:59 (*with acc. of route*), 61

Sigmundr *m.* Bjǫrn Hítdœlakappi's farmhand V:2

signa (*past* **signaði,** *pp.* **signat**) *wv.* sign with the cross; **signa sik** make the sign of the cross, cross oneself XIV:64, 68; **signdu þau sik ok sveininn** they made the sign of the cross over themselves and over the boy XXVI B:182

sigr (*gen.* **sigrs**) *m.* victory VI:185, XXII:1/4, 47/4; *with suffixed def. art.* **af sigrenum er** of the victory whereby VI:315

sigrask (*past* **sigraðisk**) *wv.* **-sk** *form* be victorious XXVI B:54

Sigríðr[1] *f.* daughter of Ketill kálfr VII B:6

Sigríðr[2] *f.* daughter of Skǫglar-Tósti VI:37, 38

Sigurðr sveinn *m.* Boy Sigurðr (the dragon-slayer), former husband of Grímhildr XI:7, 8, 24, 35, 37, 39, 40, 71, XXV:22, 26

Sigvaldi *m.* jarl of Jómsborg VI:24, 33, 103, 106, 120, 135, 137, 199 (*gen. with* **getit**), 200; **ok Sigvalda** *along with* **Frísa dolgi** *dat. object of* **fylgða ek** VI:204

Sigyn *f.* a goddess, one of the **Ásynjur**, wife of **Loki** II:10

sik *refl. pron. acc.* oneself *etc.* (*Gr* 3.2.1) I:30, 110, 119, VI:249, VIII:120, XI:18, XVI:44, 93, XIX:110, XXI:68, XXVI A:72, B:38, 190, 230

sikling(r) *m.* ruler (here = King Óláfr) VI:356 (*gen. with* **morð**), XXII:13/1, 28/3

silfr *n.* silver IX:15; *instrumental dat.* X:117, 161; money XVI:85, 141, 165, XXII:31/3

silfrbelti *n.* silver belt III:23

silki *n.* silk XIII:31

silkidúkr *m.* silken cloth XIII:3, 6, 15

silkirœma *f.* silken band, tie, garter V:56

silkitjald *n.* silken hanging *or* drapery XIII:18

sin *f.* sinew X:84, 86

sín[1] *refl. pron. gen.* (*Gr* 3.2.1) oneself, themselves *etc.* II:21, VI:147, XXVI B:181; him XXII:50/4, his XXII:54/1; **til sín** to (see) him XVI:87

sín[2], **sína, sínar** *see* **sinn**[1]

síngjarn *adj.* covetous, avaricious XXIII:4 (*understand* **eru**)

sinn[1], **sinna, sinnar, sinni**[1], **sín, sína, sínar, síns, sínu, sínum** *refl. poss.* one's, his, her, its, their *etc.* (*Gr* 3.3.4, 3.3.9 ex. 7, 12) II:3, 7, 37, 68, VIII:19, 50, 89, 120, 134, IX:2, 20, X:39, 78, XI:2, XIII:24, 36, XIV:170, 174, XV:12, XVI:7, 111, XIX:25, 38, 73, XXI: 81, 192, 205, XXII:13/2, 40/1, XXIII:2, 19, 40, 70, XXIV:16, 18, 63,

XXV:9, 55, XXVI B:55, XXVII:24 (**sínum** their); *n.* **sitt** II:105, VIII:153, XV:33, XVI:13, XIX:44, XXI:4, 51, XXII:34/3, 36/1, 42/2, XXVI:A12, XXVII:22, 38; his own XIX:43; *gen.* **síns** his, their XXVI A:85; **til síns lands** to their own country XXI:155; **sjálfs síns** his own XXII:7/4; *acc. sg. m.* **sinn veg hverr** each his own way, all in different directions XIX:84, **sinn ... hvárir** each (side) their own XXVII:14; *acc. sg. f.* **sína** his (own, separate) XXVI B:216; *acc. pl. m.* **sína** XXVI B:40; *nom./acc. pl. n.* **sín** their IV:40 (*with* **sverð**), VIII:112, XIX:42, her II:36 (*with* **epli**), *dat pl.* **sínum** their own XXVI A:46

sinn² *n.* time; **at sinni** on this occasion II:37 (probably referring to the gods' journey home rather than to the conversation between Ægir and Bragi, *i.e.* it goes with **ferð** rather than with **sǫgð**), for the time being III:94, XI:16, XII:65; **eitt sinn** on one occasion IV:76, VII B:32, XIII:4, XV:20; **um sinn** on one occasion, once XIV:143, XXIV:13; **einu sinni** (just) once XXV:49; **einhverju sinni** on one occasion *(the phrase belongs in the following* **at**-*clause)* XVI:115; **annat sinn** (*acc. of time, Gr* 3.1.5 (10)), **í annat sinn** a second time, again II:20, 148, VI:274, VII A:62, VIII:17, XXVI A:40; **í hvárttveggja sinn** each time, both times III:116; **hvert sinn ... er** every time that XII:87; **sjau sinnum** seven times XIV:69; **nǫkkurum sinnum** several times VII B:30; **sem fæstum sinnum** as infrequently as possible XXIV:12

sinni³ *n.* (= **sinn²**) time; **fyrsta sinni** for the first time XXIV:77; **annat sinni** a second time XXIV:8

síns, sínu, sínum *see* **sinn¹**

sitja (*pres.* **sitr,** *past* **sat,** *past pl.* **sátu,** *pp.* **setit**) *sv.* sit (*Gr* 3.6.9.1 (5)) I:4, 65, II:13, 23, 24, III:104, IV:4, VII B:16 (*inf. with* **skyli**), X:56, 98, XI:31, XXV:39; stay, live XIX:63; lie in wait IV:54, 78, V:11; *imp.* **sittu, sit** sit! XI:23, 29; *past* **sat** was sitting III:109, IV:7, IX:19, 102, XXI:175, stayed IV:47, X:13, 36; **saztu** you sat XXV:23; **sátu** were sitting IV:7, XXVI A:32, stayed X:26, XXVI A:118; **sátuð it Vǫlundr** did you and Vǫlundr sit X:179; **sátu vit Vǫlundr** Vǫlundr and I sat X:181 (*Gr* 3.6.9.1 (13)); *past subj.* **sæti** were sitting XIII:3; *impers. pass.* **meðan var setit** while they were sitting II:7; **sitja at** occupy XIV:5; **sitja eptir** remain sitting X:174; **sitja fyrir** waylay, ambush IV:5, 49; **sitja inni** are sitting indoors IV:39; **sitja um** lie in wait for (to attack), plot against, waylay XXIII:81; *pres. part. as noun* **sitjandi** a seated person IX:38

sitt *see* **sinn**[1]
sittu *see* **sitja**
sízt[1] *see* **síðr**
sízt[2] *prep. with acc.* since X:144
sjá[1] (*pres.* **sér**, *past* **sá**, *past pl.* **sá/sáu**, *pp.* **sénn**, *n.* **sét**) *sv.* (*Gr* 3.6.9.1
   (8), 3.6.9.3, 3.6.10) **1.** see (*Gr* 3.6.10) I:6, 28, 30, 90, 125, II:18, 54,
   64 (*twice*), 155, 156, III:1, IV:16 (*twice*), V:44, 46, 60; VI:61, 80,
   X:47, 111, XI:2, 50, XII:8, XV:106, XVI:94, XXI:30, 96, 122, 132,
   XXV:74, XXVI A:16, 29, B:10, 28; look VII A:85; watch XXVI
   B:175; realise IV:48, understand XXI:153; notice that XXI:172; **at
   sjá** to look at III:23, XXI:160; **sé ek, ek sé** I see I:66, 121, III:67,
   V:70, 74, 82, VII B:37; **sér þú** you see XXV:88; *with suffixed pron.
   and neg.* **sékka** I shall not see X:95; *pres. subj.* **sjái** I:36, may see
   XIV:55, (*impers.*) one can see XV:62; *imp. pl.* **sjáið** I:140; *past sg.*
   sá III:97, 99, 121 (had seen), IV:53, V:119, VI:75, 120, 151, 269,
   270, 306, VII A:144, XVI:95, XIX:52, 80; **þaðan sá hann** from
   there he could see XIX:102; *with suffixed pron.* **sáttu** have you seen
   IX:99; *with suffixed pron. and neg.* **sáka** I have not seen IX:100; **sá
   er** saw how VII B:35, XXVI B:189; *past pl.* **sám** XIV:26, *note*,
   XXVI B:12, **sá vér** we saw XXVI B:10; **sá** VI:61, 67, 109, 123,
   caught sight of, came within sight of XIX:51; **er þeir sá** which they
   could see XIX:71; *past subj.* **sæi** saw XII:60, XIV:35, were to look
   II:108, could see V:45, *impers.* one saw, could be seen I:115; *pp.*
   sét, sénir seen II:45, VI:196, XXV:67, XXVI B:116, obvious XXVI
   B:100; *impers.* (*cf. Gr* 3.9.3 (c)) **enn sér** one can still see, there can
   still be seen XIV:26, **sér þá** then it can be seen XVI:149, **lítt sér þat
   þá á** there will be little to show for it XVI:139, **en sjá þykir** than
   seems apparent, evident I:136, **eigi of sá á miðli** one could not
   distinguish between, foresee which way it would go VIII:110; **á at
   sjá** to look at VI:111, in appearance, visibly, noticeably XIX:12, **sjá
   á** to look upon X:100, look at XXV:72; **sá þat at** saw this as VI:213,
   XVI:71; **sjá fyrir/fyr** see to, attend to IV:67, XIX:79, look after
   XIV:127, provide for XVI:111; **sjá í** look inside X:103; **Hvat sjái
   þér til** what can you discern, discover by looking XXVI B:55; *past
   pl.* **sá til** were watching, looked on VI:60; **sjá við** beware of, be cautious
   about V:35; **viðr því sjá** beware not to, take care to avoid XXIV:82. **2.**
   -sk *form reciprocal* **sjásk** see each other IV:14, XXVI B:214; *refl.*
   um (at) sjásk (to) look around oneself (*Gr* 3.9.8.3) II:11 (*subject of*
   þótti), X:33

sjá² *pron.* (*Gr* 3.2.2, 3.8.2.1) this II:123, that XVI:125, XXI:121

sjaldan *adv.* seldom XIV:52, XXI:79; *sup.* **hit sjaldnasta** at the most seldom, at least XIV:143

sjáldr *n.* pupil (of the eye); *pl. with suffixed def. art.* XXIII:33, 34

sjálfala *adj. indeclinable* finding their own food; **gekk úti sjálfala** remained in the open feeding themselves XXI:108

sjálfr *adj. and pron.* self; himself III:114, VI:294, 298, VII A:64, B:27, 51, VIII:74, 93, 186, X:79, XII:54, XIV:30, XXII:50/4; herself XII:22, XIV:189; yourself VII A:53; itself XIII:16, 37; **sjálfan hann** the man himself VII A:103; **sjálfum sér** for himself XIV:63, **á sjálfum sér** in himself XIV:50; **sjálfri þér** to you yourself X:129; **þér … sjálfum** you yourself XXIV:85; **sjálfs síns** his own XXII:7/4; **sjálft** itself VIII:157, XIII:18; **sjálfir** ourselves XXV:103, XXVI B:105, themselves XXVII:17, *i.e.* in person VII B:58

sjálfrátt *adj. n. as adv.* **er þér sjálfrátt at** you are free to, it is up to you to, it is within your power to, you ought to be able to XXVI A:57

sjálfsáinn *adj. (pp., cf.* **sá³**) self-sown, wild XXI:50, 90

sjau *num.* seven (*Gr* 3.4.1) VI:8, 49, 53, VII A:55, 59, VIII:13, 29, 166, X:11, 26, 48, XIV:69, XIX:49, XXIV:35

sjaundi *ordinal num.* seventh *Gr* 3.4.1, XXIV:38

sjaután *num.* seventeen *Gr* 3.4.1

sjóða (*pres.* **sýðr,** *past* **sauð,** *past pl.* **suðu,** *pp.* **soðit**) *sv.* cook XXI:75; *pp.* II:19, 20, 21

sjóðr *m.* purse; **þér í sjóði** (*dat.*) into your purse *or* to you in a purse? XXII:31/3

sjóli *m.* king XXII:21/4, 50/3

sjónhverfingar *f. pl.* optical illusions, magical deceptions, false appearances II:4

sjór (= **sær**) *m.* sea VI:151; *gen. sg.* **sjóvar** VI:11, XXI:88; *acc. with suffixed def. art.* **sjóinn** VI:256; *dat. with suffixed def. art.* **sjónum** VI:296, XIII:11, **af sjónum** from the sea, i.e. from the shore? (*or add* **af eynni** *after* **eggver**) XXI:84; **með sjó** along the coast XIX:72, 90

sjóskrímsl *n.* sea-monster XXIII:63

sjúkr *adj.* ill *Gr* 3.3.9 (1), (13), (20)

skaði *m.* harm, damage I:77

Skaði *f.* daughter of the giant **Þjazi** II:61; *dat. of respect or poss. dat.* (*cf. note to* I:12) II:71

skaka (*past* **skók,** *past pl.* **skóku,** *pp.* **skekinn**) *sv.* shake XII:46 (*pres. part.*), XXV:57, 72

skal *see* **skulu**

skál *f.* bowl X:116, 160

skáladyrr *f. pl.* the doorway of the hall or main living-room IV:10 (here probably the doorway from the main room to the **stofa**)

skálaendi *m.* end of the hall XXVI B:201

Skálafell *n.* mountain 35 km south-east of Reykjavík XIX:102

Skálaholt (*modern* **Skálholt**) *n.* bishop's see in south-western Iceland VIII:159, 195, 197, XIV:89, 173

Skálaholtsland *n.* the Skálaholt estate VIII:160

skálasmíð *f.* building a hall XV:94

skáld, skald *n.* poet II:99, VII B:14, XXII:19/2; *i.e.* the speaker, Bjǫrn Hítdœlakappi V:24, 50

skáldfífl *n.* rhymester, poetaster II:160

skáldskapr *m.* poetry II:83, 87, 117, 121, XXI:78; *with suffixed def. art.* II:162

skalf *see* **skjálfa**

skáli *m.* hall (usually without dividing walls), the main living area of a medieval house X:10, XIX:62, 102; *with suffixed def. art.* III:6, XXVI A:22, 26, 29, 61, B:116, *i.e.* the roof of the hall III:73, 74 (*dat. after* **í**), **ofan allr skálinn** all the upper part of the hall XXVI B:120; **at skáli** in the house XIX:65; shed, hut for sleeping in: **sumir skálarnir** some of the sleeping huts XXI:106

skálm *f.* short (one-edged) sword XXV:57

Skálmarfjǫrðr *m.* fjord in north-western Iceland XV:41

Skálmarnes *n.* farm in north-western Iceland XV:34, 125, 131, 146

skalt, skaltu *see* **skulu**

skammr *adj.* (of time) short I:129, III:104, XIV:73; **skamma stund** for a short time XIV:5; (of physical length) XXIII:9 (*Gr* 3.9.2; *understand* **sýnir mann**), 75, 86, 87, 100; *wk. form in name of ship* **enn skammi** VI:126; *n. as adv.* **skammt** a short time XXVI A:23, a short way III:68, V:43, XII:56, XV:139, 149; **skammt at bíða** not long to wait XIV:100; **skammt eigu þeir hingat** they are not far away V:65, **átti skammt til þeira** was a short distance from them V:86

skammsýnn *adj.* short-sighted, foolish XXIV:43

Skánungar *m. pl.* the people of Skåne, Danes; *gen. with* **fundar**, (a rendezvous) with the people of Skåne VI:57

skap *n.* mind XVI:119; mood XI:68; **til skaps** *with gen.* to please someone XXVI B:74; temperament, disposition XXI:11; **hafa skap til at** be disposed to, feel inclined to XXVI B:215

skapa (*past* **skapaði,** *past pl.* **skǫpuðu,** *pp.* **skapaðr**) *wv.* create, shape II:92, XII:48, XIV:112; appoint, impose: **slíkt víti á at skapa** the same penalty should be imposed XV:61; **væri henni skapat víti** a punishment would (surely, by fate?) be imposed on her XV:117

skapfrǫmuðr *m.* 'mind-promoter'; **Hrundar skapfrǫmuðr** promoter of what is to the taste of the valkyrie, *i.e.* promoter of battle, *a kenning for* warrior, warlike man IV:89 (**hvern skapfrǫmuð** *is object of* **myndir þú kjósa**)

skapligr *adj.* suitable, fitting, due VI:197; fitting XIV:40; right XV:16

skaplyndi *n.* temper, disposition XXIII:8

skapstórr *adj.* proud-minded; **menn eru skapstórir** there are proud-minded people XV:66

skapt *n.* shaft (of spear) XXVI B:90; *pl.* **skǫpt** spears XXII:35/3

skara (*past* **skaraði,** *pp.* **skarat**) *wv.* to cause to slide; *impers.* **skaraði ljáinn** the scythe-blade slid IV:10

skarð *n.* cut, notch IV:11 (*subject of* **brotnaði**); gap, empty space VI:83

skarðr *adj.* (*pp.*) diminished, waning X:44

Skarpheðinn Njálsson *m.* XXVI B:16, 30, 39, 57, 62, 73, 80, 89, 90, 94, 95, 107, 112, 146, 189, 193, 199, 202, 206, 210, 217, 226

skarsk, skáru *see* **skera**

skatnar *m. pl.* men XXII:26/3

skattland *n.* tributary territory, dependency VI:32

skattr *m.* tribute, tax VII A:169; treasure XI:24 (**Niflunga-**)

skaut *see* **skjóta**

skegg *n.* beard II:69, IX:3

skeggjaðr *adj.* (*pp.*) bearded (i.e. a full-grown male) XXI:199

Skeggjasonr *m.* son of Skeggi Þorgeirsson, 10th-century Icelander VIII:79

skeið *f.* a large longship VI:74, 83, 103, 135; *gen. pl. with numeral* (*Gr* 3.4.2 (5)) VI:53; *dat. pl.* with warships (*with* **hǫfðu lokit**) VI:284

skeina (*past* **skeindi,** *pp.* **skeindr**) *wv.* scratch, wound; make furrows (in the sea, *i.e.* sail a ship) VII B:38; **-sk** *form for pass.* **skeindisk** was hurt III:112

skelfðr *adj.* (*pp. of* **skelfa** *wv.* frighten) afraid, fearful XXIII:65

skelfr *see* **skjálfa**

skellr *m.* resounding blow IX:129

skemmri *adj. comp.* (*of* **skammr**) shorter, lasting a shorter time XV:10

skemr *adv. comp.* for a shorter time XXVI A:84

skem(m)ta (*past* **skem(m)ti,** *pp.* **skem(m)t**) *wv. with dat.* **skem(m)ta sér** entertain oneself, amuse oneself XI:77, XXI:95

skemtan *f.* amusement, toy XII:45; enjoyment XII:86

skemtiligr *adj.* pleasant XIV:40

skepna *f.* creature XIV:40

sker *n.* skerry, rock covered at high tide (*Gr* 3.1.7.5 (4)) II:119 (*with suffixed def. art.*)

skera (*past* **skar,** *past pl.* **skáru,** *pp.* **skorinn**) *sv.* cut V:5, XXI:117; pierce XXII:20/4; cut up, flense XXI:73; carve XII:23, 32; *pp. f. pl.* **skornar** X:86; **-sk** *form* **skerask í** cut out cloth for oneself into, make oneself, dress oneself in XV:89; *for pass. past pl.* **skǫrusk** were cut (*i.e.* by swords in battle) VI:232

skerðir *m.* cutter, damager; **skerðir seims** 'damager, diminisher of riches', one who gives away gold, generous man (the king) VII A:18

skerjóttr *adj.* rocky, full of skerries; *sup.* XV:149

skíði *n.* sheath XXV:53

skíðijárn *n.* 'sheath-iron', sword XXV:53 (*pl.*)

skikkja *f.* cloak; *with suffixed def. art.* XXVI B:147

skildi, skildir *see* **skjǫldr**

skilja (*past* **skilði,** *pp.* **skilit/skilðr**) *wv.* (*Gr* 3.6.9.3 ex. 8) **1.** *intransitive* part, be separated (**við** from) III:36, XIX:13, XXVI B:172; *impers.* **skilði með þeim** they got separated XIX:51; *transitive* **skilði** parted, separated (*sc.* them) X:28, **skilja** break off XV:29; **skilja við** separate from, deprive of XXII:34/4; *pp.* **skiliðr frá** exempt from VIII:28; **skilðr við** parted from XIV:104; **skilit** divorced (**við** from) XV:28, 30, 64; **-sk** *form* **skiljask** part from each other I:64, XVI:189, *1st person pl.* **skiljumsk** VI:92; *subj.* **skilisk við** be parted from XXVI B:76. **2.** understand I:27, XIII:44; *subj.* **skili** may understand XXIV:34; deduce VIII:23, 70; **at skilja** to be understood, to be interpreted XXVI B:62; **-sk** *form with pass. meaning, with dat.* **ef þér skilz** if you understand XXIV:47; **þessi lutir skiljaz mér** I can understand these things XXIV:50. **3.** stipulate: *pp. n.* **skilt** XV:8; **skilja fyrir** announce (it) XXVII:19

skillingr *m.* shilling, coin; *in pl.* = money IX:129

skilnaðr *m.* parting II:91, III:34 (*with suffixed def. art.*), XII:38; *with gen.* parting between XXVI B:138; **skilnaðr með** parting between XXVI B:213

skilning *f.* understanding XXIV:48

skilríkr *adj.* upright, respectable XIX:102

skína (*pres.* **skínn,** *past* **skein,** *past pl.* **skinu,** *pp.* **skininn**) *sv.* shine
Gr 3.6.9.1 (11), X:91, XXII:60/3, XXIII:24; *pres. part.* shining
XXIII:27, 89, *dat. pl.* **skínǫndum** XXIII:108

skinn *n.* skin, fur; **hvítt skinn** ermine XII:35

skinnhjúpr *m.* body-garment made of skin *or* fur XXI:156

skinnslitr *m.* skin-colour, the colour of the skin, complexion XXIII:105

skip *n.* ship, boat, canoe II:105, VI:11, 44, 49, 59, 61, 65, 185, VII
A:52, 110, 135, B:36, 75, X:150, XVI:130, XIX:26, 43, XXI:3, 112;
with suffixed def. art. **skipit** VI:267, XV:146, 151, XVI:131; **á skipi**
by boat XV:43, **á skip** aboard XVI:7; **á skipi með** on the ship with,
on someone's ship XXI:15; **allt skipit fram** the whole ship forward
(of there) VI:275; *nom. pl.* **skip** XVI:129; **smæri skip** the smaller
ships VI:219; *nom. pl. with suffixed def. art.* **skipen** VI:120; *acc. pl.
with suffixed def. art.* (*with* **létu fljóta**) **skipen** VI:109; **hin smæstu
skipin, hin stœrri skipin** (*Gr* 3.3.5) the smallest ships, the larger
ships VI:217, 220; *gen. pl. with suffixed def. art.* VI:103; *dat. sg.
with suffixed def. art.* II:104; *partitive gen.* (3.4.2 (5)) VI:21, 49;
dat. pl. with suffixed def. art. **skipunum** XXI:35, 52, 97

skipa (*past* **skipaði,** *pp.* **skipat**) *wv.* **1.** occupy I:62, 69; *pp. m.* **skipaðr,**
f. **skipuð** manned I:79, VI:224. **2.** *with dat.* assign, give places to,
assemble VI:194; fill with: **skipa Lǫgberg** assign places on Lǫgberg
to XXVII:23; **skipaði** was putting him XII:43; **skipaði til um** made
arrangements, gave orders concerning/for XVI:86; **skipuðu
mǫnnum til sýslu** assigned men to tasks XIV:138, *note*; **skipaðu**
ordained, originated XXIV:62; *pp.* **skipaðr at** given the task of
XIV:138, *note*; *impers. pass.* (*Gr* 3.9.3) **er skipat** is filled XI:57, **en
þeim var skipat** than they had been assigned I:71, **er skipat** are
arranged XXIV:27; **svá skipat atkvæðum** the mode of address is
so ordained XXIV:32; **-sk** *form* **skipask** arrange oneself, position
oneself, take up one's position XXVI B:81, 84, 87; **skipuðusk fyrir**
arranged themselves, were lined up XXVI B:46. **3. -sk** *form pp.*
skipazk changed I:129, 141, XVI:108

skipan *f.* **1.** manning, complement of men VI:226. **2.** change, alteration
XIV:37

skipsbrot *n.* shipwreck XVI:149

skipta (*past* **skipti,** *pp.* **skipt**) *wv.* (*Gr* 3.6.9.3 ex. 4) **1.** *with dat.* share out, divide up II:79, 80; *impers. pass. (Gr* 3.9.3) XV:76; **skipta málum við** bandy words with, argue with XXV:33. **2.** change: **máli skipta** make a difference, be of importance VII B:55; **skipta miklu** be of great importance, be very important XV:23; **kvað þat øngu skipta** said it did not matter XXI:70; *(with acc.)* **skiptir hana in meira** it is the more important for her, it will matter the more to her XV:55; *impers. pass. subj. with dat.* **skipti með oss** our shares of something should be reversed V:62; *pp.* **skipt um við** exchanged with V:57. **3. -sk** *form* **skiptask við** deal with one another II:129; *pp.* **skipzk** changed I:135

skipti *n. pl.* dealings XIX:8

skíra (*past* **skírði,** *pp.* **skírðr**) *wv.* **1.** cleanse; baptise VII A:67, VIII:78, XXI:201. **2. -sk** *form* be baptised VII A:29; **láta skírask** have oneself baptised VIII:79

skírdagr *m.* Maundy Thursday XIV:144

skírlífi *n.* purity of life, chastity XIII:22, 28

skírn *f.* baptism VII A:50 (*gen. with* **til**), 55, 66, VIII:139, XXII:27/3

skírnarbrunnr *m.* baptismal well, font XXII:26/3

skjaldar *see* **skjǫldr**

Skjaldarey *f.* island in Breiðafjǫrðr XV:153

Skjaldbjǫrn *m.* Irish slave XIX:37

skjaldborg *f.* shield-wall, wall of shields I:11, 12 (*gen. of respect*), 16; *with suffixed def. art.* I:20

skjálfa (*pres.* **skelfr,** *past* **skalf,** *past pl.* **skulfu,** *pp.* **skolfit**) *sv.* tremble, shiver, shake I:26, 100, III:114, 115; *pres. part.* quivering XXIII:28

skjól *n.* shelter XXI:33, *textual note*

skjóta (*pres.* **skýtr** *Gr* 3.6.5.2, *past* **skaut,** *past pl.* **skutu,** *pp.* **skotit**) *sv.* **1.** *with dat. of weapon or missile and acc. of the person shot* shoot (*Gr* 3.6.6, 3.6.10) V:94, X:171 (*subj.*), XXI:175, XXVI A:37, 63, B:194; **þeiri skjóta** shoot it (the arrow) XXVI A:45; **skaut** shot it XXVI A:49. **2.** *with dat.* push, place (*understand* it) III:59; throw XIX:52; **skutu út á þá** flung them out at them XXVI B:194; **skjóta út** expel XII:19; **skjóta á fylking** draw up in battle array, get (one's troops) in battle order (*understand* them, **lið**) VII B:73; **skjóta upp** haul up, raise (on the mast) VI:104; *impers. pass. (Gr* 3.9.3) **borði var skotit** a board had been placed III:53. **3. -sk** *form* **skýzk** bounds, hops XXI:174

skjótleikr *m.* speed XXI:40

skjótliga *adv.* quickly XXIII:104

skjótr (*n.* **skjótt**) *adj.* quick XXIII:2, 4, 39, swift, speedy XXIV:30; *n. as adv.* **skjótt** quickly *Gr* 3.5.3 (4), I:116, XV:128, XXIII:25, XXVI A:70, B:61; *comp. with dat.* **dýrum skjótari** faster than animals XXI:41; *comp. n. as adv.* **skjótara** more quickly IV:15; *sup.* **skjótastr** *Gr* 3.3.9 ex. 18; *sup. n. as adv.* **sem skjótast** as quickly as possible XXVI B:84

Skjǫldólfsdóttir *f.* daughter of Skjǫldólfr *Gr* 3.1.8 ex.

skjǫldr (*pl.* **skildir**) *m.* shield (*Gr* 3.1.7.3, 3.1.7.3–5 ex. 1, 3.1.8 (4)) V:29, 37, VI:287, 296, X:44, XI:3, 26, XV:153, XXI:101, XXV:72 (his shield); *with suffixed def. art.* his shield V:100, 101, XXVI A:31, 73, B:91, 152; *gen. sg.* **skjaldar** X:150, *with suffixed def. art.* **skjaldarins** V:101; *dat. sg.* **skildi** (*object of* **skjóta**) VI:104, XI:36, XXVI A:72; **und skildi** carrying a shield V:50; **á skildi** on a shield VII A:54; *dat. sg. with suffixed def. art.* **skildinum** V:99, VI:295 (his shield); *acc. pl.* **skjǫldu** XXI:124, XXII: 38/4; *dat. pl.* **skjǫldum** II:12, XXI:112

skógarbjǫrn/skógbjǫrn *m.* forest bear, brown bear XIX:66, XXIII:6

skóggangr *m.* full outlawry XV:136

skógr *m.* wood, forest II:39, V:27, VI:10, VIII:54, XIX:68, XXI:27, 29, 94

skók, skóku *see* **skaka**

skóli *m.* school XIV:24, 26 (*with suffixed def. art.*); **þar í skóla** at school there XIV:182

skólkinni *m.* name for a wolf (perhaps 'dark-cheeked') V:51

skolla (*past* **skolldi**) *wv.* hover X:172

skór (*pl.* **skúar**) *m.* shoe XV:50

skorinn, skorit, skornar *see* **skera**

skorta (*past* **skorti**, *pp.* **skort**) *wv. impers. with two accusatives* lack; **skorti hann eigi** he was not lacking in VII B:26, **skorti þá eigi** they did not lack XXI:82; **þat einu skorti á er . . . eigi . . . at** this alone was lacking for it so that . . . did not . . . that (*i.e.* this alone prevented . . . that) VII B:87; **ekki skorti** there was no lack of VI:288; **þar skorti eigi** there were no fewer there than XIV:144

skot *n.* shot, shooting XXII:12/4 (*pl.?*)

Skotar *m. pl.* Scots VII A:16

skothríð *f.* battle with missiles, storm of missiles, attack with missiles XXI:125

skotit *see* **skjóta**

Skotland *n*. Scotland VII A:4

skotmál *n*. range (of missiles or arrows) VI:211

skozkr *adj*. Scottish *or* Irish (see note); **menn skozkir** Scots XXI:39, 42

skreppa¹ *f*. scrip, pilgrim's wallet XVI:98

skreppa² (*past* **skrapp**, *past pl*. **skruppu**, *pp*. **skroppinn**) *wv*. slip; *with dat*. **Þorgrími skruppu fœtrnir** Þorgrímr's feet slipped XXVI A:31

skriða *f*. landslide *Gr* 3.1.8 ex.

skríða (*past* **skreið**, *past pl*. **skriðu**, *pp*. **skriðinn**) *sv*. crawl through, glide along II:149, glide through the water VI:265; go skiing X:4, travel on skis X:12, 34

skrifa (*past* **skrifaði**, *pp*. **skrifaðr**) *wv*. write VIII:3, 172, 178

skrín *n*. shrine XXII:62/2

skript *f*. **1.** picture, image; *with suffixed def. art*. XIII:16. **2.** penance XIV:99, 102

skrjá (*past* **skrjáði**) *wv*. skulk; **skrjá um** sneak about IV:62

skrofhárr *adj*. with curly hair V:31

skrokkr *m*. container XXI:156

skrúð *n*. furniture XIV:10

skruppu *see* **skreppa**

skrýða (*past* **skrýddi**, *pp*. **skrýddr**) *wv*. with *dat*. adorn with XII:49

skrækja (*past* **skrækti**) *wv*. shriek, squeal (**við** at it) II:71

Skrælingaland *n*. the land of the Skrælings XXI:203

Skrælingar *m. pl.* Norse name for the indigenous inhabitants of Vínland VIII:71, XXI:118, 120, 122, 124, 126, 127, 138, 141, 149, 156, 198; **af Skrælingum** of the Skrælings XXI:144

skúa *see* **skór**

Skúli Þorsteinsson (Þorsteinssunr) *m*. Icelandic poet, late tenth to eleventh century VI:200

skulu (*pres*. **skal**, *past* **skyldi**) *pret.-pres. vb. aux*. (*Gr* 3.6.7) shall I:80, 130, 147, II:34, 40, IV:14, 50, V:40, VI:91, XXIV:40, XXVI B:19, XXVII:2; must II:109, 144, VI:326, IX:47, XXII:22/3, XXVII:31; should XI:43, XIV:90, *note*, XXVI B:16, 187; **skulu** are to XXVII:6, 10, 15; **skulu vera** are to be, are to consist of VII A:100; **hverr vera skal** who it is to be XXVII:7, 19; **skulu þeir fara** they are to go XVI:57; **skal** shall XXVI A:56, should XV:53, should be XXIV:51, is to XVI:57, XXVII:9 (2), 13, 19, must, has to XXIV:27; **þat skal eigi vera** that shall not be XXVI B:52; **skal ek** I shall XXVI A:45, B:139; **þú skalt, skalt þú, skaltu** you shall I:101, 148,

IV:70, 73, X:149, XV:87, XVI:74, XXVI B:110, 206, you will XXV:38, you must XXIV:2, 4, 8, XXVI B:175, shall you, are you going to I:21; **skulum** have to XIX:98, **skulum eigi** we are not going to XXVI B:50, **skulu vér** we shall XXVI A:54, we must XXVI B:117, **skulu vit** shall we XXVI B:166; *pres. subj.* **skyli** have to VII B:15, shall be XXVI A:23; **skylim** we should/must XXV:108; *impers. pres.* **skal taka man** a man is to be selected XXVII:4, **mæla skal** one has to address XXIV:15; *past* **skyldi** was to III:17, 106, VI:44, 148, 149, VII A:79, XV:8, 10, had to II:80, was supposed to VI:4, must II:127, XXVI A:12, ought XII:75, should I:19, III:26, VI:18, VII A:98, VIII:27, 32, 116, XII:66, XV:26, XXV:30, XXVI B:9, should be I:51 (1), would XIX:10, 53, XXVI B:164; *past 2nd person* **skyldir þú** you should V:72; *past pl.* **skyldu** must II:68 (1), 141, would II:68 (2), XIV:164, used to XIV:83; were about to, had to II:79, were to VII B:58, VIII:174, XXVI A:6, were to, had to VII A:72, IX:82, should VII B:72, VIII:140, 141, XIV:127, XIX:65, 77, ought VI:1, were supposed to (eat) IX:96; **skyldu vera** were to be II:8; **skyldum** should, ought, must VI:84; *past subj.* **skyldi** should III:112, IV:106, VIII:94, 105, 117, one should I:51 (2), they should VI:116, XXVI A:7, **skyldim** should XXVI B:171; *impers. past* they should VIII:40, 183, XXVI A:107, were to be XV:132, they were about to II:5, it will surely be XXVI B:123, **skyldi vera** was to be XV:79; **þat skyldi eigi vera** that should not be, surely not XXVI B:22, **æva skyldi** it should never have happened X:182; *past inf.* **skyldu** should III:94, V:106, XV:117, 128; **svá vera skyldu** so it should be XXVI B:9, 18, 81

skunda (*past* **skundaði**, *pp.* **skundaðr**) *wv. with dat.* cause to hurry, hasten XII:1

skutilsveinn *m.* cupbearer (a high office in the royal court, though like others, originally a menial one, waiting at the king's table; **skutill** = a small table or tray that food and drink was served from; cf. *Heimskringla, Óláfs saga kyrra* ch. 3, *ÍF* XXVIII 205–06 and note 6) XVI:116, 169

skutr *m.* stern (of a ship) VI:81 (**hánum** *poss. dat. or dat. of respect*)

skutu *see* **skjóta**

ský *n.* cloud X:172

skygn *adj.* sharp-sighted; *sup. Gr* 3.3.8.1

skyld- *see* **skulu**

skyldr (*n.* **skylt**) *adj.* related *Gr* 3.3.9 ex. 2; required (**til þess at** to do something) XXVII:3, 25; *n. as adv.* necessary, important, urgent VI:108, right VIII:6

skyldu *see* **skulu**

skylduliga *adv.* dutifully XIV:70

skyli *see* **skulu**

skyn *f.* knowledge, information; **kunna skyn á** have knowledge of XXI:74

skynda (*past* **skyndi,** *pp.* **skyndr**) *wv.* cause to hurry, hasten IX:82; *intransitive* hasten, make haste XXII:26/4

skyndiliga *adv.* quickly IV:12, 17

skynsemð *f.* reason (**til** for) XXIV:14, (**hversu** how) 27

skynsemðargrein *f.* discernment, ability to distinguish, understanding XXIII:14

skyr *n.* a kind of milk product III:98 (*with suffixed def. art.*), *see note* 22

skýra (*past* **skýrði,** *pp.* **skýrðr**) *wv.* explain XXIV:25, 54; expound; **engi skýrir** no one can expound XXII:2/3

skyrbúr *n.* dairy, the room in a farm where **skyr** and other dairy products were made or stored III:89, 90

skyrker *n.* vat *or* cask for storing **skyr** III:97, 100 (*with suffixed def. art.*)

skýrr *adj.* clear, manifest, definite VIII:31

skyrta *f.* shirt, tunic XV:27

skyti *m.* shooter, hunter X:31, 51

skýtr, skýzk *see* **skjóta**

skæri *n. pl.* shears; *with suffixed def. art., i.e.* the mane-shears V:126, 127, 131, 142

skǫfnungr *m.* shin III:113 (*with suffixed def. art.,* his shins)

Skǫglar-Tósti *m.* father of Sigríðr, queen of King Sveinn of Denmark VI:38

skǫkull *m.* (*in pl.*) harness, tackle, traces (of a draught animal) IX:82

skǫmm[1] *f.* shame VII B:72, XXVI A:87; disgrace I:53, VI:85; humiliation (**þeim** for them) XXVI A:45; **við skǫmm** in shame XXVI B:160

skǫmm[2], **skǫmmu** *see* **skammr**

skǫp *n. pl.* fate IV:96 (*subject of* **yrði góð mér,** *parallel to* **goð**); destiny, what was fated (*with gen.* **þess … at** for this that, that this should be that) VI:345

skǫpt *see* **skapt**

skǫpuð, skǫpuðu *see* **skapa**

skǫpun *f.* shape XII:21

skǫr *f.* hair (of a man's head) IX:3, X:116, 160, XXV:72; **standa of skǫr** *with dat. i.e.* preside over someone's death V:170

skǫrugliga *adv.* outstandingly well, splendidly XIV:115

skǫruligr *adj.* imposing III:23

skórusk *see* **skera**

slá (*pres.* **slær,** *past* **sló,** *past pl.* **slógu,** *pp.* **sleginn**) *sv.* (*Gr* 3.6.9.3 and ex. 7) **1.** strike XIII:13; *with instrumental dat.* strike, smite X:98; throw; **slá eldi í** set fire to II:57; *with two accusatives* strike (someone a blow) XV:21. **2.** mow II:124. **3.** hammer, forge X:37, 121, 165; make, form V:109. **4.** *impers. with dat.* **slær/sló yfir** there comes upon someone, someone is afflicted by I:44, XXI:128, (something) was cast over XXII:53/1

Slagfiðr *m.* brother of Vǫlundr X:4, 10, 13, 32, 35

slátra (*past* **slátraði,** *pp.* **slátrat**) *wv. with dat.* slaughter; *impers. pass.* (*Gr* 3.9.3) **hafði slátrat verit uxa einum** an ox had been slaughtered XXVI B:179

sleikja (*past* **sleikti,** *pp.* **sleikt**) *wv.* lick (out) VI:189

sleita *f.* quarrel; **ganga mjǫk sleitum** quarrel a great deal XXI:195

slétta (*past* **slétti,** *pp.* **sléttr**) *wv.* slap (á on it) XXI:141

sléttr *adj.* flat XXIII:10; smooth? XXIII:89

slíðrar/slíðrir *f. pl.* sheath, scabbard I:97 (*with suffixed def. art.*)

slíkisteinsauga *n.* nickname, 'polished-stone eye'? XV:39

slíkr *adj.* such III:10 (any . . . like it), VI:266, XXI:133, XXVI B:126, such a V:121, 143, VI:113, 349; this III:130, *pl.* these VII A:44; **fyr merkin slík** as a result of miracles like these XXII:58/3; **engi . . . slíkr** no . . . like him XXII:64/3; **til annars slíks** until another like it XXVI B:124; **slíkr . . . sem** such . . . as XIV:30, 74, the same as XV:61, XVI:22, the same as if XVI:75; **slíka ok** the same as III:69; **tvau verð slík** double that price XVI:24; *n. as substantive* **slíkt** such a thing I:53, *gen.* **slíks** VI:160, *dat.* **slíku** *i.e.* this XII:69; **slíkt sem** that which, what XV:117, XXVI B:37; **slíkt er, slíks sem** whatever XIV:32, XXIV:23; *n. as adv.* **slíkt sama, slíkt it sama** likewise II:10, XI:20, XIII:38; **slíkt sem** as much as, as loud as I:91

slíta (*past* **sleit,** *past pl.* **slitu,** *pp.* **slitit**) *sv.* tear (*transitive*) VIII:135; **slitu frið** *i.e.* they fought VI:239; *with dat.* break, break off VI:37

slitna (*past* **slitnaði,** *pp.* **slitnat**) *wv.* tear (*intransitive*), be torn II:33

sló, slógu *see* **slá**

slóð *f.* path, track; **kjalar slóðir** is a kenning for the sea XXVI A:94

slær *see* **slá**

slœgð *f.* cunning XXIII:56

slœgr *adj.* cunning, sly XXIII:59, 105, XXIV:53; clever XXVI A:57

sløkkva (*past* **sløkkti,** *pp.* **sløkkt**) *wv.* extinguish, put out XXVI B:229; **sløkkva niðr** damp down XXVI B:114

smádropar *m. pl.* small flecks XXIII:31

smalamaðr *m.* XV:85, 87, 90, 91 (*with suffixed def. art.*)

smalasveinn *m.* shepherd boy XV:97, 101 (*with suffixed def. art.*)

smali *m. collective* sheep, cattle XV:84 (*with suffixed def. art.*), 132

smár *adj.* small VI:61, VII A:155, XXI:103; *n.* **smátt** VII A:149; *dat. pl.* **smám** I:35, VI:297

smaragdus *m.* (Latin word) emerald XII:27

smásveinn *m.* young boy, small boy XIV:163

smáþarmar *m. pl.* small intestines XXI:175

smíð *f.* making, construction XII:1 (*with suffixed def. art.*); **í smíðinni** at work XV:20; work, object of art, piece of craftsmanship XII:8 (*with suffixed def. art.*); workmanship XII:30

smíða (*past* **smíðaði,** *pp.* **smíðat**) *wv.* forge, make (*with dat.* for someone) X:87; build XIV:25; *pres.* **smíða** are working XII:2

smiðja *f.* smithy, workshop X:95, 156

smiðr *m.* builder; worker in metal or wood; craftsman (*pl. with suffixed def. art.*) XII:3; *as nickname* III:75, 83

smjúga (*past* **smaug/smó,** *past pl.* **smugu,** *pp.* **smoginn**) *wv.* creep; **smugu í** crept through, put on XXV:58

smjǫr *n.* butter XIX:56

smæri *adj. comp.* smaller VI:26, 27, 219; lesser, of less importance, lower XXIV:75

smæstr *adj. sup.* smallest VI:217

snara (*past* **snaraði,** *pp.* **snarat**) *wv.* turn (something) quickly, twist sharply XXVI A:73; **-sk** *form* turn (oneself) quickly; **snarask til ferðar** set out immediately XV:129

snarfengr *adj.* tough to deal with V:55 (*gen. with* **hoddlestis**)

snarpr *adj.* (*Gr* 3.3.8.1) sharp, violent, fierce VI:209 (*f.* **snǫrp**); keen XXIII:38, sharp VI:238, XXII:15/4, 42/2

snarr *adj.* swift XXIII:38, keen, bold V:149 (*vocative*; **at** in something), XXII:46/3

snauðr *adj.* poor, having no possessions; unarmed? III:78

snemma = **snimma**

snera, sneri, snerisk *see* **snúa**

snerra *f.* battle V:149

snerta (*past* **snart,** *pp.* **snortit**) *sv.* touch XIII:37, 41

sníða (*past* **sneið,** *past pl.* **sniðu,** *pp.* **sniðinn**) *sv.* cut XXII:49/2; *with acc. and dat. of respect* (*Gr* 3.9.6.2) cut from someone something X:84 (*imp.*); **sníða af** cut off X:114, 158, XIV:95

snimhendis *adv.* early on VIII:79

snimma/snemma *adv.* early V:1, X:6, 110, XIV:61, XXI:96, 110, XXVI B:191; soon IX:93; too soon V:139

snjallr *adj.* wise, brave, good, clever VI:159 (*with* **jǫfra tvá**), 282, XXII:13/2, 61/2; *sup.* **snjallasti** cleverest XIV:29

snjár/snjór *m.* snow XXI:108

Snorri goði (Þorgrímsson) *m.* (died 1031) VIII:11

Snorri Sturluson *m.* historian, killed 1241 in his own cellar on the orders of Gizurr Þorvaldsson III:70

Snorri *m.* son of Þorfinnr karlsefni XXI:196

Snorri Þorbrandsson *m.* XXI:2, 3, 86, 100, 114, 126, 163. *Cf.* **Þorbrandr Snorrason**

snortit *see* **snerta**

snót *f.* woman XXII:51/2

snotr *adj.* clever, skilled (*with gen.,* at something) VI:312 (*with* **Þorketill**)

snúa (*pres.* **snýr,** *past* **sneri/snøri,** *past pl.* **sneru,** *pp.* **snúinn**) *sv.* (*Gr* 3.6.7) twist, plait IX:20; turn III:123, IV:17; *imp. pl.* **snúið þit saman** twist them together XXVI A:78; *with dat.* set off with, take VII A:168; *pp.* **ok snúinn** and there were turned (on hinges), hinged XXVI A:25 **snúnar** twisted XXIII:87; **snúum í** let us twist/wind in them (i.e. in the ropes) XXVI A:60; **snúa inn** go inside IV:12; **snúa til** prepare for, put in to II:19; make one's way to V:75, *with dat.* commit something to XXI:81; **snúa yfir** place across VII B:60; *past subj.* **at þeir sneri aptr** of their turning back III:124; **-sk** *form* **snerisk** turned over XV:106; **snýsk at** turns towards XXVI A:70; **snýsk til** points to, indicates *or* tends to XXIII:108; **snúiz til** turned into, become XXIV:59

snœrivitnir *m.* 'wolf of ropes', *kenning for* ship VI:312; *the phrase perhaps goes with* **snotr** *or with* **hugframr** *rather than with* **heldi undan**

snǫr *see* snarr

snǫrp *see* snarpr

snøri *see* snúa

soðit *see* sjóða

soðna (soðnaði) *wv. impers.* cook (*intransitive*), become cooked
II:23, 25

sofa (*pres.* søfr/sefr, *past* svaf, *past pl.* sváfu, *pp.* sofinn) *sv.* (*Gr*
3.6.5.2, 3.6.9.3 and ex. 12) sleep IX:112, X:98, XI:62, XII:71, XV:96,
104; svaf slept, was asleep XXVI A:25; *pres. part.* sofandi (*Gr* 3.3.9
(19)), sofanda (Norwegian form of *acc. pl.*) asleep XXI:156; -sk
form þeim hafi sofizk they have slept XI:66

sofna (*past* sofnaði, *pp.* sofnat) *wv.* fall asleep X:60, 131, get to sleep
X:144, go to sleep XIV:70; *impers. with dat.* sér hafa vel sofnat he
had got to sleep easily XI:67

Sogn *m.* district in western Norway VII A:129

Sokki Ormsson *m.* died in the fire at Flugumýrr III:76

sókn *f.* attack VI:254

sóknrýrir *m.* 'diminisher of attacks', successful defender, i.e. Gunnarr
XXVI A:97

sól *f.* the sun (*Gr* 3.1.7.4 (3)) VI:115, XIX:111 (*with suffixed def. art.*)

sólarfall *n.* sunset XV:97

sólargeisla *f.* sunbeam, sunshine XIX:111

sólarsinnis *adv.* sunwise, the same way as the sun; ferr (*impers.*)
sólarsinnis the motion was the same way as the sun XXI:98

sólarupprás *f.* sunrise XV:119

Sólundir *f. pl.* Solundøyar, off the west coast of Norway VII A:129

sóma (sómði) *wv.* be fitting; *impers.* befit XIV:60, be suitable for
XII:24; tignum mǫnnum sómir at þiggja it is fitting for noble men
to receive XVI:152; betr sóma be more fitting V:160

sómi *m.* honour XVI:118, 122, 170, XXII:25/4

Són *f.* name of a vat II:97, 118, 153

son, sonr, sunr *m.* son (*Gr* 3.1.7.2) III:131, VII B:6, 8, VIII:12, 45,
IX:68, 78, 84, 131, XI:44, XV:2, 135, XIX:4, 5, XXI:8, 174,
XXII:16/3, XXIV:14; *acc. sg.* son, sun IV:107, VI:144, VII B:62,
XXV:60, XXVI A:113; *gen. sg.* sonar V:115, VIII:8, sunar VI:367
(*with* falli); *dat. sg.* (-)syni VII A:99, XIII:48; *pl.* synir II:79, III:20,
IV:73, V:87, X:3, 101, XV:39, 134, XIX:2, XXII:40/1, XXVI B:46,
70; synir eins karls *i.e. they are brothers* IV:41; *acc. pl.* sonu IV:2,

71, X:2, 144, XV:126, XIX:15, XXV:9, 93, XXVI B:130, **sunu** VI:43,
syni XIV:106; *gen. pl.* **sona** XXVI B:160; *dat. pl.* **sonum** XIX:6

sopi *m.* draught, mouthful I:103

sorg *f.* sorrow, grief, anxiety XXV:4

sóru *see* **sverja**

sóti *m. name of a horse* (*SnE, Skáldskaparmál* 88), *used as a common
noun in kenning for* wolf (giantesses were said to ride on wolves)
VI:252 (*subject of* **var lítt svangr**)

sótt¹, sótta, sóttan, sótti, sóttisk, sóttu *see* **sœkja**

sótt² *f.* illness VIII:182, XVI:89

spádómr *m.* prophecy VII A:33, 48, power of prophecy VII A:61

spakr (*f.* **spǫk**) *adj.* wise (*Gr* 3.3.8.1 ex. 3) VIII:56, 61, 174; *wk. form
as nickname* (*Gr* 3.3.9 ex. 9) VIII:39, 169; *sup.* most wise VIII:9

spala *see* **spǫlr**

spámaðr *m.* prophet VII A:31, 44, 46, 61; *gen. sg. with suffixed def.
art.* VII A:39

spánn (*pl.* **spænir**) *m.* bit, chip (left by an auger); *with suffixed def.
art.* II:146, 148; **í spán** to pieces XV:152

spannarlangr *adj.* the length of a span (about 23 cm.) XXI:115

spara (*past* **sparði/sparaði**, *pp.* **sparat**) *wv.* withhold; **spara við/til**
withhold from, begrudge to (for) I:66, XIV:14; **spara at** hold back
from, grudge to XIV:17; **spara sik** spare oneself, *past inf.* **spǫrðu
sik** *in acc. and inf. construction after* **hykkat** VI:249

sparn *see* **sporna**

speki *f.* wisdom VII A:63

spekingr *m.* philosopher XXIII:94

speld *n.* square piece of wood, shutter XXVI A:25

spenna (*past* **spennti**, *pp.* **spenntr**) *wv.* clamp, fasten X:63, XI:20

spilla (*past* **spillti**, *pp.* **spilltr**) *wv.* spoil XXVI A:107; **spilla fyrir**
with dat. do someone harm V:15; **-sk** *form* be spoilt, damaged, injured
XXIV:52

spinna (*past* **spann**, *past pl.* **spunnu**, *pp.* **spunninn**) *sv.* spin; **spunnu**
they were spinning X:7, 20

spjarrar *f. pl.* leg bands, cross-garters XV:50

spjót *n.* spear III:110, V:94, XXI:114 (*pl.*), XXII:12/4, 45/4, XXVI
B:96, 194; *with suffixed def. art.* the spear V:95, his spear-head XXVI
B:90; **sitt spjót it snarpa** that sharp spear of his XXII:42/2

spjǫr *n. pl.* spears VI:202, 240 (*subject of* **gullu**)

sporðr *m.* tail (of a fish); lower (pointed) end of a (kite-shaped) shield V:101; **ok (hjó) af sporðinn** and cut off its point XXVI B:152

sporna (*past* **sparn,** *past pl.* **spurnu**) *wv.* kick, tread, step, *i.e.* travel VII A:138 (the image is of riding a horse of the sea, *i.e.* sailing)

spretta (*past* **spratt,** *past pl.* **spruttu,** *pp.* **sprottinn**) *sv.* spring (up); sprout XXV:1; **springa upp** jump to one's feet XV:68, 111

springa (*past* **sprakk,** *past pl.* **sprungu,** *pp.* **sprunginn**) *sv.* spring, burst *Gr* 3.6.9.1 (6); split, break apart XXV:56/2

spurall *adj.* inquisitive *Gr* 3.3.8.1

spurning *f.* question XXIV:22, 29

spyrja (*pres.* **spyrr,** *past* **spurði,** *pp.* **spurt**) *wv.* **1.** ask I:7, 10, 47, 73, 112, II:44, 107, 124, III:65, V:45, VI:105, 181, VII A:63, 119, XI:33, 65, XV:26, 58, 84, 112, XVI:19, 131, 160, XXI:69, XXII:22/1, XXIV:10, 11, 49, 54, XXVI B:8, 36, 185; *pres. subj. first person* **spyri** XXIV:24; **spyrja at** ask about I:3, 57, *pp. f.* **spurð at** asked about XV:13; **spyrja eptir** enquire VII A:45; *with acc. and gen.* ask someone something II:93, 101, XXIV:23, XXVI B:6. **2.** hear, learn II:111, VI:134, VII A:30, 125, VIII:105, X:41, XV:71, 92, XVI:138, XXVI A:93; learn of VII B:77, XXVI A:4. **3.** -sk *form* **spyrjask** be heard of, be reported VI:86, XXVI A:118

spyrnask (*past* **spyrndisk**) *wv.* -sk *form (reciprocal)* push against each other; **spyrnask í iljar** push against each other's soles (when lying on the stones on their backs) XXI:23

spýta (*past* **spýtti**) *wv. with dat.* spit II:90 (**í** into it, *Gr* 3.7.7), 157

spænir *see* **spánn**

spǫlr (*pl.* **spelir,** *gen. pl.* **spala**) *m.* bar *Gr* 3.1.9 ex. 9

spǫrðu *see* **spara**

staddr *pp.* (*of* **steðja**) positioned, present III:55; located, in residence XVI:93; placed, situated XV:145; engaged VII A:109

staðfestask (*past* **staðfestisk**) *wv.* -sk *form* settle XIX:3

staðfesti *f.* steadfastness XXIII:53

staðit, staðnir *see* **standa**

staðr *m.* place (*Gr* 3.1.8 (2)) I:5, 69, VIII:103, XIII:16; establishment, ecclesiastical foundation VIII:162, XIII:12, 32, XIV:25, 126, 127, 134, 143, 150; **þegar í stað** on the spot VII A:122; **í sinn stað** into their respective position(s), to their station(s) VI:162; **í marga staði** in many instances, in many respects? in many cases? XIV:117; *adv. acc.* (*or dat.?*) **þriðja stað** in a third position, station VI:163; **koma**

í stað come instead (of him), take his place XXIV:70; *with suffixed def. art.* **í staðenn** in their place, to replace them VI:222 (1), **í staðenn þess liðs** to replace those men VI:222; **annars staðar** elsewhere XIV:180, XXI:47, XXVI B:208; **nema stað/staðar** stop XV:100, 109, XXVI A:14, B:47

stafaðr *adj. (pp.)* striped VI:74 (*dat. sg. n.* **stafaðu**)

stafkarl *m.* beggar XVI:91, 122

stafn *m.* stem, prow; *with suffixed def. art.* VI:268

stafnbúi *m.* 'forecastle man', man whose station was at the prow of the ship VI:270; *pl. with suffixed def. art.* VI:274

stafr *m.* staff XVI:97

stakk *see* **stinga**

stakkgarðr *m.* haystack enclosure V:44

stál *n.* steel; *in pl.* = weapons VI:338 (*gen. pl. with* **ór éli**); *with suffixed def. art.* his weapons XXII:18/3

stálhúfa *f.* steel helmet (broad and with a brim) III:28, 95 (*with suffixed def. art.*)

stallari *m.* marshal; *as title* VI:291, 295, XXII:17/3, 45/1

stallr *m.* **1.** platform, pedestal XIII:5; *dat. sg. with* **hneit við** IV:19; **Hrungnis fóta stallr** *is a kenning for* shield (*see SnE, Skáldskapar-mál* ch. 17, where Hrungnir stands on his shield to fight with the god Þórr). **2.** stable I:2

standa (*pres.* **stendr,** *past* **stóð,** *past pl.* **stóðu,** *pp.* **staðinn/staðit**) *sv.* (*Gr* 3.6.9.3 and ex. 1) stand III:11, 15, V:122, 170, VI:290, 291, VII B:18 (*inf. with* **skyli,** *parallel to* **sitja**), X:76, 139, XI:49, XIII:1, 6, 16, XVI:58, XXIII:82; stay VII B:60, 64, XXVI B:53; be positioned XXIII:44, be situated, be placed XXVI B:117; be fixed XII:27, XXI:139; remain in force VIII:141; *pres.* **stendr** is standing XI:2, XIV:12, **stǫndum** we stand XXV:106; *past* **stóð** was standing III:97, 100, V:130, VII B:35, XXVI B:46, it stood, it stuck I:98, she stood XXV:78; *past pl.* **stóðu** stood VII A:129; *past subj.* **stœði** were standing VII B:82, XII:54, were flowing, pouring XXI:123; *pp.* **hafði staðit** had been standing XXVI A:50; **standa betr** *with dat.* (of the wind) be better positioned, blow in a better direction for someone VI:121; **standa ór** stick out of XII:18, extend, stream forth XII:13; **standa upp** get up XI:42, 64, XV:114; *imp.* **standið upp** get up VI:129, IX:86; **eru upp staðnir** have got up XI:76; **standa úti fyrir** stand (stay) outside in front of the house XXVI B:49; **standa við** *with dat.* withstand

XXI:152, oppose XXVII:8; **standa yfir** last, go on XXI:65; *pres.*
part. **standandi** standing XII:22, XIII:46; *impers.* it remains IV:102
stangir *see* **stǫng**
starf *n.* work XII:6, XXVII:38, labour XII:70
starfa (*past* **starfaði,** *pp.* **starfat**) *wv.* work; **starfa firir** work for, be
servant to XVI:5
Starkaðr Barkarson *m.* XXVI A:5
sté *see* **stíga**
stefna¹ (*past* **stefndi,** *pp.* **stefndr**) *wv.* **1.** aim for, make for V:165 (*Gr*
3.6.9.1 (14)), VII A:156; **nær stefna** lay a course close, steer *or* aim
close (metaphorically, i.e. he will avoid naming but nevertheless
indicate who it is) VI:139; **þeir stefndu** they were making their way
XXVI B:11; **þeir stefndu ina sǫmu leið** they took the same route
XXVI B:13. **2.** *with dat.* summons XV:135 (**um** for); **stefna sǫkum**
til refer cases to XV:136
stefna² *f.* meeting (**við** with) XXVII:33
Stefnir (Þorgilsson) *m.* Icelandic poet and missionary (died 1001)
VI:137
stefnulag *n.* appointment VII A:100, VII B:58
steikja (*past* **steikti,** *pp.* **steikt**) *wv.* roast X:53
steina (*past* **steindi,** *pp.* **steint**) *wv.* paint XII:7
Steingerðr *f.* (*Gr* 3.1.8 (17)) daughter of Þorkell of Tunga IV:4, 6, 16,
26, 35, 36, 64, 74, 76, 86, 92, 99, 100, 101, 111
steinn *m.* rock XXI:151; boulder XXVI A:60; (precious) stone; *in pl.*
jewellery IV:55, IX:63 (*understand* **vera**; *but see under* **breiða** *and*
breiðr)
Steinn smiðr (builder; worker in metal or wood) *m.* died in the fire at
Flugumýrr III:75
steinsmíði *n. collective* stone artefacts VIII:70
Steinsstaðir *m. pl.* a farm in Miðfjǫrðr IV:1
stela (*past* **stal,** *past pl.* **stálu,** *pp.* **stolinn**) *sv.* (*Gr* 3.6.5.2) steal, rob
(*with acc. and dat.* some one of something) IX:8 (*pass.*)
stendr *see* **standa**
sterkr *adj.* strong I:105, XXII:16/3, XXIII:58; *sup.* **sterkastr** Gr 3.3.3
ex. 5
stétt *f.* rank XXII:47/3
steypa (*past* **steypti,** *pp.* **steyptr**) *wv. with dat.* fling down III:94, XXVI
B:222; **steypa af** cast (metal) in XII:41, 59

stíga (*past* **steig/sté,** *past pl.* **stigu,** *pp.* **stiginn**) *sv.* (Gr 3.6.9.1 (2, 9)) climb, mount III:120, XV:97; *subj.* **stigi á** boarded (ship) XVI:7; **stíga af baki** dismount from a horse XV:101; **stíga niðr** step down VI:256; **stíga ór** dismount from X:45; step; **stíga hátt** i.e. raise the feet high when walking XXIII:101

Stígandi *m.* son of Kotkell XV:39, 138

stígr *m.* path; way (of life) XVI:91, 122

stikla (*past* **stiklaði,** *pp.* **stiklat**) *wv.* run along XXVI B:222

Stiklastaðir *m. pl.* site of St Ólafr's last battle in Þrándheimr XXII:35/1

stilla (*past* **stillti,** *pp.* **stillt**) *wv. with dat.* control, moderate X:76

stillingarlauss *adj.* uncontrolled, intemperate XXIII:38, 97

stillir *m.* ruler, king XXII:8/2

stinga (*past* **stakk,** *past pl.* **stungu,** *pp.* **stunginn**) *sv.* stab (*with dat. of the instrument*) II:149

stinnr *adj.* stiff, firm, unbending XXII:18/3

stjarna *f.* star *Gr* 3.1.7.1; *pl.* **stjǫrnur** II:74

stjóri *m.* ruler, leader; **dróttar stjóri** *i.e.* king (here King Ólafr) VI:362 (*subject of* **hné**)

stjórn *f.* rule, control, government XXII:5/2; authority XIV:177; **með mikilli stjórn** with firm rule XIV:2; **slíks byskups stjórn** the guidance *or* rule of such a bishop XIV:76

stjórna (*past* **stjórnaði,** *pp.* **stjórnat**) *wv.* rule over XXI:202

stjórnborði *m.* starboard (the side of the ship where the steering oar was fastened) XXI:32

stóð, stóðu *see* **standa**

stoða (*past* **stoðaði,** *pp.* **stoðat**) *wv.* avail, be of use V:90

stofa *f.* a living room *or* parlour IV:7; *with suffixed def. art.* III:78, IV:7, XXVI B:28; chamber; *with suffixed def. art., i.e.* **málstofa,** the council-chamber VII B:59, 64, 68, 70

stofna (*past* **stofnaði,** *pp.* **stofnat**) *wv.* institute, set in motion IV:48

stofudyrr *n. pl.* door of the chamber VII B:64 (*with suffixed def. art.*)

stokkna *see* **støkkva**

stokkr *m.* block (of wood) III:97; *with suffixed def. art.* plank or beam, = **setstokkinum** XXVI B:220

stolinn *see* **stela**

stóll *n.* seat; (bishop's) see VIII:159, 192, 195, XIV:5; **þar til stólsins** to that see VIII:160; **hilmis stóll** *i.e.* throne (*gen. with* **fyllar**) VII B:43

stopir *f. pl.* uneven ground, hillocks XXI:189

stórauðigr *adj.* very wealthy, of great wealth VII B:5

stórbrǫgðóttr *adj. as subst.* very wily person, one who undertakes great deeds XXV:43

stórhátíð *f.* major festival XIV:41

stórmannligr *adj.* munificent, grand XVI:174

stórmerki *n. pl.* great wonders, miracles VII A:65

stórr *adj.* big, large I:39, VI:122, VII A:155, XII:27, XXI:23, XXVI B:120; *n.* **stórt** VII A:149 (*understand* were), XXII:57/1; great I:53, 103, VI:28, 65, 72, XI:7, 35, XIII:4, XXVI A:89, B:104; **þau skip en stóru** (*Gr* 3.3.5) those great ships VI:190; *n. as adv.* severely, harshly XXII:5/4

stórtákn *n.* great miracle XIII:40

stórviðir *m. pl.* big beams, main timbers; *with suffixed def. art.* **stórviðinir** XXVI B:198

strá (*past* **stráði**, *pp.* **stráðr**) *wv.* strew (with straw, rushes, coverings etc., to make comfortable for visitors) IX:86 (*imp. pl.*)

strandar, strandir *see* **strǫnd**

strandhǫgg *n.* a raid on the shore (for supplies) VII A:110 (*gen. pl.*)

strangr/strángr *adj.* hard, harsh XXII:33/2; fierce XXII:39/2; serious XXII:43/4

straumr *m.* current XXI:53; torrent XXI:123

Straumsey *f.* 'torrent island', XXI:54

Straumsfjǫrðr *m.* XXI:56 (see note 1), 83, 161, 194

strendr *see* **strǫnd**

strengja (*past* **strengði**, *pp.* **strengt**) *wv.* fasten; **strengja heit at** make a solemn vow that XIX:10

strengr *m.* rope XXVI A:58; string, cord; *pl.* **boga strengir** bowstrings XXV:76; *pl. with suffixed def. art.* XXVI A:59

stríð *n.* strife, warfare, opposition XXII:14/4; battle (*or* distress, grief?) XXII:55/3

stríða (*past* **stríddi**, *pp.* **strítt**) *wv. with dat.* fight (against) XXII:19/4, 29/4 (*or* distress, afflict?); attack XXII:8/2; cause pain *or* harm to XXV:28; *with suffixed neg.* **at sér ne stríddit** that he has not harmed himself XXV:31

stríðr *adj.* harsh, severe XXII:49/4

strjúka (*pres.* **strýkr,** *past* **strauk,** *past pl.* **struku,** *pp.* **strokinn**) *sv.* stroke IV:17 (*i.e.* whet?)

stræti *n.* street, paved road XXV:43

strǫnd (*pl.* **strendr/strandir**) *f.* coast, shore *Gr* 3.1.7.1, 2 ex. 4, 3.1.8 (18), X:19; beach XXI:32, 186; *dat. pl. with suffixed def. art.* **strǫndunum** XXI:34; *in kenning for* heart *or* mind *or* breast **hyggju strendr** XXII:19/3

studdisk *see* **styðja**

stukku *see* **støkkva**

stuldr *m.* theft XXII:5/1

stund (*dat. sg.* **stundu**, *cf. Gr* 3.1.8 (14)) *f.* while, period of time I:129, II:21, XVI:78 *(pl.)*, 135; time II:38, IV:70, 111 (*with suffixed def. art., though of an indefinite period of time*), XXI:122; moment V:4; **þessa stund** for the time being XXI:48; **af stundu** in a short while VIII:130; **stundu síðar** after a while XV:67; **um stund** for a time IV:108, for a while XXI:105, 116; *dat. pl. as adv.* **stundum** sometimes XIV:139, from time to time XXI:180, XXIV:5, some of the time VII A:108; **stundum . . . stundum** sometimes . . . sometimes VIII:30–31, XXIII:25

stunda (*past* **stundaði**, *pp.* **stundat**) *wv.* devote oneself to; **stunda til** cultivate (someone's) friendship IV:99

stundanarmikill *adj.* very painstaking, assiduous XXIII:19

styðja (*past* **studdi**, *pp.* **studdr**) *wv.* support; **-sk** *form* **studdisk** was leaning (**við** against) XIII:19

stynr *m.* groan XXVI B:200

stýra (*past* **stýrði**, *pp.* **stýrt**) *wv. with dat.* control, rule VII A:93, XIV:1, XXIV:36 (this vb. is understood in each of the six following clauses); be in charge of XIV:26; direct: **kallar sér stýrt** declares he is being sent I:88 (*Gr* 3.9.3, 3.9.4, 3.9.5.2); steer VI:135, command (a ship) VI:105, 115, 119, 264 (*pres. subj.*, may steer)

stýri *n.* helm, steering-oar XXI:175

stýrimaðr *m.* steersman, captain of a ship XVI:3, 9

stýrir *m.* ruler, controller; controller of silver (or gold) or of the sword *is a kenning for* (generous or valiant) king (here King Óláfr) VI:347 (*subject of* **myndi koma**)

styrk *n.* support (**til** for something) XV:82

Styrkárr af Gimsum *m.* Norwegian landowner, one of Óláfr Tryggvason's supporters VI:67

styrkja (*past* **styrkti**, *pp.* **styrkt**) *wv.* strengthen, support XIV:3; *pp.* XIV:148

styrkr (= **sterkr**) *adj.* strong XXIII:84, 86

styrkt *f.* strength XXIII:50 (*gen. sg. with* **-mark**)

styrr *m.* turmoil, uproar, battle VI:356, XXV:83

stœði *see* **standa**

stœrri *adj. comp.* larger (*Gr* 3.3.8.2) VI:27, 220

stǫð *f.* place; landing-place, beach X:85 (*see note and cf.* **Sævar-staðr**), 101

stǫðva (*past* **stǫðvaði**) *wv.* stop (transitive); *impers.* (**ǫrninn** *object*) II:58

stǫndum *see* **standa**

stǫng (*pl.* **stangir**) *f.* pole II:29, XXI:127, 206; *with suffixed def. art.* II:31

støkkva (*past* **stǫkk**, *past pl.* **stukku**, *pp.* **stokkinn**) *wv.* leap, spring away VI:279, IX:107; take to flight, run away V:41 (with lines 38–39); snap, spring apart IX:50; go flying XXV:83; **fyrir** before, in the face of; **støkkva undan** leap away, escape VI:219; *pp. acc. pl.* **stokkna** sprinkled, spattered X:157

sú *pron. f.* (*Gr* 3.2.2, 3.8.2.1) she, it; that VI:30, XV:79, XXVI B:8, 149; this VIII:143; **er sú af** that is one of XXVI A:44; **sú es/er/sem** which XIV:12, the . . . which VIII:52, XXIII:33, she whom XXV:11; **sú (. . .) er** a . . . which XXIII:64, 67; **sú hǫndin** the one arm XV:122; **sú in fremri** the foremost XXVI B:92

suðr, sunnr *adv.* south(wards) *Gr* 3.5.1–3 ex. 6 (a), III:73, VI:245, VII A:5, 156, 159, 168, X:35, XV:100, XVI:13, 14, 88, XXI:105, 164; *i.e.* on pilgrimage to Rome XVI:82, 85; in the south (actually south-west) VIII:17, in the south, to the south (i.e. in the more southerly Álptafjǫrðr) XIX:29; **suðr hér** here in the south XXVI A:110; **sunnr fyrir** in the south off VI:207; **suðr fyrir land** southwards along the coast XXI:86, 121, south past XXI:105

suðrátt *f.* southerly direction; **í suðrátt** southwards XXI:43

suðrdyrr *n. pl.* southern doorway; *gen. pl.* **suðrdura** III:96; *acc. as adv.* (*acc. of route*) by the southern doorway III:81

Suðreyjar *f. pl.* the Hebrides VII A:5

suðreyskr *adj.* Hebridean, from the Hebrides XV:40

suðrganga *f.* pilgrimage to Rome XVI:165

Suðrríki *n.* 'the southern realm', southern Europe (the Roman Empire) VI:320

suðrœnn *adj.* southern, from the south X:20

suðu *see* **sjóða**

súla *f.* pillar XIX:53 (*with suffixed def. art.*)

súðþaktr *adj. (pp.)* roofed with ovrlapping boards XXVI A:24

sukku *see* **søkkva**

sumar *n.* summer (*Gr* 3.1.7.1, 5 (1), 3.1.8 (27)) II:137 (*with suffixed def. art.*), XI:5, XIV:1, XV:79, 82, XXVII:5, 26; *acc. of time* **þetta/ þat sumar** that summer IV:108, VIII:88, XV:43, **et/hit sama sumar** the same summer VIII:145, XXI:165, **annat sumar** the following summer XIX:9, (which is to be, for) the following summer XXVII:40, **it fjórða sumar** in the fourth summer XXVII:44, **sumar þat er** in the summer that XIX:47; **et næsta sumar eptir, of/um sumarit eptir** the following summer VIII:91, 179, 190, XVI:9; **um sumarit** that summer XXI:4; **þegar um sumarit** that same summer XVI:190; **af sumri** VIII:93 *see* **af**; *pl.* **sumur** VIII:59, 170, 171, XXVII:20, 43; *dat. pl.* **sumrum** XXVII:26, **um sumrum** in summer XXI:10

sumr *adj.* some, some of VI:123; a certain, some or other VI:354 (*with* **seggr**); *acc. sg. m.* **suman** II:159; *pl.* some men III:4, V:70, VI:226; *gen. pl.* **sumra** III:47, **sumra manna** of some people XXI:161; **sumir** some of them XXVI A:38; **sumir ... sumir** some ... others III:110, V:82, VII B:67, XIV:134, 167, XXI:106–07; *n. sg. for indefinite number and gender* **sumt ... sumt** VII A:149 (*understand* were)

sun, sunar *see* **sonr**

sund[1] *n.* sound, strait IV:28

sund[2] *n.* swimming; **af sundi** *i.e.* out of the water, from where they were swimming in the water VI:300; **sunds** *gen. with* **snotr** *or adv. gen.* ('by swimming') VI:313

sundr *adv.* apart; **ganga sundr** be broken VI:57; **í sundr** apart III:11, VIII:135, in two XXVI A:69, to pieces I:16, in pieces XXI:117; **gekk í sundr** broke in two V:100

sundrmœðr *adj.* born of a different mother, half-brother XXV:45

sungu/súngu *see* **syngja**

sunnan *adv.* from the south *Gr* 3.5.3 (6), VI:51, 355, X:17, XXI:111, 122; *in verse perhaps* = **fyrir sunnan**, in the south VII A:139; **fyrir sunnan** to the south of XXVI A:96

sunnanveðr *n.* a wind from the south, a southerly wind XXI:198

sunnr = **suðr**

sunr, sunu *see* **sonr**

súpa (*pres.* **sýpr**, *past* **saup**, *past pl.* **supu**, *pp.* **sopinn**) *sv.* sip *Gr* 3.6.9.2 (1)

sura *f. (Latin word)* calf (of the leg) XXIII:96; *pl.* **surae** XXIII:98

Susa *f.* Soest in Westphalia XI:3, 11

sút *f.* sickness, grief, wound (collective) XXII:54/4; grief, sorrow, pain (*with gen.* for) XXV:4

sútari *m.* cobbler (Latin *sutor*, Old English *sutere*; in later Icelandic 'tanner'); *as nickname* III:76

Suttungr (Suttungi) *m.* a giant II:111, 113, 115, 131, 136, 139, 140, 155, 158; *gen.* **Suttunga** II:119, 122, 135, 160

svá/svó *adv.* so I:110, 115, 143, II:111, 144, III:66, VI:46, 122, VIII:28, 33, 36, 50, 93, IX:105 (*with* **óðfús**), X:86, XVI:58, 127, XXII:33/3, XXVI B:8, 36; **gera/gjǫra svá** do so XXI:72, 102, XXVI B:213; **var eigi svá** was it not the case XXI:77; **þetta mun svá vera** that will be so, all right XXVI A:112; **nǫkkut svá** a little bit XXIII:59; so much I:90, XVI:184; thus *Gr* 3.5.3 (7), I:41, 64, 134 (2), VI:83, IX:131, XII:80, XIV:65 (1), XV:54, XIX:53, XXIII:1, XXIV:9, 20, XXVI B:204; like that VIII:2, XI:47, XIX:78, XXV:27, XXVI A:40; thus, in the same way III:116, like this XXI:116; similarly XII:84, XXVI B:25; as follows II:8, VI:258, VII A:10, 78, B:14, XIX:36; such IV:86, XV:141, XVI:83, XXVI B:187, such . . . (that) XXII:40/3; then X:39, XIV:65 (2), XXVI B:222; so that XXII:48/2; as if XXVI A:23; **svá fast, svá hǫrð** thus hard (fierce), hard (fierce) like this V:133, VI:254; **svá mikit** similarly large XXIII:63; **(ok) svá** (and) also III:112, V:46, VII A:7, 59, XI:11, XIII:5, XVI:186, XXII:2/1, XXVII:42, and . . . as well XXVI B:222 (1), and then, and so VI:10, VII A:156, B:75, and so on XXI:88, and so did (*i.e.* jump overboard) VI:295; **ok svá þat ef** and also (this), if XXVII:28; **svá ok** also, likewise XIV:181; **ok svá er** and so it is, and that is right VI:197; **svá er ok** that is right too V:136; **ok svá var** and so it was VI:67, and so it happened VII A:66; **en svá** than that VI:340; **svá at** (*Gr* 3.8.2.2) so that I:32, III:10, V:130, VIII:57, X:131, XI:11, XIII:4, 22, XXI:129, XXII:22/3, XXIII:25, 72, XXVI A:18, 64, 74, B:31, 76; so hard that XV:151, so harsh that XXII:6/1, such that XV:11, in such a way that II:83, VI:117, XXI:3, 117, so well that VIII:130, XIV:163, (on occasions) when VII B:32, it being the case that, at the point where VI:305, at a time when XXVII:27, this, that XXI:157, XXIV:35; **svá (. . .) at** so . . . that I:17, 26, 36, 97, II:5, 32, III:125, VI:271, 288 (1), VII A:154, B:86, X:60, 170, XII:10–11, XVI:32, XXI:23, XXIV:26, XXVI B:63, 124, XXVII:31, such . . . that I:43, XI:46, 60, XII:13, XVI:125, XXVI A:88, thus (. . .) that II:73, 127,

III:113, VI:288 (2), XV:8, XXIV:1, 32, XXVII:2, in this way . . .
that I:134, IV:65, XXI:44, in such a way that XXI:70 (*or* **svá lengst**
for such a very long time?), in this way . . . by XIV:118, in such a
way that I:109, IV:104, VI:256, VIII:133, 137, X:126, XII:79,
XXV:30, like this, that XXIV:79–80; **svá . . . at eigi** without XIV:67;
svá . . . at . . . hvárki without either VI:8; **svá at hon lét lesa** by
having them read XIV:188; **svá at hann stóð** while standing, still
standing V:142; **svá at menn viti** as far as is known X:14; **svá sem**
as VI:221, 276, VII A:58, VIII:164, X:15, XXIV:3, just as if XII:53,
XV:90, in the way that XII:7, XXIV:30, like VIII:191, XV:60,
XXI:34, XXIII:11, just like XXI:123, as if XII:14, XXIII:34 (when?),
(that it) seemed to sort of XXI:173, almost, rather, pretty well
XXIII:10; **svá sem . . . vel = svá vel sem** so well as I:15; **þat . . . svá
sem** what VIII:185; **svá . . . sem** as . . . as I:18, 79, XI:38, XII:81,
XIX:112, XXI:64, as . . . as if XII:23 (1), XXI:111, so . . . as XIV:43,
so . . . that XXVI B:48, like XXV:45, as I:118, III:33, XI:40, as if
XIII:2, just as (he did) XIII:8, such a . . . as XXVI A:57, in such a
way that (it seems that) *or* so that XXIII:102; **svá . . . svá sem** as . . .
as if XII:22; **svá . . . es** it being the case that, i.e. when VIII:95; **svá
. . . er** you being such . . . that XXI:133; **svá margir sem þeir** so
many as they were, considering how many they were V:144; **svá** *as
conj.* so that I:18 (1), 56, 96, as far as XXVI B:183

svaf *see* **sofa**

svagla (*past* **svaglaði,** *pp.* **svaglat**)*wv. impers.* gurgle III:115

svala (*past* **svalaði,** *pp.* **svalat**) *wv. impers. with dat.* cool down III:18, 27

svalt *see* **svelta**

svanfjaðrar *f. pl.* swan-feathers, (swan's) plumage X:23

svangr *adj.* hungry VI:253 (if the wolf was not hungry there must
have been plenty of fallen warriors for it to feed on and a good
battle had been fought)

Svanhildr *f.* daughter of Sigurðr the dragon-slayer XXV:9 (see note
5), 10

svanhvítr *adj.* swan-white; *as a byname* X:8; **Svanhvít** *f. as a personal
name* X:11, 13, 23, 35

svar *n.* answer, response XXIV:29; **halda upp svǫrum** be spokesman
VII B:25; **hafa eins manns svǫr í munni** have to answer for one
person, be responsible for one person XXIV:66; **eiga svǫr at veita
firi** be answerable, bear responsibility for XXIV:64, 66

svara[1] (*past* **svaraði**, *pp.* **svarat**) *wv.* reply, answer I:11, 61, 63, 107, 127, II:77, 88, 123, V:159, VI:65, VII A:48, 77, XI:25, 37, 66, XV:55, 60, 91, XVI:21, 162, XXI:100, XXIV:28, XXV:45, XXVI B:132; *past pl.* **svǫruðu** III:123, **svaraðu** VI:183; **var honum svarat** he got a reply I:8; **þar firi svara** answer about that XXIV:57; *with dat.* **því fyst svara er** answer that first which XXIV:31

svara[2] *see* **svar**

svardagi *m.* oath, solemn promise VIII:156; *acc. pl.* II:35

svarðlauss *adj.* grassless *Gr* 3.3.9 ex. 20

svartr (*f. sg. and n. pl.* **svǫrt**) *adj.* dark, swarthy XXI:11, XXIII:105, 108; black I:7, V:166, XXIII:28, XXV:12; black-haired V:86; *wk. form as nickname* VIII:8, XIV:183

sváss *adj.* beloved XXV:36

svefn *m.* sleep XIV:67, XXV:22, XXVI B:37

svefnfarar *f. pl.* 'sleep experiences', dreams; *with suffixed def. art.* your dreams V:16

sveinn *m.* (*Gr* 3.1.7.3–5 ex. 1) boy V:32; *with suffixed def. art.* III:43, 44, V:44, 45, 65, 69, 80, 85, 88, 91, XI:45, XV:90, XXVI B:169, boy child, young boy XXI:200; *as nickname* XI:7, 8, 35, 37, 40, 71; *as a term of abuse* V:121; *jocular, in address* XXVI B:109

Sveinn Haraldsson forkbeard *m.* king of Denmark (died 1014) VI:1, 5, 12, 16, 29, 38, 39, 63, 69, 75, 107, 114, 118, 127, 142, 146, 162, 183, VIII:146

Sveinn Úlfsson *m.* king of Denmark 1047–76 XVI:14, 30, 39, 44, 46, 77, 128, 136, 140, 144, 149, 161, 166

sveipa (*past* **sveip**, *past pl.* **svipu**, *pp.* **sveipit**) *sv.* wrap *Gr* 3.6.9.3; **sveipa útan** enclose, cover (*with dat.* in something) X:117, 161

sveit *f.* troop V:54, VII A:82; district XXVI A:119

sveitúngr *m. pl.* members of a **sveit**; fellow soldier XXII:30/2

svelta (*past* **svalt**, *past pl.* **sultu**, *pp.* **soltinn**) *sv.* die XXV:26

sverð *n.* sword I:132, III:54, 56, 85, IV:9, V:29, 36, 59, VI:52, 238 (*gen. pl. with* **gangr**), XI:26, XIX:33, XXI:114 (*pl.*), XXII:12/3, XXVI B:152; the sword X:81, 91; *with suffixed def. art.* the sword I:130, 137, 148, III:28, VII A:103, X:79, XIX:34, XXI:142; *with suffixed def. art.*, his sword I:94, 95, 96, III:95, XXI:140; *nom. pl.* V:156 (*subject of* **bitu**), VI:196; *acc. pl.* II:5, IV:39 (*object of* **hvetja**); *dat. with suffixed def. art.*, his sword III:98, V:58, VII B:68; *dat. with suffixed def. art. and gen. of owner* V:116; **með sverði** with his sword VII A:17; *dat. as instrumental* **sverði** with a sword VII A:102, XXV:31

sverðleikr *m.* 'sword-play', 'sword-sport', battle VII A:18 (*object of* **gerði**)

sverja (*past* **sór,** *past pl.* **sóru,** *pp.* **svarit**) *sv.* swear *Gr* 3.6.9.1 (5), 3.6.9.3 ex. 2; **sóru** swore VIII:153

Svíaherr *m.* army of Swedes VI:163

Svíakonungr *adj.* king of the Swedes; *as title* VI:35, 84, 128, 146, 163, 187, VIII:147

Svíar *m. pl.* Swedes VI:188, 213, 222

svik *n. pl.* treachery, betrayal VII A:52

svíkja (*past* **sveik,** *past pl.* **sviku,** *pp.* **svikinn**) *sv.* (*Gr* 3.6.9.2 (6)) betray, cheat II:147, VI:143 (**ór** out of, so as to make him leave); *pp.* cheated VI:4, ambushed, trapped, caught in a trap V:151

svima (*past* **svam,** *past pl.* **svámu,** *pp.* **sumit**) *sv.* swim *Gr* 3.6.9.3

svinnr *adj.* wise, shrewd XXV:32

svipan *f.* movement, force, speed I:43

svipta (*past* **svipti,** *pp.* **sviptr**) *wv.* deprive *Gr* 3.6.9.1 (7); *pp.* **sviptr** *with dat.* deprived of XXII:48/4; having lost XXII:9/4

svívirðing *f.* dishonour, affront, insult, outrage VI:36, 40, XV:25

Svíþjóð *f.* Sweden X:2, XVI:130

svó *see* **svá**

svæla (*past* **svældi,** *pp.* **svældr**) *wv.* choke with smoke III:14; **svæla inni** suffocate (someone) in their house XXVI B:67

svælumikit *adv.* very smoky, full of choking smoke III:5

svænskr *adj.* Swedish (= **sœnskr**); *acc. pl.* **svænska menn** *in acc. and inf. construction after* **kváðu** VI:244; *wk. form as title* **svænski** VI:35, 213

Svǫlðr (*gen.* **Svǫlðrar**) *m.* an island in the Baltic VI:29; *referred to as a river* VI:207; *cf.* VIII:145, *note 47*

svǫr *see* **svar**

svǫrt, svǫrtum *see* **svartr**

svǫruðu *see* **svara**[1]

svǫrum *see* **svar**

syðri *adj. comp.* more southerly III:12, XXI:170; **í Álptafirði enum syðra** in the more southerly Álptafjǫrðr XIX:28; *dat. pl.* **syðrum** III:51

syknuleyfi *n.* licence for mitigation of penalty XXVII:27

Syllingar *f. pl.* the Scilly Isles VII A:9, 28, 29, 30, 70

sýn *f.* (restoration of) sight XXII:58/3

sýna (*past* **sýndi,** *pp.* **sýndr**) *wv.* show; display XV:146; demonstrate, give an example (of) XIV:38, 50; indicate, betray XXIII:5, 9, 39, 40, 47, 57 (cf. *Gr* 3.9.8.2), 84 (cf. *Gr* 3.9.8.2), they indicate XXIII:60; reveal XXIII:3; **sýna af sér** give out, proclaim XXIII:52; **sýnir** (it) indicates, (it) is a sign of XXIII:16, 80, 85; **sýnir manninn** shows the person to be XXIII:64; *with suffixed 1st person pron* **sýndak** I showed (it) VIII:2; **sýna sik í** display (one's readiness for) something, reveal one's concern for something V:160; **sýna viðrkvæmiligt vera** show that it was fitting XIII:20; *pres. part.* **sýnandi** XIII:24; **-sk** *form* **sýnask** appear, can be seen XXIII:31; **sýnaz** appear, be apparent XXIV:79; **sýnisk mér**, **mér sýniz** seems to me XVI:120, XXIV:30, it seems to me XXVI B:28; **sýnisk honum nǫkkvot eptir sem** there seems to him to be something in what, he thought it was probably right what XVI:55; **sýnisk þeim** it seems to them XXI:146 ; **sýndisk** appeared, looked X:104, it seemed XIV:51

syngja/syngva (*past* **sǫng,** *past pl.* **sungu,** *pp.* **sungit**) *sv.* sing *Gr* 3.6.9.2 (2, 6); chant, intone XIV:64, 70; **súngu** rang, clashed, resounded XXII:56/4; **þar er spjǫr sungu** 'where spears sang' *means* in battles VI:202

syni, synir *see* **sonr**

synja (*past* **synjaði,** *pp.* **synjat**) *wv. with gen.* refuse II:140

sýnu *adv. with sup.* by far V:87

sýr *f.* sow *Gr* 3.1.7.2 (5)

sýra *f.* sour whey III:99 (*see note*), III:102 (*with suffixed def. art.*), III:103 (*with suffixed def. art.*), XXVI B:114

sýrgja (*past* **sýrgði,** *pp.* **sýrgðr**) *wv.* wail, weep aloud XXVI B:31

sýruker *n.* cask for storing **sýra** III:100 (*with suffixed def. art.*)

sýsla[1] *f.* **1.** work XIV:18; task(s) XIV:138, *note.* **2.** diocese XIV:142

sýsla[2] (*past* **sýslaði,** *pp.* **sýslat**) *wv.* do, effect; **sýsla þat** arrange it, i.e. make the decision XXVII:6

sýsligast *adv. sup.* most briskly *Gr* 3.5.3 (12)

systir *f.* sister VI:31, 47, VII A:74, IX:114, 127, X:24, XI:19, 28, 71, XIX:107, XXV:10, XXVI A:115; *gen.* **systur** XIX:39, XXV:60

systurdóttir *f.* sister's daughter, niece VII B:7 (refers to Sigríðr, not Gunnhildr)

systursonr *m.* nephew (sister's son) III:43 (*in apposition to* **sveinsins**)

sæi *see* **sjá**

sælið *n.* help at sea, (trying to) save a ship XV:146

Sælingsdalr *m.* valley in western Iceland XV:46, 84

Sælingsdalsheiðr *f.* moor between Sælingsdalr and Saurbœr in western Iceland XV:100

sæll *adj.* happy, fortunate, blessed I:9, 11, 21, 39, XIV:75, XXV:74

sæmdarmaðr *m.* man of honour, honourable *or* distinguished man XXII:28/3

Sæmundr (Sigfússon, enn fróði) *m.* Icelandic priest and historian 1056–1133 VIII:2, 145, 152

sær (= **sjór**) *m.* sea II:50, 103, 112, VI:316, XV:145; *with suffixed def. art.* II:108, VII A:157; *gen. sg.* **sævar** X:19, 85, 101

særa (*past* **særði,** *pp.* **særðr**) *wv.* wound XXVI A:51, 75, B:96

sæta[1] (*past* **sætti,** *pp.* **sætt**) *wv. with dat.* mean, signify; **hverju þat sætti** what this meant, what was the cause of this I:74; **undrum sæta** amount to a miracle *or* marvel XXII:44/2

sæta[2] *f.* *poetical term for* woman; = Steingerðr, *subj. of* **hvarf** IV:27

sæti *see* **sitja**

sætt *f.* settlement II:62, 72, 114; peace VI:56; *in pl.* compensation, atonement, settlement XIX:24; **taka sættum við** accept reconciliation with XXVI B:130

sættargjǫrð *f.* terms of settlement II:67

sættask (*past* **sættisk**) *wv.* reach agreement (**á** on something) VIII:27, XVI:56; **sættask at því at** agree on these terms, that XIX:24

sætti *see* **sæta**[1]

sævar *see* **sær**

Sævarstaðr *m.* 'Sea-stead', an island X:87; cf. **sævar stǫð** X: 85, 101

sœkja (*pres.* **sœkir,** *past* **sótti,** *pp.* **sótt**) *wv.* (*Gr* 3.6.9.3) **1.** seek (**eptir** for, *i.e.* go in search of, fetch) II:48; make an attempt on IV:46 (*subj.*); attack V:103, 132, 134, 144, VI:343, XXVI B:64; go to, attend IV:110, VII B:25; visit XIV:61; **skjótt sœkja** quickly win them (the buildings) *or* defeat us XXVI B:61; **mik fá sótt** attack me successfully, overcome me XXVI A:81; **þá sótta geta** manage to defeat them XXVI B:49, 100; *past subj.* **sœtti** might seek out IX:56; **sœkja á fund** *with gen.* go to visit XIV:139; **sœkja í hendr** make demands on, pester *or* demand (women) from? XXI:195; **sœkja at** attack IV:62, V:81, 113, VI:275, XXI:138, 146, XXVI A:37, 39, B:51, force one's way to VI:285; **sœkjum at** let us attack XXVI A:42, *past subj.* **at sœtti at** that they should attack VI:273; **sœkja heim** attack (someone) in their home XXVI B:63; **sœkja til** look for, call (on someone) for something II:130, come (to try to get something) IV:37, attend XIV:58; *pp.* **sótt verða** to be overcome VI:316; **sóttan** (to be) overcome (*with* **vann jǫfur**) VI:247, **sóttan und lok** (to have been) finally defeated, *i.e.* slain VI:303. **2. -sk** *form* **illa sóttisk þeim Gunnarr** Gunnarr was hard for them to defeat XXVI B:60; *impers. with dat.* **sóttisk þeim, þeim sœkisk** they were progressing, gaining success III:1, IV:63; **þeim mun illa sœkjask** it will be slow progress for them, they will find it tough work XXVI B:58

sœmð *f.* honour I:66 (**at honum** sign of his being a source of), XXIV:68, 73; **þeim til sœmðar sem** in honour of him who XXIV:60; **þeim til sœmðar** as a compliment to them XXIV:74

sœmðaratkvæði *n.* respectful address, honourable forms of address XXIV:61

sœmiliga *adv.* becomingly XIII:30

sœmiligr *adj.* honourable, reverend XIV:175; *sup.* XIV:165

sœmr *adj.* befitting; *comp. Gr* 3.3.3 ex. 5

sœnskr *adj.* Swedish (= **svænskr**); *wk. form as title* VIII:146

sœtr *adj.* sweet; *sup.* **sœtasti** most sweet XIII:47; *dat. pl.* **sœtustum** sweetest XII:18

sœtti *see* **sœkja**

sǫðla (*past* **sǫðlaði,** *pp.* **sǫðlat**) *wv.* saddle XV:95

sǫðull *m.* saddle V:157, X:45

sǫgð (*Gr* 3.3.9 ex. 8)**, sǫgðu, sǫgðum** *see* **segja**

sǫgn (*pl.* **sagnir**) *f.* (*Gr* 3.1.7.1 ex. 5) report III:47; **er þat sumra manna sǫgn** some people say XXI:162

sǫgu, sǫgur, sǫgum *see* **saga**

sǫk *f.* cause; suit XV:67, XXVII:7; lawsuit XV:137; accusation, charge, cause of resentment, grievance, grudge VI:30, 32, 41; **á sǫk þá** has (responsibility for) that case, that case lies with XXVII:36; **fyrir þá sǫk** for this reason IV:105, VII A:79, as a result XIV:144; **fyrir þá sǫk at** because VI:34, **firi þá sǫk . . . at** for this reason . . . that XXIV:57–58; **fyrir þessa sǫk** because of this, on account of this VI:137; **fyr sanna sǫk** for good cause V:155; **sú var sǫk til** this was the reason for it VII A:135; **fyrir sakar, fyrir (. . .) sakir** *with gen.* for the sake of, because of XII:36, XIV:97, 114, XXIV:21, because of V:46, XIV:99, XIX:3, for someone's sake, on someone's account IV:100; **fyrir mínar sakir ok fyrir þínar** for my sake and for your own XII:40; **fyrir sakir þeira er** because of those who XII:89; **fyrir sakar þess er** for this reason, that VI:317; **fyrir þær sakar** as a result of this, for all that XV:12; **fyrir þessar sakar** on these grounds XV:28; **til saka** as the offence, as the reason XV:69

sǫkótt *adj. n.* **eiga sǫkótt** have many quarrels, have much enmity (many enemies) V:3

sǫl *n. pl.* an edible sea-weed used as food; *gen. pl.* **sǫlva** IV:61

sǫmu *see* **samr**

sǫngr *m.* song *Gr* 3.1.7.5 (4); singing, chanting, music XIV:156, 162

sǫnn, sǫnnu, sǫnnum *see* **sannr**

Sǫrli *m.* brother of Hamðir, son of Guðrún and Jónakr XXV:32, 75, 110

sǫx *see* **sax**

søkkva (*past* **sǫkk,** *past pl.* **sukku,** *pp.* **sokkinn**) *sv.* (*Gr* 3.6.9.2 (2)) sink III:98 (**upp um** up over, *i.e.* so as to be covered up over), VI:256, 259, XXI:200

-t *neg. suffix with verbs* IV:42, VI:261, 342, 348, XXV:31, 64

tá¹ (*pl.* **tær**) *f.* toe *Gr* 3.1.7.2, 3.1.8 (20)

tá² *n.* pathway, trodden ground round or in front of the house XXV:1

taða *f.* hay (from the well-manured home field) III:4

tak *n.* hold, grasp; **betri honum til taks** any better for him to use XV:123

taka (*pres.* **tekr,** *past* **tók,** *past pl.* **tóku,** *past subj.* **tœki,** *pp.* **tekinn** *Gr* 3.3.8.4 (3a), 3.3.8.2–5 ex. 4, 3.6.9.1 (4)) *sv.* **1.** take (*Gr* 3.6.9.1 (4, 12, 13, 14)) II:18, 42, 52, 73, 80, III:3, IV:63, X:79, XVI:186, XIX:34, XXI:51, 115, XXVI A:40, B:107; *imp.* **tak** XII:38, *imp. pl.* **takið** XXVI B:150; **tǫkum, tǫku vér** let us take XXI:100, XXVI A:59; receive I:121, VII A:66, VIII:140, XXII:51/3, 58/3; accept XXII:27/3, XXIV:68, *with dat.* XXVI B:130, *imp.* **taki þér** XXII:25/1; take away VII B:56; take up, pick up V:157, XI:19, 44; take hold of IV:64; take possession of VII A:107, XIX:54; take on, assume VIII:58, 62, 169; adopt XVI:83, XXVI B:105; choose XXVII:4; **tók sér** chose himself XIX:94; appoint XXVII:10, 18, 50; start XI:112; undergo XIV:37; board VI:103; catch V:67, 91, 95, XIX:57, XXVI B:195; arrest VII B:51, *past subj.* **tœki** take prisoner XXVI A:8; catch (an illness) XVI:89; capture II:46, VI:297, 300 (*pp. pl.* **teknir**), XIX:36, XXVI A:9; reach X:170; touch, consume? XIII:17; strike XXVI B:92; **taka kveðju** respond to a greeting XVI:19, 157; **taka mat eða svefn** enjoy food or sleep XIV:67; **hvat**

suffixed def. art.); reckoning VIII:149; **tal af honum** what he said, his opinions (*cf.* **halda**) XXI:15

tál *f.* deceit, betrayal; *pl.* **draga á tálar** entrap, betray VI:145

tala[1] (*past* **talaði**, *past pl.* **tǫluðu**, *pp.* **talaðr**) *wv.* speak (**við** with) III:15, IV:36, XIV:33, XV:6, 58, XXII:31/1, XXVI B:40, 155; say (**við** to) XXII:15/2; speak of, discuss III:18, VII A:62, 95; **tala um** speak about, discuss IV:77, XXI:2, write about, treat of XIV:90, *note*; *impers. pass.* **um var talat at** it was discussed that III:105

tala[2] (*acc.* **tǫlu**, *pl.* **tǫlur**) *f.* speech VIII:123; *in pl.* persuasion VIII:152; reckoning VIII:8, 61; number XI:12

talðr, talði *see* **telja**

tálma (*past* **tálmaði**, *pp.* **tálmat**) *wv.* hinder XVI:70

tanngnjóstr *m.* 'Tooth-gnasher' or 'Tooth-crushed', a nickname; also the name of one of Þórr's goats (*SnE, Gylfaginning* ch. 21) IV:107

téa *see* **tjá**

tefla (*past* **tefldi**, *pp.* **tefldr**) *wv.* weave braid, do tablet weaving XIV:189

tegr/tigr/tugr (*pl.* **tigir**) *m.* (a group of) ten, a decade (*Gr* 3.4.1 and 2 (5), (9)) VIII:56, 60, 196; *with gen.* (*Gr* 3.4.2.(9)) **fjórir tigir** forty XXI:18, 164, **sjau tigir** seventy XIX:49, **tíu tigir** a hundred XXI:162; *acc. pl.* **tegu** VIII:29, **sex tigu** sixty VI:21, **sjau tigu** seventy VI:49; *dat. pl.* **nær þremr tigum** nearly thirty XXVI B:47; **sex tigum ok einu** with seventy-one VI:53 (*adv. with* **fór**); **sjau tegum vetra ens níunda hundraðs eptir** = 870 years after VIII:13; **þremr tegum vetra ens annars hundraðs eptir** = 130 years after VIII:148; **sex vetr ens fjórða tegar** 36 years VIII:194; **hálfr þriði tugr manna** half the third ten (= two tens and half the third) of men, i. e. 25 men III:79 (*Gr* 3.4.2 (9))

teitr *adj.* cheerful, happy, joyful XXII:21/2

Teitr Ísleifsson *m.* priest VIII:8, 36, 93, 144

Teitr Ketilbjarnarson *m.* 10th-century Icelander VIII:80

tekinn (*Gr* 3.3.8.4 (3a), 3.3.8.2–5 ex. 4)**, tekit, teknir, tekr** *see* **taka**

telja (*past* **talði**, *past pl.* **tǫlðu**, *pp.* **talðr**) *wv.* reckon, declare II:110; tell, report XII:63; calculate, reckon up VIII:153; count VIII:165, X:56; enumerate XXII:28/2; **telja fyrir** work out or argue in the presence of VIII:73, put to, plead to, try to persuade VIII:125; **-sk** *form* **talðisk** said that he II:132; **teljask undan** decline, refuse XXVI B:145

ténaðarmaðr *m.* assistant, deputy XIV:170

tendra (*past* **tendraði,** *pp.* **tendrat**) *wv.* kindle; **-sk** *form* **tendrask með** be kindled by (*or* in), be excited by (*or* in) XIII:23

tengja (*past* **tengði,** *pp.* **tengt**) *wv.* tie together VI:169 (*imp. pl.*)

tenn *see* **tǫnn**

tét *see* **tjá**

teygja (*past* **teygði**) *wv.* entice, lure II:38, XXVI A:15

teygjask (*past* **teygðisk**) *wv.* **-sk** *form* show oneself; **tenn hánum teygjask** his teeth are bared X:81

tíð *f.* time VIII:129; *pl.* **tíðir** divine service XIV:43, 58, 124; the canonical 'hours', prayers XIV:69; **til tíða** for services, for prayers XIV:160

tíða (*past* **tíddi,** *pp.* **títt**) *wv. impers. with acc.* desire XVI:88

tíðagjǫrð *f.* (holding of) church services XIV:152

tíðindalauss *adj.* uneventful, without incident XV:57

tíðindi *n. pl.* tidings, news, events II:14, 37, VI:89, 106, 134, XV:72, 91, XIX:74 ('what had happened'), XXVI B:6; **lǫng tíðindi** long drawn-out story IX:37; **vera myndi nǫkkur tíðindi** something must be going on, something must be up VI:124; **hvat til tíðinda hafði gǫrzk** what had happened of importance XV:121

tíðr[1] *adj.* frequent; common, popular (*with dat.* with) XIV:83; swift; *n.* **hvat títt væri** what was happening XV:112; *n. as adv.* **títt** pleasant XXV:62; quickly; *sup.* **sem tíðast** as quickly as possible, at once VI:63

tíðr[2] *m.* time VIII:8, 20

tiginn *adj.* noble, of high rank; *dat. pl.* **tignum** VI:194, XVI:152, 184; *sup.* **tignastr** XI:58, *f.* **tignust** XII:24

tigir *see* **tegr**

tignarliga *adv.* splendidly, majestically, nobly, magnificently XII:24

tigr, tigu, tigum *see* **tegr**

til 1. *prep. with gen.* to (*Gr* 3.7.2) I:1, 23, 25, 38, 46, 56, 68, 88, 98, II:3, 37, VI:5, VIII:15, 43 (2), X:10, 95, XI:64, XV:43, XVI:10, 96, XIX:30, XXI:130, XXII:27/1, XXV:56, XXVI A:1, 5, 10, B:40; towards XXIII:21; towards, to, at I:13, 35, V:129, VII A:102, XIX:71, 80, XXVII:22, 29; to the home of (cf. *Gr* 3.1.5 (13)) II:50, 95, IV:3; **til hans** at him XXVI A:71, B:90, to see him X:88, **til sín** to see him XVI:87, **til mín** to see me XVI:39, **til þín** to you XXIV:1, 3, **til þeir(r)a** at them XXVI A:45, to them XXIV:75; **til þess** about it XXII:22/4, so far XXVII:32, for this I:119; for VI:7, VII A:100, VIII:55, XIV:174, XVI:97, 189, XXII:28/4, 37/2, XXIII:27, XXVII:17; for (the purpose of) III:105, XVI:90, 165, 167, XXI:41,

XXII:1/4, XXVI A:85; for *or* until XVI:51; for, to bring about *or* until XXV:30; for (voyages to) XVI:129; XIX:43; engaged in XIV:136; to get II:17 (*see* **illr**), III:20; until VI:304, 324, XXVI B:124; about II:45, VI:331; as I:39 (to cause), II:73, 114, VII A:52; **til bogastrengs mér** as a bowstring for me XXVI A:79; **ok til** and (go) to VI:129; **gera til** earn I:61. **2.** *as adv.* towards (something), in that direction II:24, there, to that place II:112, XXI:73, up to it I:108, for it I:118, 121, 130, VIII:39, 43 (1), 89, XVI:35, for this III:105 (1), VII A:135, XXIV:3 (2), to earn it I:137, to do (it) I:126, III:17, VIII:164, of this I:115; available, possible XVI:38, 48; **til búit** prepared, ready XIX:57 (*cf.* **búa**); **taka til, takask til** *see* **taka**; **vera til** be available, be enough VI:225, be available (to do) VII B:20, XXVI B:102; **sem þú ert maðr til** as a man like you would XXVI B:112; **þat var mest til at** this was the main reason why VI:46; **hér til** for this XV:27; up to now V:77; **þangat til** up to then VIII:95; **þar til** for it (*cf. Gr* 3.9.1) VII A:98, for that event, *i.e.* at that battle VI:154; **þar til . . . sem** towards the spot where XXIII:18. **3.** *forming conjunctions* **til þess er** in order to bring about what XIV:90, *note*; **til þess er, til þess unz** until VI:45, VII A:28, VIII:25, XII:4, XXI:87, XXVI B:43, 228; **þar til er** until XI:47, XIX:33, 50, XXI:52; **svá til þess er** on until VI:10; **til þess at** in order that, so that VII A:51, VIII:163, XIV:122, 124, (in order) to XIV:26, 151, so that XIV:55, to (do something) XXVII:3, for this, that XXIV:14; **til at** for the purpose of, to XXVII:4, (in order) to XIX:47, in order that XXVI B:65

tilgjǫf *f.* bridal gift (from the bridegroom to the bride) VI:2, 4

tillit *n.* glance I:30

tilræði *n.* attack IV:8

tilskipat *pp. n.* ordained XXIV:45

tilstilli *n.* guidance, contrivance, action XIV:112

tími *m.* time XV:35; **einn tíma** on one occasion XIII:13

tína (*past* **tíndi,** *pp.* **tínt**) *wv.* rehearse XXVII:29

tingl *n.* prow-piece, a triangular piece of wood between the gunwales at a ship's prow; *gen. pl. with* **tangar** (*see* **tǫng**) VI:232

tinsmiðr *m.* a worker in tin or pewter; *as nickname* III:79

tírr *m.* glory VII A:22; fame XXV:108

títt *see* **tíðr**[1]

tíu *num.* (*Gr* 3.4.1) ten III:46, VIII:92, XV:79, XIX:36, XXI:162, XXVII:29; **tíu (hundruð)** i.e. 1200 (*Gr* 3.4.1) VIII:166, XXV:81

tíund *f.* a tenth part; a tithe, tithe-payment VIII:154, 157

tíundi *num. (ordinal) adj.* tenth *Gr* 3.4.1; **við/með tíunda mann** with nine others (*Gr* 3.4.2.(8)) XV:130, 134

tívar *m. pl.* gods IX:55

tjá/téa (*past* **téði,** *pp.* **tét**) *wv.* show X:81; describe XII:63; give an account of, enumerate XXII:13/3; **-sk** *form* **tjásk** be shown, be to be seen (*or* be used, be useful?) XIV:179

tjald *n.* tent; sheet of tarpaulin XIX:58

tjalda (*past* **tjaldaði,** *pp.* **tjaldat**) *wv.* cover, hang; *pp. n. pl.* **tjǫlduð** II:12

Tjaldanes *n.* farm on the south side of Gilsfjǫrðr XV:131

tjara *f.* tar III:4 (*with suffixed def. art.*)

tjǫrr *m. poetical word for* sword *or* spear; *gen. pl.* **tjǫrva** VII A:21

tjǫrupinnr *m.* a piece of wood covered in tar *or* a small container for tar III:2

tók, tóku *see* **taka**

tólf *num.* twelve (*Gr* 3.4.1) II:7, VII A:100, VIII:171, 193, XIV:143, 173, XV:133, XIX:48, XXII:59/4; **tólf (hundruð)** i.e. 1440 VIII:167

tólfti *num. (ordinal) adj.* twelfth *Gr* 3.4.1; **með tólfta mann** i.e. with eleven others (*Gr* 3.4.2 (8)) VIII:98, XV:75

tópt *f.* foundations, ground plan (i.e. overall length) XIX:62

Torfi Hamalsson *m.* XIX:114

tradda *see* **treðja**

traðir *see* **trǫð**

trana *f.* crane (bird) XXV:62; *with suffixed def. art.* **Tranan** name of a ship VI:105, 227; *acc.* **Tranu** (*with* **sá fljóta auða**) VI:307; *gen. with suffixed def. art.* **Trǫnunnar** VI:216

trauðr *adj.* reluctant; *n. as adv.* **trautt** scarcely XXI:54

traust *n.* protection, support XV:127

traustr *adj.* reliable, strong VI:288, XXII:17/3

tré *n.* tree II:27 (*with suffixed def. art.*); tree *or* a piece of wood XXI:150; *dat. pl. with suffixed def. art.* **trjánum** their pieces of wood XXI:97, 112 (these may have been bullroarers, which were widely used by North American Indians for ceremonial purposes); timber, wood XIII:14, 30

treðja (*past* **traddi,** *pp.* **traddr**) *wv.* cause to be trodden on (*with dat.* by) XXV:11; *pp. acc. f. sg.* **tradda** (*Gr* 3.9.7.1) XXV:69

trega (*past* **tregði**) *wv.* **1.** grieve for, lament X:138. **2.** cause to grieve, cause grief to X:168

treginn *adj. (pp.)* grievous, sad XXV:1

tregr *adj.* reluctant I:102

trésmiðr *m.* wood-carver, carpenter XII:2

treysta (*past* **treyst,** *pp.* **treystr**) *wv.* trust (á in) XXII:24/1; **-sk** *form* **treystask** dare XIV:164

tréþak *n.* wooden roof XIV:8

trítill *m.* (spinning) top; urchin; small movements XXIII:39 (*see note*)

Tristram *m.* XII:1, 3, 5, 16, 36, 38, 62, 64, 69, 70

trjánum *see* **tré**

troða (*past* **trað,** *past pl.* **tráðu,** *pp.* **troðit**) *sv.* (*Gr* 3.6.9.3) **1.** tread XVI:122 *(subj.).* **2.** stuff III:4 (*object understood; Gr* 3.9.5.1)

trú *f.* belief, religion XXII:22/3; (i.e. the Christian religion) XXI:13; faith XIV:65 (*with dat.* in?); (the) faith, *i.e.* Christianity VII A:50, VIII:78, XXIV:46; **rétt trú** VII A:68, XXIV:52; *acc.* **helga trú** Christianity XXII:25/1

trúa (*past* **trúði,** *pp.* **trúaðr**) *wv.* believe *Gr* 3.6.9.1 (8); **trúa á** believe in XXIV:33, 34; *with dat.* believe in, trust XXII:17/4 (*3rd person pres.* **trúr**?—cf. **trúr** *adj.*); *imp.* **trúið þér ok því** also trust in this XXVI B:124

trúanligr *adj.* believable XIII:40

trúr *adj.* (*Gr* 3.3.8.5 (4)) true, loyal (*with dat.* to someone) VII A:41, XXII:17/4 (cf. **trúa**); *dat. pl.* **trúm** *Gr* 3.3.8 (4) *and* 3.3.9 (5)

tryggiliga *adv.* securely XII:76

tryggr *adj.* trusty XXII:17/3

Tryggvason, Tryggvasunr *m.* son of Tryggvi Óláfsson VI:48, 77, 89, 130, 211, 215, VIII:145, XXI:37

Tryggvi Óláfsson *m.* father of King Óláfr of Norway; *gen.* **Tryggva** VI:144, 336, 367, VIII:75

trýta (*past* **trýtti,** *pp.* **trýtt**) *wv.* dangle XXV:62

trǫð *f.* (trodden) path; sheep pen? XXVI A:13; *in kenning for sea,* **fjarðmýils trǫð** VI:251

trǫll *n.* monster I:81

Trǫllaskógr *m.* 'troll forest', farm in southern Iceland XXVI A:17

trǫnu *see* **trana**

-tu = **þú** I:10, 15, 20, 125, IV:97, XXV:23, XXVI B:218; *see* **þú**

tugli *see* **tygill**

tugr *see* **tegr**

Tumba *f.* mountain on the coast of Normandy XIII:1, 11, 28

tún *n.* enclosure, farmyard, infield III:59 (*with suffixed def. art.*), V:33; court(yard); *gen. pl.* **túna** to the dwelling, abode IX:9

tunga *f.* language VI:317

Tunga¹ *f.* a farm, the home of Þorkell and Steingerðr, in Gnúpsdalr, off Miðfjǫrðr, about fifteen miles south of Steinsstaðir IV:3, 6, 107

Tunga² *f.* an area in eastern Iceland *Gr* 3.1.8

túngarðr *m.* farmyard wall, hayfield wall XV:100

tungl *n.* moon; *in kenning for* shields (referring to the way they were fastened along the sides of viking ships) **tungl tingla tangar** (*subject of* **skǫrusk**) VI:232

tunglkváma *f.* new moon XIV:80

turn *m.* tower XI:2, 48

tuttugu *num.* twenty (*Gr* 3.4.1) V:83, VIII:59, 62, 191

tvá, tvau *see* **tveir**

tveir *num.* two (*Gr* 3.4.1) V:48, VI:198, VII A:97, VIII:163, X:100, 106, XII:18, XV:94, XXI:23, 144, XXVI B:102; **tveir einir** just two XXV:81; *acc. m.* **tvá** I:74, 103, IV:2, VI:159 (*with* **jǫfra**), VIII:82, 83, X:2, XV:32, 95, XIX:62, XXI:38, 165, XXVI A:11, 78; two (warriors) XXVI A:100; **þá tvá** those two (**þá²**) *or* now, by then two (**þá¹**) XXVI A:76; *f.* **tvær** II:74, X:8, **ok tvær** and two (were) XXI:199; *n.* **tvau** I:76, II:28, 97, III:30, XIV:140, XXI:21, 199, XXVI A:76, XXVII:37, of two persons, a male and female IX:47; **tvau verð slík** double that price XVI:24; *gen.* **tveggja** VII A:154, XIV:177, **tveggja þeira** of the two of them X:120, 164; *dat.* **tveim** VIII:195, **tveimr** (to) two XXVI A:104, 105

tvímánaðr *m.* 'double month', the fifth month of summer (late August to late September); **at tvímánuði** at the beginning of double-month, i.e. in late August XV:14

tvisvar *adv.* twice III:116

tvær *see* **tveir**

tyggi *m.* ruler, king VII A:24 (*subject of* **barði** *and* **hjó**); *dat. sg.* **tyggja** (here = King Óláfr) VI:353

tygill (*dat.* **tugli**) *m.* strap *Gr* 3.1.7.2 ex. 4

týna (*past* **týndi**, *pp.* **týnt**) *wv. with dat.* lose VII A:53, XIII:36 (*pres. part.*), XVI:139, 143, 182; destroy: **-sk** *form as passive* **týnask** be lost, perish II:91, 105; *supine* (*Gr* 3.9.7.1) **týnzk** II:108

typpa (*past* **typðu**, *pp.* **typðr**) *wv.* top; **typpa um** dress around the top, put a head-dress on IX:64 (**typpum** let us put . . .), 77

Týr *m.* a god (one of the Æsir) II:9; *in kenning for* warrior (here the king), **Týr tjǫrva dýrra** VII A:21

tær *see* tá
tœki *see* taka
tǫðu *see* taða
tǫku, tǫkum *see* taka
tǫlðu *see* telja
tǫlu *see* tala²
tǫluðu *see* tala¹
tǫlvíss *adj.* skilled in mathematics and computation XIV:191, *note*
tǫng *f.* (a pair of) tongs; **tǫng tingla** a pair of ornamental strips of
    wood along the sides of ship's prow VI:233 (*gen.* **tangar** *with* **tungl**)
tǫnn (*pl.* **tenn**) *f.* tooth X:81, 120, 164, XII:57
uf *see* of¹
úfár *adj.* no few, *i.e.* many VI:365 (*gen. with* þjóðar)
ugga (*past* **uggði**, *pp.* **uggat**) *wv.* fear, be afraid III:1, VI:12
úkristni *see* ókristinn
Úlfdalir *m. pl.* 'Wolf-dales', valley in Sweden X:5, 14, 36, 42, 68
Úlfheðinn Gunnarssonr *m.* lawspeaker from 1108 until his death in
    1116 VIII:55, 169
Úlfljótr *m.* Norwegian, 9th–10th century VIII:36, 40, 44, 59
Úlfljótslǫg *n. pl.* Úlfljót's law VIII:37
úlfr *m.* wolf IV:45, VII A:15, XXV:102
Úlfr enn rauði *m.* one of Óláfr Tryggvason's men (his standard-bearer
    according to *Heimskringla, Óláfs saga Tryggvasonar* ch. 94, *ÍF*
    XXVI 344) VI:270, 274
Úlfsjár *m.* 'Wolf-lake', in Sweden X:6
Ullr *m.* a god (one of the Æsir) II:9
um¹ *prep. with acc.* (*Gr* 3.7.1) **1.** *of time* IV:101, 108, *see* **síðir, stund**;
    during, in I:87, 112, 113, II:4, IV:52, V:7 (2), XVI:9, XIX:9, 90,
    XXI:4, XXV:3, 19, XXVI A:2; at XIV:41; through(out) IV:47,
    XIX:63; **um kveldit** that evening XXVI B:4. **2.** *of place* over II:17,
    94, III:73, 99, VI:279, VII A:2, 35, X:52, XI:50, XIX:35, XXII:64/2,
    XXVI B:14, 28; across XIX:98; round II:69, 70, III:23, V:56, 109,
    VI:81, 283, VII A:156, 159, IX:64, XXI:116, 177, XXVI A:59, 60,
    B:149; **ok um** and (they went) round XXI:53; around I:110, VI:267,
    VII B:31, IX:62, XI:76, XII:82, about XII:61; all over III:45, VI:241,
    throughout XXVI A:119; by VI:268, XII:79; through III:116, IV:13,
    VII A:116, XXII:60/3 (*or* over?); past VI:45, 89; **allt um** all over,
    over the whole of VII B:24; **útan um** round the outside of XXIII:33;
    lúka um surround VI:282. **3.** *of abstract relations* about I:54, 129,

II:37, III:34, IV:60, 104, V:11, 14, VI:137, 314, 320, 333, VII A:51, 98, 134, IX:55, XII:83, XIV:90, *note*, XV:19 (as to), XIX:11, 41, XXI:3, 79, XXIV:54, XXV:68, XXVI B:38; concerning XXIV:49, XXVI A:92; on XXIV:28; in relation to I:135; with V:7 (1), XV:141; with respect to, for IV:71, XV:136, XVI:86. **4.** *in complex prepositions* (*Gr* 3.7, 3.7.1) **um fram, umfram** beyond XXIII:35, in greater measure than VII B:10; **um fram hátt** beyond measure XXIII:62; **um þvert/þverar** across I:35, III:53 (**þvert/þverar** *is a strong adjective in agreement with the accompanying noun*). **5.** *with dat.* **um sumrum** during the summer(s), in summer XXI:10. **6.** *as adv.* about it III:105, 110, IV:86, 105, V:72, X:15, XIV:34, XV:76, XXIV:9; for it XXV:103 (*or* **um²**); **vera mest um** be most significant V:9; **hér um** about this I:50, 86; *with* **-sk** *forms of verbs* (*see* 1/15 n.; *Gr* 3.9.8.3): **um búizk** arranged things around oneself I:15; **litask um, um sjásk** look around (oneself) IV:16, X:33; **þar um at sjásk** to look around (oneself) there II:11; **um at þreifask** to grope around IX:4

um² *meaningless adverbial particle with verbs* (cf. **of³**) VI:55, IX:2, 5, 10, 27, 29, 35, 38, 39, 42, 45, 56, 71, 81, 93, 101, 103, 109, 111, 124, 129, X:28, 63, 75, 82, 107, 115, 131, 140, 159, 169, XV:74, XXV:4, 10, 11, 50, 65, 69, 103 (? *or adv.* about it), 105, XXVII:28

umbergis *adv.* round about XIII:34; *as prep. with acc.* round XII:50

umbráð *n.* counsel, guidance VIII:152, 173; help, patronage XVI:3

umbsýsla *f.* management, organisation VIII:89

umbúð *f.* preparation, arrangement XXVI A:62

umbúnaðr *m.* bedding XI:63

umfram *see* **um¹, 4** (*Gr* 3.7, 3.7.1)

umgjǫrð *f.* scabbard; *with suffixed def. art.*, his scabbard I:94, 96

umhverfis/umhverfum *prep. with acc.* around (*Gr* 3.7.1) V:11, XIV:152, XXVI B:87

umkringis *adv.* around XIII:16

umrœða *f.* talk, discussion; rumour, gossip XV:19; **í allri umrœðu** in everything they said VI:318

umsjá *f.* care, guardianship, looking after XVI:6

umvandan *f.* admonition, reprimand, discipline XIV:103

und¹ *prep. with acc.* beneath IX:106; **und lok** under/into (the power of) death VI:363; *with dat.* under X:116, 160; **und hánum** beneath him (his body), i.e. from his belt IX:61; **und skildi** carrying a shield V:50; **und hjálmum** wearing helmets XXV:67; **und holmi** close to, under the shelter of, the island VI:236

und² *f.* wound XXII:40/1

undan *prep. with dat.* (*Gr* 3.7.3) from under XII:19, away from XXI:133; out from XXI:21; off XXI:27; *as adv.* away VI:215, 219, 272, 313 (*see* **halda**), XXI:130, 132, 200, XXII:11/4, XXVI B:67, 221; out XXI:20; down XXVI B:29; **undan ganga** escape V:107; **láta undan ganga** let off VII B:54; **draga undan við** get away from XXVI B:94; *see* **leysa 2**, **telja**, **þiggja**

undanbragð *n.* subterfuge, trick (in order to escape), means of escape III:92

undarliga *adv.* strangely XVI:120; wondrously XXVI B:28

undir *prep.* (*Gr* 3.7.4) **1.** *with acc.* under, underneath, beneath II:55, III:59, X:115, 159; close to, under the shelter of VI:121, 123, 133, XV:126, up to XXI:30; within range of VI:189. **2.** *with dat.* beneath I:97, XII:2, 16, XV:100, XXIII:96; below, at the foot of XIX:91, XXVI A:5; under XIV:177, 187, XXIV:65, XXVI B:152, i.e. with XIV:8; **undir sér** under him/them, under his/their authority XIV:133, 178. **3.** *as adv.* under her IX:49; **þar undir** under (the roof) there III:74, under them, underneath XI:19

undirferli *f.* underhandedness XXIII:55

undirfǫrull *adj.* underhand, cunning XI:12

undirmaðr *m.* subordinate XIV:73, 105, 119

undit *see* **vinda**

undr *n.* wonder, something strange V:17; miracle, marvel XXII:30/3, 44/2, 55/2

undrask (*past* **undraðisk**) *wv. refl.* wonder, be amazed V:143, stare in amazement XXI:105; *with acc.* be surprised at something XXI:70; **undruðusk þá** were amazed at them XXI:102

ungr *adj.* young VII A:95, XI:30, XIV:34, XXV:9, 56; young ones XXV:41; *i.e.* new XIV:79; *wk. f. form* X:18, 30, 59; when young VII A:11 (*with* **konungr**), when I was young VI:202, XXVI B:163 (*f. sg.*); *pl. with* **synir** X:100

unna (*pres.* **ann**, *past* **unni**, *past pl.* **unnu**, *past subj.* **ynni**, *pp.* **unnat/ unnt**) *pret.-pres. vb. with dat.* **1.** love (*Gr* 3.6.7) IV:61 (*inf. with* **skal ek**), VI:322, XIV:114, XV:14. **2.** grant, refuse not; **ef aðrir unna honum** if others are content that he should XXVII:46

unnit *see* **vinna**

unnvigg *n.* wave-horse, *kenning for* ship; *gen. with* **meiðr** VI:51

unz, til þess unz *conj.* until (*Gr* 3.8.2.4) VIII:25, 31, 103, 129, IX:17, XVI:87

upp *adv.* up I:6, 13, 22, 29, 45, 52, 69, 99, 109, II:22, 28, III:12, IV:62, VI:76, IX:86, X:175, XI:18, XII:10, XV:68, 106, XIX:80, XXI:130, XXIII:70 (*see* **hefja**), XXVI A:17, 29, 68, B:11; uphill IV:82; upwards XV:151, XXI:67; ashore VII A:159, B:34, 37 (*with* **ganga**), XVI:154; aboard VI:269, 273; thoroughly I:24; **á upp** on it at the top XXI:45; **upp frá** above XXI:106; **segja upp** *see* **segja; ýla upp** *see* **ýla**; *of time*, on: **upp frá þessu** from now on I:107, 147

upphaf *n.* beginning XIX:48; *pl.* origins II:88, VIII:29

upphald *n.* support XIV:30; maintenance XXIV:68; **er Guðs kristni væri mest upphald at** in which there would be the best preservation of God's Christianity XIV:126

upphaldsmaðr *m.* support(er), upholder XIV:176

upphiminn *m.* the sky above; *adv. gen.* in the sky above IX:8

uppi *adv.* **1.** up X:172, XXVI A:15; *i.e.* ashore VI:60. **2.** exhausted, gone XVI:43. **3.** evident, known about XV:150; **mun langt uppi** will be remembered, spoken of, for ever XXVI A:87, *similarly* XXVI A:102

uppréttr *adj.* upright, straight up, erect XXIII:81

Uppsalir *m. pl.* modern Uppsala, north of Stockholm, Sweden; it was the ancient seat of the Swedish kings VIII:147

úr *prep. with dat.* = **ór** from (*Gr* 3.7.3) VIII:7, 25, 36, 59, 80, 128; out of, *see* **lǫg**

urð *f.* heap of stones, gravel II:32

Urðir *f. pl.* farm in Skálmarfjǫrðr in north-western Iceland XV:41

urðu *see* **verða**

úrigr *adj.* wet XXV:41

úsiðr *m.* bad practice, immoral behaviour XXII:4/4

út *adv.* out *Gr* 3.5.3 (11), I:22, II:35, III:44, V:34, VI:20, VII B:35, X:33, XI:47, XXI:120, 132, 176, XXVI A:37, 52, B:136; outwards XXVI A:75; *i.e.* out of the hall XI:45, 74; *i.e.* from the shore VI:103, 167, VII A:59, 157, out to sea XVI:8, XXI:61, 81; *i.e.* towards the sea VII B:75, 80; **ǫll nes út** right out to all the nesses XIX:97; *i.e.* across the sea XVI:122; = westwards, *i.e.* from Europe to Iceland IV:108, VIII:25, 36, 186, XV:38, XVI:119, 189; *i.e.* from Iceland or Norway to Greenland VIII:65, 74, XVI:10; **út fyrir** out (in the sea), off it XXI:53; **út í frá** *as prep. with dat.* on the outside of, outermost of, beyond VII A:82

útan *adv.* back, away IX:107; round the outside X:117, 161; on the outside XXVI A:24; from without: **útan at** round outside up to, around I:17; abroad (from Iceland, *i.e.* in *or* to Europe) IV:108, VIII:88, 186, XVI:2; **útan af** back from (Greenland) XVI:63; **útan um** round the outside of XXIII:33; *as prep. with acc.* without XIII:48, XXIII:78; *as conj.* except XV:148; *see also* **fyr útan, fyrir útan**; cf. *Gr* 3.7.5, 3.8.2.4

útanferð *f.* journey abroad, passage abroad XVI:5 *(with suffixed def. art.)*

útar *adv.* farther out I:5

útarliga *adv.* far out, near the door (*i.e.* a position of fairly low rank) I:4

útburðr *m.* exposure VIII:140

útganga *f.* exit, going out XXVI B:157; to go out XXVI B:131; *gen. in* **biðja útgǫngu** *with dat.* ask that someone be allowed to go out III:40

úti *adv.* outside III:3, VII B:60, 63, 64, X:139, XVI:97, XXVI A:44, B:46, 53; out of doors, unsheltered, in the open XXI:108; **úti fyrir** out in front of the house XXVI B:49; out at sea XXI:21

útibúr *n.* outhouse, storehouse (entered from outside the house) IV:14

útlagr *adj.* subject to a fine (*with the amount in the dat.*) XXVII:35, 40

útlegð *f.* penalty, fine XXVII:38

útlendr *adj.* foreign VII A:87

útnes *n.* outlying, remote ness XIX:99

útrauðr *adj.* red round the edges *or* = **ótrauðr** not reluctant XXIII:37

útróðr *m.* rowing out to fish, fishing-grounds, sea-fishing XXI:84 (*acc. pl.*)

útsuðr *n.* south-west XIX:71; **í útsuðr** to the south-west XIX:80

úvígr (= **óvígr**) *adj.* invincible VI:58

úvinr *see* **óvinr**

uxi, oxi *m.* ox; *acc. sg.* **oxa** IX:95, **uxa** XIX:64, *with suffixed def. art.* **uxann** II:19, XIX:66, *gen. sg.* **oxans** II:28, *dat. sg.* **uxa** XXVI B:179, *with suffixed def. art.* **oxanum** II:25; *nom. pl.* **øxn** IX:90; *gen. pl.* **øxna** II:18

vá *see* **vega**

vaða (*pres.* **veðr,** *past* **óð/vóð,** *past pl.* **óðu,** *pp.* **vaðinn**) *sv.* (*Gr* 3.6.9.1 (1)) wade, rush VII A:157, XXII:46/1; *pp.* **vaðinn at** destitute of XXV:18

vaðmál *n.* cloth of standard quality, 2 ells wide, used as a form of currency (*Laws* I 246) XXVII:37 (*gen. pl.*)

vafði, vafit *see* **vefja**

vágr *m.* (small) bay XXI:36 (*dat. pl. with suffixed def. art.*), 181

vágrek *n.* flotsam and jetsam, driftage VII A:136

vágskorinn (*n.* **vágskorit**) *adj.* (*pp.*; *cf.* **skera**) indented with bays XXI:35

vágum *see* **vega**

vaka[1] (*pres.* **vakir**, *past* **vakði**, *pp.* **vakat**) *wv.* (*Gr* 3.6.9.2 (4)) be awake V:18, X:143; keep vigil XIV:121; **vakir þú?** are you awake? X:142

vaka[2] *f.* watch, vigil *Gr* 3.1.7.1 ex. 3

vakði *see* **vekja** *and* **vaka**[1]

vakna (*past* **vaknaði**, *pp.* **vaknat** *Gr* 3.3.8.2–5 ex. 4) *wv.* wake up IX:1, X:61, XIV:64, 67, XV:112, XXVI A:22

vakr *adj.* watchful, on the lookout (**til** for) XXIII:27

val = **vel** *adv.* well XIV:187

vald *n.* power III:17 (**til** to do it); **þat er á yðru valdi** it is/lies in your power, it is up to you XVI:36; **fær í vald jǫtunsins** gives it into the giant's charge XII:65; **með valdi** by force VII B:57

valda (*pres.* **veldr**, *past* **olli**, *pp.* **valdit**) *sv. irregular* (*Gr* 3.6.7), *with dat.* cause, be the reason for, bring about VI:23

Valdidida *m.* native king in North America XXI:203

valði *see* **velja**

Valdís *f.* former wife of Bishop Jón, separated from him when he became bishop XIV:128

valdsmerki *n.* sceptre XII:29

Váli *m.* a god, one of the Æsir II:9

valit *see* **velja**

válk *n.* restlessness, trouble XII:36, 39

válkask (*past* **valkaðisk**) *wv.* be being turned *or* rolled over, pondered XXIII:26

valkyrja *f.* valkyrie X:8

valla = **varla**

Valland *n.* France (Frankia) VII A:8, X:10

valr[1] *m.* falcon; *with suffixed def. art.* II:54, 56, *gen.* II:58

valr[2] *m.* corpses of those slain in battle XXV:106

valshamr *m.* falcon shape, falcon form II:48, 49 (*with suffixed def. art.*)

valslǫngva *f.* war-sling, catapult XXI:126

ván *f.* hope, expectation; **er ván** *with dat. of person and gen. of thing* someone has expectation of something, someone can expect something VI:195; **sem ván er** as is to be expected XXVI B:191;

vita sér ván *with gen.* know where to look for something II:132; **eigi er minni ván** it is no less than would have been expected; there is no small hope V:62; **vera eigi minni ván** there was not less expectation, it was more than likely VI:96; **létu sér eigi annars ván en** said they expected nothing else but that VIII:90; **at vánum** to be expected, as it should be XXVI B:34

vanðatíð (vandatíð?) *f.* customary times (*cf.* **vanði**) *or* obligatory (important) times (*cf.* **vandi 2**) XIV:58

vandar *see* **vǫndr**

vandi *m.* **1.** difficulty, problem XXII:26/2, 52/2. **2.** obligation, relationship; **ef mér er nǫkkur vandi á við þik** if I am under some obligation to you, if I am related to you in some way V:140

vanði *m.* custom, practice I:34, 52; habit *Gr* 3.1.8 ex.

vandliga *adv.* carefully, with care XIV:25, XXIV:2; in detail XXVI B:185; completely XIV:10

vandr *adj.* difficult *Gr* 3.3.8.4 (2); **vandr at** particular about XIV:138, *note*; *comp. n. as adv.* **mun oss vandara gert** we will be judged more strictly, more will be demanded of us XXVI B:33

vándr *adj.* wicked, evil IV:75, XII:42, 89, XIV:2, 41

vandræðaskáld *n.* 'troublesome poet' VI:322, VII A:10 (on the origin of the nickname see *Heimskringla*, *Óláfs saga Tryggvasonar* ch. 83, *ÍF* XXVI 331; *Hallfreðar saga* ch. 6, *ÍF* VIII 155)

vanhagr *m.* misdeed, error *or* disadvantage, loss? XIV:106

vanheilsa *f.* sickness VI:323

Vanir *m. pl.* a race of gods II:89, IX:58

vanmeginn *adj.* feeble, weak XXIII:41

vann, vannsk, vanntu *see* **vinna**

vanr[1] (*n.* **vant**) *adj. with gen.* lacking VI:263; *n.* **er vant** there is lacking XXV:97; **orðz þikkir vant** *with dat.* one thinks a word is lacking, one wants to have the last word XXV:34

vanr[2] (*n.* **vant**) *adj.* accustomed XII:85; **eru vanir at vera** are usually XXIII:101; **sem hann var vanr, sem fyrr var vant** as usual XII:71, XV:44, 45

vanrœkt *f.* negligence, carelessness XXIII:22

vansemð *f.* offence, insult V:161

vápn *n.* weapon V:49 (*see* **Eir**), XI:36; *pl.* I:77, III:55 (*partitive gen.*, *Gr* 3.2.6 (20)), IV:17, 63, VI:174, 257, 290, 303, XI:16, XXI:135, XXVI A:46; **undir vápn** *with dat.* within range of, to meet someone's weapons VI:189; *dat. pl.* (**með**) **vápnum** by (with) weapons, in battle VI:316, XXVI B:100

vápnabúnaðr *m.* equipment of arms VI:291

vápnaburðr *m.* wielding of weapons, weapons being used VI:288

vápnaðr *pp.* armed V:71, XIV:66

Vápnafjǫrðr *m.* fjord in north-eastern Iceland VII A:150, 166

vápnask (*past* **vápnaðisk**) *wv.* arm oneself, be armed VII B:55

vápnaskipti *n.* exchange of weapons (missiles), fighting VI:196, (**við þá** with them) XXVI B:196

vápn-Eir V:49 *see* **Eir**

vápnlauss *adj.* weaponless, unarmed V:143

vápnreið *f.* wielding of weapons, fighting VI:284 (*subject of* **varð**)

var *see* **vera**

vár[1] *n.* spring XV:29; *with suffixed def. art.* XVI:115, 128; **um várit** in the spring XIX:63, XXI:83; **eptir um várit, um várit eptir** the following spring XV:124, XIX:14

vár[2] *pron. gen. 2nd person pl.* (of) us XXVI B:80, 94

Vár *f.* a goddess IX:122

vara[1] (*past* **varði**, *pp.* **varðr**) *wv. impers. with acc.* **þá varði** they expected IV:15

vara[2] *see* **vera**

vara[3] (*past* **varaði**, *pp.* **varat**) *wv.* warn, caution; **vara þik** take care, beware, be on your guard XI:70; **-sk** *form (refl.)* **varask/varaz** beware (of), be one's guard (that), be careful (that) XXIV:2; *pres. subj.* VI:108

vára[1] *see* **várr**

vára[2] (*past* **váraði**, *pp.* **várat**) *wv. impers.* become spring XXI:110

varat *see* **vera**

varð *see* **verða**

varða (*past* **varðaði**, *pp.* **varðat**) *wv.* guard; *with acc. and dat.* keep someone from someone IV:57; be a penalty, incur a penalty VIII:142; *impers.* **hvat konu varðaði** what was the penalty for a woman XV:59; **láta varða** declare as penalty, call for the penalty of XV:136

varði *see* **verja**[1] *and* **verja**[2]; **varðisk** *see* **verja**[1]

varðmenn *m. pl.* watchmen, guards I:115

varðveita (*past* **varðveitti**, *pp.* **varðveittr**) *wv.* keep, take care of, guard V:109, XII:66

varðveizla *f.* keeping; *pl.* things to take care of, responsibilities XXI:10

vargtré *n.* 'wolf-tree' *or* 'criminal tree', gallows XXV:61 (*pl.*)

varit *see* **verja¹, verja²**

várkunn *f.* what is to be excused XXVI A:106

varla/valla *adv.* hardly V:114, XVI:105; scarcely XIV:108, XV:99, XXI:178, XXII:6/2

varmr *adj.* warm XXV:19

varna (*past* **varnaði,** *pp.* **varnat**) *wv. with gen.* refuse, withhold IV:71; **varna við** abstain from, refuse to eat or drink (*or* refuse to look upon, i.e. the person would not hold back from shedding; *cf. note* 8) XXIII:37

varnaðr *m.* goods, cargo XVI:154

varp *see* **verpa**

varr (*n.* **vart**) *adj.* wary; **varr við** aware of XII:80; **verða við ekki varr** be aware of nothing (untoward), notice nothing *or* be wary about nothing, take no precautions XXI:95; **varð þá ekki vart við þá** then there was no sign of them XXI:121 **ok vera vara um sik** and to beware about themselves, they were to be on their guard XXVI B:38; *sup.* **sem varastr** as careful as possible V:14

várr = **órr** *poss. adj.* our (*cf. Gr* 3.3.9 (21, 22), 3.9.6.1) VI:166, XIII:10, 31, XIV:166, XVI:72 (the king referring to himself), XXIV:28, 42, XXVI B:50, 72; *referring to the writer* XIV:26, *note*; *acc. sg. f.* **vára** VII A:114; *n.* **várt** X:70; *dat. sg. n.* **váru** VI:167; *acc. pl. m.* **vára** X:68; *dat. pl.* **várum** XIV:168, XXVI A:104, 110, B:99

varrir *see* **vǫrr**

vart *adv.* barely XXI:165

váru¹, váruð, várum¹ *see* **vera**

váru², várum² *see* **várr**

vas = **var,** *see* **vera**

vás *n.* hardship, suffering XII:88

vask = **var ek,** *see* **vera**

vásklæði *n. pl.* bad-weather clothes, storm-gear VII A:82

vaskr *adj.* valiant; diligent, clever XIV:178; *sup. Gr* 3.3.9 ex. 1

vástígr *m.* path of *or* to woe *or* disaster XXV:59

vatn *n.* water XIX:58; lake (*Gr* 3.1.7.1, 3.1.8 (26)) I:23, V:43 (*with suffixed def. art.,* i.e. Hítárvatn), X:5, XXI:88, 106, XXIV: 37

vatnfátt *n.* (cf. **fár** *adj.*) shortage of water; **fá vatnfátt** get short of water XIX:55

vatnsstrǫnd *f.* lake-shore X:6

vátr *adj.* wet, moist, XXIII:39

vátta (*past* **váttaði,** *pp.* **váttat**) *wv.* bear witness to, attest VI:172, 304

váttr *m.* witness VIII:113, 142, XV:68

vax *n.* wax; **varð vax eitt** turned completely to wax, *i.e.* became a weakling VII A:141

vaxa (*past* **óx,** *past pl.* **óxu/uxu,** *pp.* **vaxinn**) *sv.* (*Gr* 3.6.9.1 (1), 3.6.9.3 ex. 8) grow, increase VII B:12; *pp. n.* **vaxit** *with dat.* grown with, covered with VIII:20; shaped (**svá sem** like) XXIII:11

vaxtar *see* **vǫxtr**

veðr *n.* weather XV:48; storm *(with suffixed def. art.)* XV:145; *adv. acc.* **fagrt veðr** in fine weather VI:26; wind VI:124; *with suffixed def. art.* **veðret** the wind VI:121; **meira veðrit** the more wind, the wind (to be) stronger VI:27

veðreygr *adj.* weather-eyed, having an eye for the weather X:31, 51

vefa (*past* **vaf/óf,** *past pl.* **váfu/ófu,** *pp.* **ofinn**) *sv.* weave *Gr* 3.6.9.1 (1); *pp. f. pl.* **ofnar** woven (*with dat.* by) XXV:25

vefja (*past* **vafði,** *pp.* **vafit**) *wv.* **1.** *with dat.* wrap, tie XXVI B:146; *impers. pass.* (*Gr* 3.9.3) **ok vafit** there were tied V:56, **en vafit spjǫrrum** with cross-garters wrapped round XV:50. **2. -sk** *form pp.* **vafizk** become entangled III:23

vega (*past* **vá,** *past pl.* **vágu,** *pp.* **veginn/vegit**) *sv.* kill (*Gr* 3.6.9.1 (2)) III:83, VIII:83 (*supine* **vegit**), XXV:99; fight (**við** against) VI:158; *pp.* **vegit** fought XXV:106; **veginn, vegit** slain, killed XXVI A:75, 115; **vega at** attack, strike at V:110; **vega tveir at mér** if the two attack me IV:44

veggr *m.* wall; **á vegginum** (on the roof) above the top of the wall (of the house) XXVI A:44; **af vegginum** from (the roof) above the top of the wall XXVI A:75

veggþili *n.* wall-panel; *pl.* II:11

vegligr *adj.* grand, magnificent *Gr* 3.3.9 ex. 5; *sup. n. as adv.* **sem vegligast** as grandly as possible VII A:34

vegr *m.* way; distance X:52; **á marga vega** in many ways III:9, VIII:125; **á einn veg** in the same way VII A:118; *adv. acc.* **hvern veg** in what way, how V:84; **þann veg** (= **þannig**) this-wise, like this (**sem** as if) XXI:159, in that way XXVI B:62, that way, similarly XXII:8/3; **annan veg** in a different way VIII:40, otherwise XIV:107, in any other way XXVI B:65; **á nǫkkurn veg** in some way XIV:112; **sinn veg hverr** each his own way, all in different directions XIX:84;

alla vega from all sides VI:255; *adv. gen.* **tveggja vegna** in two directions, on both sides VII A:155

veiða (*past* **veiddi,** *pp.* **veiddr**) *wv.* hunt, catch V:63 (*subj.* that I may catch), 64, X:4

veiðifǫr *f.* hunting expedition XXI:9

veiðimaðr *m.* huntsman, hunter XXI:9

veiðr *f.* hunting X:31, 51; *pl.* fishing catches, hunting catches, game XXI:61 (*with suffixed def. art.*), 84; **nǫkkut af veiðum** something to catch *or* hunt XXI:62

veifa (*past* **veifði,** *pp.* **veift**) *wv. with dat.* wave, swing: *impers. pass.* **var veift trjánum** their pieces of wood were waved XXI:97, 112

veifun *f.* swinging from side to side, waving; **veifanar orð** unreliable report, rumour VI:358

veik, veiksk *see* **víkja**

veill *adj.* ailing, wretched; *wk. form as nickname* XXVI A:115

veit *see* **vita**

veita (*past* **veitti,** *pp.* **veitt**) *wv.* give IV:51, V:105, 129, 132, VII B:27, XV:107, XXII:21/4, XXV:45, XXVI A:116; **ok veita** and giving XIV:138; be given XXIV:27; grant XXVI A:103, 105; *pres. part.* **veitandi** granting XIII:46; provide XIV:29; carry out XXVI A:62; make, put up V:143, VII B:87, XXI:130, make (an attack) on someone IV:8, V:137; make, take (an oath) II:35 (*subj.*); perform, hold XIV:124; **veita svǫr firi** be responsible for XXIV:64; *impers.* cause: **hefir oss erfitt veitt** it has proved difficult for us XXVI A:102; *with dat.* help XIX:18, XXV:47

veizla *f.* feast, banquet XI:59, XV:79, XIX:9; *pl.* **veizlur** a nobleman's right to receive entertainment from landowners VII B:3 (*see note*)

veizt *see* **vita**

vekja (*past* **vakði,** *pp.* **vakðr**) *wv.* wake (*transitive*) XV:106, XXV:22; rouse XXVI A:47

vel *adv.* well (*Gr* 3.5.2, 3.5.3 (9)) I:15, 79, 108, II:3, 85, VI:68, VII A:81, VIII:93, 179, IX:58, 82, X:38, XV:23, XVI:12, XIX:8, XXI:63, XXIV:49, XXV:106, XXVI A:38, 88, B:33, 76; very much XVI:133; well, very much *or* very (*see* **trúa** *and* **trúr**) XXII:17/4; kindly, warmly VI:46; courteously XI:14, XVI:19, 158; valiantly VI:273; nicely XXIII:89; quite XXIII:66; easily XXI:23, soon XI:34, 67, XIII:39; **vel má ek** I am content to XXVI B:74; *with comp.* much, many, considerably V:49; **lætr þat vel vera** agrees, says it is a good idea II:142; **vel er** it is good XV:73, it is a good thing XXVII:7; **vel ek** happy me! *or* all right! X:134; **svá vel at sér** so noble-minded, of such fine character XXVI B:63. Cf. **fara**, **verða**

vél *f.* trick, cunning plan II:142; artifice, cunning things, subtle things X:99

veldi *n.* rule, domain, territory ruled over (*with gen.* by) VI:149; kingdom XXII:63/4; power XIV:2, XXIV:65

veldr *see* **valda**

velja (*past* **valði**, *pp.* **valit**) *wv.* choose *Gr* 3.6.5.2, XIV:15, 27, 101; select XXII:28/4

Vellankatla *f.* 'boiling crater', at the north-eastern corner of Ǫlfossvatn, about 4 km from Lǫgberg VIII:104

velli *see* **vǫllr**

venda (*past* **vendi**, *pp.* **vendr**) *wv. with dat.* turn VI:134

vendiliga *adv.* carefully, minutely, in detail VII A:63

venja (*pres.* **venr**, *past* **vanði**, *pp.* **vaninn**) *wv.* accustom; make a habit (of doing something) IV:3

vér *pron. 1st person pl.* we (*Gr* 3.2.1) VI:81, 183, 184, 195, VIII:132, 135, IX:59, X:71, 72, XIII:7, XV:23, XXI:177, XXII:24/1, XXIV:34, 40, XXVI B:7, 10, 33; *referring to the writer* V:104, XIII:44, XIV:26, note, 72, 154, *to the speaker* X:154 (Vǫlundr), XV:54?, XVI:36, 37 (or to Auðunn and the bear?), *to the poet* XXVI A:93

vera/vesa (*pres.* **er/es**, *past* **var/vas**, *past pl.* **váru/vóru**, *past subj.* **væri**, *pp.* **verit**) *sv. irregular* be (*Gr* 3.6.7, 3.6.10) *inf.* I:19, 62, 63, 109, 117, 125, 143, 145, II:8, 85, 143, VI:1, 214, IX:79, XI:9, XIII:21, XVI:10, 40, XXV:52, XXIII:12, 36, 101, XXVI A:2, 112, B:16, XXVII:2, to be XXIII:104, XXIV:31, XXVI A:19; **okr vera** to be (should be) for us (sc. to follow) XXV:102; **hverr vera skal** who it is to be XXVII:6, 18; stay IV:50, XV:18, XIX:88, 90, XXI:59 (2), 94, 162, 164, 193 (2), 208, XXVI A:109, 116, B:4; live VIII:151; **þar at vera** being there III:126; **ekki vera mega** could not be true III:123; **þess er var** such as there was, such as he had XVI:6; *pres.* **em** am VII A:87, 91, XXIV:25, XXV:16, XXVI B:67; **þú ert** you are XVI:32, XXVI A:57, B:112; *with suffixed pron.* **ertu** you are I:105, V:10, VII A:41, XXVI A:22, B:94, are you I:10, IX:24, XVI:61, you will be XVI:142; **er** I:26, 36, 56, 81, 90, 94, 102, 125, 132, 133, 146 (2), VI:140, 160, XI:10, XXVII:7, 11, he is XXII:62/3, it is VI:331, 340, XXV:51, there is I:53, XXV:7, it will be IV:45; **er**

þat that will be VI:85, it is VI:167; **nú er þeim út at ganga ǫllum er** now all those are to go out to whom XXVI B:135; **hvat er** what's up IX:23; **hvárt er** can it be XVI:32; **illt er** it is bad IX:25; *with dat. (poss.) 1st person pron. suffixed* **erum** (= **er mér**, I have) IV:28; *with suffixed neg.* **era** is not X:77, **erat** there is not (no) X:170, XVIII:122ra20; *pl.* **eru** I:78, VI:106, IX:108, X:83, XI:11, XXIII:7, XXV:104, XXVI A:16, 104, **ro** X:64, **eru nú til** there are now available XXVI B:102, **Nú eru** If there are XXVII:16; *with suffixed neg.* **erut** will not be IV:42; *1st person pl. referring to the speaker* **erum** I am IV:33, **erumk** XVIII:122ra15; *pres. subj.* **sé** I:46, 143, VI:183, XVI:53 (is evidently), would be XXVI B:66, should be XXIV:32, may be XIII:46, XXIV:71, is XXI:100, XXIII:1, XXIV:22, XXVI B:14, 29, XXVII:3, 27, am XXIV:19, *2nd person* **sér** VII A:41, XVI:40, XXIV:85, stay XXVI A:110, **sért** I:136, *1st person pl.* **sém vér** let us be XIII:45, *3rd person pl.* **sé** V:72, **séu** should be I:83, are XXIII:25, **sé augun mikil** if the eyes are large XXIII:33; *imp.* **ver** be XI:69, **ver þú** stay! VII B:63, **ver hér** stay here XVI:76. *imp. pl.* **verið** stay XXII:25/4; *past* **var** was I:3, 7, 23, 71 (2), II:2, VI:8, 252, 333, IX:1, XIX:4, XXI:7, XXII:1/3, XXV:7, he was (*Gr* 3.9.5) III:65, it was XV:13, there was XV:32, XXI:27, XXV:63, **vas** VIII:11; *with suffixed neg.* **vara** was not V:54, it was not XXV:5, **varat** it was not XXV:62; *past pl.* **várum** we were V:48, **þér váruð** you were XXVI B:70; **váru/vóru** were II:5 (*subject understood*), III:3, IX:53, XI:17, XV:6, XIX:2, XXII:3/2, XXIV:70, there were X:3, XV:15, XXI:17, 91, XXVI A:13, had been X:116, 160, (found they) were, had arrived XIX:28, **sem þar váru** as there were there XXVI B:61; **váru þat, þat váru** these were (*cf.* I:26–27, *note*; *Gr* 3.9.8.2) III:113, XV:143; *past subj.* **væri** was I:7, 113, III:20, VI:14, VIII:28, 29, 42, 57, XV:113, XXI:69, XXVI A:51, B:8, there was XIII:31, would be I:123, XV:116, XVI:73, XXV:98, might be XIV:15, should be XIV:138, *note*, there should be VIII:163, it was III:122, VI:298, (he) was VII A:35, were X:105, XV:59, XXI:44, XXIV:44, XXVI A:53, XXVI B:88, were, should last XV:10, it were IX:14, 15, XXI:160, XXIV:45, **at þú værir** that you should be XVI:73, **ok værir** and that you should be V:14, **fleiri væri** there would be (*or* were?) more XXIV:42, **þar væri** there were there XXI:153; *pp.* **hafa verit** (to) have been II:75, VIII:29–30, XXVI B:168, XXVII:42, **hafi verit** have been, were

V:15; **hafði (hǫfðu, hafðu) verit** had been IV:108, VI:42, 47, XV:32, XIX:48, XXI:9, had been staying VIII:82; **hefði verit** has been XV:150; **var á** there was on it XXVI A:52; **vera af** *see* af; **væri at** was in, was to be gained from XIV:125; **vera at at** be occupied *or* busy in XVI:131; **váru eptir** were left, remained VI:218, **hafi þar eptir verit** stayed behind there XXI:162; **vera fyrir** portend V:8; **vera í** be engaged in XXI:9; **var í** was wearing V:56, lived in, resided in VIII:40; **vas í** stayed in VIII:189; **vera með** stay with XVI:8, 113, XXI:208; **vera til** be there, be to come VI:72; relate to XXIV:28–29 (cf. *Gr* 3.9.8.2), **var til** was available, was enough VI:225; **vera mest um** be most significant, be most troublesome V:9; **vera úti fyrir** be out there (on that side) XXVI B:221; **væri við** were present VII B:27; **váru við** were at it XXVI A:43; *pres. part.* **verandi** being, continuing to be XIII:46; *as aux.* *forming pass.* (*Gr* 3.9.7.2), *inf.* I:37, II:19, III:14, *pres.* I:79, 137, II:1, 37, 145, VI:199, 355, VIII:5, 14, 17, IX:8, XI:15, XXII:59/1, XXVII:39; *pres. subj.* **sé** are XXVII:7, should be XXIV:14, **ok sé** and that they may be XXVI A:104, **sé mælt** it is spoken ('it is then not the king alone that is addressed') XXIV:80, **svá sé** as if it is XXVI A:23, *past* I:18, 29, 118, II:20, III:83, IV:102, VII B:69, X:43, XI:36, XV:12, XVI:7, XIX:23, 34, 86, XXII:19/1, XXV:10, 24, 67, *impers.* I:8, 71 (1), 113, II:3, 6 (2), XV:4 (2), *past pl.* II:8, VI:151, IX:81, XV:17, *past subj.* **væri** should be XIV:137, 138, *note, pp.* **hefi verit** V:77, **hǫfðu/hefði verit** had been I:48, XIX:88; *as aux. with pp. of intransitive verb forming perfect* (*or past perfect*) (*Gr* 3.9.7.1) I:128, II:50, IV:20, 48, V:2, 60, 163, VI:14, 337 (*inf. in acc. and inf. construction*), 361, IX:24, X:59, XVI:17, XIX:81, XXI:30, 69, XXII:9/3, XXIII:26; **var komit** it was come *or* (people) had arrived IX:93; **eru komnir** are arrived XXV:68

veraldar *see* verǫld

veraldligr *adj.* worldly XIII:42

verð *n.* price XVI:22, 24

verða (*past* **varð,** *past pl.* **urðu/vurðu,** *past subj.* **yrði,** *pp.* **orðinn,** *n.* **orðit**) *sv.* (*Gr* 3.6.7, 3.6.9.3 ex. 1) **1.** become I:105 (*pp.* **orðinn**), II:28, 35, 36, 43, 47, 99, III:25, 129, IV:66, 72 (*subj.*), V:117, VII A:35, 49, 140, VIII:47, 53, IX:48, 51, XII:79, XIV:89, 144, 187, XV:108, 140, XVI:125, XIX:83, XXIV:69, XXV:16, XXVI A:31; come to be III:5, V:156 (*inf. with* **myndak**), VI:283, 296 (get), VIII:4,

29, 61 (**verða dauðr** = die), XVI:12, XIX:12, 77, come about V:132; happen VIII:126 (1); happen to be III:74; take place VIII:25, XIX:22, XXI:125, XXV:83, XXVI B:214; **þat skal verða aldri** that shall never be XXVI A:56; **verða má svá enn** it may still happen XVI:143; turn out to be V:100, 145, VI:209, 345 (*inf. with* **mundut**), VIII:135, XXVII:7; *inf.* **verða** it happens XIX:78; *pres.* **verðr** will be XXVII:34, is turning out XXVI B:138; **verðum eigi** let us not be VI:70; **varð** was, became, turned out to be XIV:108, 169, XV:123, XIX:102, XXI:78, 137; **engi varð** there was no VII B:74; **varð þat ekki** that did not happen, he could not XV:111; *pres. subj.* **verða ek** if I could get X:134 (*cf. note*); **þó at svá illa verði** though it should turn out so badly XVI:147; *past subj.* **yrði** would have been IV:95, he might become, he could become XXVI A:28; *pp.* **vel er orðit** it has turned out well I:108; **sem áðr er orðit** as it has already turned out XI:41; **er á orðit fyrir mér** I have a serious problem, I have got into a difficulty XVI:64; **varð þar af** there became from it, it turned into II:98; **hvat varð af** what became of, what has happened to X:148; **varð ekki af** nothing came of (it) III:124, VII B:73; **ekki verðr af oss** we are getting nowhere XXVI A:42; **verða at** come to, lead to VIII:126, come to be, be accepted as II:114; **varð at** there was at this, there arose from it VI:131; **mundu at orðit** would have resulted from it XV:122; **vándum mǫnnum varð at** for wicked men they caused XIV:41; **verða at bana** *with dat.* put someone to death X:153; **verða fyrir** be in the way, get in the way V:128, be subject to, be the victim of XV:113; **verða í** there turn out to be in them IV:103; **varð í því** there came about in this VI:220; **verða til** come about, happen XXIV:7, be available, be there VII B:88; **verða vel** do well, get on well XXI:62; *imp. pl.* **verðið vel við** put up with it bravely XXVI B:123; *past subj.* **yrði við** reacted to it, took it, bore it III:107; *impers.* **verðr** it gets XXIII:20, **varð** it got XXI:52, **varð þá ekki vart við þá** then there was no sign of them XXI:121, **varð þeim** they became IV:15, **varð ǫllum illt af** they all got ill from it XXI:76, **fyrir yrði** something was there III:110, 112; *impers. pass.* **svá var honum kalt orðit** he had become so cold III:126; *see* **mismælt**; *as aux. of pass.* (*Gr* 3.9.7.2) VI:315, 316, VIII:35, 56, X:107, XXI:144, XXVI B:78, *impers.* **yrði tekit við** might be accepted VIII:90, **mun getit verða** XIV:130, **verðr mælt** it is spoken, one speaks XXIV:79. **2.** **verða, verða at** *with inf.* must III:43, have to, be forced to I:89,

VI:272, XVI:43, **mun/munu verða at** will/shall have to XXVI B:79, 101; **verðr vera** will have to be XI:40; **varð fram at ganga at** it had to come on to XXII:33/4; **varð at fram fara at** turned out to happen that? had to happen that? VIII:177; *impers. with inf.* it is necessary, we must III:39

verðr[1] (*n.* **vert**) *adj. with gen.* worth; **þótti þeim meira um vert** they found it more valuable XIV:34; **betr en ek sé verðr** more than I deserve XXIV:19

verðr[2] *see* **verða**

vergjarn *adj.* eager for men; *sup.* very eager for men, quite man-crazy IX:51

verja[1] (*past* **varði,** *past pl.* **vǫrðu,** *pp.* **varit**) *wv.* **1.** *impers. with dat.* **er varit** someone is dressed V:84. **2.** defend *Gr* 3.6.6 ex. 5, XXI:140, XXII:41/3, XXVI A:88, 89; guard XII:55; *with dat. and acc.* bar someone from something VIII:106, deprive someone of something XXII:10/4; **verja ǫðrum til aldrlaga** encompass others' deaths XXV:30 (*or* **verja**[2]?) **3.** enfold, put one's arms round X:25; **verja faðmi** enfold in an embrace X:21. **4.** -**sk** *form* **verjask** defend oneself: *past* **varðisk** V:130, 142, XXVI A:37, 93, *past pl.* **vǫrðusk** VI:255

verja[2] (*past* **varði,** *past pl.* **vǫrðu,** *pp.* **varit**) *wv. with dat.* invest, lay out (**til** in/for) XVI:189, XIX:31; **verja sverði ǫðrum til aldrlaga** use a sword to bring about other people's deaths? XXV:30 (*or* **verja**[1]?); *impers. pass.* **er hingat er bezt varit í Nóreg** which is the most advantageous to exchange here in Norway, which is of the greatest value to bring to Norway XVI:173

verk *n.* work II:134, XIV:191, deed I:145, V:161, VII A:49 (*pl.*), VII B:86, XIV:39, 51; **góð verk** good works XIV:55

verkandi *m. (pres. part.)* worker, user, *in kenning for* warriors, **Heðins baugs serkjar verkendr** VI:262 (*subject of* **sukku niðr** *and* **gerðut við vægjask**)

verkfœri *n.* tool XIV:135

verkmaðr *m.* workman, labourer II:132

verknaðr *m.* task(s) XIV:138, *note*

verkreiði *m.* work equipment XIV:136

verma (*past* **vermði,** *pp.* **vermðr**) *wv. transitive* warm III:127

vernda (*past* **verndaði,** *pp.* **verndat**) *wv.* protect; *pres. part.* XIII:43

verpa (*past* **varp,** *past pl.* **urpu,** *pp.* **orpinn**) *sv.* throw *Gr* 3.6.9.1 (1); cast up, raise (**at** for) XV:154; **verpa frá sér** *with dat.* throw down

XXII:50/1; *impers. pass. with dat.* **hǫndum þínum orpit** your arms thrown XXV:88

verr[1] *m.* husband IX:97; man XXV:100; **vers** your husband's (Sigurðr's) XXV:25; **kjósa sér at ver** choose as one's husband IV:91

verr[2] *adv.* worse *Gr* 3.5.2, X:169; **mjǫk er verr** it is much worse VI:340; *sup.* **verst** worst *Gr* 3.5.2

verri *adj. comp.* worse *Gr* 3.3.8.3, XXV:29; **hit verra** what was worse, the worse course XXI:13; *sup.* **verstr** worst *Gr* 3.3.8.3

versagjǫrð *f.* verse-making, composition (probably in Latin) XIV:156

vert *see* **verðr**

verǫld *f.* world VI:113; *gen.* of this world, secular XXIV:55

vesa = **vera**

vesall *adj.* wretched, miserable I:12

vestan *adv.* from the west V:53, XV:125, eastwards XV:77; from the west of Europe (to England) VII A:9; **fyr vestan, fyrir vestan** *with acc.* west of (*Gr* 3.5.3 (7), 3.7.1) VIII:19, XV:36; **fyrir vestan fram** on past to the west of it XXI:167; **vestan** *with gen.* west of XXV:61

Vestfirðir *m. pl.* the Western Fjords (of Iceland) XV:16

Vestfirzkr *adj.* from the Western Fjords (of Iceland) XV:2

Vestmannaeyjar *f. pl.* Westmann Islands ('Islands of the Irishmen'), islands off the south coast of Iceland VIII:92, XIX:86

vestmenn *m. pl.* Irishmen XIX:87

vestr *n.* the west; **í vestr** to the west XXI:169; *as adv.* (in the) west VIII:69; west(wards) VII A:10, XV:34, 84, XIX:72, 75, 90; in a westerly direction VII A:148, XV:131; to the west (of Europe; actually in an easterly direction here; see *Saga-Book* XXV, 72–82) VII A:8; to the west V:6 (*i.e.* to Dalir, in the west of Iceland, where Þorsteinn Kuggason lived; actually north of Hítardalr); **vestr frá** to the west of XIV:25; **vestr fyrir** west past XV:146; **vestr fyrir land** west along the coast VII A:153, XIX:55; **vestr til Saurbœjar** to Saurbœr in the west XV:75; **útan vestr þar í fjǫrðum** abroad (to Norway) from those fjords in the west (i.e. from the Western Fjords) XVI:2; **vestr um landit** west round the country VII A:156

Vestribyggð *f.* Western Settlement (the more northerly settlement on the western coast of Greenland) XXI:20

vestrvíking *f.* raiding in the British Isles XIX:32

vesǫld *f.* misery XII:36; *pl.* XII:40, 88

vetfangr *m.* scene of action V:162

vetr *m.* winter (*Gr* 3.1.7.4 (1)) VIII:82, 189, XV:32, XIX:29, 90; *acc. of time* **þann vetr** for that winter XXI:107; **vetr annan** for a second winter XIX:89; **hinn þriðja vetr** for the third winter XXI:194; *with suffixed def. art.* **of/um vetrinn** during the winter XV:124, XVI:4, XIX:9, XXI:59, 208, **of/um vetrinn eptir** during the following winter VIII:173, XIX:20; **at vetri** at the beginning of winter II:138; **vetri miðr en** one year short of VIII:192; *nom. pl.* **vetr** years XIX:49; *acc. pl. with suffixed def. art.* **um vetrna** in winter, during the winters XXI:160; *acc. pl. of time* years I:74, VII A:27, VIII:190, 194, X:11, 26; *gen. pl.* **vetra** (*Gr* 3.4.2 (5), (6), (7)) years III:22, 46, V:32, VIII:13, 16, 29, 56, XIV:173, XV:4, XVI:7, XIX:49; *dat. pl.* **fám vetrum síðarr**, **síðar fám vetrum** a few years later VIII:17, 143; **tólf vetrum síðar** twelve years later VIII:193; **tveim vetrum meir en** two years over VIII:196

vetrhús *n. pl.* the buildings used in the winter, *i.e.* the main farm buildings XV:88, 94

vexti *see* **vǫxtr**

við, viðr *prep.* (*Gr* 3.7.4) **1.** *with acc.* to, against II:31, 56, V:157 (1), VI:30, 41, 199 (1), 228, VIII:146, X:37, XIX:16, from XXII:34/4, 65/4, to XXII:15/2, XXIV:18, XXV:79; with II:98, IV:4, VI:90, 197, X:146, 177, XII:84, XV:129, XXII:54/3, XXIII:52, XXV:33, XXVI B:40; towards XIV:49, XXII:1/3, 42/4, XXIV:21; close to III:7, 85, XXVI A:30, 89; by, near XXI:175, XXVI A:115; by, beside V:157 (2), VI:253 (**viðr**; *phrase goes with* **fœrðuð Barða**), VII A:52, B:64, X:172, XI:17, XIX:60, 92, 103, XXIII:18; on the coast of XVI:177; off VI:28, XIX:15, XXI:170; with, in relation to I:66, 71, II:72, 73, V:161, 162, VIII:89, 114, 117; **við mek** with me, to me XXIV:26; in connection with VI:199 (2), XVI:155; in connection with, from I:84; using VI:122, XXVI B:117; with the help of VI:118; accompanied by V:93, VII B:60; in company with VIII:22; in (the light of) X:44, together with XXII:43/1 (*postposition*); **með honum við sex menn** with a group of six men in all with him (with him, accompanied by six men?) V:94; at, engaged in II:6; in response to II:30, because of II:43, at XXII:53/2, XXVI B:36; **við þetta** at this XV:112, XXI:128; **við þat** thereupon, after that, in spite of that III:87, at that, in response to that VIII:86; **kenna við** *see* **kenna**. **2.** *with dat.* against I:17; from XXIII:37 (*see* **varna**); towards, at XXI:173; in response to IX:103; for, in return for XVI:22; **taka við** *see* **taka**. **3.** *as adv.* at this I:14,

II:71 (*see* **skrækja**), IV:104 (*see* **víkja**), XXV:90, XXVI A:18, at it
XXVI B:95; by it XXI:120 (2); at the same time, as well XXI:120
(1); against VI:166, against it I:41, against them VI:261, XXVI A:82;
with (each other; *see* **eiga**) I:104, II:13; close by VI:215 (**viðr**); **vera
við** be present VII B:27; **þar við** (in return) for it XVI:25; **þar viðr
auka**, **við auka** add to it VIII:3, 40

viða (*past* **viðaði**) *wv.* cut wood (**til** for) VIII:54

víða *adv.* widely, to many places II:94, in many places VII A:2, 16,
126, XIV:179, XVI:138, XIX:35, XXI:16, extensively VIII:35

Viðarr *m.* a god (one of the Æsir) II:9

viðfǫng *n. pl.* supplies XXVI A:53

Víðimýrr *f.* farm in Skagafjǫrðr, northern Iceland III:129, XIV:133

viðr¹ *m.* tree; tree *or* wood XXV:18; forest X:29; timber V:27, XXVI
A:24; wood X:55; piece of wood, rod XII:30; **viðr hauðrmens** 'timber
of the sea' *is a kenning for* ship XXVI A:98; *dat.* **viði** with trees VIII:20;
acc. pl. **viðu** trees II:32

viðr² = **við**

víðr *adj.* wide XXIII:62; extensive XXII:29/2; **á víðum velli** in the
open IV:43

Viðrir *see* **hand-Viðrir**

viðrkvæmiligr *adj.* fitting XIII:39; **at sýna viðrkvæmiligt vera** to
show that it was fitting XIII:20

við(r)taka *f.* resistance VI:286, defence XXI:131

viðrtal *n.* conversation (*with gen.* between) XXVI B:39

viðskipti *n. pl.* dealings, encounter VII A:57

Vífill *m.* slave XIX:72, 91; *dat.* **Vífli** XIX:100

Vífilsfell *n.* mountain 20 km south-east of Reykjavík XIX:101

vífilstoptir *f. pl.* a farm near Reykjavík (= Vífilsstaðir) XIX:101

víg *n.* killing, slaying II:60, XIX:3, XXII:37/2, XXV:101, XXVI A:21,
118; battle VI:246, X:12; *dat.* **vígi** by force of arms VIII:106; *dat.
sg. with suffixed def. art.* V:158

vígfrœkn *adj.* bold in battle XXV:100

Vígi *m.* a dog VII A:123

vígja (*past* **vígði**, *pp.* **vígðr**) *wv.* **1.** consecrate; *imp. pl.* **vígið** IX:122;
bless IX:120; **vígja til** ordain as VIII:187, 191, 194, consecrate to
VIII:195. **2.** **-sk** *form* **láta vígjask til** let oneself be consecrated, be
ordained (as) VIII:184

vígmóðr *adj.* wearied, exhausted by fighting XXVI A:94

vígr *adj.* able to fight V:31

Vígslóði *m.* Manslaughter Section (of the Law), 'Treatment of Homicide', dealing largely with offences against the person (injuries, assaults, killings; see *Laws* I 139–74) VIII:178

Vík *f.* Oslofjord XVI:41

vika *f.* week VIII:92, 197; **viku fyrr** a week earlier (in the year) VIII:96; **at tíu vikum sumars** when ten weeks of summer remained, i.e. in late July XV:79; **fyrr en tíu vikur eru af sumri** before ten weeks of summer have passed XXVII:29; **þrjár vikur í samt** for three weeks together, for three whole weeks running XXI:121

Víkarsskeið *n.* the coast to the west of the mouth of the Ǫlfoss river, south-western Iceland (modern Skeið) VII A:159

víkja (*past* **veik,** *past pl.* **viku,** *pp.* **vikinn**) *sv.* **1.** turn (back) V:91; **víkja út** turn back out XVI:102; *transitive with dat.* turn, direct XXIV:49; *impers. with dat.* **svá víkr við** it turns out in such a way IV:104. **2.** -**sk** *form* **víkjask;** *past* **veiksk undan** turned himself away, dodged (out of the way) V:128; **veiksk við** responded to XV:128

víl *n.* misery; a hard task IV:56 (*object of* **hafa**)

vili *m.* wish: *acc.* **vilja** VI:22, will XIV:117; *dat.* **vilja** purpose XXII:34/2; desire, compliance XIV:90, *note*; joy: *gen.* **vilja** X:61, 143, *dat.* **vilja** XXV:18

vilja[1] (*pres.* **vil/vill/vil(l)t,** *past* **vildi,** *pp.* **viljat**) *wv.* (*Gr* 3.6.7, 3.6.9.1 (11), 3.6.9.2 (3)) wish, want, be willing (to, for) I:27, 31, 47, 68, 83, 85, 121, II:36, 48, 91, 108, 127, 160, III:33, 34, IV:68, V:113, 158, VI:8, 23, VII A:120, B:14, 21, VIII:22, 133, XI:50, XII:65, XIV:187, XV:125, XVI:39, 47, XXI:80, 113, XXII:4/3, XXIV:54, XXVII:8, 16; want to, try to II:129, XV:111, XXI:136; mean to, try to I:95, V:98; be trying to II:146; intend to IV:70, V:125, XIX:63; intend to, be going to VII A:57, 102, 159, VIII:106, XII:58, XIX:21; **vil ek** I wish XXII:31/3, XXVI B:157, I will XXIV:25, 29, I desire that I:147, XXVI B:59; **ef ek vil** if I want to XXVI B:24; **vil ek eigi** I do not wish, I do not intend VIII:101; **eigi vil ek** I am not williing XXVI B:132, **eigi vil ek þat** I do not want that XXVI B:210; *with suffixed pron. and neg.* **vilkat ek** I do not wish XXV:33; *2nd person sg.* **þú vill** IX:117, XVI:39, XXVI A:66 (you insist on), **þú vil** XVI:80, **þú vilt** you wish XIV:10; **villt þú** will you, are you willing to XXVI B:130; *with suffixed pron.* **viltu** you want I:15, if you are willing VII A:88, are you willing I:60, 62, **villtu** will you XVI:22, XXVI A:103, do

you want XVI:24, 80, do you wish XVI:29, **villdu** you want to go
XVI:137; *3rd person sg.* **vill** wishes XXVI B:72, XXVII:23, 45 (1),
wants XXVI A:66; **eigi vill** does not want VI:94, he will not XIX:78;
vill eigi is determined not to V:146, is not going to VII B:29, is not
willing to VI:95; **nú vill hann** but if he is willing XXVII:45; *pl.*
vilið þér if you are willing II:25; **vilja** want (to have) XXVII:14; **ef**
vilja if they want to XXVII:51; *past* **vildi** would XIX:42; wished it
to be XXV:27; **vilda** wanted XXVI B:172; **eigi vilda ek at þú** I
would like you not to V:14; **vildu heldr** they would rather XXVI
B:63; **vildu æ fram** always wanted to advance VI:258; *pres. subj.*
vili II:124, **né ek vilja** nor would I wish (nor for which I would
wish?) X:169, *pl.* **vili** XXVII:20; *past subj.* **ef þú vildir eigi** if you
had not wished XVI:83; *past subj. pl.* **vildim** V:64, **vildi eigi** did not
want it VIII:130; **ef þeir vildi** if they liked VI:103; *impers.* (of fate;
see **auðna**) III:92; *past inf.* **vildu** XXVI B:155
vilja² *see* **vili**
viljaðr *adj. (pp.)* (well) disposed, kind (*with dat.* **þeim** to them)
    XXIV:71
villa *f.* error; fantasy XXII:43/4 ('made a big mistake'?); delusion,
    heresy, i.e. heathendom XXII:25/3
villdu, villtu *see* **vilja**
villustígr *m.* false path XXIV:46
Vilmundr Þórólfsson *m.* abbot at Þingeyrar 1133–48 XIV:180
vilnask (*past* **vilnaðisk**) *wv.* -sk *form with gen.* wish for, desire X:146
vín *n.* wine XI:59; **at víni** over his wine XXV:71
vin *see* **vinr**
vinátta *f.* friendship VII A:122
vínber *n.* grape XXI:50 (*pl.*)
vinda (*past* **vatt**, *past pl.* **undu**, *pp.* **undit**) *sv.* twist, wind (**af** off)
    XXVI A:63, **vindum af** let us wind off XXVI A:60
vindáss *m.* winding-pole (put between two ropes and twisted to tighten
    them) XXVI A:60 (*acc. pl.*)
Vinðir *m. pl.* the Wends VI:283, VII A:140
vindkaldr *adj.* 'wind-cold', made cold by winds XXV:61
vínker *n.* wine-goblet XXI:50, *textual note*
Vinðland *n.* Wendland (parts of modern Poland and north-eastern
    Germany) VI:6, 13, 19, 21, 25, 28, 48, 320, VII A:27
vindr *m.* wind XIV:38

vindþurr *adj.* wind-dried X:55

vingask (*past* **vingaðisk**) *wv.* make friends (**við** with), get on good terms with, show affection for VI:318

vingjarnliga *adv.* friendlily XV:88

Ving-Þórr *m.* a name for Þórr ('swing-Þórr') IX:1

Vínland *n.* the name given by the Vikings to (some part of) the northeast coast of North America VIII:71, XXI:2, 4

vinna[1] (*past* **vann,** *past pl.* **unnu,** *past subj.* **ynni,** *pp.* **unninn,** *n.* **unnit**) *sv. irregular* (*Gr* 3.6.9.1 (6)) **1.** perform II:137; achieve VII A:49; **vanntu** you brought about XXV:94; work (at): **vinna hannyrðir með** work embroidery with pictures of, make embroidered pictures of XIV:189; fight (a battle) VI:236; defeat, overcome VI:315, XXVI B:58, 197; **at vinna** to overcome (*with* **hafa fœtr**; *or* **at vinna** [**sverð**] = fight hard) IV:81; *with dat.* resist, prevail against, withstand X:183, 184; **at vinna** to perform *with* **hafa víl** IV:56; **hafa œrit at vinna** have enough work to do, have plenty to do, have a hard enough job VI:92; **vinna eiða at** swear oaths by X:149; *with acc. and adj. or pp.* cause someone to be, make someone something VI:247, **vinna (menn) sára** cause men to be wounded XXVI A:97; **vinna á** *with dat.* injure someone III:120, XV:114; **vinna til** earn, deserve, achieve, accomplish I:140; **allt til vinna at** do everything (anything) in order that (so that) XXVI B:65; **ef þetta er til unnit** if this is achieved to earn it I:137; **ekki fyrir unnit** no preparations *or* provision had been made for it XXI:60. **2.** -**sk** *form* **hánum vannsk** *with dat.* lasted him VI:324; **honum vinnsk eigi fróðleikr til þess** (his) knowledge does not extend so far in him XXVII:32

vinna[2] *f.* work, labour XIV:134

vinr/vin *m.* friend III:33, VIII:109, 182, XI:46, XII:77, XIX:23

vinstri *adj. comp.* left XI:55

vinsæld *f.* popularity; *pl.* XXI:14

vinsæll *adj.* popular XV:36, 42; *comp.* **vinsælli** more popular *Gr* 3.3.9 ex. 22; *sup.* **inn vinsælsti** the most popular, a very popular VII B:10

vintr = **vetr** (*archaic form or a loan-word from some other Germanic language*) XXI:194, *textual note*

vínviðr *m.* (grape)vine(s) XXI:91

virða (*past* **virði/virti,** *pp.* **virðr,** *n.* **virt**) *wv.* **1.** value (*Gr* 3.6.9.1 (7)) VIII:153, 156; *with gen. of amount of price or value* **virða mik engis** value me at nothing, show no respect to me XXVI B:70; value,

regard XXVI B:113; consider, esteem, rank, honour (**þik** yourself)
XXIV:85; judge, decide, conclude XXI:157. **2. -sk** *form impers. with
dat.* **virðisk** it seems to someone (**sem** as if, that) V:15; **þeim virðisk
landit betra** they thought the land looked better XIX:29

virðar *m. pl.* men XXII:60/1; *vocative* you men XXII:25/3

virðing *f.* honour; **góð virðing** high honours XVI:117

virðuligr *adj.* magnificent XIV:12; worthy XIV:128

virtu *see* **virða**

vísa[1] *f.* verse, stanza IV:17, 26, 53, 77, V:16, 148, 164, XIV:84, XXVI
A:92

vísa[2] (*past* **vísaði,** *pp.* **vísat**) *wv. with dat.* direct (**í** towards) VII A:115;
vísa ífrá *with dat.* refuse *or* forbid to someone XXIV:53; **vísa til**
indicate XXIII:55, 81, *with dat.* direct someone to XIX:42

vísaván *f.* certain expectation VIII:126

vísi/vísir *m.* ruler X:67, 147 (Vǫlundr), XXII:60/2 (Sveinn Knútsson)

víss *adj.* certain; **hvers víss yrði** of what he could become certain,
what he could find out XXVI A:28; *n. as substantive* **at vísu** indeed
XV:98. Cf. **víst**

vissa, vissi, vissu *see* **vita**

vist *f.* habitation, dwelling VIII:69; board and lodging XVI:4; *in pl.*
food XIV:146, XVI:45, 47, 51

víst *adv.* (*n. of* **víss**) indeed, to be sure I:102,141, XXII:14/3, XXIV:25;
for certain VI:82, XXVI B:73; **svá var víst** it was indeed so XVI:181

vit *pron.* 2nd person dual (*Gr* 3.2.1) I:63, 65, V:79, IX:47, XVI:108,
XXIV:47, XXV:99, 103, 106, XVII B:166, 167; **vit Hǫttr** (*Gr* 3.9.6.1)
Hǫttr and I I:64; **vit Vǫlundr** Vǫlundr and I X:181; **vit Grímr** Grímr
and I XXVI B:16

vita (*pres.* **veit,** *past* **vissi,** *pp.* **vitat**) *pret.-pres. vb.* **1.** know (*Gr* 3.6.7,
3.6.9.1 (10), 3.6.9.3 ex. 7) I:111, 128, 144, II:132, V:7, 126, VI:14,
108, VII A:65, IX:7, XIV:59, XV:73, XVI:106, XIX:110, XXI:80,
XXIV:26, XXVI A:26, 50, B:73; know to be, feel, find X:62; **veit
ek eigi, eigi veit ek** I do not know VI:325, XXVI A:66; **veit ek ei at**
I am not sure whether XXIV:22; **eigi má ek þat vita** I cannot see, I
am not sure V:80, I canot bear it XVI:121; see, find out XXVI A:28;
vitið þér þat you find that out XXVI A:35; **varla mátti hann vita**
he could not bear to know XIV:108; *with acc. and inf.* **mik veiztu
verða** you will know that I am becoming IX:51; **vér megum víst
vita** we shall certainly know it VI:82; *pres. subj.* **viti** will know

XXVII:32, may know I:56, **þótt ek vita** even if I knew XXVI A:56, **svá at menn viti** as far as is known X:14, *pl. 1st person* **es vér vitim** whom we know VIII:151, *pl. 3rd person* **viti til** know of I:112; *past* **vissi** knew XV:114; **hitt vissa ek** this I found out XXVI A:35; **vissi ... fram** could see into the future IX:58; *past pl.* **vissu** knew about II:3, XIV:51; *inf. (after* **skyldi**) find out, see III:107; **þykkjask vita** feel sure VI:134, VII A:59, VII B:54; *impers.* **hvat má vita** what can one know, how can one be sure I:135, **hvat vissi til** what was known about II:45. **2.** *with gen.* indicate, betoken, lead to IV:22

víti *n.* punishment XV:117; penalty XV:61, torment, trouble IV:25 (*gen. object of* **vita**); vengeance V:35

vitja (*past* **vitjaði,** *pp.* **vitjat**) *wv.* visit I:77; *with gen.* go to see, go to attend X:12; visit XIV:143

vitni *n.* witness, testimony VI:324

vitr (*acc.* **vitran**) *adj.* wise II:93, VI:165, XIV:40, 51, XXIII:77, XXIV:79; clever VII A:119; sensible XXIV:60; *sup.* **vitrasti** *Gr* 3.3.5 ex. 3, 3.3.8.1 ex. 3

vitrlega *adv.* wisely XXIV:45

vitugr *adj.* intelligent, sensible, clever XXIII:86

vizka *f.* wisdom XXIII:17, 53

vóð = **óð,** *see* **vaða**

vóndzligr *adj.* evil, harsh, terrible XXII:60/1

vóru *see* **vera**

vurðu *see* **verða**

vægð *f.* mercy, giving way, yielding; *dat. sg.* with mercy or giving way VI:246

vægjask (*past* **vægðisk**) *wv.* **-sk** *form* yield, give way (**við** in the face of their enemies) VI:261

væl *f.* trickery, deception XXIII:55

vængr *m.* wing VII A:154 (*pl. with suffixed def. art.*), XII:33; *acc. pl.* **vængi** I:76

vænligast *adv. sup.* most promising *or* useful XXIV:30

vænn *adj.* (*Gr* 3.3.8.4 (1)) handsome V:30; fine, splendid XXII:38/2

vænta (*pres.* **væntir,** *past* **vænti,** *pp.* **vænt**) *wv.* expect (that) I:105, XXI:61; *with dat. of person and dat. of thing* expect something for someone, expect that someone will achieve something XV:148; *with gen.* expect XXIV:23; *impers.* **væntir mek** I expect, I have expectation of, I anticipate VI:91

værl, værir *see* **vera**

værugjarn *adj.* fond of rest and warmth XXVI B:168

Vætildr *f.* North American native woman XXI:202

vætr *pron.* nothing IX:104; *as adv.* not at all IX:112, X:183, 184

vǫkðu *see* **vekja**

vǫllr (*dat.* **velli**, *pl.* **vellir**) *m.* field *Gr* 3.3.7.1, 2 (4); ground; *with suffixed def. art.* III:45, XXVI A:28, 32, 71; *dat. sg.* **at velli** to the ground XXVI A:101; **á víðum velli** in the open IV:43; *acc. pl.* **vǫllu** space, battlefield? XXII:29/2

Vǫlundarkviða *f.* a poem about Vǫlundr X:*title*

Vǫlundr *m.* legendary smith X:1, 4, 11, 13, 16, 25, 36, 42, 52, 55, 67, 90, 125, 134, 136, 146, 147, 152, 169, 173, 179, 181; *elliptical gen.* **at Vǫlundar** at Vǫlundr's home X:79; *poss. dat.* (*Gr* 3.9.6.2) **Vǫlundi til smiðju** to Vǫlundr's smithy X:95; *dat. pl. as common noun* by craftsmen XXV:25 (see note)

vǫndr *m.* stick, thin rod, wand; *with suffixed def. art.* XII:32; *in kenning for* sword, **vǫndr hjalts** V:40

vǫrðr *m.* guardian, defender; *in kenning for* warrior (*see note*) **vǫrðr vápn-Eirar** V:48 (vocative)

vǫrðusk *see* **verja**[1]

vǫrn *f.* defence V:143, VI:315, XXVI A:92, 102; *dat. sg. with suffixed def. art.* **vǫrnenni** VI:255

vǫrr (*pl.* **varrir**) *f.* lip XXIII:57

vǫrusekkr *m.* sack of wares *Gr* 3.1.9 ex.2

vǫtnum *see* **vatn**

vǫxtr (*gen.* **vaxtar** *Gr* 3.1.7.1 ex. 5) *m.* size VII B:9; *dat. sg.* **vexti** in size III:23, V:30, XXI:11; **at vexti** in shape XII:11

yðar/yðvar *pron. 2nd person pl. gen.* (*Gr* 3.2.1) your I:59, 63, of you XXI:135

yðarr/yðvarr *poss. adj.* your (*pl.*) *Gr* 3.3.6 (11), 3.3.9 ex. 4, 3.9.6.1, XXI:78; *acc. sg. m.* **yðarn** XIV:56; *gen. sg. f.* **yðarrar** XXIV:21; *n.* **yðart** XIV:55, XXVI B:71; *dat. sg. n.* **yðru** (*i.e.* of you Icelanders) XVI:138; *n. pl.* **yður** XIV:56

yðr *pron. 2nd person pl. acc., dat.* (*Gr* 3.2.1) you, to you, for you I:53, XXVI A:105, for yourselves XXVI B:20; *in addressing king* XVI:63, 118, yourself XXIV:11

ýdróg *f.* bowstring VII A:19

ýfask (*past* **ýfðisk**) *wv.* **-sk** *form* become angry or hostile XXII:7/1

yfir *prep.* (*Gr* 3.7.4); *with acc.* above, over, upon I:44, II:22, 109, III:26, 54, XI:47, XIII:3, XXII:53/1, XXVI B:164; above XXI:128; across V:42, 163, VII B:61, XV:47, 100, XXV:41, XXVI A:4; *of time,* for XXI:65; *with dat.* about XIX:75, above XXIII:5; *as adv.* across *Gr* 3.5.3 (2), VI:25; about it IV:77; over him XXV:26; **yfir ofan** up on the top XXIII:10; **þar yfir** above it, on top of it III:100

yfirboð *n.* command, authority, rule XIV:177

yfirbœtr *f. pl.* compensation, atonement II:63, 73, V:161

yfirfǫr *f.* visitation XIV:1

Yggr *m. a name for* Óðinn; *gen.* **Yggs** *used elliptically to mean* 'Óðinn's business', *i.e.* fighting *or* poetry, *which is the object of* **ne leggjum fyr lið** IV:24

ykkar, yk(k)r *dual pron.* (*Gr* 3.2.1) your, you, to you IV:50, X:107; **ykr þjóðkonunga** (*acc. with* **eptir er þrungit**) you great kings XXV:14; *used for pl.* I:17; **með ykkr Njáli** with you and Njáll XXVI B:173

ykkarr *poss. adj. dual* your *Gr* 3.3.8.1, 3.3.9 (22), 3.9.6.1; *f.* **ykkur** your XXV:10, **ykkur beggja** of you both X:167; *dat. sg. n.* **ykru hváru** to each of you XXV:34

ýla (*past* **ýldi**, *pp.* **ýlt**) *wv.* howl; **ýla hátt upp** raise a great howling *or* screaming XXI:123

ýmiss *adj.* various, XVI:129; *n. pl.* **þau ymsi** they in turn II:70

ynði *f.* happiness, bliss XII:86

yngri *adj. comp.* younger (*Gr* 3.3.8.2) IV:2, XIV:158, XXVI B:70

ynni *see* **unna** *and* **vinna**

yrði *see* **verða**

yrkja (*pres.* **yrkir,** *past* **orti,** *pp.* **ort**) *wv. irregular* (*Gr* 3.6.9.3) compose (poetry) II:161, V:164, VII A:137, XXI:79, XXVI A:92; *impers.* **yrkja skyldi** there should be composed VII A:134

ýtar *m. pl.* men XXII:18/2, 63/2

ýtri *adj. comp.* outer; *acc. n. as adv.* **it ýtra** on the outside, on the fringe IV:63; **hit ýtra** on the outer (seaward) side VI:59; *sup.* **ýztr** outermost, on the outside, on top VII A:82, furthest out (from the centre) VI:217

þá¹ *adv.* then *Gr* 3.5.3 (3, 10, 12), 3.5.1–3 ex. 6 (a), I:8, 14, 50, 82, 95, 98, 108, 131, II:7, 71, 72, III:5, V:47, 92 (by then), 101, VI:3, 73, 232 (*followed by* **þá er**), VII B:63, 71, IX:16, 31, 48, 59, 72, X:174, XI:23, 54 (of place), XV:21, XVI:12, XIX:22, 30, 57, XXI:26,

102 (1), 121 (1), XXII:11/3, XXV:20, XXVI A:5, 37, B:15, 50, XXVII:6, 10, 45, 50; at that time VIII:21, 37, 38, 165; at this time VI:8, 38 (2), VII B:6, XV:38; at the time VI:317; then, at any given time VII B:21; by that time XIX:48; **ok þá var** and (which) then (*or* thereafter) was XIX:27; **þá ok þá** at every moment I:37; *introducing main clause after* er-*clause* (*Gr* 3.8.2.1) II:5, 47, 79, III:27, V:44, 163, VI:271, XIX:65, 68, XXI:42, 117; *after* **þá** er-*clause* II:95, III:2, VI:227, 269, 273, 294, VII A:140, VIII:82, XII:78, XXVI B:70; *after* **þá es** VIII:35, 194; **þá . . . es/er** VIII:92, IX:1, XIX:83, 113; **þá . . . er . . . þá** (*second* **þá** *pleonastic*) XXIV:76–77; **þá . . . ef** VIII:124, XXIV:79, XXV:74; **þó . . . þá . . . þó . . . þó** at XXIV:22–24; **þá . . . þau er** (= when *or* if they) **. . . heldr en** XXIV:14–15; *after* **nú er** XVI:95; *after* **ef** XXIV:8, 16, 47, 67, XXVI B:25, 78, 214, XXVII:4, 15, 32; **ef . . . ok . . . þá** XXVII:9 (*see* ok); *after conditional vb. with inverted word order* II:25, *after* **Nú** *and conditional vb. with inverted word order* XXIV:1, XXVII:46; *after* **eptir þat** VI:298, **eptir þat er** VI:302; *after* **hvatki es** VIII:5; *after* **meðan**-*clause* V:111, VI:225; *after* **til þess at** VII A:51; *after* **síðan er** VII A:92; *after* **svá sem** VI:221; *after* **sem** (= when) XII:70, 81; *after* **með því at** VIII:3; XXIV:29, 73; *after* **þó at** VI:118, XIV:146, XXIV:85; *after* **þó** XVI:137; **þá** *as conj.* when 1:30, 138, 144; **þá er/es** *as conj.* (*Gr* 3.8.2.1) when II:21, 56, 94, 111, III:1, 59, 131, IV:10, VI:25, 48, 54, 75, 185, 205, 226, 234, 250, 269, 272, 281, 294, VII A:30, 138, B:31, VIII:16, 188, XI:64, 73, XII:77, XIV:159, XV:4, XIX:52, XXI:30, 37, XXIII:82, XXV:19, XXVI A:26, B:70, XXVII:18, 43; while VI:59, 240; **þá . . . er** when XVI:39, by the time . . . , XV:138

þá² *pron.* (*Gr* 3.2.2) *acc. f. sg., acc. m. pl.* that, this, these, those, them *etc.* I:92, 107, II:90, 113, IV:4, 5, 15, 16, 105, V:8, 42, 60, 87, VI:34, 38 (1), 102, 124, 172, VII A:137, B:9, 25, VIII:89, 118, XI:9, 66, XV:153, XIX:21, 72, 82, 84, XXI:70, 102 (2), 121 (2), 129, 134, 158, XXII:22/1, XXIII:104, XXIV:74, XXV:76, XXVI A:47, B:49, 100, 104, 195, 197, XXVII:36; **á þá** at them XXVI B:194; **þá Þorkel nefju** Þorkell nefja and those with him (*acc.*) VI:120; **við þá Leif** against Leifr and Íngólfr XIX:16; **þá Hjǫrleif** Hjǫrleifr and the others XIX:67; **þá er** *as rel. pron. acc. f. sg.* which, whom (*Gr* 3.8.2.1) VI:4, 324, X:154; *acc. m. pl.* VIII:83, 132 (those who), XIV:172, **þá es/er** VIII:87, XXIII:85, **þá . . . er** those . . . that XXIV:28, **þá alla es** all those who VIII:78, **þá sem** those who XIII:25, whom XIV:166

(normally **þeir sem**; perhaps the influence of Latin grammar; cf. *Gr* 3.8.2.1); **þá er ... af** those (**lǫgmenn**) from whom XXVII:34

þá³ *see* **þiggja** VI:9, XVI:5, 162

þaðan *adv.* from there *Gr* 3.5.3 (5), III:38, VII A:3, 68, 156, 158, VIII:104, 107, X:46, XIX:102, XXI:21, XXVI A:38; *i.e.* from Norway VIII:15, 28

þagall *adj.* silent *Gr* 3.3.8.1 ex. 3

þagna (*past* **þagnaði,** *pp.* **þagnat**) *wv.* fall silent; *past pl.* **þagnuðu** VI:131

þágu *see* **þiggja**

þak *n.* roof; *with suffixed def. art.* **þakit** XXVI A:63

þakðr, þakið *see* **þekja**

þakka (*past* **þakkaði,** *pp.* **þakkat**) *wv.* thank *Gr* 3.6.10; *with acc.* say thanks for XVI:135; *subj.* **Guð þakki yðr** *with acc.* may God thank (reward) you for XVI:118

Þakkráðr *m.* slave of Níðuðr X:175

þambarskelfir *m.* nickname, either 'paunch-shaker' or 'bow-string-shaker' VI:301, VII B:1, 2, 39

þang *n.* seaweed (*in a kenning for the* sea) VII B:40

þangat *adv.* (*Gr* 3.8.2.1) thither, to that place, there I:5, 7, 34, 113, V:79, VIII:65, 67, XIX:81, XXI:17, XXVI A:39, to it V:97, XXVI B:42; onto it (that ship) VI:225; **þangat sem** to where I:99, V:118, XVI:92, 187, XXI:174; **þangat til** up to then VIII:95; **þangat heim** into the precincts there XIV:150

Þangbrandr *m.* Saxon missionary priest VIII:77

þann *pron. acc. m. sg.* (*Gr* 3.2.2, 3.8.2.1) that VIII:120, XXV:94, XXVI B:62, **þann enn** this (*Gr* 3.3.5) XXII:15/4; it (the sword) X:95; that man V:155, XVI:185, him XXII:27/2; **þann mann** this man XIX:34; **þann er** who XIV:56, whom XXIV:40, someone who XXIII:74, which XI:24, **þann (...) er/es/sem** that one (...) who I:43, VII A:33, B:38, XI:9, the one who (*object of* **nefna**) VI:142, the ... who VI:156, the ... which VIII:103, X:78, XVI:33, 118, XXIII:35, **þann sem ... á** the ... on whom XXVII:10; **í þann tíð ... es** at the time when VIII:8–11; **þann vetr** for that winter XXI:107; **þann veg** that way, similarly XXII:8/3, **þann veg ... sem** thus ... as if XXI:159

þannig, þannug (= **þann veg**) *adv.* there, to that place II:55, XIV:42; in this way, thus XXII:38/3

þar *adv.* (*Gr* 3.5.3 (2), 3.8.2.1) there, in that place I:3, 4, 6, 7, 23, 26,

70, 73, 92, 116, II:11, 12, III:3, V:157, VI:11, VIII:46, IX:93, X:5, 87, XI:10, XIII:4, XV:19, 151, XVI:4, XIX:32 (1), XXI:24, 48, 204, XXII:43/2, XXV:110, XXVI A:6, 107, B:2; present XXVII:28; on it (*i.e.* that ship) VI:130; at it (the battle) XXII:35/3; to that place I:74, II:41, VI:14, VIII:107, X:31, XV:25, XXI:73, XXVI B:5; to *or* in that place XXI:108 (1); to that point IV:101; in this matter V:162, VIII:30, 91, 113, on that topic XXIV:28; **þar var** there was there XXI:32, 53, **þar váru** there were there X:7, XXI:168, it was (there) X:8; **þar eru enn** are still there XIX:95; **ef þar er** if there it is XXIII:97; **þar á** on it III:24, XII:37, on that ship XXI:17; **þar á landi** in that country VIII:69; **þar af** therefrom, from them II:6; **þar at** at the point (in the story) where II:16; **þar at boðinu** at that feast XIX:13; **þar austr** there in the east, in Norway VIII:87; **þar frá** from this III:39; **þar fyrir** ahead there XXVI A:16, in front of them XXVI A:25, for this reason XII:35, **þar firi** about that XXIV:57; **þar hjá honum (þeim)** next to him (them) there III:7, 8; **þar í** into them *or* it III:3, 4, XIX:32, in it III:24; **þar í anddyrit** into the doorway there III:21; **þar í skógum** in those woods VIII:53–54; **þar í ofan** down into it XXVI B:229; **þar inn** in there, into it (the **lopt**) XXVI B:117; **þar innan borðs** on board that ship VI:81; **þar með** along with it I:42, and in addition XIV:44; **þar . . . meðal** between them (the eyebrows) XXIII:19; **þar næst** next, secondly VI:315; **þar ór** out of it II:92; **þar til** (cf. *Gr* 3.9.1) for it VII A:98, for that event, *i.e.* at that battle VI:154; **þar um landit** throughout that country VII A:72; **þar undir** under them XI:18; **þar úti** outside there III:37, XXI:108, XXVI A:44; **þar við** for it XVI:25; **þar viðr** thereto, to it VIII:3; **þar** *as conj.* since, whereas XIV:34; where XXVI B:16; **þar er, þar sem** *as conj.* (*Gr* 3.8.2.1) where II:108, VI:202, 267, VIII:44, X:172, XII:20, XV:155, XIX:59, XXI:29, 91, 128, to where II:124, VII A:85, VII B:79, XVI:15, in which XI:17, in a place which XIX:85, from where V:60, XV:145, when VI:292, XVI:69, as VI:265, while, whereas V:11, XIV:116, where, if, in a person in whom XXIII:30; **þar sem heita/heitir** in a place called II:115, XIX:82; **þar . . . sem/es/er** where VIII:17, 19, 52, 65, XIX:53, 54, XXI:92, to where XV:152, XVI:34, the place where XIX:86; **at þar er** to where VI:271, **þar at sem** to *or* at where XXVI B:89; **hér . . . þar er Hǫttr er** here where Hǫttr is, *i.e.* out of Hǫttr I:146; **þar til sem** to where II:150, XXIII:18; **þar til er** until XI:47, XVI:126, XIX:33, 50, XXI:52, XXVI A:89

þarf *see* **þurfa**

þars *conj.* since XVI:53

þat, þau *pron. n.* (*Gr* 3.2.1 and 2) it, the, that, this, those, they *etc.*
I:28, 51, 98, 123, 124, 145, VI:26, 27, 107, 227, VIII:6, 29, 38,
XI:34, 35, XV:25, XVI:23, XIX:23, XXI:3, 5, XXII:23/2, 30/3,
XXIII:4, 39, 54, 97, XXIV:4, XXV:5, XXVI A:4, 19, 35, 43, B:72,
230 (that place, *sc.* **gróf**), XXVII:6; that one I:69; it I:76, 77, 81, 88,
94, 112, 115, 142; this VI:270, 334, IX:57 (as follows); **er þat** it is
XXI:161; **ok er þat** and that is XXVI B:33; **þat var** it was XXI:37,
these were VI:300; **þat váru, váru þat** *with pl. complement* (*Gr*
3.9.8.2; *cf.* I:26–27, *note*) it was III:113, they were X:7; **þat hefir**
there has XXV:6; **þá var þat ekki hús** then there was no building
XIV:157; **þat orða** this (in the way) of words, these words IX:5;
þat it (*Gr* 3.3.5) IX:50; **engi þau** any of those XXIV:3; **þat (...) at**
this (namely) that X:41, XXI:126, XXIV:2, 12, 44, XXVI A:47, 76,
that which, what XXV:80, such a . . . that XXVI B:53; **ok þat at** and
this too, that XI:3; **þat er/es** which X:92, XIV:157, XV:132, XVI:90,
XXIII:13, 77, one that XXIII:14, that which VI:118, VIII:45, what
XV:23, XVI:156, XXVI B:20, as much as XII:1; **þat es af því** such
that from it, from which VIII:70; **þat . . . er** what XVI:67, XXVI
A:66, B:113, that . . . when XXVI A:106; **þat sem** which XV:33,
XXVI B:121, that which, what XIV:57, XV:149, to what VII B:21;
þat allt er everything that XXIV:25; **þat nef er** a nose which XXIII:51;
þat er þá væri whatever might make XIV:14; **þau er/es/sem** which
VI:107, 110, VIII:117, XXIII:24, XXIV:7, XXV:104, XXVI A:57,
which, when they, if they XXIV:15, those that XXI:192, XXIII:42, 47,
XXIV:6; **þau . . . er . . . þau** such as VIII:175; *n. pl.* **þau** *referring to
a man and a woman or men and women* (*Gr* 3.9.6.1) IV:13, 77, 106,
VI:11, 46, VII A:95, X:11, XV:9, 18, 29, 40, 41, 133, XXI:40, 162,
XXVI B:22, 165, *to a herd of horses consisting of a stallion and
some mares* V:6; **þau Guðrún** he (Þorvaldr) and Guðrún XV:5; **þau
Kormak** her and Kormakr IV:14; **þau Einarr** she and Einarr VII B:78

þáttr *m.* (*Gr* 3.1.7.2 (3)) strand, member XXV:15; story, section of a
story, episode I:149, XVI:*title*; section of the law XXVII:34; *acc. pl.*
þáttu alla all sections of the law XXVII:31

þau *see* **þat**

þaut *see* **þjóta**

þegar *adv.* immediately, straightway *Gr* 3.5.3 (8), 3.5.1–3 ex. 6 (a),
I:2, 97, II:28, III:54, V:102, 113, 129, 141, 162, VI:13, VII B:69, 78,

VIII:97, IX:70, XI:20, XIV:118, XV:68, 151, XVI:18, XIX:16, XXVI
B:64, 91, 206; **ok þegar** and (was) immediately XXVI B:92; **þegar
eptir** immediately behind, immediately after III:64, XXVI B:204,
211; **þegar í stað** on the spot VII A:122; **þegar um sumarit** that
same summer XVI:189; *as conj.* **þegar** when, as soon as XXVI A:4,
as long as III:20; **þegar er** (*Gr* 3.8.2.1) when IV:52, XIV:64, 67,
160, as soon as V:94, XV:9, XVI:106

þegit *see* **þiggja**

þegja (*past* **þagði,** *pp.* **þagat**) *wv.* (*Gr* 3.6.9.2 (4, 5)) be silent I:41, 92;
imp. **þegi þú** desist from speaking IX:69

þegn *m.* servant, follower or officer of a ruler, subject, warrior, man
VI:342 (*subject of* **sóttu**), XXII:37/4, 46/3; **þegnar** your servants,
i.e. we XXII:23/1

þeim, þenna, þennan, þeir, þeira, þeirar, þeirra, þeir(r)i *pron.* (*Gr*
3.2.1 and 2) that, this, these, those, they, their, them *etc.* I:31, 34, 89,
90, 110, 111, 112, VIII:2, 5, IX:9, 69, XI:15, XV:8, 39, XIX:2, 8, 10,
XXI:4, 5, 20, 137, XXII:11/2, 16/2, 21/3, XXIII:7, 71, XXV:22, 95,
XXVI A:4 (2), 19, B:4, XXVII:9, 11, 12, 17, 21, 35; **þeir** they, i.e.
those people XXIII:72; **ok þeir** together with those, and also those
V:88; **þeim** that person XVI:152; to/for them XXII:10/2, for them
XXVI B:3, **með þeim** between them XXVII:13; **þeira** of them
XIX:69, **til þeir(r)a** to them XXIV:55, 75, XXVI B:122, at them
XXVI A:49; **ein(n) þeira, einn af þeim** one of them X:21, XIV:169,
XXI:150; **tveggja þeira** of the two of them X:120, 164; **hvárr þeira
. . . annan** each of them . . . the other XI:46; **þeim** *poss. dat.* XIII:3;
**þeir er/es, þeir sem, þeira er, þeirar er, þeiri er, þeim er, þeim
sem** *as rel. pron.* (*Gr* 3.8.2.1) (those) who, which I:78, 132, II:7, 14,
V:27, 57, VI:1, 255, 299, 303 (*referring to* **margs manns**), VIII:47,
140, X:64, 135, 156, XII:60 (**enginn . . . þeir er** no one who), XIII:7,
48, XIV:182, XV:66, 104, XXI:87, XXIII:32, XXVII:16, those people
who XXIII:69, 100; **þeirar sem** of that woman who XIII:21, 41;
þeirar er with which XIV:114; **þeira (. . .) er** of those who XIX:87,
XXII:32/3; **þeim er** to anyone who XIV:90, *note*, those (ships) which
VI:218, **af þeim er** from those who XXI:154, **at þeim er** at those
who XXVI B:220; **þeirra manna er** from among those men whom
XXVII:12 (*with* **taka,** *line* 10); **ór þeim . . . er . . . í** from the . . . in
which XXVII:4–5; **þeir . . . er** those (. . .) who XXIV:62, XXVI
B:63, 119, XXVII:13; **þeir er . . . þeim er** those who . . . those who

XXI:195–96; þeir . . . er . . . með those with whom XXVII:15; þeim . . . er those . . . which XXIII:61; þeirar . . . at such a . . . that VI:91; þeir brœðr the brothers XXVI B:5, *similarly* XV:71, XIX:9; þeir bragnar those men XXII:20/3; þeir Skrælingar the Skrælings XXI:118; þeir *with a singular name* (*Gr* 3.9.6.1): þeir Hǫttr he and Hǫttr I:70; þeir Hólmsteinn brœðr Hólmsteinn and his brothers XIX:15; þeir Gizurr he and Gizurr III:8, at þeim Gizuri up to Gizurr and the others XXVI A:32; þeir Hjǫrleifr Hjǫrleifr and the others (that were not slaves) XIX:64; með þeim Þorvaldi with Þorvaldr and his men XXI:15; þeir Einarr Einarr and the other man III:59; þeir Jón Jón and Guðmundr III:95; þeim Ingólfi Ingólfr and Leifr XIX:18, *similarly* XIX:20, 47; þeir Auðunn Auðunn and the king XVI:130; þeira Bǫlverks of (between) him and Bǫlverkr II:140; þeira Sæmundar of him and Sæmundr VIII:152; þeira Bergþórs of Bergþórr and Hafliði VIII:173; með þeim Haraldi between him and Haraldr VII B:3, *similarly* XIX:12; þeir Þorkell Þorkell and his men, Þorkell and his companions VI:109; þeir Gizurr Gizurr and his party VIII:103; þeir Flosi Flosi and his party XXVI B:87, 120; þeir Karlsefni Karlsefni and his party XXI:89, 119, með þeim Karlsefni with Karlsefni and his party *or* with Karlsefni and Snorri XXI:17; þeir Sveinn konungr King Sveinn and his companions VI:109; þeim Óláfi konungi King Óláfr and his men VI:276; þeir Ósvífr tveir both he (Þórðr) and Ósvífr XV:94; synir þeira Kotkels the sons of Kotkell and his wife XV:134; *with two or more names* (cf. *Gr* 3.9.6.1) þeira Einars ok Eindriða of Einarr and Eindriði VII B:84; þeir Gizurr ok Hjalti VIII:88, 111, *similarly* XV:39, XIX:4, 6, 91, XXI:2, 41, 66, 114, 163, XXVI A:4, B:2, 24; þeira Þórðar ok Guðrúnar between Þórðr and Guðrún XV:19, 80; þeira Teits . . . ok Þorkels . . . ok Þóríðar VIII:8–11, *similarly* XIX:7, XXVI B:193; þeir *anticipating subject* (hirðmennnir) XVI:100 (1). Cf. *Gr* 3.9.6.1

þek *see* þik

þekja¹ (*past* þakði, *pp.* þakðr/þakiðr) *wv.* thatch, roof, cover (af with) VI:152, XIV:10; *pp. f.* þakið re-roofed XIV:13

þekja² *f.* roof; *with suffixed def. art.* XXVI A:32, 53, 68, B:220

þekkja (*past* þekði, *pp.* þekðr) *wv.* recognise IX:124, X:82; þekði mann realised that there was a man XVI:101; -sk *form* þekkjask agree to, accept XVI:77

Þelamǫrk *f.* Telemark in Norway XIX:3

þengill/þeingill *m.* ruler (Eiríkr jarl) VI:280 (*subject of* **hét**), (King Óláfr Tryggvason) VI:361, (Óláfr Haraldsson) XXII:27/1, 49/1, 65/1 (*in address*)

þenna/þennan *pron. acc. m. sg.* (*Gr* 3.2.2) this VIII:100, XII:51, XV:35, XVI:182, XXII:26/2, XXV:79

þér *pron. 2nd person dat. sg. and nom. pl.* (*Gr* 3.2.1) you, yourself I:55, 64, 124, 125, 128, IV:83, VII A:50, IX:79, XIII:23, XVI:111, 120, XXI:134, XXII:25/1, XXIV:13, 85, XXVI A:35, 57, 83, B:20, 55; to you IX:14, X:180, XI:25, XV:92, XVI:24, XXII:65/1; towards you XVI:75; for you XXV:27, XXVI A:80, B:113, for yourself IX:71; *nom. pl. in addressing a king* X:154, XVI:118, XXII:32/2, XXIV:11, 20; *in addressing one's father* XXIV:22, 54; **sjálfri þér** to you yourself X:129; **þér einum** to you alone X:124; *poss. dat.* **þér af hǫndum** from your hands IX:116; **þér í sjóði** into your purse (*or* to you in a purse, *since* **sjóði** *is dat.*) XXII:31/3

þess, þessa, þessar, þessara, þessarar, þessi, þessir, þessu, þessum, þetta *pron.* (*Gr* 3.2.2) this, that, these, those I:15, 24, 25, 27, 30, 36, 39, 45, 54, 55, 61, 68, 119, 127, 128, 132, 137, VIII:3, 5, XI:10, XIII:9, XIV:185, XV:13, 25, 39, XVI:5, 33, XIX:11, 48, XXI:40, 41, 80, 179, XXII:34/1, 46/4, XXIV:26, 36, XXVI A:62, 68, 92, B:25, 30, 62; it I:138; **til þess** about it XXII:22/4; **þetta** *with pl. vb.* V:69, XXV:112 (*Gr* 3.9.8.2); **þetta allt** all this XXVII:30; **þessi** that man (the one who had been killed) I:64; **þessu** (*i.e.* **silfri**) XVI:143 (1); **upp frá þessu** from now on I:107, 148; **þess** for that X:97; **þessa** for this XXVI A:85; **þess er var** such as there was XVI:6; **þess er** who XVI:45, which XIX:27; **þess er** from this that XVI:144, of one who XIII:75; **þess manns er** a person who XXIII:81; **þessu er** that which XVI:37; **þess at** (of) this, that XXVI B:85; **til þess at** for this, that XXIV:14; **þess . . . at** for this, that VI:342 (*with* **skǫp verða**), XIII:8; **þau er . . . ok þessi er** those that . . . and these that XXI:192–93; **þess at meir** all the more VII A:43; **þessir** these men XXVI B:64; **þessir lutir eru þeir enn er** there are these things in addition that XXIV:76; *acc. m. pl.* **þessa** these ones XXIII:65; **til þess** so far XXVII:32 (*see* **vinna**)

þeygi *adv.* not at all XXII:47/1

þí *see* **því**

Þiðrekr af Bern *m.* Theoderic the Great (died AD 526), king of the Ostrogoths XI:*title*, 43, 45, 56, 64, 65, 69, 73, 75

þiggja (*past* **þá,** *past pl.* **þágu,** *pp.* **þegit**) *sv.* (*Gr* 3.6.9.3) receive XVI:4, XXIV:61; accept XVI:152; **þá af** received from XVI:5; **þá at** accepted from VI:9, XVI:162; **þiggja undan** get (someone) let off VIII:89; *pres. part.* **þiggjandi** receiving (them) XIII:48

þik/þek *pron. 2nd person sg. acc.* (*Gr* 3.2.1) you I:107, 129, 136, X:169, XVI:69, XXVI B:94, 144; **þek** XXIV:12 (*object of* **henda**), 48; yourself IX:46, XXIV:83, XXVI A:84

þik(k)ja *see* **þykkja**

þín[1] *pron, 2nd person* (of) you XXVI B:80; **til þín** to you XXIV:1, XXVI B:215

þín[2], **þína, þínar** *poss. adj.* (*cf. Gr* 3.3.9 (21)) your I:135, IV:71, X:145, XI:70, XVI:25, 33, XXV:24, 36, XXVI A:87, B:132

þing *n.* meeting; **darra þing** *is a kenning for* battle XXII:54/2; assembly, conference II:44, VII A:72, 73, 79, B:25, 26, IX:53; *with suffixed def. art.* II:46; i.e. the Alþingi VIII:104, 108 (*with suffixed def. art.*), XV:12, 43, 46, 65, XXVII:40, **í þingi** of the assembly XXVII:44; local assembly in Iceland VIII:45, XIX:108

þingboð *n.* summons to an assembly VII A:72

Þingeyrar *f. pl.* monastery in northern Iceland XIV:180

þingfararkaup *n.* assembly attendance tax or dues VIII:168

þinglausnir *f. pl.* the close of the assembly XXVII:30

þingskǫp *n. pl.* assembly procedure XXVII:5, 26

þingvǫllr *m.* assembly-field, the site of the assembly, Alþingi (southwestern Iceland) VIII:106 (*with suffixed def. art.*)

þínir, þinn, þinna, þinnar, þinni, þíns, þínu, þínum *poss. adj.* (*cf. Gr* 3.3.9 (21) and ex. 11) your I:12, 144, IX:41, 71, X:127, 128, 158, XXII:47/4, XXIV:2, 85, XXV:87, 88, XXVI A:78, B:113

þistill *m.* thistle *Gr* 3.1.7.5 (1)

þit *pron. dual* (*Gr* 3.2.1) you; **þit móðir mín** you and my mother XXVI A:79; *used for pl.* I:52, 54

þitt *poss. adj.* (*Gr* 3.3.9 (21)) your I:145

þjalfi *m.* noose, encircler; *in kenning for the* sea, **þjalfi þangs** VII B:39 (*object of* **skeina**)

Þjazi *m.* a giant II:41, 50, 52, 59, 61, 74, 75, 81

þjóð *f.* people, nation VI:179, VII A:26 (*pl., object of* **hjó**), B:22 (*subject of* **lýtr**), VIII:70; men VI:279 (*subject of* **stǫkk**), people VI:365 (*gen. with* **gœði**), XXII:10/3, 65/4

þjóðá *f.* mighty river; *pl.* **allar þjóðár** *subject of* **skulu rinna upp**

IV:85 (*the older pl. form* **-áar** *would provide an additional syllable and make the metre more regular*)

þjóðgata *f.* high road XXIV:46

þjóðkonungr *m.* king of the people or country, great king XXV:14 (*cf.* **þjóðá**)

þjóðleið *f.* main sea-route, normal route VI:87 (*acc. with* **siglir**)

Þjóðólfr (Arnórsson) *m.* 11th-century Icelandic poet VII B:14

þjófnaðr *m.* theft XV:136

þjófr *m.* thief VII B:52, XV:129, XXIII:53

þjóhnappr *m.* buttock V:146

þjóna (*past* **þjónaði**, *pp.* **þjónat**) *wv. with dat.* serve XIII:12, 25, XXIV:40; attend to, provide for: **at þjóna** looking after XIV:137; *pres. part.* **sér þjónandi menn** people serving her XIII:45

þjónusta *f.* service XIII:46, XXIV:65

þjónustumaðr *m.* servant XII:66

Þjórsárdalr *m.* valley in south-western Iceland VIII:80

þjóta (*past* **þaut**, *past pl.* **þutu** *pp.* **þotinn**) *sv.* sound, blow XXV:65 (a horn)

þó *adv.* yet, nevertheless, even so I:18, 27, 102, 145, II:4, III:63, IV:66, V:6, 7, 122, 144, VI:102, 200, 254, 288, 293 (*i.e.* in spite of being valiant), 316, VII B:3, 31, 72, XI:68, XII:73, XV:5, 14, XVI:49, XXI:12, 73 (in spite of the fact that?), 144, 177, XXII:27/3, XXIII:37, 102, XXIV:22, 51, XXVI A:90, B:101; but XXI:76; however VIII:81, XVI:64, XXI:62, XXIV:12, 23, 57, XXVI B:23, 58; **þó ... þótt** even ... if IX:14; **ok þó** and yet were (*Gr* 3.9.5.2) VI:299, but only XV:139; **eða þó** or rather, or in spite of everything VI:328; **þó** *as conj.* even though, although XVI:137, XXII:65/1; **þó at** *conj.* (*Gr* 3.8.2.2) even if, although VI:4, 85, 117, VII B:27, XVI:147, 177, XXIII:83, XXIV:3, 24, 84, even though VI:226, XIV:145, XVI:35; **þó ... at** even ... if IX:15; **þó ... þó at** still ... even if XIV:91–93

þola (*past* **þolði/þoldi**, *pp.* **þolat**) *wv.* endure XXII:6/2; suffer XII:36, 40, 88; **hann þolði eigi** he could not bear III:126; *with acc. and dat.* put up with something from someone VII B:29; **þola illa** take it badly XXVI B:121

þollr *m.* tree; *in kenning for* man *or* warrior, **hjalms þollr**, *i.e.* Bjǫrn Hítdœlakappi V:171

þopta *f.* thwart, rowing bench (on a ship) VI:279

þora (*pres.* **þorir**, *past* **þorði**, *pp.* **þorat**) *wv.* dare (*Gr* 3.6.9.2 (3))

Þóríðr *f.* daughter of Snorri goði, died 1112 VIII:11
Þórir *m.* Norwegian sea-captain XVI:3, 5, 9
Þórir hundr Þórisson *m.* XXII:8/3, 10/1, 42/1, 43/1, 44/1, 45/4, 51/1.
   Cf. **Hundr**
Þórir kroppinskeggi *m.* 10th-century Icelander VIII:48
Þorkatli *dat. of* **Þorkell**
Þorkell *m.* nicknamed **dyrðill**, one of Óláfr Tryggvason's followers
   VI:165
Þorkell (*dat.* **Þorkatli**) *m.* neighbour of Gunnarr XXVI A:8, 10, 14, 17
Þorkell Elfaraskáld *m.* XXVI A:92 (*see note*)
Þorkell Gellisson *m.* Ari's uncle, 11th century VIII:10, 33, 73
Þorkell máni Þorsteinsson *m.* lawspeaker 970–84 VIII:46, XIX:109
Þorkell *m.* nicknamed **nefja**, Óláfr Tryggvason's half-brother VI:105,
   300, 304; **þeir Þorkell** Þorkell and his men, Þorkell and his
   companions VI:109; **þá Þorkel nefju** Þorkell nefja and those with
   him (*acc.*) VI:120; *archaic nom.* **Þórketill** VI:313
Þorkell hvelpr *m.* brother of Auðr XV:80
Þorkell smiðr *m.* one of the incendiaries at Flugumýrr III:83 (*see note*)
Þorkell í Tungu *m.* father of Steingerðr IV:4, 8, 11, 48, 50, 63, 67,
   107; *dat.* **Þorkatli** IV:100
Þorkell of Víðimýrr *m.* XIV:133
Þorkell *m.* son of **Þorkell í Tungu** IV:107
Þórketill *see* **Þorkell nefja**
Þorlákr Rúnólfsson *m.* 1085/86–1133, bishop at Skálaholt 1118–33
   VIII:1, 183, 194, 195
Þorlákr Þorleifsson *m.* III:43 (*in apposition to* **sveinsins**)
Þorleifr enn spaki Hǫrða-Kárason *m.* 10th-century Norwegian VIII:39
Þorleifr (Ketilsson) hreimr ('cry, noise, shriek') *m.* died 1289; married
   to Gróa's sister III:44
Þorleikr (Þórarinsson) *m.* 11th-century Icelander VIII:183
Þormóðr *m.* priest VIII:92
Þormóðr Bersason (Kolbrúnarskáld) *m.* XXII:19/1, 41/1
Þormóðr Hamalsson *m.* XIX:114
Þormóðr Þorkelsson *m.* XIX:113
Þóroddr Gamlason *m.* XIV:17
Þóroddr goði (Eyvindarson) *m.* 10th-century Icelander who lived at
   Hjalli in Ǫlfus VII A:167
Þórólfr munkr frá Þverá *m.* III:57

Þórólfr tinsmiðr (pewterer) **Þorfinnsson** *m*. III:79

Þórr *m*. a god (one of the Æsir) II:8, IX:34, 59, 65, 69, 72, XIV:81 (**Þórs dagr** = Thursday), XXI:79

Þorskafjǫrðr *m*. fjord in north-western Iceland XV:36

Þorsteinn *m*. farmer in the Western Fjords of Iceland XVI:3, 4

Þorsteinn (Bǫðvarsson) *m*. 10th-century Icelander VIII:79

Þorsteinn genja *m*. III:47

Þorsteinn Gyðuson *m*. descendant of Auðunn XVI:191

Þorsteinn Ingólfsson *m*. **goði**, 10th-century Icelander VIII:45. XIX:108, 109

Þorsteinn Knarrarsmiðr *m*. XXII:43/1, 49/1

Þorsteinn Kuggason *m*. friend of Bjǫrn Hítdœlakappi V:6

Þorsteinn *m*. (uxafótr? — see Oddr*ÓT* chs 71, 73), one of Óláfr Tryggvason's followers VI:300

Þorvaldr Eiðsson *m*. enemy of Bjǫrn Hítdœlakappi V:94, 96

Þorvaldr Eiríksson *m*. XXI:8, 15, 174, 176, 179, 175–80, *textual note*

Þorvaldr (Gizurarson) *m*. Gizurr's father (died 1235) III:32

Þorvaldr Halldórsson *m*. XV:1, 2, 6, 7, 15, 17, 18, 20, 21, 30, 31

Þorvaldr kroppinskeggi *m*. 10th-century Icelander VIII:49

Þorvaldr hinn veili *m*. XXVI A:115

Þorvarðr *m*. husband of Freydís Eiríksdóttir XXI:7

Þorveig *f*. a sorceress IV:1, 68, 72, 105

Þorveigarsynir *m. pl*. the sons of Þorveig, Oddr and Guðmundr IV:Ch. 5, *heading*, 7, 38, 49 (*acc. pl*. **-sonu**), 62, XVIII:121vb28

þótt[1] *conj*. although V:82, 104, VII B:55, XXI:153; even though VI:263, VIII:130, IX:14, X:154, XV:129, XVI:142, 167, XXVI A:56, B:52, 209; even though, whether or not V:106, XXV:108

þótt[2], **þótti, þóttisk, þóttu, þóttusk** *see* **þykkja**

þráðu *see* **þreyja**

Þrándheimr *m*. district of northern Norway, modern Trøndelag VII B:2, 24

þrausk *n*. rustling noise, rummaging I:5

þraut *f*. test, difficulty, trouble XXII:60/1; trial *or* struggle; **at þraut varð fram at ganga** it was going to have to come (on) to a (final) trial XXII:33/4; battle: **þrautar gildr** mighty *or* doughty in battle XXII:42/1

þreif *see* **þrífa**

þreifa (þreifaði, þreifat) *wv*. grope; **um at þreifask** to grope around (oneself) IX:4

þrekstórr *adj.* great in strength and endurance XXII:27/1
þremr *see* **þrír**
þrettán *num.* thirteen (*Gr* 3.4.1) III:22
þreyja (*past* **þráði,** *pp.* **þrát**) *wv.* long for *Gr* 3.6.9.3, yearn X:27
þreyngja (*past* **þreyngdi,** *pp.* **þreyngt**) *wv. with dat.* oppress, trouble, ill-treat, attack XXII:47/2
þreyta (*past* **þreytti,** *pp.* **þreytt**) *wv. with acc.* contend in VII B:28
þreyttr *adj. pp.* tired III:53
þriði *num. adj.* (*Gr* 3.4.1) (the) third II:81, III:79, X:4, XXII:8/4; **hinn þriði** XIV:181, 183, XXIV:36; *acc. sg. m.* **þriðja** VI:163 (*or dat.*?), hinn/enn **þriðja** XIX:90, XXI:194; **ok jarl enn þriðja** (*with* **vá við,** *parallel to* **jǫfra tvá**) and a jarl (who was) the third (enemy) VI:161; *dat. sg. m.* **þriðja** II:153, **þriðja degi í viku** the third day in the week, i.e. Tuesday VIII:197; *nom. sg. f.* **en/in þriðja** X:9, 24; *acc. sg. f.* **ina þriðju** XXVI A:43
þriðjungr *m.* third part; **at þriðjungi** by a third XXV:55; **at þriðjungi hverr við annan** each in a third share with the other, sharing with each other three ways VI:149
þrífa (*past* **þreif,** *past pl.* **þrifu,** *pp.* **þrifinn**) *sv.* grab, grasp I:13, V:101, XXII:42/2, XXVI A:49, 69
Þríhyrningr *m.* three-peaked mountain in southern Iceland XXVI A:5
Þríhyrningshálsar *m. pl.* the ridges of Þríhyrningr XXVI B:11
þrír *num.* three (*Gr* 3.4.1) II:16, III:105, 109, X:3, XIX:49, XXI:49; *m. acc.* **þrjá** II:152, IV:53, VIII:83; *f. acc.* **þrjár** II:151, X:6, XXI:121; *n.* **þrjú** VI:98, 126, IX:97, XXI:44, 65, XXVII:20; *gen.* **þriggja** VI:162, XVI:7; *dat.* **þremr** I:69, VIII:148, 196, XXVI B:47, XXVII:26, 35, 41
þrítøgr *adj.* thirty years old; **tveim vetrum meir en þrítøgr** i.e. thirty-two VIII:196
þrívetr *adj.* three years old XXI:197
þrjá(r), þrjú *see* **þrír**
þrjótlyndi *n.* stubbornness XXIII:76
þrjózka *f.* defiance XXII:23/1
þrjózkr *adj.* defiant, rebellious XXII:46/3
þróask (*past* **þróaðisk,** *pp.* **þróazk**) *wv.* prosper, increase in wealth VIII:162
þrotna (*past* **þrotnaði,** *pp.* **þrotnaðr**) *wv.* dwindle, come to an end; *pres. part.* dwindling XXIII:107

þróttharðr *adj.* strong in valour VI:343

þróttr *m.* valour, courage (*gen. with* orð) VI:180; strength XXV:55

þrúðugr *adj.* mighty IX:65

þrungit *see* þryngva

þrútinn *adj. (pp.)* swollen, inflamed XXII:33/3

Þrymheimr *m.* the mountain home of the giant Þjazi II:42

Þrymr *m.* a giant IX:19, 22, 41, 85, 98, 119, 125

Þrymskviða *f.* a poem about Þrymr IX:*title*

þryngva (*past* þrǫng, *past pl.* þrungu, *pp.* þrungit) *wv.* push, press; *impers. pass.* eptir er ykr þrungit you have been pushed to the rear XXV:14

þræll *m.* slave II:124, 131, VIII:47, XIX:36; *with suffixed def. art.* XIX:55, 64; liegeman, vassal XII:66

þræta (*past* þrætti, *pp.* þrætt) *wv.* quarrel (um about it) III:110; dispute, deny VI:129

Þrœndir/Þrændir *m. pl.* people of Þrándheimr XXII:10/1, 14/4

Þrœnzkr *adj.* Trondish, from Þrándheimr (Trøndelag, Norway) VI:157

þrǫngr *adj.* narrow XXIII:93; *n. pl.* þrǫng narrow ones (*sc.* ears) XXIII:46; *n. as adv.* þrǫngt close together XXVI:44; *comp.* þrǫngri *Gr* 3.3.8.2

þrøngva/þrøngja (*past* þrøngði, *pp.* þrøngðr) *wv.* press XXIII:5

þú *pron. 2nd person sg.* (*Gr* 3.2.1) you I:10, 16, 105, 130, 136, 142, 144, 145, IX:26, 36, 69, 71, X:152, XI:23, XV:24, XVI:22, 32, XXII:31/4, 47/1, XXIV:2, 83, XXV:21, XXVI A:47, 110, B:171; *in address to God*, thou XXIV:18; attu = at^2 þú XXVI B:218; *suffixed to verbs* bittu IX:46 (*see* binda); ertu I:10, IX:24, heyrðu IX:6, láttu IX:116, muntu I:20, IX:11, sáttu IX:99, saztu XXV:23, segþu IX:37, veiztu IX:51 (*see* vita), viltu I:15, þarftu XXIV:8

þungi *m.* heaviness, weight; vera til þunga be of any weight XV:147

þungr *adj.* heavy VI:287; weighty, serious XXII:52/2; stern XXII:14/3; *n. as adv.* ganga oss þungt go hard (*or* badly) for us XXVI B:196

þunnhærðr *adj.* thin-haired XXIII:3

þunnr *adj.* thin VII B:48, XXII:49/2, XXIII:8, 49, 57

þurfa (*pres.* þarf, *past* þurfti, *past subj.* þyrfti, *pp.* þurft) *pret.-pres. vb.* need (*Gr* 3.6.7) VI:27, XVI:51, 53; þurfa at *with inf.* VI:188, XXI:71, XXVI B:110; þarf at rœða needs to be spoken *or* discussed XXIV:75; *with suffixed pron.* þarftu you need XXIV:8; eigi þurfu þér (*Gr* 3.6.9.1 (14)) you need not XVI:111; *pres. subj.* þurfi

XXIV:13; *past subj.* **þyrftu** needed, might need XIV:59; have need (of it) IV:51; *with gen.* VI:108, VII A:110; **þurfa við** be necessary XIV:138, *note*; **þurfa við** *with gen.* be in need of something V:4, XXI:40; **þurfti meira við þat** he needed more help for this, it was a bigger job XVI:155; **alls muntu þess við þurfa** you will need all of that XI:72; *pres. part.* **þurfandi** *Gr* 3.3.9 ex. 25, XIII:47

þurka (*past* **þurkaði**, *pp.* **þurkat**) *wv.* dry; *pres.* are drying XI:18

þurs *m.* giant IX:19, 41

þursligr *adj.* giant-like XXI:11

þúsund *f.* thousand (years) (*Gr* 3.4.1, 3.4.2 (5)) VIII:149, XIX:49

þvá (*pres.* **þvær**, *past* **þó/þváði**, *past pl.* **þógu**, *pp.* **þveginn**) *sv./wv.* wash (*Gr* 3.6.9.3) I:24

þvarr *see* **þverra**

Þverá (Munka-Þverá) *f.* a monastery in Eyjafjǫrðr, northern Iceland III:58

þverliga *adv.* absolutely, flatly II:140; *comp.* **þverligar** more definitely, more emphatically IV:30

þverr *adj.* across; **þvers fingrar breitt** the breadth across a finger XXI:117; *see under* **um**

þverra[1] (*past* **þvarr**, *past pl.* **þurru**, *pp.* **þorrinn**) *sv.* (*Gr* 3.6.9.1 (1)) diminish, be sated VII A:25

þverra[2] (*past* **þverði**, *pp.* **þverðr**) *wv.* decrease (transitive), cause to lessen XXV:55

þversýning *f.* optical illusion, magical delusion XXI:147 (*pl.*)

þvertré *n.* cross-beam, joist XXVI B:116, 201; *with suffixed def. art.* XXVI B:219

því, þí *pron. n. dat.* (*Gr* 3.2.1, 2) the, this, that, it I:95 (*i.e.* his sword), 122 (*i.e.* the beast), IV:64, 66, 72, 73, 75, 86, V:129, VI:19, 23, 322, VII B:28, 77, XIII:24, XIV:87, XV:4, XVI:41, XIX:58, XXI:3, XXVI B:32, XXVII:28; with this XVI:162, XXIII:6; *object of* **jǫkk** VIII:4; *object of* **játa** II:27, 125; **því er** this that (*object of* **ráða**) II:23, which XIX:33, what XXVII:8, 16; **því . . . es/er** that which XXIV:31, such . . . as VIII:126; **því at** of/in this that XXVI A:116; **því . . . at** this . . . that XXVI B:163; **at því at** on this, that XIX:25; **á því** for this (affair) XXII:26/1; **af því** from this VIII:23, as a result VIII:53; **þat es af því** from which VIII:70; **af því at** because (*Gr* 3.8.2.2) VI:290, 314, VIII:98; **at því es/er** according to what VIII:14, 73, XIX:110 (as far as?); **frá því er** from where V:43, about that which XXIV:75; **í því**

in this, by doing this I:53, VII A:50, in this, as a result of this VI:220, at this moment XXVI A:16; **með því at** according as VIII:2, since XXIV:22, 29; **því er . . . með** with which XIV:66; **því nær** about that time? almost (*with* **næstr**)? VIII:58; **því næst** next I:90, V:119, VI:109, XI:43, XXI:180; **því næsta** close to that, almost, practically I:49; **því líkast sem** exactly like XXI:97; **því ǫllu** everything XV:147; **því at einu** only then XIV:141; *dat. of comparison* **því fleira** with more than that XVI:175; **því** *as adv.* therefore II:161, XIV:187, XXIII:94, for this reason, so XIII:45, so (*or dat. with* **í gegn**?) VIII:179; for what (reason), why I:10, XXI:69, 133; **því meira . . . er** the more . . . that IV:58; **því auðveldara . . . sem fleiri** the easier . . . the more V:67; **því, því at** *as conj.* because, for 1:31, 33, 85, 136, III:16, 31, 125, IV:37, 82, V:21, 65, 70, 80, 92, 114, 126, 131, VI:2, 4, 12, 184, 209, VII B:71, XXIV:11, XXVI B:20, 48, 59, 62, for VII A:35, X:130, XII:73, 74, XIV:42, 138, 140, 156, XV:65, 76, 149, XVI:111, 123, 148, 152, 185, XIX:104, XXI:15, 34, 40, 137, XXIII:35, 60, XXIV:27, XXV:80, XXVI A:81, 106, since XIX:81, 87; **því . . . at** for this reason . . . that XXVI B:57

þvílíkr *adj.* similar (**sem** to that which) VI:291; such VI:317, XXIII:34, 36

þýðask (*past* **þýddisk**) *wv.* -sk *form* **þýðask til** pay attention to; be made responsive to XXIV:41; **undir þýðask** attach/apply to oneself XXIV:53

þykkhærðr *adj.* thick-haired XXIII:4

þykkja¹/þykja/þikkja (*pres.* **þykir/þykkir/þikkir**, *past* **þótti**, *past subj.* **þœtti**, *pp.* **þótt**) *wv.* (*Gr* 3.6.9.1 (15), 3.6.9.3, 3.9.4) **1.** *with dat.* seem (to someone) I:29, 146, II:11, 40; be thought XIV:16; *pres. pl. with suffixed neg.* **þykkjat** do not seem VI:348; be considered (*with dat.*, by someone), one considers, thinks something IV:111, V:3 (1), VII A:119, VII B:55 (*past subj.*); **þykkir** it will seem X:127; **þótti vera** was considered to be XVI:190; **þykki(r) mér, þyki(r) mér, mér þikkir/þykki** seems to me (*Gr* 3.6.9.1 (15)) I:145, II:75, 85, 121, IX:109, XXIV:31, seems to me to be VIII:132, seems to me to behave like VIII:102; **þótti þér þat** did that seem to you XVI:69; **munu þér at þykkja** will seem to you in it, you will find it II:77, **þér munu þykkja** you will think XV:92, **þat þótti þeim** it seemed to them XXVI A:19; **þótti þeim vera** they thought it was XXI:150; *past subj.* **þœtti** should seem XXIV:55; *impers. with dat.* **þykki/**

þykkir it seems XV:23, XXIV:57; **mér þykkir/þikkir** it seems to me to be IX:92 ('it seems to me there is lacking only Freyja'), XXVI B:172; **þiki mér sem** it seems to me as if XXVI B:29; **þykkir ykru hváru** you each think XXV:34; **en sjá þykir** than seems apparent, evident I:136; **þykir honum sem** it seems to him as if I:37; **þótti** it seemed V:3 (2; understand **at**?), X:93; **við þótti þurfa** it seemed, they felt were necessary XIV:138, *note*; **honum þótti, þótti honum** he thought (it) VIII:26, XXI:152; **þótti henni** it seemed to her XII:78; **þótti þeim** they found it XIV:34; **þótti mǫnnum** people thought it I:71; *past subj.* **þœtti** it seemed XV:16; **þœtti mér sem** I would have thought that XXI:135; **mér þœtti líkligt at** I would have thought it likely that XXI:134; **firi þykkja** be displeased XXIV:11; **mindi mér fyr þikkja í** I would be displeased XVI:84; **þykkir mikit fyr** one finds it difficult: **svá mikit sem honum þótti fyrr fyr** difficult as he found it before XVI:99; **þykki mér** it seems to me *with nom.* (they *understood*) *and inf.* XXIV:50; **honum/þeim þótti** *with nom.* (*and inf.*) (*Gr* 3.9.4) II:126, VIII:162. 2. **-sk** *form* **þikkjask** consider oneself, feel oneself XVI:151, 179; **þykisk hann** he thinks that he I:27; **munu þeir þykkjask** they will think that they VI:196; **þóttisk** thought that he V:85, thought he was V:114, felt (himself) I:33, felt that he VI:1, 30, 41, felt that he was VI:3; **hann þóttisk eigi mega** he felt he could not III:10; **þóttisk eiga hefna** felt he needed to avenge VI:36; **þóttiz þú** you thought that you XXV:28; **þóttusk hafa** thought they had V:63, 144, XXI:51; **sjá þykkjumk ek** it seems to me V:137; **ek þikjumsk sjá** I seem to see XXVI B:28; **þóttusk sjá** thought they could see XXI:191, they realised, felt sure XXI:153; **þykkjask finna, þykkjask vita** feel sure VI:134, VII A:59, 118, B:54, XVI:101; **þykjask kenna** feel they recognise I:136; **ek þœttumk** I would think myself (to be) XXV:74

þykkja[2] *f.* thought, mood; *dat. sg.* in mood XXII:14/3

þykkr (*pl.* **þykkvir**) *adj.* thick XXIII:6, 22, 48; *sup. n. as adv.* **sem þykkvast** as closely together as possible XXVI B:84

þylja (*past* **þulði,** *pp.* **þuliðr/þulinn**) *wv.* recite, chant, mumble, mutter XXI:68

þyngja (*past* **þyngði,** *pp.* **þyngðr**) *wv.* weigh down, make heavy XXIII:97 (*subj.*)

þyrðu, þyrða, þyrði *see* **þora**
þyrfti, þyrftu *see* **þurfa**

Þyri *f.* daughter of Haraldr bluetooth VI:2, 4, 6, 31

þyrma (*past* þyrmði, *pp.* þyrmt) *wv.* spare, show mercy to, show respect to, reverence; **hverjum í er at þyrma** who ought to be paid respect (regard?) to V:135

þær *pron. f. pl.* (*Gr* 3.2.1, 3.2.2) they, them, those X:10, 19, 116, 160, XII:85, XIV:90, *note*, XXIII:18, 94, XXVI B:6; those very XIX:96; **þær er/sem** *as rel. pron.* VI:2, IX:96, XI:15, XIV:179, XIX:71, XXVII:38, those which XXIII:48, those . . . which XXII:3/1; *in apposition to two names* (cf. *Gr* 3.9.6.1) III:39; **þær . . . es** such . . . as VIII:127

þœtti *see* **þykkja**

þǫgull *see* **þagall**

þǫkk *f.* liking, agreement VI:22; thanks XVI:75

þǫn *f.* tenter, stretcher (frame for preparing animal hides) III:3

æ *adv.* always VI:258, XXII:1/3, for ever X:94; constantly XXV:62

æðra *f.* words *or* sounds of fear *or* despair XXVI B:123

æðrask (*past* æðraðisk) *wv. refl.* be afraid, hesitate VI:84

ær *f.* ewe; *pl.* **ær** IV:45 (*subject of* **sœki**)

Ægir *m.* a giant, personification of the ocean II:1, 75, 85, 86, 121; *dat.* II:11, 13, 14; *as common noun for* sea *in kenning for* ship, **ægis dýr** V:39

æsiligr (œsiligr) *adj.* vehement, furious XXII:55/1

Æsir *m. pl.* a race of (heathen gods II:3, 7, 15, 16, 43, 44, 62, 68, 122, 156, IX:53, 66; *with suffixed def. art.* II:54, 59; *gen. pl.* **Ása** IX:17, 33, 49, 57, *with suffixed def. art.* **Ásanna** II:72, 163; *dat. pl.* **Ásum** II:63, 100, 161 (*with suffixed def. art.*), IX:23, 25, XXII:24/3

æsta (*past* æsti, *pp.* æst) *wv.* request VIII:109, 164 (**til** to do, to arrange); *with gen.* **æstir** you wished for/desired XXV:86

ætla (*past* ætlaði, *pp.* ætlaðr/ætlat) *wv.* think I:79, III:125, XII:11, XXIV:32, XXVI B:58; **þat ætla** think this XXVI B:66; **þat ætla menn** this is believed to be XXI:206; reckon, believe (them to be) XXI:192; expect III:31 (*with dat.*, for someone), VI:316; intend, plan I:19, 39 (*pp.*, *understand* **vera**), III:37, XVI:13, 94, XXI:2, 4, XXVI B:138, 176; **þat hefi ek ætlat** that is what I had intended XXVI B:78; decide VII A:132, VIII:86, XVI:37; decide to go XXI:155; propose XXVI A:38; *with suffixed pron.* **ætlaðak** I had intended XVI:63; **ok ætlar** (ætlaði) **at** intending to, meaning to V:127, VII A:150; **ætlar þú** do you think XVI:32; *with acc. and inf.* (*Gr* 3.9.4) **vér ætlum** we believe XV:54; **kvazk ætla** said he thought

XV:115; **ætla hóf fyrir sér** know what is sensible for oneself, keep within one's capabilities VI:167; **ætla til** make for, intend to go to VII A:9, believe, assume, take it (**svá** like this) I:134 (*imp.*); **ætla til móts við** intend (to go) against, plan to attack XIX:14; *pp.* **til ætlaðr** appointed, detailed, selected (for this) III:105, 107, (to do something) IV:38; **sé til ætlat** it is destined/fated XXVI A:23

ætlan *f.* intention, purpose IV:64, XII:73; opinion VIII:8

ætt *f.* family VII A:90, XXV:15; race? IX:126; descent XIV:132

ætta, ætti *see* **eiga**

ættvísi *f.* (knowledge of) genealogy, family relationships V:138 (*with suffixed def. art.*)

æva *adv.* never X:182

ævi *f.* life, destiny VI:333 (*the phrase belongs with* **sagði**)

æztr (œztr) *adj. sup.* highest XXII:63/4

œði *f.* frenzy (of rage *or* madness) XXIII:108

œgir *m.* terrifier; **ýdrógar œgir** *is a kenning for* bowman, archer, warrior, here the king VII A:19

œpa (*past* **œpti,** *pp.* **œpt**) *wv.* cry out, shout I:90; **œptu á** shouted at it XXI:173; **œptu hátt** uttered/made loud cries XXI:206

œrinn (*n.* **œrit,** *pl.* **œrnir**) *adj.* enough *Gr* 3.3.9 ex. 4; *n. as substantive* VI:91; *dat. n. as substantive* **œrnu** (with) enough, sufficiently XXIV:57; *n. as adv.* sufficiently I:30; **œrit hǫfugt** hard enough XIV:92

œskja (*past* **œskti,** *pp.* **œskt**) *wv.* wish XIV:169; **betr œskja** wish it to be better, wish for more XII:9

Œynir *m. pl.* Eynir, inhabitants of two islands near Trondheim; *gen.* with **konungr** VI:50

ǫðlask (*past* **ǫðlaðisk**) *wv.* -**sk** *form* gain for oneself IX:117

ǫðlíngr *m.* nobleman, king XXII:2/4, 63/1

ǫðru, ǫðrum *see* **annarr**

ǫflugr *adj.* powerful X:171

ǫfund *f.* malice, envy IV:60 (*object of* **ala**), XXIII:46, 49

ǫfundsjúkr *adj.* envious, jealous XXIII:65; *acc. sg. m.* an envious person XXIII:91, 103

ǫfunda (*past* **ǫfundaði,** *pp.* **ǫfundat**) *wv.* envy XIV:160

Ǫgmundr (Þorkelsson) *m.* 11th-century Icelander VIII:191

ǫgurstund *f.* X:182 *see note*

ǫl *n.* ale IX:94

ǫld *f.* people VI:203, 337 (*subject of* **kveðr**), VII A:144 (*subject of* **sá**) ǫldnu *see* **aldinn**

ǫldungr *m.* elder; hero XXVI A:101

Ǫlfossá/Ǫlfusá *f.* river in the south of Iceland VIII:19, XIX:91, 96

Ǫlfossvatn/Ǫlfusvatn *n.* lake near Þingvǫllr, now called Þingvallavatn; it is Iceland's largest natural lake VIII:103, XIX:103

Ǫlfus *n.* district in the south-west of Iceland VII A:167

ǫlgerðarmaðr *m.* brewer of ale III:58

ǫll, ǫllu, ǫllum *see* **allr**

Ǫlmóðr enn gamli *m.* XIX:17

ǫlreifr *adj.* merry with ale XXV:63 (*understand* were)

Ǫlrún *f.* a valkyrie X:9, 10, 12, 34, 74

ǫlskál *f.* ale-cup XXV:83

ǫlstafn *m.* ale-vessel (**stafn** stem (of a ship) = ship *by synecdoche*); *a kenning for a* bowl *or* cup (*part of a kenning for* woman) IV:83

Ǫlvaldi *m.* a giant II:77

ǫnd *f.* soul XXVI B:182; his soul XXII:63/1

ǫndóttr *adj.* piercing, frightful IX:108

ǫnduðusk *see* **andask**

ǫndugissúlur/ǫndvegissúlur *f. pl.* high-seat pillars, the pillars that had supported the roof on either side of the high seat in Ingólfr's home in Norway XIX:52, 73, 92, 95, 96

ǫndverða/andverða *f.* beginning; **firi andverðu** in the beginning XXIV:59; **frá andverðu** in the first place XXIV:62

ǫnnuðusk *see* **annask**

ǫnnur, ǫnnr *see* **annarr**

Ǫnundr Kolsson of Trǫllaskógr *m.* XXVI A:17

ǫr *f.* arrow *Gr* 3.1.7.5 (4), XXI:175, XXII:2/3, XXVI A:37, 44; *acc. sg. with suffixed def. art.* **ǫrina** XXI:176, XXVI A:49

ǫrmum (*Gr* 3.1.7.1 ex. 3) *see* **armr²**

ǫrn *m.* eagle (*Gr* 3.1.8 (5)) II:24; *with suffixed def. art.* II:24, 30; *dat. sg.* **erni** *Gr* 3.1.7.2 ex. 4, *with suffixed def. art.* **erninum** (*dat. of respect or poss. dat.* (*cf. note to* I:12), 'the eagle's') II:30; *gen. sg. with suffixed def. art.* **arnarins** II:31, 58, 155; *pl.* **ernir** XXV:107

Ǫrn = **Fótar-Ǫrn**

Ǫrn *m.* son of Þorkell of Víðimýrr XIV:132

Ǫrn (*gen.* **Arnar**) Bjǫrnólfsson *m.* father of Ingólfr XIX:4, 11, 39

ǫrr *adj.* generous XIV:109, XXII:1/1; *wk. acc. m. sg.* **ǫrva** VII B:37

ǫsnum *see* **asni**

ǫsp *f.* aspen (tree) XXV:16

ǫx *see* øx

ǫxl *f.* shoulder II:33; **yfir ǫxl sér** over his shoulder XII:55

øðli *n.* origin, extraction VII A:90

øngr/aungr *pron. neg.* no one, no = **engi** (*Gr* 3.2.4)

ørindi *n. pl.* = **erindi** IX:40

ørlǫg *n. pl.* fate; war? X:18, 30

ørvænt *adj. n. as adv.* beyond expectation VIII:85; **aldri ǫrvænt** never unlikely, always to be expected V:3 (*understand* **at** that?)

ørœfi *n.* desert; harbourless coast VII A:163, XVI:138, XXI:32

øx/ǫx *f.* axe XXI:149, *with suffixed def. art.* XXI:150, 152, XXVI B:91; *acc. sg.* **øxi** VII A:102; *gen. sg.* **øxar** VII B:48, *dat. sg.* **øxi** XXII:49/2 (*instrumental*), XXVI A:17

Øxará *f.* river flowing into the north side of Ǫlfusvatn XIX:97

øxn, øxna *see* **uxi**

SUPPLEMENT I: GLOSSARY AND INDEX OF NAMES TO EAST NORSE TEXTS
(*NION* 2, XX A–D)

GLOSSARY AND INDEX OF NAMES TO EAST NORSE TEXTS (*NION* 2, XX A–D)

No references will be found in this glossary of East Norse texts to *NION* 1 (*Grammar*) since Old Danish and Old Swedish can differ considerably from Old West Norse. The abbreviations used, however, are the same as those found in the *Grammar* and the main glossary. A second or third occurrence of a word in a line is indicated by (2), (3). Cross-references are provided where there may be difficulty in identifying the entry form.

Grammatical information is included as appropriate. Case forms, for example, are given for text A, and where relevant for C, but only sparingly for B or D since morphological case does not play a significant part in either. The distinction made between masculine and feminine in text D is notional, while grammatical gender of any kind is hard to discern in B (see B, notes on the language 12). The gender of some place-names is undiscoverable (e.g. Alexandria).

The same alphabetical order is followed as in the main glossary. No attempt has been made to normalise the entries, and they are given just as they appear in the texts. Where different grammatical forms of a word occur the order is normally *m., f., n.; sg., pl.; nom., acc., gen., dat.*; and for verbs *inf.; 1st, 2nd, 3rd; sg., pl.; pres., past; indic., subj.; pp.* Certain grammatical forms are considered unmarked and are often, or as a rule, not noted: *sg.* in nouns, adjectives and pronouns, *nom. sg.* in nouns and pronouns, *nom. m. sg.* in adjectives and *indic.* in verbs.

a *prep.* on B:3; **sum allum snællum sambykkis a** on which all sensible people agree A:19

aar *n.* year B:2

af[1] *conj.* if B:8, 11 (2), 15, 22

af(f)[2] *prep.* from, of B:1, 5, 8 (2), 10, 11, 24, C:4, 18, 20; off, from B:32, C:8; according to A:17; by D:11; of, about D:14; **ther aff** about it C:16; as *adv.* away A:18

affat *adj. n.* wanting, deficient A:14

aftæn *m.* evening, eve B:3

aldrigh *adv.* never D:11

aldræ see **all**

aldærmen *m. pl.* masters of guilds B:3

alexandria Alexandria D:15

all *pron. adj.* all D:8; **oll** B:8, 27; *n. sg.* **olt** B:20; *nom. m. pl.* **allir** all, everyone A:10; *m. pl.* **alle** all C:7; *pl.* D:14; **ollæ** B:4; *gen. pl.* **aldræ** A:20; *dat. pl.* **allum** A:3, 12, 19; **allom** C:11

almænni *n. dat.* (the) common people A:6

alsø *f.* probably to be identified with Als, an island in the southern part of Lille Bælt, Denmark C:4

alzwærdugsth *adj. n. sup.* **thet er alzwærdugsth at throo** it is most worthy (for people) to believe D:7

and(h)re see **annær**

annæn see **annær**

annær *pron.* (*num.*) *adj.* second A:22; **annæn** another B:14, 17, 22; *m. pl.* **andre** other C:5, 21; *pl.* **andhre** D:5; **hwar annan** each other C:30

apostelæ *m. pl.* apostles D:5

arf *m.* inheritance B:7, 8, 16, 25, 26

arf skift *n.* division of inheritance B:8

aruing *m.* heir B:9

at¹ *prep.* as *adv.* **þungi ær. at** is burdensome A:13

at² *conj.* that C:12, D:1, 4, 5, 8 (2), 12 (2); **for thi at/forthy at** because B:6, D:11; **swa at** so that, in order that C:25; **tho at** even if B:13

at³ *particle with inf.* to D:8; **till at** to D:12

athælkunæ børnæ *n. pl.* children born in wedlock, legitimate children B:11

attundi *num. adj.* eighth A:26

attæ *num.* eight A:21

Augustine *m.* (St) Augustine D:1

balkær *m.* chapter, section (of the law) A:22, 23, 24

baptisthæ see **johanni baptisthæ**

barn *n.* child B:19; *pl.* **børn** B:13, 22, 26; to the children B:18; *pl.* **børnæ** B:21

barn løt *m.* child's share (of an inheritance) B:24

baþi *conj.* both A:6

benkt *m.* Bengt (this person is otherwise unknown) C:4

bestoodh *sv. past sg.* fought C:14

bewiisthe *wv. past sg.* demonstrated D:6

biscopp *m.* bishop D:15

bleff *sv. past sg.* remained C:32

bok *f.* (law)book A:20; *acc.* A:4, 12; *dat.* A:15

bordh *n.* table C:9; *nom. pl. def.* **bordhin** the tables C:27

breff *n.* letter D:16; *pl.* **breffwe** D:3

breffwe see **breff**

brollups kost *m.* wedding expenses B:23
brollæp *n.* wedding B:17
brollæps dagh *m.* wedding day B:17
broo *f. acc.* bridge C:15
brutin see **sønder brutin**
brysthyggiu *f. dat.* conviction A:18
by *m.* town B:8
byggiæ *wv. 3rd pl. pres.* live A:4, 20
bygningæ balkær *m.* section (of the law) dealing with farming and the community A:26
bymens see **bymæn**
bymæn *m. pl.* men of the town, burghers B:4; *gen. pl.* **bymens** of the burghers B:1
Byrghir *m.* King Birgir of Sweden (1290–1318), crowned 1302 A:3
Byrghiri iarli *m. dat.* Earl Birgir, *de facto* ruler of Sweden 1250–66 A:17
byriæs *wv. 3rd sg. pres.* -s *form* begins B:1
bør *wv. 3rd sg. pres.* behoves; **bør thet sik ey** it is unfitting D:12
børn(æ) see **barn**
Cyrillus[1] *m.* (St) Cyril (*c.*315–86), Bishop of Jerusalem (*c.*349–86) D:1
Cyrillus[2] *m.* (St) Cyril (*c.*380–444), Bishop of Alexandria (412–44) and prominent theologian D:15
dagh *m.* (see **brollæps dagh**) B:17; *pl.* **daghe** days D:16; **dagh** days' B:30
danmark *f.* Denmark C:20
danske *adj. m. pl.* Danish; **the danske** the Danes C:3
diwr see **offe**
doo see **døør**
drap *n. acc.* killing A:24
driffwen see **wt diffwen**
dør *f.* door C:28
døør *sv. 3rd sg. pres.* dies B:8, 13; *3rd sg. past* **doo** died C:16
e *adv.* ever, always; **e mæth** as long as B:19, 26; **æ til** right until C:16
een *num. indef. art.* a(n) C:13, 19, D:14; *nom. f.* C:1; *acc. f.* **ena** a certain C:15; *acc. n.* **eth** a(n) C:23; **ien** one B:9, 11, 24; *n.* **ient** a(n) B:29
eenfaldughe *adj. pl.* simple D:13

eldiærn *n.* fire-steel B:30

ellær see **ællr**

en(n) see **æn**

enghen *neg. pron. adj.* no D:7; **ænik** B:32; *n. sg.* **ekki** nothing B:11; *pl.*(?) D:9; **mæth engi logh** with no legal authority B:13

en waldughær *adj.* sole-ruling, absolute A:2

er see **wæræ**

Erikinum hælghæ *m.* St Eriker, who was king of Sweden *c.*1156–60 A:16–17

Etake *n.*(?) an estate in Västergötland, modern Ettack/Ettak, a small community in Vartofta härad C:1

ey see **æi**

eþsøre *n.* oath to defend the peace of the country (Sweden) sworn by the king and other leaders A:22

faangær *sv. 3rd sg. pres.* gets B:11; **fæær** B:19; *3rd sg. past* **fæk** got, obtained B:21; *3rd pl. past* **fingo** got C:9

fathær *m.* father B:12, 14, 17, 18, 26; *gen. sg.* **fathærs** B:24

fatøkum *adj. dat. pl. as substantive* **almænni til styrls baþi rikum ok fatøkum** for the direction of the common people, both rich and poor A:6; **fatøkum til wærnær** for the defence of the poor A:7

fierþi *num. adj.* fourth A:24

fingo see **faangær**

fiyrsin *num. adv.* four times (see B, notes on the language 13) B:2

fiyræ *num.* four B:3

flere *adj. comp.* (in non-*comp.* sense) many C:5

flokkum *m. dat. pl.* sections, paragraphs (of the law) A:5

flænsborgh *f.* Flensburg B:1, 4

folki *n. dat. sg.* people A:1, 2

for(e) *prep.* for, of A:2; *of time*, before B:17; ago D:16

forfæþrum *m. dat. pl.* predecessors A:16

for glømer *wv. 3rd sg. pres.* neglects B:20

forklaræ *wv. inf.* establish D:12

for thi see **forthy**

forthy *conj.* because D:11; **for thi** B:6

fra *prep.* from; **fra wors hærræ aar** *contamination of* from the birth of our Lord *and* in the year of our Lord B:2

friþær *m. gen.* **spakum til friþær** for the peace of the law-abiding A:8

fromer *adj.* doughty C:19

frugh *f.* lady; **a fyrmer wor frugh aftæn** on the festival of the Assumption (the earlier of the principal feast days of the Virgin Mary; see B, note 1) B:3

full *adj.* complete, fully equipped B:9

fylghiæ *wv. inf.* follow A:16

fyndir *f. acc. pl.* finds, findings (of lost property) A:24

fyr *adv.* previously B:6; already B:22; **førre** before D:11

fyrmer[1] *adj. comp.* earlier (see **frugh**) B:3

fyrmer[2] *adv.* previously A:20

fyrsti *num. adj.* first A:2, 21; *acc. n. pl.* **fyrstu** A:1

fæk see **faangær**

fæmpti *num. adj.* fifth A:25

færth see **iorthæ færth**

fæthærn *n.* paternal inheritance B:12

fæær see **faangær**

førre see **fyr**

føræ *wv. inf.* move, take B:32

gaf see **giuæ**

gaghin *n.* gain, growth B:27

gangæ *sv. inf.* go; **af fathærs løt ut gangæ** come from the father's share B:24

gardhin *m. acc. sg. def.* the farm C:15

gawo see **giuæ**

gif see **giuæ**

gift man *m.* husband B:23

giptæ mal *n. acc. pl.* marriage(s) A:23

gitum *sv. 1st pl. pres. (as aux. with pp.)* **hwat wir gitum til satt. ællr aff takit** whatever we can add or remove A:18

giuæ *sv. inf.* give B:14; *3rd sg. pres. subj.* **gif** is to give, shall give B:18; *3rd sg. past* **gaf** gave B:5; **gawo** (*3rd pl. past*) **sik alle godha trøst** felt confident, felt themselves to be safe C:7

giæstning *f. acc.* provision of accommodation A:25

giømæ see **gømæ**

giøtæ *m. gen. pl.* of the Geats A:3

glømer see **for glømer**

goodh *adj.* good, fine C:13; *acc. f. sg.* **godha** (see **giuæ**) C:7

gooz *n.* goods, property B:26, 32; **gwoz** B:20; *pl.*(?) **gotz** fiefs C:24

gotz see **gooz**

gudelighet *f.*(?) devoutness, piety D:8

Gvþ *m.* God A:1

gwoth *adj. n.* good, solid B:18

gwoz see **gooz**

gømæ *wv. inf.* **giømæ** protect, preserve A:22; *inf.* -**s** *form* **gømæs** be observed A:7; *3rd sg. pres. subj.* **gømæ** is to keep, is to look after B:19

haffde/haffdhæ/haf(f)do see **hauær**

haffs *n. gen.* (the) sea A:4

haffwe see **hauær**

hafn *f.* harbour B:32; **hauæn** B:31

hafth see **hauær**

hald *n.* succour, protection C:23

haldæs *sv. inf.* -**s** *form* be kept A:7

halft *adj. n.* half B:21, 22

hallande *n. dat.* Halland C:18

ham see **han**

han *pron.* he B:19, 20, 22, C:14, 16, 20, D:5, 15, 16; *oblique case* **ham** B:29; *gen. as poss. adj.* **hans** his A:2, 11, 23, B:20, 21 (*refl.*), 21 (2), D:10

hauæn see **hafn**

hauær *wv. 3rd sg. pres.* has B:11; **hæuær** B:22; **haffwe** (*pres. pl.*) **ther vndher paa** are astonished about it D:2; *past sg.* **haffdhæ** (*as aux. with pp. forming past perfect*) had D:2; **haffde** (*3rd sg. past*) **them kæra** held them dear, held them in affection C:26; *3rd pl. past* **haf(f)do** had (*as aux. with pp. forming past perfect*) C:8, 23, (*as aux. with pp. forming past perfect*) 29; *3rd pl. past* **hafth** B:6

hedherligh *adj.* honourable D:15

helgesthe *adj. sup. wk.* most holy D:10

helighet *f.*(?) holiness D:4

herra *m.* (as title) Sir C:4, 13, 18; **wors hærræ** (*gen.*) **aar** the year of our Lord B:2

hertoghen *m. nom. sg. def.* the duke C:24; *dat. sg. def.* **hertoghanom** C:23; **hærtugh** Duke B:4

hesta *m. pl.* horses C:29

heþin *adj.* heathen A:11; *nom. m. sg. wk.* **heþne** A:14; *dat. m. sg.* **heþnum** A:11

hin *def. art.* A:14; *dat. m. sg.* **inum** (see **Erikinum hælghæ**) A:17

hittum *wv. 1st pl. pres.* find A:11

huilkin *pron. acc.* (as expression of wonderment) **huilkin kamp** what a fight! C:14; *n.* **hwicketh** which (things) D:6

hun *pron.* she B:9, 10, 11, 22

husbond *m.* master of the house, husband B:8

husfrugh/husfrø *f.* wife B:8, 14

hwannær *adv.* whenever B:12, 32

hwar see **hwær**

hwat see **hwo**

hwicketh see **huilkin**

hwit see **palne**

hwndrada *num.* hundred C:6

hwo *pron.* **hwo sum** whoever B:29; *acc. n.* **hwat** what(ever) A:18; **hwat (. . .) ær** whatever A:11, 14

hwær *pron.* each B:14, 18; **hwar annan** each other C:30

hælade *m.* warrior C:13, 19

hælghæ see **Erikinum hælghæ**

hændhe *wv. inf.* **oss skall enghen vndher oc thwiffwell hændhe ther om** we shall not experience any amazement or doubt about it D:9

hænt *wv. pp. pl.* fetched C:31

hær *adv.* here B:1

hærræ see **herra**

hærtugh see **hertoghen**

hæuær see **hauær**

hørdhe *wv. pp. pl.* heard D:11

i *prep.* in A:11, 12, 14, 16, B:4, 8, 31, C:10, D:3, 4, 5, 15 (2); at A:15; in(to) B:21, C:29; into A:21, B:32; on B:29; on (to) B:29 (2); of D:15; **j** in D:8

iarli *m. dat.* Earl A:17

iauæn *adj.* equal B:9; as *adv.* **iauænt** equally B:21

iek *pron.* I D:8, 12, 13; *oblique case* **mik** D:4, 16

ien see **een**

inum see **hin**

iorthæ færth *f.* funeral B:24

iorþir *f. acc. pl.* land and farming A:25

iutland *n.* Jutland B:5

j see **i**

jeronimus *m.* (St) Jerome D:4

jnnan *prep.* in, at C:1; *of time*, within, at C:2

johanni baptisthæ *m.* John the Baptist D:4–5

jærthegnæ *n. pl.* miracles D:10

kamp *m. acc.* battle C:14

karsson see **wlff karsson**

kirkiu balkær *m.* ecclesiastical section (of the law) A:21

kirkiu laghum *n. dat. pl.* ecclesiastical law A:15

kiøp see **løsøræ kiøp**

klæthær *n. pl.* clothes B:10

koll *m. acc.* **lupu hwar annan vm koll** ran each other down, knocked each other over C:30

komo see **kummær**

kompne see **kummær**

kost *m.* provisions, sustenance B:30; (see **brollups kost**) B:23

krankær *adj. comp. wk.* (the) worse, (the) poorer B:11

krauæ *wv. inf.* demand B:12; *3rd pl. pres. subj.* may demand B:13

kristnu ræt *m. dat.* Christian law A:14

kummær *sv. 3rd sg. pres.* comes, arrives B:32; *3rd pl. past* **komo** were coming C:12; *pp. m. pl.* **kompne** come, arrived C:3

kunungær *m.* king A:3; *acc.* **kunung** A:22; *gen.* **kununx** A:3, 22; *dat.* **kunungi** A:17

kunæ *f.* wife B:17, 21

kæra *adj. m. pl.* dear C:26; *sup. wk.* **kæresthe** dearest D:1

lagh *n. pl.* law A:5, 7, 8; *acc.* A:1; *gen.* **lagha** A:10; *dat.* **laghum** A:5, 16; *pl.* **mæth engi logh** with no legal authority B:13

laghmaþær *m.* law speaker A:2

laghsaghu *f. dat.* enunciation of the law, oral law A:12

laghæ balkæ *m. acc. pl.* sections, parts (of the law) A:21

laghæ yrkir *m.* lawmaker A:10

latit see **læt**

leffneth *m.* life D:10

legghe *wv. inf.* **ther till legghe** add to them D:13

lente *wv. 3rd sg. past* granted (as fiefs) C:24

ligherwiiss *adv.* **ligherwiiss som** just as if D:2

lighnes *wv. pres.* **-s** *form* resembles D:5

liighæ *adj.* equal, comparable D:4

liuær *wv. 3rd sg. pres.* is (still) alive B:8, 12

logh see **lagh**

lotæ see **læt**

lupu *sv. 3rd pl. past* ran C:30

lykkia see **utæn lykkia**

læt *sv. 3rd sg. past* let, caused A:14; **lotæ** (*3rd pl. past*) **scriuæ** had written, caused to be written B:4; *pp. n.* **latit** put C:29

læthæ *adj. pl.* of little weight, trifling D:13

løsøræ kiøp *n. acc. pl.*(?) buying of goods and chattels A:25

løt *m.* share B:9, 24

løøst *wv. pp. n.* **aff sik løøst** taken off, removed C:8

ma *pret.-pres. vb. 3rd sg. pres.* may, can B:32; *3rd pl. pres.* **mugh** B:12; *3rd pl. past* **matto** could, were able C:25

maat *m. acc.* food C:9

magnusæ *m. gen.* King Magnus of Sweden (1275–90), nicknamed *ladulås* 'barnlock' supposedly because he forbade his nobles, during their travels around the country, to claim maintenance from the peasants A:3; *dat.* **magnusi** A:17

mal see **giptæ mal**

man *m.* man C:10; *gen. pl.* **mannæ** of men, of people A:20; *dat. pl.* **mannum** to men, to people A:12; *as indefinite subject* **man** one A:21

manghe *adj. pl.* many D:16; *as substantive* many people D:2

margh *adj. f. sg.* many a C:28, 32

mark *f.* mark (monetary unit) B:14

matto see **ma**

megtughe *adj. pl.* powerful D:6

mellom *prep.* between C:15; **mellum** A:4, 6; **mell** B:26

mere *adj. comp.* more (in number) C:6; *sup. as substantive* **mest** most B:9

meth see **mæth**[1]

mothær *f.* mother B:13; *gen.* **mothærs** B:24

moyses *m.* Moses A:1

mugh see **ma**

mykæt *adj. n. as substantive* (how) much B:18

mæn *conj.* but D:7

mænneske *n.*(?) *pl.*(?) people D:11

mæth[1] *prep.* with B:13, 30; together with B:21, 22; with, by B:5; **meth** with D:6; **mæþ** with, through A:1; with, containing A:4; **ær . . . mæþ** with which A:22

mæth² *conj.* while B:19, 26

mæthærn *n.* maternal inheritance B:13, 18, 19

mæthælst *adj. sup. wk.* (in non-*sup.* sense) average, middling (one) B:10

mæþ see **mæth¹**

naath *f.* grace B:5

nogeth *pron. n.* something D:3; *pl.* **noghre** any D:13

nyth *adj. n.* new D:3

nytæ *wv. 3rd pl. pres. subj.* are to enjoy, are to have the benefit of B:23

næfnæ *wv. 3rd sg. pres. subj.* is to cite, is to summon B:18

næfst *f. acc.* punishment, chastisement A:8

næra *wv. inf.* support, maintain C:25

nøkæs *wv. 3rd sg. pres. -s form* (if their property) diminishes B:27

oc see **ok¹** and **ok²**

offe diwr *m.* Offe 'animal' (see C, note 4) C:21

offwergiffwe *sv. inf.* dismiss, drop D:14

ognær *f. gen.* dread, terror A:8

ok¹ *conj.* and A:1, 4 etc., C:4, 5 etc.; **oc** B:2, 3 etc., D:3, 5 etc.

ok² *adv.* also A:2; furthermore A:14; **oc** also D:5 (3)

oll/ollæ/olt see **all**

orlof *n.* permission B:33

o ræt *m. acc.* wrong, injustice A:7

o snællum *adj. dat. pl. as substantive* (the) unwise, (the) foolish A:9

o spakum *adj. dat. pl. as substantive* (the) unruly A:8

ospent *wv. pp. f.* unfixed, unbuckled C:32

o þarfft *adj. n.* unnecessary, unsuitable A:13

paa *prep.* **ther . . . paa** about it D:2

palne hwit *m.* Palne 'white' may have been a member of a landowning family in Thy, northern Jutland (cf. Pipping 1926, 336–7) C:4

par *n.* pair B:11; *pl.* B:10

peder porsse *m.* Peder Porsse (see C, note 4) C:18

penning *m.* (in) money B:15

plata *f.* breastplate C:32; *acc. pl.* **plator** C:8

porsse see **peder**

ran *n. acc.* robbery A:24

rasker *adj.* able, vigorous C:19

rasklika *adv.* quickly C:27, 31

rathmen *m. pl.* (town) counsellors B:3

raþ *n. acc.* counsel, deliberations A:18

riddare *m. pl.* knights C:5

ridhande *sv. pres. part.* riding C:12

rikum *adj. dat. pl. as substantive* (the) rich A:6

roþæræt *m. acc.* special legal provisions governing life on board ship during time of war A:23

rymde *wv. pp. m. pl.* **waro . . . rymde** had fled, had escaped C:22

ræt *m.* law B:23; *acc.* right, justice A:7; (see **o ræt**) A:7

rætningær *f. gen.* correction A:10

rætwisir *adj. m. pl.* just, honest A:10; *dat. pl. as substantive* **rætwisum** (the) just, (the) honest A:9

saat *sv. 3rd sg. past* sat C:10; *3rd pl. past* **satho** C:9

saer *n. acc. pl.* wounds A:24

saffdh see **sighe**

sagde/sagdo see **sighe**

sagh see **sighe**

saghþum see **sighe**

samma *adj. acc.*(?) *f. sg. wk.* same C:2; *wk.* **samæ** B:23

samþykkis *wv. 3rd sg. pres.* -**s** *form, with dat.* **sum allum snællum samþykkis a** on which all sensible people agree A:19

samæ see **samma**

samæn sættiæ *wv. inf.* put together, compile A:19

sanctus *Latin adj.* (the) holy D:1

sandhet *f.*(?) truth D:8, 12

sanneligh *adv.* truly D:7

sannesthe *adj. sup. wk.* (the) most veritable D:8

satho see **saat**

satt see **sættiæ**

saw *sv. 3rd sg. past* saw D:15

scal see **skal**

scra see **skra**

scriuæ *sv. inf.* **lotæ scriuæ** had written, caused to be written B:4; *2nd sg. past* **skreffsth** wrote D:3

scul see **skal**

sial *f. acc.* soul A:21

sighe *wv. inf.* **sighe aff** tell about D:14; *pres. sg.* **sigher** says D:1; **sagde** (*3rd sg. past*) **ther aff** told about it C:16; *1st pl. past* **saghþum** stated, said A:20; *3rd pl. past* **sagdo** said (see C, notes on the language 6) C:11; *pp. m.*(?) **sagh** stated B:23; *n.* **saffdh** told D:2

siit see **sin**

sik *refl. pron. oblique case* themselves (see **giuæ**) C:7, (see **løøst**) 8, 9; 'itself' (see **bør**) D:12

sin *refl. poss.* her B:23; *f.*(?) his B:5; *acc. f. sg.* **sinæ** one's A:22; *n.* **siit** its B:19; **sint** his B:32; **sith** his D:15; *dat. n. sg.* **sinu** his A:1; *acc. m. pl.* **sina** their C:29

siundi *num. adj.* seventh A:25

siþærsti *adj. sup. wk.* last A:26

siælwær *adj.* himself A:1

skal *pret.-pres. vb. 3rd sg. pres.* shall, is to A:21, B:20, 24; **scal** B:14; **skall** shall (see **hændhe**) D:9; *1st sg. pres.* **skall** should D:13; *2nd sg. pres.* **skalth** should, must D:1; *1st pl. pres.* **skulum** shall A:15, 19; *3rd pl. pres.* **skulu** shall, is to A:5, 7, 8; **scul** shall, are to B:29

skathæ *m.* loss B:27

skift see **arf skift**

skiftæs *wv. inf. -s form* be divided B:21; *3rd sg. pres.* **skiptis** is divided A:20

skiold *m.* shield B:15

skip *n.* ship B:29, 31, 32, 33

skipaþi *wv. 3rd sg. past* made, compiled A:1; *pp. n. pl.* **skipaþ** drawn up, compiled A:6

skipman *m.* member of the crew B:32; *pl.* **skipmen** (the) crew B:29; *gen. pl.* **skipmenz** (the) crew's B:33

skipthiuf *m.* thief on board ship B:28

skiptis see **skiftæs**

skipwistir *f. acc. pl.* the provisioning of ships levied by the king for aggressive or defensive war A:23

skiæl *n. pl.*(?) **til . . . skiæl** as a distinction, to distinguish A:6; *n. pl.* **skæll** grounds, reasons D:6, 11, 13

skra *f.* (law) scroll, legal code B:1, 6; **scra** B:4

skreffsth see **scriuæ**

skutin *sv. pp. n. pl.* pushed aside C:27

skæll see **skiæl**

slike *adj. nom. m. pl. as substantive* such people C:21

snællum *adj. dat. pl. as substantive* (the) wise, (the) sensible A:9; wise, sensible (see **samþykkis**) A:19; (see **o snællum**) A:9

som *conj.* as (see **ligherwiiss**) D:2, 15; who D:9; which D:4, 10, 14; **sum** as A:14, B:24; which (see **a**) A:18; **hwo sum** whoever B:29

son *m.* son A:3; **syn** B:14

spa see **wiger**

spakum *adj. dat. pl. as substantive* (the) peaceable, (the) law-abiding
    A:8; (see **o spakum**) A:8

spiyt *n.* speer B:15

stal *m. acc.* stable C:29

stark *adj.* strong C:19

stathfæst *wv. 3rd sg. past* confirmed B:5

stathæligh *adj.* town, for the town B:6

sthoræ *adj. pl.* great D:10, 12

stiyp mothær *f.* stepmother B:22

striidh *f.* battle C:1

strøms see **sæw strøms**

styrls *f. acc.* guidance A:6

styræman *m.* captain (i.e. captain's) B:33

stæl *sv. 3rd sg. pres.* steals B:29

sum see **som**

summi *adj. nom. m. pl.* **the . . . summi** some of them C:29

swa *adv.* thus, in the same way A:2; such A:14; so D:12; **swa at** so
    that, in order that C:25

swena *m. pl.* squires C:5, 30

swerike *n. acc.* Sweden C:22

sweæ *m. gen. pl.* of the Swedes A:3

swørth *n.* sword B:15

syn see **son**

sywffn *f.* vision D:14; *n.(?) pl.* visions, revelations D:6

sændhe see **sændir**

sændi see **sændir**

sændir *wv. 3rd sg. pres.* sends A:2; *3rd sg. past* **sændi** sent A:1; *past
    sg.* **sændhe** D:4, 16

sæng *f.* bed B:10

sætti *num. adj.* sixth A:25

sættiæ *wv. inf.* (see **samæn sættiæ**) A:19; **sættæ** place, put B:29; *1st
    pl. pres.* **sætium** (will) place, (will) include A:12; *pp. n.* **gitum til
    satt** can add A:18; *n. pl.* prescribed A:5

sæw strøms *m. gen.* the name of a river on the border between the
    provinces of Uppland and Västmanland A:4

sømdær *f. gen.* **rætwisum ok snællum til sømdær** to the honour of
    the just and the wise A:9

sønder brutin *sv. pp. f.* broken to pieces C:28

takær *sv. 3rd sg. pres.* takes B:9, 14, 17; *3rd sg. pres. subj.* **takæ** is to take B:9, 10; *3rd pl. pres. subj.* are to take B:21; *pp. n.* **gitum . . . aff takit** can take away, can remove A:18

tha *adv.* then B:20, C:2, 10, 22, 27, 31, D:12; **þa** A:10, 19

then[1] *pron.* that C:10; *n.* **thet** it B:19, 20, D:7, (see **bør**) 12; that B:20 (2); *nom.*(?) *n.* **þæt** that A:13; *acc. n.* A:12, 13 (2), 15; *gen. n.* **thes** its D:12; *pl.* **the** they B:6, 12, 19, 23, C:22, 25, (see **summi**) 29; **thee** C:17; *gen. as poss. adj.* **thera** their C:8 (*refl.*), 30, 31; **theræ** B:12 (*refl.*), 13 (*refl.*), 22, 26; **thers** theirs B:27; *oblique case* **them** them B:5, C:11, 24, 25 (*refl.*), 26, (see **hauær**) 26 (2), D:3, 5, 14; *dat.* **þem** them, those A:3

then[2] *def. art.* B:10, 23, D:14; *acc.*(?) *f. sg.* C:2; *nom. m. sg.* **þæn** A:21; *pl.* **the** (see **danske**) C:3, (see **vplænzske**) 12

ther *adv.* there C:12, 14, 32; **ther aff** about it C:16; **thær yuær** in addition B:9; **ther . . . paa**, **ther . . . vppa**, **ther om** about it D:2, 7, 9; **ther till** (see **legghe**) D:13; *as conj.* where, when D:3; **thær** B:17; **þær** where A:20; which D:16; **thær** who B:9; which B:4, 20; that, as B:23

thi see **forthy**

thinnæ *pron.* this B:4; *nom. f. sg.* **þæssi** A:20; *acc. f. sg.* **þessæ** A:4, 13; *dat. f. sg.* **þæssæri** (for expected *gen.*) A:15; *dat. pl.* **þæmmæ** A:16

tho *adv.* nevertheless B:14; *as conj.* **tho at** even if B:13

thre *num.* three B:14; *n.* **thry** B:10; *gen.* **thrigi** B:30

thrigi see **thre**

throo *wv. inf.* believe D:8

thry see **thre**

thu *pron. 2nd sg.* you D:1, 2, 3, 4, 6

thusænd *num.* thousand B:2

thwiffwell *m.*(?) doubt D:7, 9

thy *adv.* therefore D:13

thynæ *poss. adj. 2nd sg.* (modifying *pl.*) your D:3, 11

thær see **ther**

tidhande *n. pl.* tidings, news C:11

tiidh *f. acc.*(?) time, period C:2

tiit *adv.* thither, there C:3

til *prep.* to A:9, C:22; for A:6, 7, 8, 9 (2), 19; for, as B:19; (followed by clause) in evidence of B:18; **till** (followed by *inf.* phrase) D:12;

as conj. **æ til** right until C:16; *as adv.* **ær til** exists B:15; **till** (see **legghe**) D:13; **til satt** (see **sættiæ**) A:18

till see **til**

til økiæ *wv. inf.* add A:15

timæ *m. dat.* time, era A:11

tiughæ *num.* score, unit of twenty B:2

træno *n. dat. sg. def.* the tree C:10

trøst *f. acc.* confidence (see **giuæ**) C:7

tu *num.* two B:10, 21

tuhundræth *num.* two hundred (to be analysed as two separate words **tu hundræth**) B:2; **twhundradhe** (**tw hundradhe**) C:17

tundær *n.* tinder B:30

twhundradhe see **tuhundræth**

uilium see **will**

um *prep.* about A:22, 23, 24, 25, 26; **vm** about, concerning B:7, 16, 25; **vm koll** (see **koll**) C:30

upbyriæn *f. dat.* beginning A:15

upplænzkum see **vplænzske**

ut *adv.* out B:18, (see **gangæ**) 24

utæn lykkia *wv. inf.* exclude A:13

vbygd *wv. pp.* uninhabited B:29

vhørligth *adj. n.* unheard of, strange D:3

vm see **um**

vndher *n.* wonder, amazement (see **hauær**) D:2; *pl.*(?) (see **hændhe**) D:9

vndherligh *adj.* miraculous D:14; *pl.* **vndherlighe** D:6, 10

vplænzske *adj. m. pl.* Upplandic, of Uppland; **the vplænzske** the Upplanders, the men of Uppland C:12; *dat.* **upplænzkum** A:5

vppa *prep.* **ther . . . vppa** about it D:7

vskift *wv. pp.* unapportioned, not shared out B:26

vtæn *prep.* without B:33

wald *n.* power (see C, note 6) C:24; **wold** B:5

waldughær see **en waldughær**

war/ware/warin/waro see **wæræ**

wari/warum/warþt see **wors**

wi *pron.* we A:11; **wij** D:9; **wir** A:12, 13, 15, 16, 18, 19, 20; *oblique case* **oss** us D:8

wiger spa *m.* Wiger (the) prophetic, Wiger (the) wise, otherwise unknown A:11; *gen.* **wigers** Wiger's A:5

wiid see **with**

wij see **wi**

wilium see **will**

will *wv. 1st sg. pres.* will, want to D:13; *1st pl. pres.* **uilium** will, wish to A:13; **wilium** A:16; *3rd pl. pres.* **wilæ** want B:12, 19

wintær *m. pl.* winters B:2, 3

with *prep.* with B:9, 22; **wiid** at, by C:9; *as adv.* **þurfpti æi . . . wiþ** one would not need, would not be needed (see **þurfpti**) A:10

withe see **withæ**

withner *wv. pres. sg.* testifies D:15

withæ *pret.-pres. vb. inf.* know D:1; **withe** *pres. pl.* D:9

witnæ *n.* testimony B:18

wiþ see **with**

wlff karsson *m.* Ulf Karlsson, a Swedish nobleman and trusted servant of King Magnus C:13

wold see **wald**

woldemar *m.* Duke Valdemar (IV) of Southern Jutland (born *c.*1262, duke 1283–1312) B:5

wordo *sv. 3rd pl. past (as aux. forming pass.)* were C:27

wors *poss. adj. gen. m.* of our B:2; *f.* **wor** our (see **frugh**) B:3; *dat. f.* **wari** A:17; *acc. n.* **warþt** A:18; *dat. pl.* **warum** A:16

wrangum *adj. dat. pl. as substantive* (the) unjust, (the) dishonest A:9

wt driffwen *sv. pp. m.* driven out C:20

wæl *adv.* well C:25, 26; **wæl hwndrada** a good hundred C:6; **wæl twhundradhe** a good two hundred C:17

wænther *wv. pres. sg.* expect D:8

wærnær *f. gen.* defence, protection A:7

wæræ *sv. irregular inf.* be *(as aux. forming pass.)* A:5, 8, 14; *3rd sg. pres.* **er** is D:7; **ær** A:12 (2), 13, 14 (2), 21, 22, 23, 24, 25, 26, *(as aux. forming pass.)* B:23, 26; **ær til** exists B:15; *3rd pl. pres. subj.* **wæræ** are to be, shall be B:27; *3rd sg. past* **war** was A:2, 11, C:1, *(as aux. forming pass.)* 20, D:4; *past pl.* **ware** were *(as aux. forming pass.)* D:11, 12; *3rd pl. past* **waro** C:17, *(as aux. forming pass.)* 31; were, had *(as aux. with pp. forming past perfect)* C:3, 22; *3rd pl. past subj.* **warin** were A:10

yrkir see **laghæ yrkir**

yuær *prep.* **thær yuær** in addition B:9

þa *adv.* see **tha**

þarfflikt *adj. n.* beneficial A:12

þarfft see **o þarfft**

þarwæ *f. gen. pl.* benefit A:19

þem see **then**[1]

þessæ see **thinnæ**

þingmal *n. acc. pl.* assemblies and court procedure A:26

þiuffnæþ *m. acc.* theft A:24

þriþi *num. adj.* third A:23

þungi *m.* **þungi ær. at** is burdensome, is difficult A:13

þurfpti *pret.-pres. vb. 3rd sg. past (with gen.)* **þa þurfpti æi lagha wiþ** then one would not need laws, laws would not be needed A:10

þæmmæ see **thinnæ**

þæn see **then**[2]

þær see **ther**

þæssi see **thinnæ**

þæssæri see **thinnæ**

þæt see **then**[1]

æ see **e**

æfn *n.*(?) means, wealth B:15

æi *adv.* not A:10; **ey** B:6, D:12

ælskade *wv. 3rd sg. past* loved C:26

ællr *conj.* or A:18; **ellær** B:17, 18, 26

æn[1] *conj.* but A:8, 9; **en** B:19, 23; **enn** B:12

æn[2] *adv.* even C:6

ænik see **enghen**

ær *conj.* who A:2, 4, 20; which A:12, 21 (2); **hwat (. . .) ær** whatever A:11, 14

æren *f. def.* (his) glory D:5

ærffþir *f. acc. pl.* inheritance A:24

økiæ see **til økiæ**

økæs *wv. 3rd sg. pres.* **-s** *form* (if their property) increases, grows B:26

øland *n.* island B:29

øpte *wv. 3rd sg. past* shouted C:10

ørss *n. pl.* chargers, steeds C:6, 17, 31

øþmorþæ (gender and case uncertain) the name of a forest on the border between the provinces of Gästrikland and Hälsingland A:4

SUPPLEMENT II: GLOSSARY AND INDEX OF NAMES TO RUNIC TEXTS (*NION* 2, XVII A–G)

GLOSSARY AND INDEX OF NAMES TO RUNIC TEXTS (*NION* 2, XVII A–G)

This list is organised on the same principles as the main glossary. There are, however, no designated entry forms; only forms that occur in the inscriptions are given. References are to lines in the normalised texts of the inscriptions.

á *prep. with dat.* in E:7

aft *prep. with acc.* after, in memory of A:1, B:1, 2, 3, C:1, 2; after B:5; **at** after, in memory of E:1

ailti *wv.*(?) *3rd sg. pres. subj.* removes(?), may remove(?) B:4

Alla *m. acc.* Alli B:1; *gen.* Alli's B:2

alla *adj. acc. f. sg.* all, the whole of C:2

annan *pron. acc. m. sg.* another B:5

Arinbjǫrg *f. acc.* Arinbjǫrg D

ást *f.* love G2

at[1] see **aft**

at[2] *prep. with dat.* (see **verði**) B:4; for, in search of E:3

auk *conj.* and A:2, B:2, C:1, 2, 3, E:4; **ok** G3:2

austarla *adv.* in the east E:4

austr *adv.* in the east A:1

bað *sv. 3rd sg. past* ordered, commanded C:1

bróður *m. acc.* brother E:1

dani *m. acc. pl.* (the) Danes C:3

Danmǫrk *f. acc.* Denmark C:2

dóu *sv. 3rd pl. past* died E:6

dragi *sv. 3rd sg. pres. subj.* drags, may drag B:5

dróttin *m. acc.* lord B:3

drængila *adv.* manfully E:2

eða *conj.* or B:5

eigi *pret.-pres. vb. 3rd sg. pres. subj.* **Óðinn þik eigi** (may) Óðinn own you G3:4

en *conj.* and, but B:3

eptir *prep. with acc.* after, in memory of D

es *conj.* who B:4, C:2

fáði *wv. 3rd sg. past* wrote, painted A:2

faður *m. acc.* father B:2, C:1

fial *sv. 3rd sg. past* (*inf.* **falla**) fell A:1

fiarri *adv.* far E:3

fóru *sv. 3rd pl. past* went, travelled E:2

fyrir *prep. with dat.* of, in F:2

fyrr *adv.* earlier F:1

gáfu *sv. 3rd pl. past* gave E:5

goða *m. acc.* leader (see B, notes) B:1

góðum *adj. dat. pl.* good G3:2

Gorm *m. acc.* GormR (Gormr the old, Danish king of the mid-tenth century, father of Haraldr bluetooth) C:1

GrímulfR *m.* GrímulfR A:2

gulli *n. dat.* gold E:3

gǫrva *wv. inf.* **bað gǫrva** ordered (people) to make, ordered to be made C:1; *3rd sg. past* **gærði** made A:1, C:3; *3rd pl. past* **gærðu** B:2

hans *pron. gen. as poss. adj.* his B:3

Haraldr *m.* Haraldr bluetooth (Danish king and ultimately king of Denmark from somewhen in the 940s(?) to *c*.985) C:1, 2; **Harald** *acc.* Haraldr (brother of Ingvarr the far-travelled) E:1

haugr *m.* mound, cairn F:1

heil(l) *adj. m. or f. sg.* hale, well G3:1

heldr *conj. with comp.* **fyrr . . . heldr** earlier than, before F:1

hennar *pron. gen. as poss. adj.* her F:1

hinn *def. art.* the D

hlaðinn *sv. pp. m.* built, thrown up F:1

hugum *m. dat. pl.* spirits G3:2

hvatir *adj. nom. m. pl.* bold F:2

hæiðverðan *adj. acc. m. sg.* noble, worthy of honour (see B, notes) B:1–2

í *prep. with dat.* in G3:2

Ingvars *m. gen.* of Ingvarr E:1

kona *f.* wife B:3

konungR *m.* king C:1

kristna *adj. acc. m. pl.* Christian C:3

kross *m. acc.* cross D

kumbl *n. pl.* monument (consisting of more than one element) A:1, B:2, C:1

kvinnu *f. acc.* wife D

kyss *wv. imp. sg.* kiss! G2

lét *sv. 3rd sg. past* **lét ræisa** had raised E:1

liðs *n. gen.* of (the) host, of (the) body of men (see B, notes) B:1

Loðbrókar *f. gen.* Loðbrók's (see F, notes) F:1
menn *m. pl.* men F:2
meʀ *prep. with dat.* with A:2
mik *pron. acc.* me G2
mín *poss. adj. nom. f. sg.* my G2
móður *f. acc.* mother C:2
myntari *m.* moneyer G1
Norveg *m. acc.* Norway C:3
ok see **auk**
Óðinn *m.* Óðinn G3:4
pipar *m. acc.* pepper G1
Ragnhildr *f.* Ragnhildr B:1
reisti *wv. 3rd sg. past* raised D; *inf.* **læisa** had raised E:1
retta *m. dat.* pervert (see B, notes) B:4
rúnaʀ *f. acc. pl.* runes B:3, 4
ræisa see **reisti**
ræist *sv. 3rd sg. past* (*inf.* **rísta**) carved B:3
sá (*demonstrative*) *pron.* he A:1, B:4; that C:2
Sandulfr *m.* Sandulfr D
satti *wv. 3rd sg. past* placed B:1
sé *sv. irregular 2nd sg. pres. subj.*(?) (see G, notes) may you be G3:1;
 3rd sg. past (*as aux. forming pass.*) **var** was F:1; *3rd pl. past* **vóru**
 were F:2
sem *conj.* as F:2
sendir *wv. 3rd sg. pres.* sends G1
sér *refl. pron. dat.* themselves F:2; **séʀ** for himself C:2
Serklandi *n. dat.* Serkland (see E, notes) E:7
sinn *refl. poss. acc. m. sg.* his A:1, B:3 (2), C:1; her B:3, E:1; their
 B:2; *acc. f. sg.* **sína** his C:2, D
sjá *demonstrative pron.* this F:1; *acc. m. sg.* **þenna** D; **þennsa** E:1;
 þennsi B:1, 4; *acc. f. pl.* **þassi** these B:3, 4; *acc. n. pl.* **þausi** B:2, C:1
slíkt *adj. n. sg. as substantive* such (a thing) F:2
Sóti *m.* Sóti B:3
Stygguʀ *m.* Stygguʀ (see A, notes) A:1
stæin *m. acc.* stone B:1, 4, E:1
sun *m. acc.* son E:1; **sunu** A:1; *nom. pl.* **syniʀ** sons B:2; **synir** F:1
sunnarla *adv.* in the south E:6
svarti *adj. nom. m. sg. wk.* black D

synir/syniʀ see **sun**
Sǫlva *m. gen. pl.* of the Sǫlvaʀ (see B, notes) B:1
Tolla *f.* Tolla (see E, notes) E:1
vann *sv. 3rd sg. past* won C:2
var see **sé**
véa *m. acc.* priest (see B, notes) B:1
ver *m. acc.* husband, man B:3
verði *sv. 3rd sg. pres. subj.* **at retta sá verði** may he become as a
     pervert, be reckoned a pervert B:4
vígi *wv. 3rd sg. pres. subj.* hallow B:4
Víkingʀ *m.* Víkingʀ A:2
vǫru see **sé**
þassi see **sjá**
þausi see **sjá**
þegn *m. acc.* thane (see B, notes) B:2
þeir *pron.* they F:1, 2; **þæiʀ** E:2; *n. pl.* **þau** these (see A, notes) A:1
þenna/þennsa/þennsi see **sjá**
þiggi *sv. 3rd sg. pres. subj.* receive, take G3:3
Þorkell *m.* Þorkell G1
Þórr *m.* Þórr B:4, G3:3
Þórví *f. acc.* Þórví (generally known in Icelandic sources as Þyri,
     wife of King Gormr the old) C:2
þú *pron. 2nd sg.* you G3:1; *acc.* **þik** G3:3, 4; *dat.* **þér** G1
ærni *m. dat.* (*nom.* **ǫrn**) eagle E:5
Øyvind *m. acc.* Øyvindʀ A:1
Øyvísli *m. dat.* Øyvísl A:2